ROUTLEDGE LIBRARY EDITIONS
BROADCASTING

Volume 27

MEDIA USE IN THE INFORMATION AGE

MEDIA USE IN THE INFORMATION AGE

Emerging Patterns of Adoption and Consumer Use

Edited by
JERRY L. SALVAGGIO
AND
JENNINGS BRYANT

LONDON AND NEW YORK

First published in 1989 by Lawrence Erlbaum Associates, Publishers

This edition first published in 2024
by Routledge
4 Park Square, Milton Park, Abingdon, Oxon OX14 4RN

and by Routledge
605 Third Avenue, New York, NY 10158

Routledge is an imprint of the Taylor & Francis Group, an informa business

© 1989 Lawrence Erlbaum Associates, Inc.

All rights reserved. No part of this book may be reprinted or reproduced or utilised in any form or by any electronic, mechanical, or other means, now known or hereafter invented, including photocopying and recording, or in any information storage or retrieval system, without permission in writing from the publishers.

Trademark notice: Product or corporate names may be trademarks or registered trademarks, and are used only for identification and explanation without intent to infringe.

British Library Cataloguing in Publication Data
A catalogue record for this book is available from the British Library

ISBN: 978-1-032-59391-3 (Set)
ISBN: 978-1-032-64380-9 (Volume 27) (hbk)
ISBN: 978-1-032-64386-1 (Volume 27) (pbk)
ISBN: 978-1-032-64385-4 (Volume 27) (ebk)

DOI: 10.4324/9781032643854

Publisher's Note
The publisher has gone to great lengths to ensure the quality of this reprint but points out that some imperfections in the original copies may be apparent.

Disclaimer
The publisher has made every effort to trace copyright holders and would welcome correspondence from those they have been unable to trace.

MEDIA USE in the INFORMATION AGE:
Emerging Patterns of Adoption and Consumer Use

Edited by

Jerry L. Salvaggio
Whataburger, Inc.
Corpus Christi, Texas

Jennings Bryant
University of Alabama

LEA LAWRENCE ERLBAUM ASSOCIATES, PUBLISHERS
1989 Hillsdale, New Jersey   Hove and London

Copyright © 1989 by Lawrence Erlbaum Associates, Inc.
All rights reserved. No part of this book may be reproduced in
any form, by photostat, microfilm, retrieval system, or any other
means, without the prior written permission of the publisher.

Lawrence Erlbaum Associates, Inc. Publishers
365 Broadway
Hillsdale, New Jersey 07642

Cover, production, and interior
design: Robin Marks Weisberg

Library of Congress Cataloging-in-Publication Data
Main entry under title:

Media use in the information age.

Includes index.
  1. Telecommunication—Social aspects. I. Salvaggio
Jerry Lee. II. Bryant, Jennings.
HE7631.M43 1989   302.2'34   88-3857
ISBN 0-89859-968-7

Printed in the United States of America
10 9 8 7 6 5 4 3 2 1

Contents

Preface   xi

Introduction   xv
H.J. Hsia

**PART I
THE NEED FOR NEW RESEARCH METHODS**

1
Assessing Exposure to the New Media
James G. Webster   3

Why Study Exposure?   4
Challenges Posed by New Media   8
Emerging Solutions   12
Concluding Remarks   16

2
Problems and Potential of Forecasting the Adoption of New Media
Bruce Klopfenstein   21

Brief History of Forecasting   22

Definitions of Forecasting 23
Technological Development
  and Forecasting Methods 24
Technological Forecasting 24

3
The Effects of New Technologies on Communication Policy
Christine L. Ogan 43

VCRs: A Political Issue 44
Satellite Pirating and Communication Policy 52

PART II
ADOPTING AND USING THE NEW COMMUNICATION MEDIA

4
A Framework and Agenda for Research on Computing in the Home
Charles W. Steinfield, William H. Dutton, and Peter Kovaric 61

Perspectives on Computing in the Home 68
Toward a Research Agenda 78

5
Teletext in the United Kingdom: Patterns, Attitudes, and Behaviors of Users
Bradley S. Greenberg 87

Introduction 87
Methods 89
Results 90
Conclusions 101

6
Interactive Electronic Text in the United States: Can Videotex Ever Go Home Again?
James S. Ettema 105

Videotex at Valley Forge 105
Some Lessons Learned From the Ventures in Videotex 107
"Firsthand": An example of the Perils of the Information Business 111
Further Explorations in Electronic Text 116

7
A Quantitative Analysis of the Reasons for VCR Penetration Worldwide
Joseph D. Straubhaar and Carolyn Lin — 125

Reasons for VCR Penetration   126
Methods   133
Results   136
Conclusions   143
Appendix   145

8
Uses and Impacts of Home Computers in Canada: A Process of Reappropriation
André H. Caron, Luc Giroux, and Sylvie Douzou — 147

The Home Computer as Innovation   149
Method   150
Results   151
Conclusions   159

9
Adoption and Use of Videocassette Recorders in the Third World
Joseph D. Straubhaar and Douglas A. Boyd — 163

VCR Context: Electronic Media in the Third World   164
Mechanisms of VCR Diffusion   174
Conclusion   175

PART III
EMERGING MODELS OF MEDIA USE IN THE INFORMATION AGE

10
Uses and Gratifications of Videocassette Recorders
Alan M. Rubin and Charles R. Bantz — 181

Method   185
Results   188
Discussion   191

11
Television Audience Behavior: Patterns of Exposure
in the New Media Environment
James G. Webster   197

Changes in the Media Environment   *197*
Audience Behavior in the New Media Environment   *203*
Implications of Emerging Patterns of Exposure   *210*

12
Implications of New Interactive Technologies for Conceptualizing
Communication
Carrie Heeter   217

Review of Traditional Conceptualizations   *218*
Dimensions of Interactivity   *221*
Implications of Interactivity   *225*

13
A Behavioral Systems Framework for Information Design
and Behavior Change
Richard A. Winett and Kathryn D. Kramer   237

Behavioral Systems Framework   *239*
Research Leading to the Development
   of the Framework   *243*
Current Project   *247*
Some Future Direction   *253*

14
An Annotated Statistical Abstract of Communications Media
in the United States
Dan Brown and Jennings Bryant   259

Introduction   *259*
Synthesis   *298*

Author Index   *303*

Subject Index   *311*

Contributors

Charles R. Bantz • *Department of Communication, Arizona State University, Tempe, AZ 85287*

Douglas A. Boyd • *College of Communication, University of Kentucky, Lexington, KY 40205*

Dan Brown • *Department of Communication, East Tennessee State University, Johnson City, TN 37614*

Jennings Bryant • *Department of Broadcast and Film Communication, University of Alabama, Tuscaloosa, AL 35486*

André H. Caron • *Department of Communication, University of Montreal, Montreal, Quebec*

Bradley S. Greenberg • *Department of Telecommunications, Michigan State University, East Lansing, MI 48824*

Sylvie Douzou • *Department of Communication, University of Montreal, Montreal, Quebec*

William H. Dutton • *The Annenberg School of Communications, University of Southern California, University Park, Los Angeles, CA 90007*

James S. Ettema • *Department of Communication Studies, Northwestern University, Evanston, IL 60201*

Luc Giroux • *Department of Communication, University of Montreal, Montreal, Quebec*

CONTRIBUTORS

Carrie Heeter • *Department of Telecommunications, Michigan State University, East Lansing, MI 48824*

H.J. Hsia • *Institute for Communications Research, Texas Tech University, Lubbock, TX 79409*

Bruce Klopfenstein • *Radio-Television-Film Department, Bowling Green State University, Bowling Green, OH 43403*

Kathryn D. Kramer • *Psychology Department, Virginia Polytechnic Institute and State University, Blacksburg, VA 24061*

Carolyn Lin • *Department of Radio-TV, Southern Illinois University at Carbondale, Carbondale, IL 62901*

Christine L. Ogan • *School of Journalism, Indiana University, Bloomington, IN 47405*

Alan M. Rubin • *School of Speech Communication, Kent State University, Kent, OH 44242*

Charles W. Steinfield • *Department of Telecommunications, Michigan State University, East Lansing, MI 48824*

Joseph D. Straubhaar • *Department of Telecommunications, Michigan State University, East Lansing, MI 48824*

James G. Webster • *Department of Radio/TV/Film, Northwestern University, Evanston, IL 60201*

Richard A. Winett • *Psychology Department, Virginia Polytechnic Institute and State University, Blacksburg, VA 24061*

Preface

When, in the 1960s and early 1970s, the inevitability of new communications technology became clear, scholars were content to study the new media from one of two perspectives. The first perspective resulted in speculative essays generally prejudicial to the potential side effects of the new technology. The second perspective was represented in essays that extolled the new technology. Most of these essays contended that the new media would revolutionize education, entertainment, and culture in general — all to the ultimate benefit of postindustrial man. Although both perspectives were valuable, neither offered empirical analysis of the new media.

The chapters included here represent an attempt to fill this void with a more empirical approach to the new media. The chapters written for this book reflect both the unprecedented number of technologies that have been unveiled in the 1980s and the multifaceted attempts by scholars to cope with the questions raised by their adoption.

The new generation of research on communications technology is challenging the relevance of traditional mass communication theories in light of the unique characteristics of the new media. Scholars are also far more sensitive to the manner in which new media are adopted and used by consumers. The new generation of research is also no longer characterized by two or three methodologies. In this book, alone, a half dozen research methodologies are used.

The growth and complexity of communications technology is amply described by Hsia in the Introduction. Virtually all of the authors agree that the new media offers a diversity of content. The question is: What are the cultural and social effects when audiences are offered such a vast array of programs? Webster, in chapter 1, suggests fragmentation and polarization are likely effects of the introduction of innovative media.

To what degree are the more informational media, such as teletext, videotex, and personal computers (PCs) being embraced by consumers? Executives have argued that the failure of Viewtron and Gateway does not augur well for the adoption of videotex by the American public yet videotex continues to be developed in Western Europe and in Japan. The failure of videotex may not have so much to do with the fact that it is an information media rather than an entertainment media as it is a matter of capital investment and long-range commitment — two things American entrepreneurs are short on. Ettema (chapter 6) points out that although it may be some time before consumers adopt videotex, major organizations are now heavy users. News organizations such as Dow Jones use interactive media extensively.

Where teletext has caught on it is clearly having an impact on other media. Greenberg (chapter 5) suggests that radio and newspapers have been adversely affected by England's teletext system, whereas television has gained.

Research methods, like technologies, can become obsolescent almost before they are adopted. The interactive nature of many of the new media requires the researcher to adopt a broad range of research perspectives. Webster's (chapter 11) study of cable television and audience behavior underscores some of the dimensions where the old and new media differ. Heeter (chapter 12) develops a model that includes six dimensions of interactivity and relates them to cable television.

Winett and Kramer (chapter 13) argue that communication scholars have incorrectly related attitudes, perceptions, and beliefs to behavior in their studies of media. The authors offer a new framework designed to cope with diverse media, information campaigns, and the development of technology.

Uses and gratifications continues to be a viable methodology for the study of adoption and use. Rubin and Bantz (chapter 10) demonstrate the effectiveness of uses and gratifications for the investigation of VCRs.

Steinfield, Dutton, and Kovaric (chapter 4) demonstrate the difficulties of conducting research on home computing and offer a framework and agenda for future research. Their study should be especially helpful to those seeking to learn how a technology impacts on its environment.

The study of new media technologies has resulted in an increased use of forecasting methodologies by researchers. To some degree, forecasting methodologies are replacing more traditional research paradigms. The question is: How effective are existing forecasting methods? Klopfeinstein (chapter 2) demonstrates that the track record of forecasters has not been effective.

PREFACE

A number of scholars have sought to identify the significant variables that influence adoption and use of new media. Gender, age, income, and education are the more obvious variables under consideration. In this volume, Ogan's (chapter 3) study cites national policy as a key variable.

The personal computer has emerged as a symbolic key that many believe can open the door to prosperity in the information society. Caron, Giroux, and Douzou (chapter 8) suggest that PCs are often adopted for their symbolic value. They argue that the consumer's perceptions and motivations influence their reaction and eventually their purchasing decisions.

In addition to PCs, the ubiquitous VCR is coming under close scrutiny by communication scholars. Straubhaar and Lin (chapter 7) have undertaken an ambitious research project that involves the study of VCR penetration on an international basis. The authors found that income and price, other media, and urbanization and television content diversity are the major variables influencing VCR growth. Straubhaar and Boyd (chapter 9) provide an analysis of the use of VCRs in the Third World.

In the final chapter (14), Brown and Bryant offer a statistical overview of all the major media. Scholars will find this chapter particularly useful as a means of seeing growth patterns and correlations at a glance.

The study of how communications technology is adopted and used in the home is more important now than ever because the new technologies in question represent only the tip of the iceberg. As memory chips become capable of holding more data and microprocessors become more powerful, existing technologies will take on increased functions and new technologies will offer even more impressive capabilities. The VCR, the television set, and the video disc still utilize the old 8-bit microprocessor and 64K and 256K memory chips. The capabilities of communication technologies will grow exponentially when they are based on 32-bit microprocessors and 4 megabit memory chips.

We are especially grateful to the contributors of this volume. In every case, scholars were willing to offer original chapters reflecting the most up to date research on the subject.

Jerry L. Salvaggio

Introduction

H. J. Hsia
Texas Tech University

Every technological advance in communication has been labeled a *revolution*, accompanied by the coinage of new terms, such as *information revolution*, *communication revolution*, and *media revolution*. "The attribution of revolutionary status to changes in communications technologies has a long history" (Slack, 1984, p. 77). Whether it is revolution or evolution, all changes have one thing in common: They are related to a new form of communication. Combined with a host of technical changes, the new media emerge. The term *new media* means different things to different people. The new media can be one or any combination of cable, interactive cable, low-power television, subscription television, communication satellites, high-definition television, teletext, videotex, cellular telephone, multipoint distribution service, direct broadcast satellite, tele-shopping, tele-conferencing (Singleton, 1986), in addition to the ubiquitous television, telephone, and fashionable videocassette recorder. New media may include many devices and systems, whether existing or yet to be born.

Each known new medium was launched with glowing expectations of revolutionizing mass and personal communication. Perhaps the seemingly most promising medium—videotex—had a spectacular commencement and has suffered humiliating setbacks. Videotex can be either an interactive cable television or a telephone through an interactive communication device (usually a modem), linked to a data or program source controlled by a personal computer. Two major videotex services, Knight-Ridder's Viewtron and Time-Mirror's Gateway, after losing $80 million altogether, exited from the scene ("Two Videotex," 1986). The first commercial videotex system in the nation, BISON (Belo Information System ONline) demised in 1982, and the frequently touted QUBE system, "the promise of the future," also bid an untimely farewell to communication (Morse 1982). International Business Machine (IBM) and Merrill Lynch announced the funeral of their joint adventure of the International Market-Net, which was to provide financial information on a worldwide basis (Carroll & Swartz, 1987). Misfortune has befallen three other prominent videotex systems: Keycom in Chicago folded its consumer operation but kept its business operation; Covidea is disintegrating; and Trintex—the most promising of all videotex systems, jointly founded in the 1984 by IBM, Sears, and CBS (CBS has already withdrawn)—is fighting for its survival ("Videotex Exodus," 1987).

All videotex systems, and perhaps, all new media, as Gross (1986) said of teletext, "appear to be a solution looking for a problem" (p. 168). Not surprisingly, that was the verdict about broadcast television not too long ago (Martin, 1982, p. 120). Teletext, a one-way electronic bulletin board, has been almost written off in this country but is flourishing in Great Britain. The Ceefax (pronounced see 'fact') system has been used heavily by professionals (Mosco, 1982, pp. 74-75). By all indications, videotex systems are successful in Britain, France, Canada, and other countries (Rapparini & Sabatelli, 1982). Teletel, the nationwide videotex system in France, is a phenomenal success. Using Minitel terminals supplied by the government, Teletel links the public to a variety of computerized services. It has enjoyed a growth rate of 125% every year since 1984 (from .2 million in 1984, .45 million in 1985, 1.3 million in 1986, to an estimated 2.8 million in 1987; Ricklefs, 1986). Teletel is truly a full service system; as more and more database operators and information providers join the system, the user base continues to grow.

Apparently, the success of Teletel can be traced to: (a) massive government support and commitments; (b) a wide variety of information and services offered to the public; and (c) free rental for the minitel terminal. Nor are there extra fees or charges for using the telephone unless a private videotex service is used. For videotex to be successful, three ingredients must be present: (a) inexpensive service, (b) information provided must be worth buying, and (c) information providers must be able to make substantial profits (Martin, 1982, pp. 120-121). But we may hasten to add: user's fear or inhibition of using the terminal must be reduced by gradually introducing them to similar electronic devices (e.g., games). Corporate adoption of new media systems should make more and more people familiar with electronic devices (Jeffries-Fox & Jeffries-Fox, 1984). Today most major firms have already installed corporate videotex systems, capable of linking customer's orders, reviewing product information, and examining customer records. Only when these services are offered will the public gradually adopt videotex services. At the present time, only 34% of all U.S. households own a personal computer. Of those, 18% are expected to connect to videotex services before 1995 (Guzda, 1985).

Judging from past diffusion and adoption rates of some new media, the slow adoption rate of new media is not surprising. It took newspapers more than 100 years and the telephone 70 years to achieve 50% penetration, whereas television needed 30 years to reach 20% adoption (Dozier & Rice, 1984). But new media adoption may be much faster, as more recent innovations have diffused more rapidly (Olshavsky, 1980). The adoption rate of new media might not please their advocates, but promising signs can be seen from three main areas: (a) problems with established media, (b) the ever-newer new tech, and (c) the unlimited connectivity of the new media that can be linked to, coupled with, and integrated into satellites, telephones, optical wire, major and minor appliances, and anything that is electrical or electronic. The development of these areas is a stimulant to the eventual emergence of the all-encompassing household communication-information system to support three sybsystems: Home Administration, Communication, and Entertainment (HACE).

PROBLEMS WITH ESTABLISHED MEDIA

Computers today have invaded every domain; no sanctuary is free from the intruder. Seen in offices, factories, homes, and even on motorcycles, the computer is thought to be capable of doing everything but making love. Wrong! "People might even come to prefer sex with robots programmed to cater to their own desires to the uncertainties and difficulties of the real thing.... If one can have sex with audioanimatronic robots with artificial personality interfaced with one's subconscious desires via a personality inventory program" (Spinrad, 1984, pp. 81-82), how long before there will be a drastic change in mass communication, communication theory, and research?

"Newspapers are doomed," many prophets said when radio was about to become popular in the early 1920s. Many authoritative figures predicted the same fate for newspapers when television was about to take off in the early 1950s. Despite the challenges of radio and TV, newspapers not only survived but prospered because radio and TV stimulated the public's interest in news. Newspapers survived—not because newspapers put up a tenacious defense against the onslaught of radio and TV, but because the invasion of radio and TV took place entirely in another dimension—the temporal dimension—which complemented and supplemented the spatial dimension of print media.

Printed media offer a degree of temporal freedom not found in the broadcast media, although the use of VCRs is changing the inherent limitation of radio and TV. The broadcast media's temporal limitation assures the continued dominance of newspapers over other media in every market as far as advertising revenue is concerned.

Another disadvantage of radio and TV is that neither can offer detailed information or in-depth analysis. An even more glaring drawback of the broadcast media is that no broadcast program allows random access, because they must be sequentially presented in accordance with schedules. With newspapers, readers can read the last page first and they can also skip, stop, and restart reading at their own will. In addition to audience control, print media also have the advantage of "referability." Readers can refer back to a particular article or advertisement within the shelf-life of a publication. Such a privilege is not conferred upon the TV viewer or the radio listener.

In contrast to these limitations of broadcast media, print media have their well-known qualities: timeliness, flexibility, portability, broad and intensive coverage, localized dissemination, and fast production. All of these are reasons for the survival of the printed media in the electronic age. However, newspapers and magazines have their own equally well-known deficiencies: short life, cluttering, intensive labor, hasty readership, and costly production. Production costs for all established media are high, even though costs for print media are relatively low as compared with TV. But enormous efforts are required to prepare anew each issue of newspapers and magazines, including editing, proofreading, typesetting, layout, printing, and distribution, not to mention the cost of newsprint, ink, and mat or plate production. In contrast to television and radio, few newspapers have nationwide readership (notable exceptions are the *Wall Street Journal*, the *Christian Science Monitor*, the *New York Times*, and the *USA Today*). They circulate within a particular geographical area.

Each Mass Medium Has Its Own Deficiencies

All established media, including newspapers, are modern dinosaurs, mammoth in production cost, labor, and time. Their fatal weakness is a fundamental problem that cannot be solved until the marriage of the home computer and database systems becomes possible. Mass media, as the name implies, are working on the cafeteria concept, publishing or broadcasting a variety of features, ads, news, and programs for the masses and hoping that some of their offerings might be read or viewed. Despite the refined art in market segmentation and targeting, all use the "shot-gun" approach, aiming at no one in particular but anticipating that certain programs or ads will hit some of their target audience, as probability theory might indi-

INTRODUCTION   xix

cate. In the absence of the new media, weaknesses of all established media can be overlooked. But now there is a better alternative: the new media. How the transformation from the established media to the new media may be brought about depends on advertising—the major source of revenue for media, old and new. With no other alternative, advertisers must laboriously go through a number of labor-intensive, costly chores to get their message across to the public.

After looking over the scene of newspapers and the gradual drop of advertising revenues for all media, Sachar (1982) commented: "The net result of the various new video technologies, regardless of their individual success, will be increased competition for the established media—commercial television as well as newspapers" (p. 1). Competition will become increasingly threatening to established media, because the ever-newer new tech will enhance the versatility of the new media and gain more advertising revenue for the new media.

THE EVER-NEWER NEW TECH

Underneath all the super-satellites, each allowing 25 million users (Burdine, 1981), are thousands of databases, information centers, communication networks, and videotex systems with a multitude of communication facilities and computers. The proliferation of communication devices can be simply traced to the semiconductors, memory chips, and microprocessors that have made computers smaller, faster, more versatile and powerful. Each succeeding generation of the computer is far more powerful and versatile than the one just a year or so older. Newer and better communication devices and programs appear almost every day, as seen from high tech and computer journals and magazines.

The Supercomputer and the Super Microcomputer

Computer technology is advancing in quantum leaps. Cray, ETA, and Japanese manufacturers all produce supercomputers, some of which can perform up to several "gigaflops" (billions of floating operations per second.) Super-computers will soon be merged with artificial intelligence and built-in voice-and-pattern recognition technology. The microcomputer has moved from 8 bits, to 16 bits, to 32 bits, with 1 to 10 megabytes of internal memory. A desk-top microcomputer is now more powerful than the third generation IBM-360 and will improve its power and versatility to perform unheard-of feats. Local area networks (LAN), linking microcomputers together within a local area, will soon be a standard feature in new buildings. Automated offices will be found at not only large corporate headquarters but also small firms, as multiuser microcomputers will be gradually adopted and installed. On the ground, fiber optic networks are criss-crossing the nation and eventually will "network" all parts of the country. Simultaneously, satellites are circling the earth, linking home computers and videotex systems, providing instant international news, TV networks, and educational services.

Software and Memory

Both software and hardware are increasingly sophisticated and friendly. The simplicity in using the computer is, to a large extent, inversely related to the complexity of programs. Complex programs generally require a large memory and speedy processing that is accomplished mainly by miniaturization. Vertical recording, capable of storing 50 to 100 times more data in the same space, is expected to be the dominant form of memory storage in the 1990s.

The most important innovations in communication may be attributed to digitalization, fiber optic transmission, and bulk downloading. *Digitalization* refers to the conversion of analog signals to the binary form so as to permit programs, ads, data, voice, and even television commercials to be stored in computer memory. Digitalized information can be easily edited, changed, enhanced, programmed, transmitted, and retrieved. *Fiber optics* provides theoretically thousands of channels, and *bulk down-loading* permits a program to be transmitted in bulk rather than sequentially over the transmission line. At the end of the process the transmitted program can be stored and then sequentially presented on the screen for human consumption.

The new optical scanner (Stanton, Burns, & Venit, 1986), or the page reader, is based on digitalization. The scanner converts the image of a document into digital electronic codes that can be stored, retrieved, enhanced, and modified. Its obvious advantages are: economical storage spaces and control of paper (document) explosion. Millions of words, when digitalized, can be processed, transmitted, and retrieved instantly.

Voice Recognition and Talk Writer

The page reader works with finite, predetermined digits and letters of distinctive forms, sizes, shapes, and fonts. Voice recognition must contend with random, infinitely varied patterns of linguistic sounds. A simple command like "Open Sesame" can be a complex problem if the voice is affected by a common cold or a few highballs. Simple voice recognition has been used for some time. For example, an airline baggage handler can call out

INTRODUCTION   xxi

the destination "Chicago," "Dallas," or "Seattle" to the computer that directs the luggage on the conveyer belt to the appropriate gate (Sandberg-Diment, 1987). Voice recognition will become even more sophisticated in the 1990s and is likely to be incorporated in all new media.

Inexorably, The Digital World

In the digital electronic world, the performance and features of hardware can be modified by software, instead of labor-intensive and costly redesigning and remaking. Digital processing allows greater amounts of information to be stored in small, less expensive memory than does analog processing (Roman, 1983). Both audio and video signals can be digitalized, upon random request, to deliver sound and pictures superior to today's TV and radio. Picture alignment, ghosts, color/contrast, and enhancement can be controlled. In the 1990s consumers can have their TV, movie, and text edited, combined, and transported electronically.

The computer will increasingly be linked to various devices within the home. In this way, the computer will play a central role in household management. Eventually, digitalization may move into the uncharted seas, such as the resurrection of John Wayne or Marilyn Monroe. An actor's vital statistics, movements, features, and characteristics can be fed into a supercomputer and programmed to create new dramatic scenes.

THE CONNECTIVITY OF THE NEW MEDIA

Because of the marriage of telecommunications and computer technologies, the new media can couple to most electronic and electrical devices to create amicable relations between human and computer—we can instruct our robot to "Bring me a cup of coffee," and command it to "Vacuum the floor." The new media will become more adaptable, versatile, and *marriageable* so as to link, interact, and control a host of home administration, communication, and entertainment systems.

Databases and Videotex

Future growth of the new media may depend on the development of databases. Databases are the supermarkets of information societies. More formally, a database is a collection of systematically compiled information to which many users can access selected information. The information may be sorted, analyzed, and displayed for a particular purpose. Nearly 10,000 privately owned bulletin-board systems (databases) are available for free public access (Roberts, 1984). Looking at *Computer Data Report*, the newsletter of Information USA's Computer Data Services, we can find a host of new and expanded database services every issue.

Most databases are accessed through either teletext or videotex. Teletext (or teletex) is a one-way broadcast system through cable or telephone via the modem (the moderator–demodulater or telephone coupler), to the home computer or computer terminal, whereas videotex is an interactive (two-way) system. The degree of videotex interaction depends on system sophistication (in both hardware and software). More formally, teletext/videotex are systems for the widespread dissemination of textual and graphic information by wholly electronic means, for display on low-cost terminal under the selective control of the recipient, and using control procedures easily understood by untrained users (Tyler, 1979). On the other end invisible to the user is a database or a number of interconnecting database systems. Although teletext is simpler and far less capital and labor intensive than videotex, it is already technologically obsolete.

Offering much more than information storage and retrieval, databases provide instantaneous analysis tailor-made for a particular user. The principal advantage of a database system may be simply stated: Any layperson without computer knowledge and programming skills can obtain the desired information. A good example is IBM's Structured Query Language that allows a user to retrieve information by typing in English-like commands on a computer terminal. A more refined system allows the user to touch the terminal screen for selected information to be printed, transferred, merged, and analyzed.

Besides storage, retrieval, and analysis of data, databases provide a systematic structure to integrate all phases and functions of an organization, a profession, or a field. Databases via videotex are increasingly a forerunner of an integrated system of administration, communication, control for management, marketing, advertising, production, and distribution.

New forms of satellite communication, such as VSAT (very small aperture technology) allow efficient, convenient, and inexpensive communication networks to develop in the corporate world. Major corporations and government agencies are using VSATs for instantaneous information retrieval, electronic mail, video teleconferences, and interoffice voice, data, and video networking.

Information networks are now capable of interconnecting systems using different computers. Many major organizations have installed a PBX, the computer controlled private branch exchange, to link all the data processing and word processing equipment as well as telephones. There are now wired houses, wired buildings, and eventually will be wired nations. Probably the first wired nation with terminals everywhere interconnected with many videotex database systems will be Japan which has devoted billions

INTRODUCTION

to this enterprise (AMCB, 1983), substantiating Salvaggio's (1982) predictions that Japan would be the leading nation in communication technology, and the first nation to build a national information system and to make two-way video and audio available.

Conditions for the Growing New Media

The emergence of the new media also depends on the reduction of costs involved in retrieving news articles, programs, or ads from the databases systems, and the availability of a variety of database systems for the users. The exponential drop in computer prices and the attraction of advertising revenue for entrepreneurs will increasingly attract advertisers. With today's media, an advertiser or ad agency has to go through many time-consuming chores of market segmentation, targeting, creative work, production, and scheduling, just to advertise. All are costly and labor intensive. An interactive computerized news and advertising system would eliminate almost all these chores and allow the users to dictate what ads or articles they wish to see. In addition, many favorable conditions are present and some predictions are appropriate for the growth of the new media.

First, despite the fact that advertising expenditure shares of the gross national product had been held more or less constant (1.99%, 2.35%, 1.96%, and 2.06% for 1950, 1960, 1970, and 1980 respectively), the total shares of advertising revenues for all media but TV and "Miscellaneous" have been declining since 1950 (Weilbacher, 1984, pp. 23–27). All print media have been losing ground. By all indications, the trend will continue for reasons that will be made apparent soon.

Second, the new media are likely to go through a slow starting stage similar to the development of radio and television. It took almost a whole decade for radio and television to reach the first 1 million sets in use (Sterling, 1984, Table 600c).

Third, the adoption of computers should increase as the postwar-baby generation (or the Yuppies), who exhibits little or no computer phobia, moves into the consumer stage. Their babies (the computer generation or the information generation) are even more accustomed to using computers than their parents. As the computer user bases expand year after year from now on, advertisers may be inclined to shift their media decision in favor of the new media. Furthermore, a database network offers a host of advantages when compared with established media as expounded previously.

Fourth, both computer hardware and software are increasingly "user friendly." Enormous strides have been made in reducing the user's confusion and improving the ease of operating the computer and the videotex system. Voice-activated computers will further improve the user friendliness and versatility of computers.

Fifth, database systems are following the adoption patterns experienced by radio and television, languishing at first, gradually taking off, and eventually enjoying an explosive growth—that can be seen from trends in broadcasting and newer technologies (Sterling, 1984). As databases and videotex systems on a worldwide basis become more available and accessible, the computer penetration into the majority of households is almost assured.

Sixth, computers are giving birth to many subcultures: investment, game, computer graphics, and others. They eventually will become widespread, because computer culture is not restricted to time, geography, sex, religion, age, race, creed, social taboo, or other traditional barriers that might bar many potential members from joining. Although with many false starts, the eventual popularization of videotex systems is simply a matter of time.

Seventh, regardless of how fast videotex and database systems may grow, the obsolescence of print media is, at least, premature. The virtues of simplicity, flexibility, inexpensiveness, portability, and the tradition of print media cannot be simply replaced by any electronic means—what will happen if there is no electricity? However, print media are likely to adopt a dual strategy: (a) the gradual conversion to computerized news gathering, editing, paginating, and printing, and (b) the delivery of an electronic newspaper.

Eighth, the total advertising revenue grow proportionately with the gross national product, and revenue gains of each established medium must be obtained at the expense of others. The new media, regardless of how successful they might be, will take away only a negligible amount of advertising revenue in its beginning from existing media (Weaver, 1983, pp. 96–100). If the new media follow the growth patterns of radio and television which in the early stages of their development (in the late 1920s and early 1950s respectively) were dismissed as a new toy, hobby, or product searching for a market by many detractors, they will gain more advertising revenue at the expense of established media. With more revenue, the new media will provide even newer and better services that will further increase their revenue.

Ninth, operators in advertising database systems or electronic yellow pages are still groping for the best marketing, content, and advertising mixes. Future development of an advertising videotex system is likely to go from the simple to the complex and from the less capital-intensive to more capital-intensive through six stages:

1. Classified ads restricted to more lucrative classifications like autos, houses, and jobs.
2. Classified ads of all categories.
3. Retail ads with texts and primitive graphics.
4. Retail ads with pictures and graphics.

INTRODUCTION

5. On-demand retail ads when digitalization of audio and video as well as fiber optic network is popularized.
6. On-demand commercials and other information.

Tenth, many new professions and jobs will be created, not necessarily at the expense of current media and advertising jobs. Evolving just like the TV industry that in its infancy was mainly staffed by personnel from the radio industry, the new media will absorb a large number of professionals from the existing communication industry. Because of the demands of the new media, mass communication as an academic discipline must undergo an evolutionary change as well.

Eleventh, when campuses are wired and students and instructors provided with microcomputers linked to databases both on and off campus, all instructions except those of a few laboratory courses can be given and taken through videotex systems. Nearly half of all elementary and junior high students and about one third of high school students make use of computers in school, and one fourth of teachers use computers regularly (Becker, 1987). Almost all advertising, communication, journalism, public relations, speech, and telecommunication courses can be readily computerized. Consequently, education can be freed from both geographical and temporal restrictions.

Twelfth, when voice, video, and data merge as the result of digitalization, joint research projects should enjoy an unprecedented growth. A host of universities have embarked upon the adoption of the so-called "wired" university. Now BITNET (BIT: because it's there) allows faculty members to exchange and co-author papers for publication via computer terminals, linking a large number of universities and institutes. Similar networks for academic and professional research of cooperative nature eventually will become popular on many campuses. Higher education may be divided into "face-to-face" and "not-to-face," and not-to-face is the on-line education in the so-called Quiet Revolution (Meeks, 1987).

Communication Education

The relentless onslaught of new technology gives communication professionals and academicians no choice but to change and to influence the resultant changes. Changes in communication curricula will not only involve the course formats, sequences, and contents, but influence the growth and direction of the new media. What changes and how much change might take place are at present pure speculations; however, what is forthcoming might be also enlightening: All print media might be wholly or partially processed through computer bases in 1990. Thus, communications courses will have to use or channel through computers. How to use computer databases and computer-aided instructions must be examined as well. It is high time for communications, advertising, journalism, and telecommunications schools and departments to:

1. Examine all courses for possible additions, deletions, or revisions in light of the Home Administration, Communication, and Entertainment System (HACES).
2. Work out tentative but comprehensive curricula for each of the communication majors (i.e., advertising, films, journalism, photojournalism, public relations, speech, and telecommunication).
3. Re-emphasize basic skills in English, statistics, and writing in addition to computer literacy and operation.

Because of new technology, the communications profession is also rapidly undergoing some fundamental changes. After World War II when broadcasting media, particularly television, developed at a rapid pace, many changes had taken place (i.e., specializations in various brances of TV). New tech will certainly bring about more specializations in new media jobs and change current curricula to meet the needs of communication in the future. How we prepare a communication graduate for the new-tech world is becoming crucially important.

Electronic and print journalists are the very minority in any news organization or advertising agency. Other jobs account for 90% of the personnel in newspapers, TV stations, public relations firms, advertising agencies, and movies. No one has a crystal ball to see what kind of graduates the world may need in the future. This offers more, not fewer, reasons for taking a critical look at what kind of talents will be needed for the emerging new medium.

CONCLUSION

Catering to HACES users are thousands of videotex systems, each supported by many database systems. For the systems operators, videotex is far less labor-intensive and far more cost-efficient than any established medium apart from the initial capital layout. For the advertisers, videotex systems linking HACES are capable of producing and updating news and advertising with minimum effort and cost, representing the ultimate rifle approach. For the users, HACES are tailor-made, as it can group, index, compare, and test all sorts of information. Most important of all, the new media allow users to be their own masters or mistresses to determine the programs and information they desire at the time of their own choice.

Within the next generation or so, "electronic newspapers" or "electronic publishing" may be compared with the invention of printing in significance. Combined with digitalized on-demand TV, the eventual integration of news and advertising will begin and the marriage between print and broadcast media will be consummated. When this is so, the impact on education, and particularly on communications, can very well be traumatic to many and exhilarating to some.

REFERENCES

AMCB. (1983). 2000: The information society. *Asian Mass Communication Bulletin, 13*(3), 7.
Becker, H. J. (1987). Using computer for instruction. *Byte, 12*(2), 149–162.
Burdine, B. H. (1981). Satellite communications. In M. Lehman & T. Burke (Eds.), *Communication technologies and information flow* (pp. 34–54). New York: Pergamon Press.
Carroll, P. B., & Swartz, S. (1987, January 2). Imnet venture of IBM, Merrill Lynch to close. *The Wall Street Journal*, p. 2.
Dozier, D., & Rice, R. (1984). Rival theories of electronic newsreading. In R. Rice (Ed.), *The new media* (pp. 103–128). Beverly Hills, CA: Sage.
Gross, L. S. (1986). *The new television technologies* (2nd ed.). Dubuque, IA: William C. Brown.
Guzda, M. K. (1985, August 3). Ad bureau soothsayer. *Editor & Publisher*, pp. 16–17.
Jeffries-Fox, B. C., & Jeffries-Fox, S. (1984). Interactive video communication. In S. Thomas (Ed.), *Studies in mass communication and technology* (vol. 1, pp. 238–248). Norwood, NJ: Ablex.
Martin, J. (1982). *Viewdata and the information society*. Englewood Cliffs, NJ: Prentice-Hall.
Meeks, B. N. (1987). The quiet revolution. *Byte, 12*(2), 183–190.
Morse, R. C. (1982, June 28). Videotex in America: The birth of electronic newspapering. *Editor & Publisher*, pp. 41–48.
Mosco, V. (1982). *Push button fantasies: Critical perspectives on videotex and information technology*. Norwood, NJ: Ablex.
Olshavsky, R. (1980). Time and the taste of adoption of innovations. *Journal of Consumer Research, 6*, 425–428.
Rapparini, R., & Sabatelli, R. (Eds.). (1982). *Videotex and the press*. Oxford, England: Learned Information.
Ricklefs, R. (1986, February 24). French connections: France plugs into a national videotex system. Telecommunications: Technologies. *The Wall Street Journal*, p. D28.
Roberts, S. K. (1984, July 19). New culture growing out of computers. *USA Today*. p. B3.
Roman, J. W. (1983). *Cablemania: The cable television sourcebook*. Englewood Cliffs, NJ: Prentice-Hall.
Sachar, E. B. (1982). Reflection on the future of the daily newspaper. *Investment Research*. New York: Goldman Sach Corporation.
Salvaggio, J. L. (1982). An assessment of Japan as an information society in the 1980s. In H. F. Didsbury, Jr. (Ed.), *Communications and the future* (pp. 88–95). Bethesda, MD: World Future Society.
Sandberg-Diment, E. (1987, February 22). Can machines be good listeners? *The New York Times*, p. F16.
Singleton, L. A. (1986). *Telecommunications in the information age* (2nd ed.). Hagerstown, MD: Ballinger.
Slack, J. D. (1984). Survey the impacts of communication technologies. In B. Dervin & M. J. Voigt (Eds.), *Progress in communication science* (Vol. 5, pp. 74–109). Norwood, NJ: Ablex.

Spinrad, N. (1984). Home computer technology in the 21 century. *Popular Computing*, 3(11), 76-82.
Stanton, T., Burns, D., & Venit, S. (1986, September). Page-to-Disk Technology. *PC Magazine*, pp. 128-177.
Sterling, C. H. (1984). *Electronic media: A guide to trends in broadcasting and newer technologies 1920-1983*. New York: Praeger.
Two videotex heavyweights quit—$80 million light. (1986, March 31). *Business Week*, pp. 31-32.
Tyler, M. (1979). *Electronic publishing: A sketch of the European experience. Teletext and viewdata in the U.S.: A workshop in emerging issues* (Background papers). Menlo Park, CA: Institute for the Future.
Videotex exodus continues. (1987, January). *Presstime*, p. 44.
Weaver, D. H. (1983). *Videotex journalism: Teletex, viewdata, and the news*. Hillsdale, NJ: Lawrence Erlbaum Associates.
Weilbacher, W. M. (1984). *Advertising* (2nd ed.). New York: MacMillan.

I
THE NEED FOR NEW RESEARCH METHODS

1

Assessing Exposure to the New Media

James G. Webster
Northwestern University

Assessing exposure to media is at the heart of much communications research. Such measurements are the primary indices of a medium's presence in our lives, its potential to influence our thoughts and actions, and its prospects for growth or decline. For these reasons, the media and related industries spend millions of dollars each year to document, analyze, and project patterns of exposure. Similarly, scholars who hope to understand the role of media in modern societies can scarcely afford to ignore exposure as a central component of their studies.

As this volume attests, a new generation of electronic media has attracted the attention of both entrepreneurs and academics. Although many forms of these new media are just emerging, it seems likely that assessments of exposure will be pivotal in determining their economic survival and gauging their social significance. In fact, the accurate measurement of exposure may be a more important component of research in new media studies than in analyses of older, more traditional forms of media.

Although many of the established techniques for measuring exposure to electronic media can be applied to these newcomers (e.g., Webster & Wakshlag, 1985), such transplanted methods are not always successful. In part, this is because the unique characteristics of new media pose new, largely unprecedented, problems of measurement. Beyond inherent differences between old and new, however, the consumers of research are asking more detailed and demanding questions about the nature of exposure.

This chapter summarizes the various applications of research on exposure, identifies the attributes of new media that complicate these efforts, and discusses possible solutions. Emphasis is on those forms of media where consumer use is not routinely monitored by a central computer. Centrally monitored communications media, such as office automation networks, pay-per-view cable, and on-line data retrieval systems, necessarily produce records of consumer use. Although the analysis of these databases can be a formidable task (e.g., Rice & Rogers, 1984), the actual measurement of exposure is typically not a problem. Rather, the chapter focuses on media where the production of an ongoing record of use is not an integral part of the technology. Here, assessments of exposure are more problematic, involving issues of measurement, sampling, and in some cases, politics.

WHY STUDY EXPOSURE?

The job of assessing exposure to new media would, of course, be pointless if such information had no value. The entire enterprise takes on meaning only when it is related to the various applications of the data. In fact, the questions that we pose shape the process of research by directing our attention to those aspects of exposure that seem most important. The applications of research, then, define what are generally considered to be the important issues of measurement and largely determine the allocation of intellectual and economic resources devoted toward solving preceived problems. It is, therefore, appropriate to begin by addressing the question: Why study exposure?

Industry Applications

If one were to consider the sheer volume of research on media exposure, the industry uses of such data would easily exceed all other applications. Since the earliest days of broadcasting, the commercial interests involved needed some way to document the extent of audience attendance. Unlike other forms of media, however, the broadcast audience had a unique, intangible quality. As a result, firms devoted to the new business audience measurement came into existence (Beville, 1985a). Today, companies specializing in ratings research are an integral part of the industry at all levels, supplying networks, stations, advertisers, agencies, and much of the creative community with data on the size and composition of electronic media audiences.

The driving force behind this concern with audiences is, of course, commercial broadcasting's reliance on advertising as a means to make money. The attention of those who are attracted to a particular program or station, can then be sold to an advertiser. Generally speaking, larger audiences command higher prices. So, for example, a television network that can add one rating point to its annual prime-time average could realize over $50 million in additional revenues (Rubens, 1984). This economic fact of life has, at least for television, placed a premium on attracting large, and necessarily heterogeneous audiences. It has also fueled an intense competition among the networks to be "number one" in the ratings, as measured by a count of television households. Although the composition of audiences has affected their saleability, segmentation schemes have historically been limited to a few broad demographic or geographic distinctions. For the most part, simple information on the incidence of exposure has been sufficient to underwrite the functions of selling and programming the electronic media.

These requirements left their mark on the procedures used to measure exposure. For a good many years, two measurement techniques have been the principle tools of ratings research; meters and diaries (Webster & Wakshlag, 1985). Meters, devices that electronically monitor the condition of television sets, have been the preferred technique for estimating the size of network audiences. Because the original metering devices did not require the active participation of respondents, meter data were free of the problems associated with self-reports of behavior. Their most important drawback, however, was that they could track only the tuning behavior of a household. Exactly who within the home was watching a given set was impossible to determine. As a result, meter data were devoid of demographic information, save for what could be inferred from the characteristics of the household itself.

The solution to the problem of who is watching has, traditionally, been to combine meter data with the self-reports contained in diaries filled out by a separate sample. These little booklets provide a log for viewers to note the program choices of each family member, or guest, over the course of a week. Diaries can also be used alone, and are the principle method for estimating audiences, market to market, in both television and radio. There are, however, a number of problems associated with diary-based data. Most significant in the context of this discussion, is the difficulty respondents seem to have noting which channel, in a multichannel environment, they are actually watching. It is generally recognized, therefore, that diary data will underrepresent the audience for cable networks (Beville, 1985a; Webster & Wakshlag, 1985).

Despite these limitations, meter and diary data have, in varying combinations, provided measures of exposure to media sufficient to meet the essential demands of industry. Above all, they have supplied continuous documentation of the sheer volume of exposure; mass audiences, consuming radio and television programming as it is served up to them.

What these techniques do not produce is any record of how individuals consume media over an extended period of time. Without using other methods, for example, it is impossible to know whether a person who watches a program one week sees it again the following week. Nor do the usual tools of ratings research produce information about the quality of exposure. Whether people actually attend to, or enjoy, what they select is not determined by conventional diaries or meters (Webster & Wakshlag, 1985).

The absence of this information should not be taken to mean that industry researchers would find the data useless. Certainly more detailed longitudinal studies on the fact of exposure would be of value to media planners concerned with the reach and frequency of various advertising campaigns. Even information about the quality of exposure might be used to improve the effectiveness of advertising (Holt, 1985; Krugman, 1985). Unfortunately, such information has been difficult and expensive to obtain. So when the utility of these data was weighed against their cost, the usual fare of the ratings services seemed, if not ideal, at least adequate.

Three factors, however, have operated to change the equation of cost versus utility. First, the emergence of new media, some with great potential to affect the nature of advertising, has underscored the limitations of traditional measurement techniques. Second, the same technological juggernaut that has made many of the new media themselves possible, has enhanced the capabilities of hardware used to measure audiences (Rubens, 1984). Third, the advertisers and their agencies have grown more sophisticated and demanding in their use of media research. There is an increased appetite for timely and precise data on the composition of media audiences (Killion, 1987). Together, these have given considerable impetus to developing the techniques for assessing exposure to media discussed at the end of the chapter.

Academic Applications

Academe's interest in exposure to media is more varied than industry's. In some ways, scholarly research on exposure is as diverse as the academic disciplines that concern themselves with the study of media. So, for example, assessments of exposure might be of interest to marketing researchers, economists, broadcast educators, critics of popular culture, policy analysts, or social scientists studying the uses and effects of media. It is useful, however, to draw a distinction among academics on the basis of the questions they ask and, in turn, the kinds of data they actually analyze.

The areas of academic research dealing most directly with exposure are those that examine the operation and regulation of industry. Marketing and advertising researchers, typically located in schools of business, have devoted considerable attention to describing and predicting patterns of exposure (e.g., Barwise & Ehrenberg, 1984; Gensch & Shaman, 1980; Headen, Klompmaker, & Rust, 1979; Henriksen, 1985; Rust, 1986). Here, research

1. ASSESSING EXPOSURE TO THE NEW MEDIA 7

is focused on questions of media reach, frequency, and schedule evaluation, often with the purpose of developing mathematical models of audience behavior. Other, closely related, analyses of viewer behavior have tried to advance a more general understanding of how and why television is consumed (Barwise, Ehrenberg, & Goodhardt, 1982; Goodhardt, Ehrenberg, & Collins, 1987; Webster, 1985a; Webster & Wakshlag, 1982). Additionally, there have been analyses of media exposure intended to inform or comment upon policy making (e.g., Ehrenberg, 1986; Webster, 1982, 1984b).

All of these studies concentrate on the specifics of exposure as it occurs "in the field." Quite often, they make use of information collected by ratings companies or other industry research services. These data offer academics tremendously rich and detailed accounts of the incidence of exposure. Yet, as with all secondary analyses, the available data limit the scope of investigation. Research is necessarily confined to those variables contained in the database, and those that can be easily added after the fact. No direct evidence on the quality of exposure, or the factors that motivated exposure in the first place is generally available.

More familiar to academics in schools of communication, perhaps, are studies of "selective exposure," and media "uses and gratifications." The inclination of individuals to selectively expose themselves to media content consistent with their actions or beliefs has long been an important component of the "limited effects" model of media influence (Chaffee & Hochheimer, 1985). More recently, theories of selective exposure have been expanded to include the preceived utility of information and assorted affective states as determinants of exposure (e.g., Zillmann & Bryant, 1985). The relevant research is typically conducted in "laboratory" environments where the causal connections that are posited can be tested in rigorous experimental designs. Gratificationists, too, have taken a rather deterministic approach to media use (McQuail & Gurevitch, 1974), imputing media consumption to a variety of individual needs. Here, however, the bulk of research has occurred outside the lab (Zillmann, 1985).

These research traditions have, for one reason or another, approached assessments of exposure differently than industry researchers. The controlled environment of experimental research has allowed the use of measurement techniques that would, outside the lab, be impractical or of questionable validity (Webster & Wakshlag, 1985). With few exceptions, field studies have devoted far more attention to the presumed causes or effects of media use than to the precise measurement of exposure (Miller, 1987). In any event, these research efforts have concentrated more on the factors that surround exposure than on actual patterns of exposure in the "the real world." Nevertheless, exposure has a central place in these theories of communication that will undoubtedly figure in research on new media.

Exacting assessments of exposure in more general works on the media's role in society have, historically, been of less importance. This has been true for two reasons. First, social theorists and critics of popular culture often have been inclined to view mass media as a pervasive, uniform influence on society. To the extent that variation in the consumption of media messages existed, these have seemed trivial distinctions for larger questions of social control and cultural homogenization. Second, with attention now focused on television as the most powerful of the media, it is increasingly common to encounter arguments that viewers are largely indifferent to the choices they do have (e.g., Gerbner & Gross, 1976). Such passivity further promotes a uniformity of media use.

As a result, to the extent that exposure is dealt with at all, it is usually summarized as time spent with a given medium. Whether these assumed homogeneities, and the resultant indifference to patterns of exposure, will be appropriate to newer forms of media is, in fact, one of the more important questions that social theorists will have to grapple with in the coming years (see chap. 11 by Webster for a discussion of these issues).

CHALLENGES POSED BY NEW MEDIA

For those in industry and academe who value precise assessments of exposure to media, the technological changes that are afoot pose serious new challenges. In an effort to bring some organization to this topic, identified here are two fundamental distinctions between old and new media that underlie many of the emerging problems of measurement.

Message Abundance

One of the hallmarks of new media is that, as a group, they vastly increase the number of messages that exist in the media environment. A.C. Nielsen (1987), for example, has reported a steady growth in the number of television channels available to the average American household. Clearly, cable, VCRs, videotex, home computers, and the like, contribute to a mushrooming of media messages. Whether this change is anything more substantive than a growth in the number of choices available to consumers can be debated, but for purposes of measurement, this simple numerical expansion causes a substantial research problem.

Nor is it an increase in the quantity of media messages, alone, that is problematic. It would be one thing if this new abundance was uniform across society, if everyone had access to the same array of messages. But that is not the case. For reasons of technology, regulation, and economics (Webster, 1986), new media are differentially available to the public. Different households, even those in close physical proximity, may now operate in quite different media environments.

CABLE CONVERSION CHART

Section	District (Cablevision)	Annapolis (United Cable)	Anne Arundel (Jones Intercable)	Baltimore County (Comcast)	Calvert (Jones Intercable)	Charles (Jones Intercable)	Columbia (Howard Cable)	Frederick (Cablevision)	Gaithersburg (Cablevision)	Lexington Park (United Cable)	Montgomery (CableTV Mont.) Red System/Blue System	Prince George's (MetroVision)	Prince George's (Prime Cable)	Station	Alexandria (Jones Intercable)	Arlington (Cable TV Arlington)	Dale City-W'bridge (CV of PW)	Fairfax (Media General)	Fort Belvoir (Columbia Cable)	Leesburg (Prime Cable)	Loudoun (Prime Cable)	Manassas (Cablevision)	Pt. William/Lake Ridge CV	Reston (WCC)
	DISTRICT	MARYLAND													VIRGINIA									
D.C. Area Broadcast	4	4	4	—	4	4	4	4	4	4	21/4	A4	B4	4	4	4	4	4	3	4	4	4	4	2
	5	5	5	25	5	5	5	5	5	5	5/5	A5	B5	5	5	5	5	5	6	5	5	5	5	6
	7	7	7	—	7	7	7	7	7	7	24/7	A7	B7	7	7	7	7	7	8	7	7	7	7	10
	9	9	9	—	9	9	9	9	9	9	26/9	A9	B9	9	9	9	9	9	10	9	9	9	9	11
	20	28	3	30	20	6	20	6	3	A10	65/40	A20	B20	20	20	20	12	20	12	11	2	20	6	12
	26	26	6	3	18	3	33	8	8	12	23/26	A8	B26	26	26	26	10	26	20	10	3	26	19	3
	32	32	21	39	19	—	32	24	6	—	29/32	A10	B19	32	32	38	36	32	32	6	6	32	20	24
	23	—	—	—	42	31	—	—	—	—	85/50	A28	B23	50	35	50	24	50	—	48	50	52	40	28
	—	—	—	—	—	—	—	—	—	—	—/—	—	B24	53	19	10	34	53	11	8	12	53	21	13
	—	—	—	—	21	—	—	36	—	—	—/—	A31	B21	56	34	54	—	56	25	32	11	56	—	23
	—	—	—	—	—	—	—	—	12	—	—/—	A33	—	66	37	—	19	52	22	19	10	60	22	16
Baltimore Area Broadcast	44	2	2	12	2	36	2	2	2	3	2/2	A2	B2	2	28	2	—	41/4	9	41	—	2	16	17
	45	11	11	21	11	35	11	11	11	11	11/11	A11	B11	11	29	11	—	11	16	42	—	11	17	18
	46	13	13	23	13	33	13	13	13	13	13/13	A13	B13	13	30	13	—	13	7	43	—	13	18	20
	33	22	12	22	22	2	29	3	—	—	19/22	A16	B22	22/67	22	22	—	22	13	12	8	22	—	14
	—	—	—	—	—	—	6	—	—	—	—/—	B14	—	24	—	—	—	—	—	—	—	—	—	—
	24	30	10	14	16	—	30	12	10	A8	80/45	A23	B27	45	45	45	—	45	30	44	—	—	—	15
	—	35	22	33	—	—	35	—	—	—	—/—	A15	B25	54	—	—	—	54	—	—	—	—	—	—
Premium Cable	12	33	14	—	29	24	—	—	—	—	—/—	—	A12	American Movie Classics	2	—	16	88	—	—	—	43	39	—
	49	—	—	—	—	—	—	—	—	—	17/20	—	B30	BRAVO	42	49	—	71	—	—	—	42	—	—
	47	—	32	8	24	19	—	14	L	7	14/17	—	B33	Cinemax	31	18	14	76	—	21	42	29	35	—
	10	18	33	—	41	14	25	15	—	6	115/16	—	B35	Disney Channel	40	21	18	65	23	40	45	30	32	—
	—	—	—	—	—	—	—	—	—	—	—/—	—	B36	Galavision	—	—	—	115	—	—	—	—	—	—
	3	16	35	5	38	17	22	16	H	2	113/14	A21	B29	Home Box Office	8	16	21	74	19	18	41	28	2	B10
	11	20	34	17	23	32	26	19	—	12	16/19	B2	A24	Home Team Sports	38	6	20	86	—	—	47	41	37	—
	48	21	30	—	40	21	18	—	—	—	15/18	A19	B34	The Movie Channel	—	—	22	81	24	20	43	46	34	B8
	—	—	—	2	37	—	—	—	—	—	—/—	—	B37	Playboy Channel	—	—	—	—	31	—	—	—	—	—
	2	—	18	20	39	—	23	—	—	—	114/15	A17	B32	Showtime	23	14	15	67	2	17	44	44	33	27
Non-Premium Cable	27	23	29	35	31	23	36	32	—	—	1/36	B13	A28	Arts & Entertainment	16	35	23	70	—	47	34	48	31	B13
	—	—	14	—	—	—	—	—	—	—	—/—	—	A5	Associated Press	—	—	—	108	—	—	—	—	—	19
	—	—	—	—	—	—	—	—	—	—	—/—	—	A5	AP Business Plus	—	—	—	107	—	—	—	—	—	—
	6	33	—	—	6	15	—	—	—	—	7/27	B16	A13	Black Entertainment	47	41	—	57	—	—	30	24	—	—
	13	14	27	28	28	34	12	26	J	10	10/10	B11	A14	Cable News Network	6	12	2	80	21	29	24	8	24	B11
	38	24	38	11	33	25	31	35	D	—	28/31	B3	A35	CBN Cable Network	44	23	28	69	26	27	26	6	23	—
	30	34	28	10	61	29	14	17	—	—	66/41	B12	A15	CNN Headline News	24	15	31	82	33	33	35	10	8	25
	15	31	19	18	27	—	16	34	E	—	82/47	B9	A19	C-Span	36	52	33	17	—	45	21	25	26	26
	14	20	40	37	—	—	—	—	—	—	83/48	—	A20	C-Span II	27	53	—	19	—	—	—	—	—	—
	—	—	—	—	—	—	—	—	—	—	—/—	—	—	Country Music Television	—	—	—	111	—	—	—	—	—	—
	17	6	20	38	34	22	—	40	—	—	69/44	B10	A33	Discovery	43	34	30	96	5	16	32	47	—	—
	25	10	26	16	25	10	3	21	G	B8	6/6	B17	A32	ESPN	12	24	6	85	36	22	23	34	13	B2
	28	—	—	15	37	8	36	—	—	—	31/34	B24	A9	Financial News Network	33	61	16	99	15	34	27	38	—	—
	—	—	—	—	—	—	—	—	—	—	—/—	—	—	Genesis	—	—	—	113	—	—	—	—	—	—
	—	—	15	—	15	16	21	—	—	—	—/—	A30	—	Home Shopping Network	49	—	—	83	—	39	15	27	—	—
	18	—	—	—	34	—	—	—	—	—	81/46	—	A3	Learning Channel	—	34	—	97	—	35	18	49	36	—
	—	—	—	—	—	—	—	—	—	—	—/—	—	—	Liberty Network	—	—	—	116	—	—	—	—	—	—
	37	25	16	24	32	18	34	27	—	—	40/37	B8	A29	Lifetime	14	46	26	72	35	28	20	15	25	22
	16	—	8	10	10	15	15	29	—	—	70/55	B9	B10	Local Government	34	35	—	16	4	—	—	1	—	—
	43	12	31	34	35	13	10	18	R	B11	8/8	B16	B6	Music TV	13	3	13	77	28	38	28	33	14	B3
	19	23	25	19	30	11	28	22	F	B13	68/43	B4	A17	Nickelodeon	15	48	11	64	27	2	33	16	27	B13
	—	—	—	—	—	—	—	39	—	—	—/—	A36	A31	PTL	—	—	37	117	—	30	—	18	—	—
	—	3	—	26	—	—	—	—	28	—	25/28	B23	A21	QVC—Shopping	—	27	—	84	—	—	—	—	—	—
	—	—	—	—	—	—	—	—	—	—	—/—	—	A6	Radar Weather	—	—	—	102	—	—	—	—	—	—
	—	—	—	—	—	—	—	—	—	—	—/—	—	A4	Sports Tracker	—	—	—	—	—	—	—	57	—	—
	—	—	—	—	—	—	—	—	—	—	—/—	—	A2	TEMPO	—	—	—	98	14	36	19	54	29	—
	41	27	36	27	36	20	—	25	—	—	27/30	B7	A26	The Nashville Network	—	40	27	109	—	31	31	23	15	—
	—	—	—	—	—	—	—	—	—	—	67/42	—	—	Trinity Broadcasting Network	—	—	—	114	—	—	—	—	—	—
	31	—	—	—	—	—	—	—	—	—	9/29	A32	A27	Univision—SIN	48	51	—	58	—	—	—	—	—	—
	42	—	—	29	—	12	—	38	—	—	30/33	B20	A10	Video Hits-1	46	39	29	110	—	46	29	39	—	—
	8	8	23	9	26	26	27	20	K	B9	20/23	B6	A34	USA Network	11	25	25	75	17	3	25	31	11	B6
	—	19	—	—	—	27	—	—	—	—	—/—	A25	—	WGN, Chicago	—	—	—	89	—	26	17	—	—	—
	22	—	24	32	—	30	19	—	I	—	22/25	A34	B28	WWOR, New York	25	19	17	79	29	25	—	21	12	—
	21	17	17	3	17	28	17	23	C	A6	12/12	A35	B8	TBS, Atlanta	17	17	8	87	18	24	16	17	10	21
	36	29	39	13	8	—	24	33	—	—	39/35	B21	A7	Weather Channel	21	36	35	101	34	23	22	14	28	—

FIG. 1.1 Cable conversion chart (compliments of *The Washington Post*)

Figure 1.1 illustrates how, in one market area, message abundance has manifested itself. Certainly, many new services have come into existence, but in the aggregate they form an uneven patchwork of coverage. For example, Black Entertainment Television, which began operation in 1980, is unavailable to many cable subscribers, and on only two systems does it have the same channel designation. Even local stations can fall victim to this treatment.

Imagine now, this situation replicated across some 7,000 cable systems serving over 200 market areas. Add to that the availability of VCRs that can themselves alter channel assignments, transplant telecast content, and introduce "library" materials into the mix, and you begin to have some sense of the potential complexities of the new video media environment.

This abundance of messages has a number of consequences for those attempting precise assessments of media exposure. The first has already been identified. The accuracy of self-reported media use suffers as the number of channels and services proliferate. As a practical matter, this has had the greatest impact on the quality of diary data. The primary diary keeper, usually a head of household, may understandably confuse one superstation with another, misidentify channel 26 because the cable system carries it on channel 15, fail to note a brief look at the news headline service, or simply be unaware of a child viewing the increasingly common second or third set.

Academic researchers, who have been more inclined to use some sort of telephone survey to assess exposure in the field (Webster & Wakshlag, 1985), face the same problem. Unaided recall obviously becomes more troublesome. On the other hand, trying to aid respondent memory by offering a comprehensive roster of all the alternatives that fit each and every media environment is, if not impossible, extremely unwieldy.

Meters, of course, are not susceptible to the same kind of reporting errors. Here too, however, message abundance presents a problem. Strictly speaking, conventional meters monitor the use of channels. It is still necessary for rating services to identify what was on a given channel at a given time. When a viewer's choices were limited to three networks and an independent or two, this was a manageable, if somewhat onerous, task. The patchwork of coverage produced by new media, the differential availability of channels, the variation in channel enumeration, and an increasing incidence of stations offering non-network programming, combine to greatly complicate the business of identifying channel content.

Not suprisingly, the job of tracking what is carried on each channel of each cable system can become a major activity of a rating service. To that end, A.C. Nielsen has instituted a special service called the Cable On-Line Data Exchange (CODE). CODE identifies channel capacity and signal carriage information for each of 8,000 cable headends across the United States

(Beville, 1985a). It is interesting to note that the units of analysis in this database are not actual cable systems. Rather, CODE maintains records for the more numerous "programming entities" referred to as headends. This is done because roughly one in five cable systems is large enough to carry different services, in different configurations, in different areas of its market. These data require constant updating, and are, on average revised every 6 months (Webster, 1985b).

Finally, there is the serious practical problem of managing all the data that measuring new media use inevitably generates. Even if meters precisely monitor channel use, and content of each channel is clearly identified as it is telecast, this information must still be manipulated in a timely and efficient manner. Although the hardware of modern computers is certainly up to the task, as is often the case, the software lags somewhere behind. Turning the continuous stream of data bits flowing in from 1,000, or more, households into a research product that is accurate and valued by its consumers is a formidable job to say the least (Killion, 1987).

Message Transience

An ability to alter the transience nature of messages is a second fundamental characteristic of new media. Among video media, the principle agent of change is the VCR. This household appliance has gone from being virtually nonexistent at the beginning of the 1980s, to being in over half of American homes as of 1987. If one assumes, as many analysts have, that this innovation will be adopted as rapidly as color television, then by the end of the 1980s, VCR penetration will stand at 60% of U.S. households (Beville, 1985b).

VCRs allow their users to break the lock-step scheduling that once seemed an inherent part of video media. This activity is labeled either *time-shifting*, simply replaying telecast material at a more convenient time, or *library-building*, adding to or drawing from a larger collection of works (Levy & Fink, 1984). In some ways, the fact that media messages may now be consumed at a time and place of an individual's choosing, is a more profound change than the message abundance previously described. The latter makes tracking exposure more difficult, but does not change the basic character of the act. The former may alter the very quality and definition of exposure.

To industry researchers, changes in message transience require answers to two very pragmatic questions. When does exposure really occur, and to what is the individual actually exposed? As VCRs proliferate, these questions become especially salient, because the answers determine what advertiser-supported media have to sell. For example, if some portion of the audience videotapes a program they are not actually watching, should they be included in a ratings report of the program's audience? On one hand, they have not viewed the program's commercial messages on the timetable intended by the advertisers. In fact, it is inevitable that some who taped the program will never replay it (Levy & Fink, 1984). Even among those who play the tape, it is possible viewers will *zap, zip*, or otherwise avoid commercial messages (Heeter & Greenberg, 1985; Kaplan, 1985). On the other hand, some viewers will watch the program, perhaps more attentively than usual, perhaps more than once.

Nor should changes in the transience of media messages be viewed only as the concern of narrow business interests. The same technology that allows consumers to rearrange broadcast schedules and to skip advertising, provides them with opportunities to explore a relatively broad range of content offerings. This newfound power to ignore some types of material, and perhaps overindulge in others would seem to have important implications for research in selective exposure, media gratifications (Levy & Fink, 1984), and international communication (see chap. 9 by Straubhaar & Boyd).

EMERGING SOLUTIONS

The very richness and complexity of the new media environment that compels more precise assessments of exposure, makes that job more difficult to accomplish. Nevertheless, progress is being made. Not surprisingly, industry researchers are leading the way. The commercial interests that depend on documenting exposure to electronic media, have an enormous stake in how measurement problems are solved, and the financial resources needed to develop solutions. Discussed here are areas in which work is being done.

Measurement

The problem of actually measuring exposure to media is one area that has received a great deal of attention. The most promising developments involve a new generation of metering devices that can cope with the complications introduced by new media. Among the enhanced capabilities of these devices are their abilities to identify the individuals who are viewing the set, monitor the various uses of a VCR unit, and collect data on household purchases obtained by having respondents scan the universal product code on items they bring home.

All these capabilities can be built into a new type of meter that is, generically, referred to as a *peoplemeter*. A. C. Nielsen and Arbitron, the two major U.S. ratings companies, have introduced their own versions of this device. Similarly, Audits of Great Britian (AGB), an international marketing research firm that has people meters operating in Europe and Asia, has attempted to establish such a service in the United States. It remains to be seen whether the market for ratings data can support all these services.

Despite some differences in design, all peoplemeters do basically the same thing. The device operates as does a conventional meter, monitoring set activity. In addition, however, such meters have small keypads that can be moved around the room like a remote control device. Sitting atop the set is a second unit, usually having illuminated numbers that correspond to the keypad. Every member of the household is assigned a number. They are instructed that, when they begin watching television, they should press their button. When they finish watching, they should press their button again. Under some systems, an on-screen prompt will periodically flash, seeking confirmation that the enumerated viewers are still present. At the end of the day, data stored in the unit are retrieved by computer over telephone lines, where they are matched to whatever viewer characteristics are on file (Webster, 1984a). Because these devices require individuals to constantly affirm their use of the set, they are sometimes called *active* peoplemeters. *Passive* peoplemeters, that could unobtrusively identify a viewer's presence, are further from implementation. Devices that use sonar or infrared sensors to accomplish this purpose, however, are being tested (Lu & Kiewit, 1987).

People meters appeal to media researchers for a variety of reasons. In principle, they provide the person-specific information contained in diaries with the speed and accuracy of conventional meters. Further, because a peoplemeter will presumably stay in a household for years, it is possible to track an individual's consumption of media over an extended period of time. These attributes are especially important to advertisers who are increasingly concerned with reaching precisely defined target markets. Certainly, the enhanced ability of the devices to clearly and continuously associate audience demographics with cable channel use is of great importance to many of the newer media services. Specialized, advertiser-supported cable networks, like music video (e.g., MTV or VH-1), are especially dependent on demonstrations that a certain audience demographic can be delivered to the advertiser. Even older media may be affected. It has been suggested, for example, that the increased availability of demographic data might cause the broadcast networks to de-emphasize traditional audience maximization objectives in favor of seeking more saleable audience subsets (Barnes & Thomson, 1988; Poltrack, 1986).

A number of problems still remain, however. Peoplemeters are no better than the devices they supplant at ascertaining the level of attention that viewers pay to the content they have chosen. It has been argued that measuring attentiveness is of growing importance, especially for advetisers, in the "noisy" environment of new electronic media (Holt, 1985). Neither can peoplemeters, as they are presently designed, monitor viewing outside the home. To measure the use of small battery powered sets, it might still be necessary to use a conventional diary, or a portable "electronic diary" into which respondents would enter information with keystrokes (AGB, 1986).

Electronic Labels

For all their technological sophistication, the new metering devices are, in and of themselves, incapable of identifying what content is actually appearing on the screen. This problem looms large in the new media environment. One promising solution involves placing some sort of "electronic label" on programming that is invisible to the viewer, but readable by a machine.

As a practical matter, one of two strategies has been employed. AGB has developed a VCR monitor that leaves an electronic "fingerprint" on any material that is recorded by a unit so equipped. The fingerprint identifies the date, time, and appropriate channel number as a program is recorded. When and if that program is replayed, the monitor reads this information. The same unit also monitors the status of the recorder as it is replayed, making it possible to pinpoint instances where content is zipped by the use of fastforwarding.

Although this approach represents a potentially significant improvement in our ability to track the use of VCRs for timeshifting, it still requires that the rating company knows what was on the channel at the time recording took place. Further, videotapes drawn from a library would be indistinguishable from one another with labels applied in this matter.

An alternative approach is to place a uniform set of labels on all content, much as consumer goods are now identified by a universal product code. There is, in fact, a way of doing that. A.C. Nielsen and the three major broadcast networks have collaborated to create a system called the Automated Measurement of Lineups (AMOL). Under this system, each program fed by the networks carries a unique electronic label in an unused portion of the signal. A decoding unit in each market picks up this information and automatically alerts Nielsen whether local affiliates have preempted the network feed (Rubens, 1984).

In principle, such a system might be extended to include all video media. Unique, but universally readable, codes could be imposed on all broadcast programs and cable programs, as well as the tapes sold and rented through video stores. In practice, this could be prohibitively expensive and require unrealistic levels of cooperation among the numerous competitors in the video marketplace. Conceptually, however, it remains an appealing way to solve the dilemma of identifying the content on the screen.

Sampling

Little has been said, so far, about issues of sampling. Yet, probability sam-

1. ASSESSING EXPOSURE TO THE NEW MEDIA 15

pling is an essential ingredient in making accurate assessments of exposure. No measurement or data-coding techniques, however powerful, will produce acceptable estimates of exposure unless they are based on an adequate sample. The fundamental attributes of new media, the abundance and variable transience of messages, present enormous, if predictable, problems for sampling.

As any student of survey research knows, when the population you are studying becomes more varied, larger sample sizes are required to maintain a given level of precision in estimating parameters. Further, all things being equal, studying a small population requires a sample equal in size to that needed for a large population. Both these factors have substantial consequences for how one must go about estimating new media audiences.

At the national level, sample sizes have had to be increased. In 1983, A. C. Nielsen, which for many years maintained a panel of 1,200 metered households, added 500 homes to the sample (Beville, 1985a). As new media proliferate and people, rather than households, become the standard unit of analysis, much larger samples will be required. To provide sufficiently precise estimates of various demographics groups, national peoplemeter samples will have to include 4,000 to 5,000 households (AGB, 1986). If the same devices are also to collect product purchase information, providing the "single source" of data prized by many advertisers, even larger samples will be needed.

Placing sophisticated hardware in such a large sample of homes is obviously expensive. At the national level, however, one or more services might find enough customers to justify the costs. At the local level, the economics of measurement and sampling place practical limits on what can be provided. Arbitron and A.C. Nielsen have conventional metered panels in the largest U.S. markets. These samples typically include 300 to 500 households. Representatives of the networks argue that twice that number is actually needed to provide stable household audience estimates (Rosenthal, 1986). Accurate measurement of channel use in even smaller populations is especially problematic. For example, a cable system might want to sell time for local advertising. Yet as Rubens (1984), has pointed out, the cost of measuring specific cable systems could exceed the cost of programming them. Without such documentation, however, effective selling is difficult.

Questions of sample size aside, the new media also require that increased attention be paid to how samples are designed and weighted (Rubens, 1984). Media that cater to relatively heterogeneous mass audiences have found such matters to be of limited importance. Estimates of the audience for more specialized services, such as music video and minority language channels, however, are quite sensitive to even minor variations in these procedures.

Surrounding all these issues of measurement, labeling, and sampling, are problems that will be resolved more as a function of marketing and politics than of methodological research. The vice president of A.C. Nielsen's Home

Video Index, is reported as saying that the mainstay of his activity is industry politics (Livingston, 1986). Disputes can range from seemingly inconsequential matters about how peoplemeter data are to be edited, to the design of samples, to how tape-delayed viewing is reported, to the timing with which certain services are introduced. What might seem to be trival issues can have significant financial implications for the providers and consumers of media research. Because both the media, and the techniques by which their use is measured, appear to have entered an extended period of change, political skirmishes are likely to be a premanent feature of the landscape. Indeed, such corporate battles can themselves be the stuff of interesting research (e.g., Beville, 1985a; Meehan, 1984).

CONCLUDING REMARKS

The fact that so much work on assessing exposure to media is done by and for industry exerts a substantial influence on the process of identifying problems and developing solutions. Quite naturally, the commercial interests involved have focused much of their attention on those new technologies that would, for good or ill, affect the business of advertiser-supported media. Those media that need not constantly report precise patterns of exposure have received less attention. So, for example, the use of subscriber-supported services like premium cable channels, or the time spent running programs on a home computer does not, from the industry's perspective, require elaborate documentation of exposure. Indeed, Rubens (1984) has gone so far as to suggest that only those new technologies that seek advertising revenues raise measurement issues at all. Although that verdict seems a bit conservative, even for industry researchers, it does reflect a real bias in their approach to the new media. That bias is, in turn, evident in this review.

Scholarly interest in assessing the consumption of new media is, as this volume demonstrates, a bit more eclectic. Academics may, for a variety of reasons, be interested in measuring exposure to new media, be they advertiser-supported or not. Broadly speaking, the problems that confront industry, confront academe as well. All new media act to create an environment of abundant messages, delivered through complex and variable structures, to a diverse population that can increasingly determine the time and place of exposure. Estimating the actual incidence of exposure to these media is a formidable job.

Fortunately, many of the new media that are of concern to communications researchers generate data on exposure. Electronic text services and centrally monitored computer networks often leave some trace of how and when they were used, although these records and their analysis are certainly not without problems (e.g., Ettema, 1985; Rice & Rogers, 1984).

There is, however, an increasingly troublesome dimension to academic work on exposure to new media. All of the kinds of data described here are proprietary. The detailed, long-term tracking done by the rating companies and the records of consumer use kept by other entertainment or information services exist for the benefit of the firms that produce or buy the research. For one reason or another, those who own the data are frequently disinclined to share the information with academe. Of course, scholarly research efforts can and will continue to collect their own data on exposure. Yet, for the reasons discussed earlier, accurate assessments will be ever more difficult and expensive propositions.

This situation presents real dangers to the quality of academic work on exposure. On one hand, to gain and keep access to propriety data, scholars may have to tread lightly on some issues, becoming a part of the political battles that surround media and their measurement. Such compromises can diminish the range and value of scholarly research. On the other hand, a failure to study emerging patterns of exposure for want of data that exist in abundance, would be tragic. Knowing how and when exposure takes place will be central to understanding media use in the information age. Striking a balance between academic independence and the need to use proprietary data may prove to be one of the more difficult aspects of assessing exposure the new media.

REFERENCES

A.C. Nielsen Co. (1987). *Nielsen report on television*. Northbrook, IL: Author.

AGB. (1986). *AGB television research*. New York: Author.

Barnes, B. E., & Thomson, L. M. (1988, May). *How will network television respond to peoplemeters?* Paper presented at the meeting of the International Communication Association, New Orleans.

Barwise, T. P., & Ehrenberg, A. S. C. (1984). The reach of TV channels. *International Journal of Research in Marketing, 1*, 34–49.

Barwise, T. P., Ehrenberg, A. S. C., & Goodhardt, G. J. (1982). Glued to the box?: Patterns of TV repeat-viewing. *Journal of Communication, 32*(4), 22–29.

Beville, H. M., Jr. (1985a). *Audience ratings: Radio, television, cable*. Hillsdale, NJ: Lawrence Erlbaum Associates.

Beville, H. M., Jr. (1985b). The audience potential of the new technologies: 1985–1990. *Journal of Advertising Research, 25*(2), RC3–RC10.

Chaffee, S. H., & Hochheimer, J. L. (1985). The beginnings of political communications research in the United States: Origins of the "limited effects" model. In M. Gurevitch & M. R. Levy (Eds.), *Mass communication review yearbook* (Vol. 5, pp 75–104). Beverly Hills, CA: Sage.

Ehrenberg, A. S. C. (1986, February). Advertisers or viewers paying? *ADMAP Monograph*.

Ettema, J. S. (1985). Explaining information system use with system-monitored vs. self-reported use measures. *Public Opinion Quarterly, 49*, 381–387.

Gensch, D. H., & Shaman, P. (1980). Models of competitive ratings. *Journal of Marketing Research, 17*, 307–315.

Gerbner, G., & Gross, L. (1976). Living with television: The violence profile. *Journal of Communication, 26*(2), 173–199.

Goodhardt, G. J., Ehrenberg, A. S. C., & Collins, M. A. (1987). *The television audience: Patterns of viewing* (2nd ed). Westmead, UK: Gower.

Headen, R., Klompmaker, J., & Rust, R. (1979). The duplication of viewing law and television media schedule evaluation. *Journal of Marketing Research, 16*, 333-340.

Heeter, C., & Greenberg, B. S. (1985). Profiling the zappers. *Journal of Advertising Research, 25*(2), 15-19.

Henriksen, F. (1985). A new model of the duplication of television viewing: A behaviorist approach. *Journal of Broadcasting & Electronic Media, 29*, 135-145.

Holt, S. A. (1985, July). The audience rates television—Qualitative ratings and commercial effectiveness. In *Research and planning: Information for management*. Washington: National Association of Broadcasters.

Kaplan, B. M. (1985). Zapping—The real issue is communication. *Journal of Advertising Research, 25*(2), 9-12.

Killion, K. C. (1987). Using peoplemeter information. *Journal of Media Planning, 2*(2), 47-52.

Krugman, D. M. (1985). Evaluating the audiences of the new media. *Journal of Advertising, 14*(4), 21-27.

Levy, M. R., & Fink, E. L. (1984). Home video recorders and the transience of television broadcasts. *Journal of Communication, 34*(2), 56-71.

Livingston, V. (1986, March 17). Statistical skirmish: Nielsen cable stats vex cable net execs. *Television/Radio Age*, p. 56.

Lu, D., & Kiewit, D. A. (1987). Passive peoplemeters: A first step. *Journal of Advertising Research, 27*(3), 9-14.

McQuail, D., & Gurevitch, M. (1974). Explaining audience behavior: Three approaches considered. In J. Blumler & E. Katz (Eds.), *The uses of mass communications* (pp. 287-301). Beverly Hills, CA: Sage.

Meehan, E. R. (1984). Ratings and the institutional approach: A third answer to the commodity question. *Critical Studies in Mass Communication, 1*, 216-225.

Miller, P. V. (1987, May). *Measuring TV viewing in studies of television effects*. Paper presented at the meeting of the International Communication Association, Montreal.

Poltrack, D. (1986, December 29). Viewpoints. *Television/Radio Age*, p. 103.

Rice, R. E., & Rogers, E. V. (1984). New methods and data for the study of new media. In R. Rice (Ed.) *The new media: Communication research and technology* (pp. 81-99). Beverly Hills, CA: Sage.

Rosenthal, E. M. (1986, March 31). Disparity between metered TV ratings firms hits fan again. *Television/Radio Age*, p. 62.

Rubens, W. S. (1984). High-tech audience measurement for new-tech audiences. *Critical Studies in Mass Communication, 1*, 195-205.

Rust, R. T. (1986). *Advertising media models: A practical guide*. Lexington, MA: Lexington Books.

Webster, J. G. (1982). *The impact of cable and pay cable on local station audiences*. Washington, DC: National Association of Broadcasters.

Webster, J. G. (1984a, April). Peoplemeters, In *Research & Planning: Information for management*. Washington, DC: National Association of Broadcasters.

Webster, J. G. (1984b). Cable television's impact on audience for local news. *Journalism Quarterly, 61*, 419-422.

Webster, J. G. (1985a). Program audience duplication: A study of television inheritance effects. *Journal of Broadcasting & Electronic Media, 29*, 121-133.

Webster, J. G. (1985b). *Television broadcast signal carriage on U.S. cable systems*. Washington, DC: National Association of Broadcasters.

Webster, J. G. (1986). Audience behavior in the new media environment. *Journal of Communication, 36*(3), 77-91.

Webster, J. G., & Wakshlag, J. (1982). The impact of group viewing on patterns of television program choice. *Journal of Broadcasting, 26*, 445-455.

Webster, J. G., & Wakshlag, J. (1985). Measuring exposure to television. In D. Zillmann & J. Bryant (Eds.), *Selective exposure to communication* (pp. 35–62). Hillsdale, NJ: Lawrence Erlbaum Associates.

Zillmann, D. (1985). The experimental exploration of gratifications from media entertainment. In K. Rosengren, L. Wenner, & P. Palmgreen (Eds.), *Media gratifications research: Current perspectives* (pp. 225–239). Beverly Hills, CA: Sage.

Zillmann, D., & Bryant, J. (1985). *Selective exposure to communication*. Hillsdale, NJ: Lawrence Erlbaum Associates.

2

Problems and Potential of Forecasting the Adoption of New Media

Bruce Klopfenstein
Bowling Green State University

Recent history has demonstrated that the successful introduction of new communication media products and services (see Singleton, 1986) may be the exception rather than the rule. Yet, optimistic forecasts for such new technologies are easily found (e.g., Klopfenstein, 1985; Koughan, 1981) and are often wrong. Cable television penetration grew more slowly in the late 1970s and early 1980s than many had forecast just a few years earlier (Krugman & Christians, 1981). Experts forecasted in 1980 that by 1985 teletext and videotext would penetrate 7% and 5% respectively of American households (Tydeman, Lipinski, Adler, Nyhan, & Zwimpfer, 1982). Klopfenstein (1985, 1986) found the various market forecasts made in the 1970s and early 1980s for consumer adoption of videodisc players were overly optimistic, whereas those for videocassette recorders were far too pessimistic. Many forecasts for adoption of direct broadcast satellite services were overly optimistic, whereas forecasts for "backyard" satellite receivers were virtually nonexistent even as the market for them developed (e.g., Barbieri, 1984). Forecasts for new media services like teleconferencing optimistically predicted 100–200fold increases in installations and service from 1980–1990 (Svenning & Ruchinskas, 1984).

Forecasts for new media are used and produced by both communication scholars and media practitioners. In academic circles, optimistic growth projections for new media technologies often are cited as if to justify research on some aspect of that new technology (see examples in Encel, 1977; Greenberger, 1985; Rice, 1984; and Rogers, 1986). In this sense, such forecasts help to set the new technology research agenda. New media forecasts are also used to help media corporations in their strategic planning. Finally, media forecasts may be useful for those developing regulatory policies for both new and existing media (Setzer, Franca, & Cornell, 1980, is one example).

Although forecasts for the new media continue to be produced from a number of sources and are widely cited, few communication scholars, industry managers, or policy makers are experts in forecasting. Despite the slow growth of some of the new media in the recent past, continuing technological developments promise to create more new media in the future (Klopfenstein, 1987). If this is so, the demand for forecasts can be expected to increase in the future. As Wheelwright and Makridakis (1985) pointed out, "when there is little uncertainty in the environment and things turn out largely as expected, there is much less need for formal forecasts, whereas in a turbulent environment with high uncertainty, the need for such forecasts is great" (p. 3).

The purpose of this chapter is to introduce some of the methods of forecasting especially as they relate to the new media. An understanding of some of the strengths and limitations of these methods will better enable the forecast consumer to judge the relative merits of others' forecasts. Knowledge of the more common forecasting methods and sources of forecasting literature will enable the communication scholar and media practitioner to better prepare their own forecasts when called on to do so in the future. Although this chapter is not a thorough review of the literature, references to some applications of forecasting to media are included.

BRIEF HISTORY OF FORECASTING

Although efforts to predict consumer adoption and use of new media date back at least to the last century (see Pool, 1983, for examples of forecasts for the telephone), the first formal forecasting methods were developed just prior to World War II. These methods, based on statistical procedures on time-series data patterns, were primarily intended to model those patterns rather than to predict their course into the future. After World War II, application of these and new models specifically to forecasting problems accelerated. Commercial econometric forecasting firms were founded in the 1960s, and the computer allowed the use of increasingly complex forecasting models (Makridakis, 1986).

Since the early 1960s, commitment to forecasting in organizations of all types had grown steadily (Wheelwright & Makridakis, 1985). The accuracy of many formal forecasts was not (and, indeed, could not be) studied until the 1970s. Ascher's (1978) work remains as the landmark study of past technological forecasts. The founding of the *Journal of Forecasting* in 1982 and the *International Journal of Forecasting* in 1985 are further indications of both the relative youth and recent growth of the forecasting field.

DEFINITIONS OF FORECASTING

Forecasting is a subset of the more general field of futures research. *Futures research* may be defined as "any activity that improves understanding about future consequences of present developments and choices" (Amara & Salancik, 1972, p. 415). Forecasting is directly involved with predicting the likelihood of one of several possible future states.

Godet (1979, 1983) compared forecasting with other futures research concepts as seen in Table 2.1. One often overlooked difference is that between forecasting and planning; a plan is the objective of a future goal, whereas a forecast is some expectation about the future. Godet (1983) believed the future should *not* be seen as a predetermined line and argues for the use of the "prospective" approach to forecasting. This approach

> accepts that there is a multiplicity of possible futures at any given time, and that the actual future will be the outcome of the interplay between the various protagonists in a given situation and their respective intentions. How the future evolves is explained as much by human action as by the influence of causalities. (p. 183)

Whether one embraces Godet's prospective approach or not, some acknowledgment of the unpredictability inherent in forecasting is critical.

Many of the forecasts for consumer adoption of new media would fall into the categories of conjecture, projection, and prediction in Table 2.1. Others seem more closely related to prophesy. Godet's definition of forecasting reflects the attempt to move forecasting beyond the realm of art

TABLE 2.1
Godet's (1983) Summary of Futures Definitions

Conjecture: Probable hypothesis.
Projection: Extension into the future or variation of past trends.
Prediction: Statement of fact before the event. (Delphic oracle.)
Prophesy: Prediction by divine inspiration.
Prospective Analysis: All-embracing, qualitative and quantitative voluntarist, multiple scenarios. (Largely a Latin concept.)
Forecasting: Assessment with a degree of confidence (probability) of trend over a given period; quantitative, deterministic, based on past data and a number of assumptions.
Futurology: All aspects of research on the future. (An Anglo-Saxon Concept)
Scenarios: Coherent series of assumptions.
Planning: Practical means of achieving a desired future.

and into science. Many Europeans like Godet, however, argue for the use of largely qualitative techniques in futures research, and often against deterministic methods. This chapter examines both.

TECHNOLOGICAL DEVELOPMENT AND FORECASTING METHODS

As noted by Linstone and Simmonds (1977), the most important step in forecasting is the initial formulation of the right questions. There are a multitude of specific methods that may be applied to address various forecasting tasks. What are the methods and how may they be applied to new media forecasting? It partially depends on the development stage of the medium. Bright (1973a) laid out a progression of the stages in technological development that is also helpful for selecting an appropriate forecasting technique. The stages are listed in Table 2.2.

Although this is an oversimplification, generally the more appropriate forecasting methods move from qualitative to quantitative as the technology progresses from the laboratory to widespread acceptance in the marketplace. In addition, consideration moves over time from investigation of the source of the innovation to its eventual users. That is, the unit of analysis moves from the technology to the eventual user. This is due to the general lack of available data when the technology is first developed; as experience in the marketplace is gained, sales data and research on user behaviors and attitudes become available. As a new media technology progresses from an idea to market acceptance, more market data become available and different forecasting approaches are more appropriate. Thus, different forecasting strategies may be employed for different stages in the development of any new technology, including those surrounding new media. The following discussion of forecasting methodologies will begin with those most appropriate for the early stages of technological development (e.g., stages 1–5 in Table 2.2) and move to those most appropriate when widespread adoption begins to occur (stages 6–8).

TECHNOLOGICAL FORECASTING

Technological forecasting (TF) is most useful in the earliest stages of new media development. Joseph Martino (1983) is a leading expert of TF. He defined it as "a prediction of the future characteristics of useful machines, procedures, or techniques" (p. 2). Because TF is used to predict the long-term development of technology, its methods are generally qualitative. TF may be used to predict technological breakthroughs as yet unachieved.

TABLE 2.2
Bright's (1973a) Stages in the Process of Technological Innovation

Stage: Identified by	Comment
1: Scientific suggestion, discovery, recognition of need or opportunity	Latter source seems to be origin of majority of contemporary innovations.
2: Proposal of theory or design concept.	Implying crystallization of theory or design concept that is ultimately successful; usually culmination of much trial and error.
3: Laboratory verification of theory or design concept	Demonstration of existence or operational validity of concepts suggested in previous stage; may be difficult for manager to assess because thing demonstrated usually is phenomenon rather than application.
4: Laboratory demonstration of application	Principle is embodied in laboratory "breadboard" model of device (or sample material or its process equivalent) showing theory of stage 2 reduced to (hopefully) useful form.
5: Full-scale or field trial	Concept has moved from laboratory bench into its first trial on large scale; succession of prototypes follows, leading eventually to saleable model.
6: Commercial introduction of first operational use.	First sale of operational system; may be deliberate or unconscious premature application of previous stage and so be replete with debugging problems and subsequent changes in technology.
7: Widespread adoption as indicated by substantial profits, common usage, and significant impact.	Admittedly, not sharply defined; individual firm might choose to classify as recovering its R&D investment through profits on sale of innovation or simply through achievement of profitability; naturally, one might define this as given percent displacement, or as given percent of adopters.
8: Proliferation	Technical advice is applied to other uses; or principle is adapted to different purposes; this stage may begin much earlier.

Among the methods of TF are monitoring, Delphi, scenarios, historical analogy, and growth curves.

Monitoring

It is possible to forecast technological change before it has any effect on existing technology. A method of technological forecasting based on seeking signals of technological change as they occur is known simply as *monitoring* (Bright, 1973b). Monitoring may be employed to detect the first stages of Bright's (1973a) process of technological innovation. The environment is monitored to detect the initial development, progress, and the likely consequences of new technological advances. Monitoring goes beyond scanning the environment as it includes evaluation and continuous review.

Keeping track of paper topics and attendance at engineering conferences (such as the Society of Motion Picture and Television Engineers) is one example of early detection in monitoring. If one topic gathers a great deal of attention, the forecaster must decide whether wishful thinking, a "bandwagon effect," or major progress are responsible for the interest. Although traditional technological lead times are growing shorter, it remains generally true that if it is not in the research labs today, it will not be on the market for 5 or 10 years (Renfro & Morrison, 1983; see also Graham, 1986).

Recent history has shown that announcements of corporate interest and/or investment in new media is not necessarily a sign of genuine progress (e.g., announced corporate joint ventures in videotex). Whirlpool (Davis, 1973) has had considerable success with monitoring and continues to use it today. Naisbitt (1982) used a form of monitoring to produce his popular *Megatrends*.

Delphi

Delphi is not a forecasting procedure per se; it is a vehicle for improving group action (Martino, 1985). Applying the Delphi technique to long-term forecasting became one of the most popular TF methods by the early 1970s (Linstone & Turoff, 1975; *Technological Forecasting and Social Change*, 1975, is devoted to Delphi.) It was originally developed by Olaf Helmer and others at the RAND corporation. Delphi was created to gather expert opinion about developing new technologies with which little or no "real-world" feedback yet exists. The general lack of available knowledge about a new technology requires the consultation of experts in the field. In Delphi, a panel of experts are identified and asked to reply to several rounds of questionnaires about the technology under study.

Delphi has three characteristics that distinguish it from interpersonal group interaction: anonymity, iteration with controlled feedback, and statistical group response (Martino, 1983, p. 16). Delphi is intended to overcome undesirable psychological factors typically found with a group of experts such as specious persuasion, unwillingness to abandon publicly expressed opinions, and the bandwagon effect of majority opinion (Dalkey & Helmer, 1963). Although Delphi is usually a mail survey, Turoff (1972) showed long ago that it may also be done by computer conferencing (Waggoner & Goldberg, 1986, is a recent example).

After the first round has been tabulated, successive survey instruments not only ask questions but supply participants with aggregate results of the previous round. This allows the experts to take into account the views of others and forces "outliers" to defend or modify their position(s). After a total of three to five rounds, consensus forecasts are reached while some lingering disagreements may remain. The first round's questions are general with successive rounds becoming more particular. Delphi tries to establish the experts' single most likely predictions, and this is considered its strength. Studies have shown that group predictions have smaller errors than individual predictions do (Parente, Anderson, Myers, & O'Brien, 1984).

The advantages of Delphi are its ability to forecast any technology, its use of experts who may have information and insights not otherwise available, and the relatively high degrees of reliability and validity that may be obtained especially given a large enough panel. (Hill & Fowles, 1975, address reliability and validity issues in Delphi.) The disadvantages include determining who the panelists will be, possible biases shared by the panelists (both if their common backgrounds encourage similar thinking and/or if they represent a vested interest in the technology), reliability problems when the panel is too small, and the time needed to complete it (especially when using four or five rounds). Sackman (1975) provided a controversial, negative critique of Delphi that is rebutted in an issue of *Technological Forecasting and Social Change* (see, for example, Coates, 1975).

An example of a Delphi forecasting study related to new media is one undertaken on the videodisc player in the mid-1970s. The U.S. Navy was interested in the expected development of videodisc player technology especially as it related to education and training applications. It commissioned a Delphi study to project the development of videodisc technology to 1986 (Daynes, 1976). A panel of 55 experts from corporations working on videodisc players, education, engineering, and the media participated in all four rounds of the study. The study correctly concluded that the videodisc would be successfully applied in education and training, prices of both videotape and videodisc machines would decrease, more than one disc format would be in use in 1986, and videodisc movies would not be the most popular use of the technology. Interestingly, little consensus was reached on the expected cultural and economic impacts of the videodisc player.

It is difficult to assess the accuracy of this study although its projections were made for 1986. For example, although the study projected 5% videodisc penetration into U.S. home's by 1986, this was a fairly conservative forecast compared to others made in 1976 (Klopfenstein, 1985). In that sense, the Delphi study really was more accurate than other forecasts even though in absolute terms is was too optimistic. The participants also predicted that medium-specific software (including videodisc "periodicals") would be necessary for videodisc adoption. Had the videodisc player been introduced by 1977 and had music videodiscs been available in quantity, perhaps the videodisc's fate would have been different (and this forecast study more "accurate").

Scenarios

In many instances, several paths for a technology or new medium may seem plausible. Rather than develop a singular forecast that predicts only one outcome, the forecaster instead may prepare a set of probable future scenarios. Scenario construction may be seen as more of a tool in planning rather than as a forecasting method per se (Beck, 1982), but scenarios assume there is more than one probable future (the view shared by Godet, 1983, and others). They may take into account different regulatory, technological, and economic/market conditions. Corporate decision making in the development of a new media technology is another variable of importance (Graham, 1986).

Much of the early work on scenario writing was developed by Herman Kahn of the Hudson Institute. As noted by Makridakis and Wheelwright (1978):

> *Scenario writing* takes a well-defined set of assumptions, then develops an imaginative conception of what the world would be like if these assumptions were true. In this sense, scenarios are not future predictions by themselves. Rather they present a number of possible alternatives, each one based on certain assumptions and conditions. It is up to the decision maker to assess the validity of the assumptions in deciding which scenario is most likely to become reality. (p. 496)

Although Kahn's development of the scenario method was intended for identifying probable paths of macroeconomic or political developments, it is applicable to new media forecasting as well. The problem of forecasting home video technologies, for example, was ripe for scenario writing. One scenario might have assumed VCR prices would remain high, whereas videodisc player (VDP) and software prices would be low. Another scenario could have assumed VCR prices would come down to a point where the less versatile VDP lost any low cost advantage. Another variable that could have been included is the availability of pay programming on cable that might be a complement to the VCR, but be an alternative or even a substitute for the VDP. Scenarios accept the multiplicity of possible outcomes.

McPhail and McPhail (1986) is a recent example of the construction of scenarios to forecasting in telecommunications. The study was commissioned by the Canadian government. Three general elements were included: technology and services; market structures; and regulation. Within each of these elements, probable developments were constructed from data gathered via literature searches and from various authorities in the telecommunications industry. Finally, what were considered to be the most likely combinations of all the developments based on expert opinion were merged into five final scenarios. Policy makers can monitor actual developments to see which scenario seems to be most appropriate and may even devise regulations to encourage movement down the most favored path.

Historical Analogy

One of the simpler ways to forecast the growth of a new technology is by

2. FORECASTING THE ADOPTION OF NEW MEDIA

an analogy to a previous or existing technology. The analogy assumes the new technology will follow the growth patterns established by the earlier technology. Thus, the growth pattern of color television sales might be expected to follow that of black-and-white television. As Martino (1983) pointed out, however, there is no inherent necessity in the outcome of historical situations, no two historical situations are alike in all respects, and historically conditioned awareness may change the way people actually behave.

Although the analogy between the growth of black-and-white and color television growth seems quite appropriate, color sales actually lagged well behind those of black-and-white set sales. Few television shows were broadcast in color, few stations had the capacity to broadcast in color, and most people waited until their black-and-white set failed to replace it with a color set. A more current example is the growth of VCR adoptions. Although VCR growth has been similar to that of color television, it is not unreasonable to suggest that VCR penetration may never reach that of color television. At the same time, the VCR has diffused more rapidly than did color television (Klopfenstein, 1987).

Klopfenstein (1985) found many forecasts used historical analogy to forecast sales of videodisc players. The forecasts that used this analogy simply assumed that the VDP would diffuse at a rate similar to that of color television. This is really a supply-side approach; little consideration was given to the demand side of the forecasting problem. In summary, historical analogy may be used as a guide to forecasting the growth of new media, but one must be very careful to consider all variables when making comparisons between two or more technologies.

Growth Curves

History suggests that when a technology is new, growth is slow due to initial technical difficulties. Once these are overcome, growth in performance and market acceptance is often rapid. The result is the familiar S-shaped growth curve (also associated with diffusion theory. Mathematical diffusion models that include communication variables are summarized later.) In the marketing literature, the curve is applied to the product lifecycle theory (Nicholls & Roslow, 1986).

Growth occurs in three stages: (a) initially slow as the technology has to prove itself over existing technologies (stage 6 in Table 2.2), (b) explosive growth as its superiority is demonstrated and awareness of the technology becomes widespread (stage 7), and (c) growth levels off as technological or socioeconomic limits are reached (stage 8). Twiss (1984) cautioned that:

> The S or logistic curve . . . is not a law of nature; it is merely a pattern of development that has been observed so frequently in the past that there is strong circumstantial evidence to assume that it will be repeated in any fu-

ture development. In spite of this evidence, it should not be forgotten that the curve is shaped by human decisions and these can vary in their application. (p.21)

Adoption curves of communication hardware (telephones, radio sets, black-and-white television sets, color sets, and now videocassette recorders) have each followed a variation of this curve. Indeed, sales of television sets is a favorite example of growth curve forecasting in many forecasting texts. Martino (1983) included an example of applying growth curves to the diffusion of cable television.

Technological substitution is another means of technological forecasting using growth curves. Fisher and Pry (1971) found that once a new technology had captured about 5% of an existing technology's market, there was a high probability that it would completely replace that technology eventually. The pattern of substitution also follows a logistic (or S) curve. Finally, the ratio of the volume of new products (f) to the volume over that of the displaced products (1-f) appears as a straight line when plotted on semilog paper.

For example, color television sets were substituted for black-and-white television. Twiss (1984) included an example of the substitution process in Britain (where highly accurate set rental data are available). The substitution of digital for analog technology is another potential application of Fisher and Pry (1971). Audio compact disc technology is beginning to replace existing phonograph technology. Digital tape-recording will probably replace both analog video- and audio-recording.

Meade (1984) discussed some problems with using growth curves in forecasting. Although curves may be found to fit historical data rather well, he said, they are not necessarily good for predicting future growth patterns. For example, Meade cited one study (Hutchesson, 1967) that discovered two curves fit existing data equally well but produced widely divergent forecasts. Meade included a similar example also using color television growth in Britain.

Issues in Technological Forecasting

Martin (1977) pointed out the pitfalls of much technological forecasting. He noted that it is often difficult for us to look beyond the technological limits in which we currently reside. Applications of technology are also difficult to see; the computer, for example, seemed limited to scientific calculations. Few if any foresaw the widespread use of personal computers especially for word processing.

Some technological developments are simply not predicted ("technological surprises"). Forecasters often underestimate the time needed for a new technology to replace an existing one or the complexity involved in the development of other technologies. Graham (1986), for example, gave an account of the unforeseen obstacles RCA faced in developing its videodisc player. Legal and political constraints also must be recognized.

Very few studies of technological forecasting accuracy are found in the literature. Wise (1976) analyzed more than 1,500 technological predictions made from 1980-1940 by a wide variety of "forecasters." He found little difference in the accuracy of experts and nonexperts in forecasting a given field. Pool (1983) looked at past technological predictions made for the telephone during a similar period: 1876-1940. He concluded that economic and marketing considerations were the most important predictors of actual telephone development and that "the best forecasts made about the telephone arose from . . . analyses by people who both understood the technology and sought to assess how to implement it in a way that would pay" (p. 156). Withington (1985) looked back at his forecasts for the evolution of computer technology to conclude that forecasts that are market-driven (i.e., matching unmet user demands with technological potentials) are the most reliable. Given the nature of the economy in the United States, these findings perhaps should not be too surprising.

Ascher (1978) conducted the most comprehensive analysis of past technological forecasts currently available. He investigated the accuracy of over 165 forecasts in six subject areas. He found, for example, that 9 of 12 forecasts for computer technological capabilities erred optimistically. Among Ascher's key findings regarding the inaccuracy of forecasts is that of "assumption drag" — the continued use of assumptions long after their validity has been contradicted by empirical data. Clearly forecasts today should take past errors into account.

New Product Forecasting

Once a new medium is introduced (e.g., Bright's stages 5-7), feedback from the marketplace can be used instead of expert opinion. A myriad of new product forecasting models have been developed in the marketing literature. Because the new media may be thought of as new products, many of these marketing models may be applied to forecasting consumer adoption of them. New product forecasts are made based on consumer buyer intent surveys, the product lifecycle (development, introduction, growth, maturity, decline), the diffusion of innovations, and time-series analysis where sales data are available. Wind, Mahajan, and Cardozo (1981) included various approaches to new product forecasting and Assmus (1984) reviewed various new product forecasting models.

Consumer Buyer Intent Surveys

Many forecasts for new products (and audience adoption of new media technologies) are based on the results of consumer attitude and/or purchase intention surveys. Intention-to-buy surveys are notoriously unreliable. Fishbein and Ajzen (1975, see also Ajzen & Fishbein, 1977), for example, have investigated the tenuous relationships between attitudes, intentions, and actual behavior. They have found that strong correlations between actual behavior and intended behavior only occur when measures of both variables closely correspond in terms of (a) the *action* to which they refer, (b) the *target* toward which the action is directed, (c) the *context* in which the action occurs, and most importantly (d) the *time* at which the behavior is performed.

Forecasts that are based on buyer-intent surveys are susceptible to such validity problems. Consumers often are asked whether they would adopt a new product *before* the product is actually on the market. The research of Fishbein and Ajzen suggested that such research is not likely to have much predictive accuracy. Foxall (1984) noted that by the time a new product is made available, unexpected events often will have intervened. In summary, consumer surveys are most appropriate in forecasting when the new product (or medium) is already on the market (Bright's stage 7).

The new interactive media may be used to catalog actual uses as opposed to reliance on self-reported use. Rice and Rogers (1984) discussed the computer-generated data made possible by some new media. Ettema (1984) included some empirical evidence along these lines. In comparing data gathered via a videotex system with self-reported usage, Ettema found a relatively low correlation between the two (r ranged from .33 to .39 for three usage variables). The peoplemeters being introduced in television audience research are also showing significant differences in television program viewership from the self-reported diary method (Beville, 1986).

Von Hippel (1986) went beyond buyer-intent surveys to suggest that research on the first or "lead" users of new products (similar to those labeled by diffusion research as *innovators*) can be used to identify novel (and perhaps unpredictable) applications. These applications may lie outside the bounds of the producers' (and researchers') expectations for use of the product. In forecasting adoption of new media, this serves as a reminder that innovators and early adopters may reveal uses not expected or apparent to researchers. Although the applications of the lead users may not be typical of later adopters, the investigator should not assume that the adopter necessarily will use the new medium as expected. Rogers (1983) referred to this process as re-invention in diffusion theory.

Time-Series Analysis

Time-series analysis is reserved for situations in which empirical evidence (e.g., sales figures) are already available. It involves statistical techniques that seek to identify and to explain any regularity or systematic variation in the series of data due to seasonality, cyclical patterns that repeat every few years, trends in the data, growth rates of these trends, and inherent randomness in the data (Chambers, Mullick, & Smith, 1974). Box-Jenkins is one of the more popular time-series analysis approaches. A wealth of literature is available on such sales forecasting techniques that are not repeated here, but they are less useful in their applications of new media forecasting at least until a few years' sales figures are available.

Accuracy of New Product Forecasting

The literature that reports the accuracy (actual sales vs. forecast sales) of new products is large and growing. In a landmark study, Tull (1967) investigated the accuracy of various companies' new product forecasts and found an average forecast error of 65% for new product unit sales and 128% for new product profits. A multitude of similar studies has appeared since. Klopfenstein's (1985) examination of 29 forecast studies made from 1968–1984 for home video products (videocassette recorders and videodisc players) revealed similarly, overly optimistic forecasts for videodisc players but overly pessimistic forecasts for VCRs. Klopfenstein (1985) and Schnaars and Berenson (1986) came to similar conclusions about why market forecasts had succeeded and failed. Schnaars and Berenson's analysis is based on 90 forecasts in the business press (*Business Week, Fortune, and The Wall Street Journal*) for what were expected to be "growth" markets including cable television, quadraphonic audio, CB radios, color television, videogames, and personal computers.

Diffusion of Innovations and Forecasting

Although few forecasting texts include it as a means for forecasting, the diffusion of innovations can be applied to forecasting the adoption of new media. Rogers (1983) provided an exhaustive review of diffusion research. He defined diffusion as the process by which an innovation is communicated through certain channels over time among the members of a social system. Rogers (1986) examined several new communication technologies from a diffusion perspective including case studies of the adoption of computers, electronic mail, automatic teller machines, and others.

Among the objects of research within the diffusion tradition are the innovation-decision process (knowledge, persuasion, decision, implementation, and confirmation), innovativeness and adopter categories (innovators, early adopters, early majority, late majority, and laggards), and the rate of adoption. Rate of adoption is the relative speed with which an innovation is adopted by members of a social system. Five attributes of innovations are relative advantage, compatibility, complexity, reliability, and observability. Each has been found to correlate positively or negatively with potential adoption. By identifying and measuring these attributes, forecasters may predict probable adoption or rejection of new media.

Bolton (1983), for example, applied diffusion theory to predict the likely consumer rejection of a prototype videotex system. He added risk to the five attributes just given associated with adoption decisions. Bolton discovered from a purchase probability instrument administered to consumers in test homes *over time* that respondents rated the service negatively on five of the six perceptual attributes. Thus, Bolton predicted rejection of the product should it be introduced as designed. Indeed, the sponsors of the system chose not to market it.

When plotted cumulatively over time, the pattern of adoption results in the S-shaped curve previously discussed. Once the adoption of an innovation takes place, estimates of its eventual diffusion may be made based on this curve. Diffusion of innovations may be applied to the marketing of new products. The diffusion model represents the spread of the innovation among potential adopters as a mathematical function of elapsed time since its introduction. Mahajan and Muller (1979) and Wind et al. (1981) review the general use of diffusion and forecasting models. Beville (1966) applied diffusion theory (and the product life-cycle theory) retrospectively to discover the factors that were responsible for the adoption of color television sets.

Several mathematical diffusion models have been posed based on the Bass (1969) type of diffusion model (see also Tigert & Farivar, 1981). The diffusion process begins with the first adopters, or "innovators," who are then imitated by others. Bass (1969) proposed the following diffusion (sales growth) model for consumer durables (including, for examples, color television):

$$S(T) = pm + (q = p)Y(T) - (q/m)[Y(T)]^2$$

where the constant p is the "coefficient of innovation" and the constant q is the "coefficient of imitation" to reflect word-of-mouth communication between adopters. The constant m represents the number of potential first time adopters, $Y(T)$ is the cumulative number of previous adopters at time T, and $S(T)$ is the predicted number of adopters in the period T. The same model may be expressed as:

$$S(T) = a + bY_{t-1} + cY^2_{t-1}$$

where a estimates $q - p$ and c estimates $-q/m$. From the statistical sales data for a given innovation, a multiple regression may be performed.

The model has been applied to new media technologies in the literature. Dodds (1973) used the Bass model to project new subscriptions to cable television beyond 1972. He found that the model fit the actual data from 1963–1972 and concluded that the market was rapidly approaching saturation. This is an example of how a forecasting method can easily go wrong. The static Bass model as employed by Dodds did not take into account the rapid changes in cable's regulatory and economic environment that were about to take place.

More recently, Lancaster and Wright (1983) applied the Bass model to British VCR sales growth to 1989. Although the model predicted that sales would peak in 1984, actual data (Euromonitor, 1984) indicated a 50% decrease in 1984 after a flat 1983. Although the authors did not know how well their forecast would compare with actual sales, they did include three caveats in the article: (a) the forecast is only a guide to the future because it shows the market in only a limited number of ways omitting minor (and potentially important) variables, (b) the prediction will only be good within limits because yesterday's data are being used to predict the future, and (c) human judgment remains an important element in prediction.

Mahajan and Peterson (1985) reviewed in detail a number of related mathematical diffusion models. Heeler and Hustad (1980) found the Bass model to be of limited usefulness in the early stages of a new product's diffusion.

Accuracy in Forecasting

Twiss (1980) has pointed out that accuracy should not in and of itself be the only criterion of forecast utility. Moyer (1984) picked up on Ascher's work to address possible reasons why forecasts often fail to predict future events accurately. Moyer offered reasons for the failure of long-term forecasting that include oversight of underlying (social) forces, failure to consider technological substitution, common assumptions held by forecasters, and intentional forecaster bias.

The basic assumptions on which a forecasting method is based are the key to useful and hopefully more accurate forecasts (Ascher, 1978). Godet (1983) argued that three key factors are responsible for many forecasting mistakes: (a) inaccurate data coupled with unstable models; (b) lack of a global, qualitative approach; and (c) explanation of the future in terms of the past. Godet advocated the use of scenarios due to the unpredictability of human actions and interactions. Twiss (1984) similarly argued that "although the techniques of forecasting may sometimes appear as scientific relationships, they are in reality only a model of how human beings are behaving" (p. 21). Like Godet, Twiss suggested that managers should be concerned with a number of possible outcomes rather than one forecast possibility. The number of poor forecasts for new media lends support to the views of Godet and Twiss.

Evidence is growing that application of more than one forecasting method to a problem results in higher forecast accuracy. This is true for both qualitative and quantitative methods. Mahmoud (1984) concluded his review of the literature on forecasting accuracy by concluding that simple forecasting methods are as accurate as complex ones, which is good news to those not well versed in forecasting methodologies.

Applying Forecasting to New Media

Forecasting remains both an art and a science. When forecasting new media, care must be taken not to be overly optimistic about the likelihood of consumer adoption. Forecasts from the late 1970s and early 1980s for consumer adoption of videotex, subscription television, interactive cable, and direct broadcast satellites attest to the problem of optimism. Many of these were market forecasts that used a top-down "method" to identify a potential market (e.g., all U.S. television households) and predict saturation of the market within x years.

In the case of new technologies, the developers (both the engineers and the corporate sponsors) begin with a near monopoly on knowledge. They are inherently optimistic about the technology's future or they would not be developing it. Often, the time the new technology will take for development and the rate of market acceptance are both underestimated. As aptly noted by Twiss (1984), "It is far easier to visualize an 'end-state' scenario for when the new product is mature than to assess the path by which it will reach the mature state" (p. 19). Carey and Moss (1985) have shown the time it took for various communication technologies to diffuse. These data can help stem the optimism that seems to blind forecasters to the requisite time needed before mass adoption can take place (for example, color television diffused slowly from 1954–1960 and the VCR diffused slowly from 1975–1979).

There are also instances, however, when new media grew more rapidly than predicted. Indeed, Olshavsky (1980) has shown that other recent household innovations have diffused more rapidly than past innovations. Radio, black-and-white television, "backyard" satellite receivers, and videocassette recorders diffused more rapidly than originally forecast. Miniature, portable television sets may become the next technology to surprise us with rapid diffusion and its potential impact on television viewing behavior.

One of the difficulties in forecasting consumer adoption of new media (or anything else for that matter) is that his or her decision to adopt is not as rational or calculated as those of organizations. This makes his or her decision less predictable. In addition, although many industrial products are developed in response to user needs (Von Hippel, 1986), new media are often the result of technology and market push rather than consumer demand. That is, equipment manufacturer and/or software (or program) providers often introduce new technologies because they are available, not because consumers expressed an a priori need for the technology. Such has been the case with videotex, teletext, the videodisc player and even home computers. A key for the forecaster is try to determine the possible wants and needs for the medium.

Different forecasting methods are appropriate for different new media—not because the media are different as much as each medium is in its own, unique stage of diffusion and may have its own alternative, complementary, and substitute technologies (see Klopfenstein, in press). A long-range forecast also has to consider social and economic changes as well as the changes associated with the new medium in question.

Once a new medium has been introduced, user data can be collected for application to forecasting. Some measure of the user's satisfaction with the new technology may be taken. This is in addition to simple frequency of use statistics. As adoption begins to accelerate, the forecaster should begin to search for limits. Cable television in its present form, for example, is unlikely to be adopted by more than about 55% of all television households (Beville, 1984). Quantitative techniques are appropriate as market sales/adopter data becomes available.

The last task for the forecaster is to evaluate the interaction between the new media and the old. History has shown that older communication media adapt to the new rather than become extinct. Even as this analysis is undertaken, the forecaster must continue to monitor the environment for signals of new technologies. The process has come full circle.

Regardless of the stage in which the technology under study falls, the forecaster must accept some unpredictability. There will be intervening events that cannot be anticipated with any certainty. The best way out of this dilemma is the construction of scenarios. In this way, forecasters will enhance their efforts to be accurate and forecast users will be alerted to the likelihood of more than one possible path. The utility of the forecast may be more important than its absolute accuracy.

Finally, forecasting must be viewed as a process. The forecasting problem must not be viewed as static—it is not. The forecaster should modify the forecast as necessary, by taking into account the actual developments when they occur (thus addressing the problem of assumption lag noted by Ascher, 1978). The forecast is most valid at the point it is made. New technologies can be expected to change the media environment on a continuous basis. The need for forecasting will continue. Improvement in forecasting will come even as we learn from past forecasting mistakes.

REFERENCES

Ajzen, I., & Fishbein, M. (1977). Attitude–behavior relationships: A theoretical analysis and review of empirical research. *Psychological Bulletin, 84,* 888–918.

Amara, R. C., & Salancik, G. R. (1972). Forecasting: From conjectural art toward science. *Technological Forecasting and Social Change, 3*, 415-426.

Ascher, W. (1978). *Forecasting: An appraisal for policy-makers and planners*. Baltimore, MD: The Johns Hopkins University Press.

Assmus, G. (1984). New product forecasting. *Journal of Forecasting, 3*, 121-138.

Barbieri, R. (1984). DBS: If wishes were dishes. *Channels, 4*(4), 48.

Bass, F. M. (1969). A new product growth model for consumer durables. *Management Science, 15*, 215-227.

Beck, P. W. (1982). Corporate planning for an uncertain future. *Long Range Planning, 15*(4), 12-21.

Beville, H. M., Jr. (1966). *The product life cycle theory applied to color television*. Unpublished masters thesis, New York University, New York.

Beville, H. M., Jr. (1984, July 9). VCR penetration: Will it surpass cable by 1990? *Television/Radio Age, 31*(25), 27-31, 108-11.

Beville, H. M., Jr. (1986). Peoplemeter will impact all segments of TV industry. *Television/Radio Age, 34*(7), 53-57.

Bolton, T. (1983). Perceptual factors that influence the adoption of videotex technology: Results of the Channel 2000 field test. *Journal of Broadcasting, 27*(2), 141-153.

Bright, J. R. (1973a). The process of technological innovation — An aid to understanding technological forecasting. In J. R. Bright & M. E. F. Shoeman (Eds.), *Guide to practical technological forecasting* (pp. 3-12). Englewood Cliffs, NJ: Prentice-Hall.

Bright, J. R. (1973b). Forecasting by monitoring signals of technological change. In J. R. Bright & M. E. F. Shoeman (Eds.), *Guide to practical technological forecasting* (pp. 238-256). Englewood Cliffs, NJ: Prentice-Hall.

Carey, J., & Moss, M. (1985). The diffusion of new telecommunication technologies. *Telecommunication Policy, 9*(2), 145-158.

Chambers, J. C., Mullick, S. K., & Smith, D. D. (1974). *An executive's guide to forecasting*. New York: Wiley.

Coates, J. F. (1975). In defense of Delphi. *Technological Forecasting and Social Change, 7*(2), 193-194.

Dalkey, N. C., & Helmer, O. (1963). An experimental application of the Delphi method in the use of experts. *Management Science, 9*(3).

Davis, R. C. (1973). Organizing and conducting technological forecasting in a consumer goods firm. In J. R. Bright & M. E. F. Shoeman (Eds.), *Guide to practical technological forecasting* (pp. 601-618). Englewood Cliffs, NJ: Prentice-Hall.

Daynes, R. R. (1976). *Videodisc technology use through 1986: A Delphi study* (Report No. NPRDC TR 77-11). San Diego, CA: Navy Personnel Research and Development Center.

Dodds, W. (1973). An application of the Bass model in long-term new product forecasting. *Journal of Marketing Research, 10*, 308-311.

Encel, S. (1977). Telecommunications. In T. Whitson (Ed.), *The uses and abuses of forecasting* (pp. 248-266). New York: Holmes & Meier.

Euromonitor. (1984). Videotape recorders. *Market research Great Britain, 24*, 1-10.

Ettema, J. S. (1984). Videotex for market information: A survey of prototype users. In J. Johnston (Ed.), *Evaluating the new information technologies. New directions for program evaluation* (Vol. 23, pp. 5-21). San Francisco: Jossey-Bass.

Fishbein, M., & Ajzen, I. (1975). *Belief, attitude, intention and behavior*. Reading, MA: Addison-Wesley.

Fisher, J. C., & Pry, R. H. (1971). A simple substitution model of technological change. *Technological Forecasting and Social Change, 3*, 75-88.

Foxall, G. R. (1984). Consumers' intentions and behaviour. *Journal of the Market Research Society, 26*(3), 231-241.

Godet, M. (1979). *The crisis in forecasting and the emergence of the prospective approach.* Elmsford, NY: Pergamon Press.
Godet, M. (1983). Reducing the blunders in forecasting. *Futures, 15*(3), 181-192.
Graham, M. (1986). *RCA and the videodisc player: The business of research.* New York: Cambridge University Press.
Greenberger, M. (Ed.). (1985). *Electronic publishing plus.* White Plains, NY: Knowledge Industry Publications.
Heeler, R. M., & Hustad, T. P. (1980). Problems in predicting new product growth for consumer durables. *Management Science, 26*(10), 1007-1020.
Hill, K., & Fowles, J. (1975). The methodological worth of the Delphi forecasting technique. *Technological Forecasting and Social Change, 7*(2), 179-192.
Hutchesson, B. N. P. (1967). Market research and forecasting for the chemical industry: The state of the art. *IMRA Journal, 3,* 242-260.
Klopfenstein, B. C. (1985). Forecasting the market for home video players: A retrospective analysis. *Dissertation Abstracts International, 46,* 546A. (University Microfilms No. 85-10588).
Klopfenstein, B. C. (1986). Forecasting the market for home video players: A retrospective analysis. In T. A. Shimp, S. Sharma, G. John, J. A. Quelch, J. H. Lindgren, Jr., W. Dillon, M. P. Gardner, & R. F. Dyer (Eds.), *1986 AMA marketing educator's conference proceedings* (pp. 267-272). Chicago: The American Marketing Association.
Klopfenstein, B. C. (1987). New technology and the future of the media. In A. Wells (Ed.), *Mass media and society* (4th ed., pp. 15-36). Palo Alto, CA: D. C. Heath.
Klopfenstein, B. C. (in press). Forecasting consumer adoption of information products and services — Lessons from home video forecasting. *Journal of the American Society for Information Science.*
Koughan, M. (1981). The state of the revolution 1982. *Channels, 1*(2), 23-29, 70.
Krugman, D. M., & Christians, C. (1981). Cable television: Promise versus performance. *Gazette, 27* 193-209.
Lancaster, G. A., & Wright, G. (1983). Forecasting the future of video using a diffusion model. *European Journal of Marketing, 17*(2), 70-79.
Linstone, H. A. (Ed.). (1975) *Technological Forecasting and Social Change, 1,* 2.
Linstone, H. A., & Simmonds, W. H. C. (Eds.). (1977). *Futures research: New directions.* Reading, MA: Addison-Wesley.
Linstone, H. A., & Turnoff, M. (1975). *The Delphi method: Techniques and applications.* Reading, MA: Addison-Wesley
Mahajan, V., & Muller, E. (1979). Innovation diffusion and new product growth models in marketing. *Journal of Marketing, 43*(4), 55-68.
Mahajan, V., & Peterson, R. (1985). *Models for innovation diffusion* (Sage University Paper Series on Quantitative Applications in the Social Sciences, 07-048). Beverly Hills, CA: Sage.
Mahmoud, E. (1984). Accuracy in forecasting: A survey. *Journal of Forecasting, 3,* 139-159.
Makridakis, S. (1986). The art and science of forecasting. *International Journal of Forecasting, 2,* 15-39.
Makridakis, S., & Wheelwright, S. C. (1978). *Forecasting: Methods and applications.* New York: Wiley.
Martin, J. (1977). *Future developments in telecommunication.* Englewood Cliffs, NJ: Prentice-Hall.
Martino, J. P. (1983). *Technological forecasting for decision making* (2nd ed.). New York: North-Holland.
Martino, J. P. (1985, March). Looking ahead with confidence. *IEEE Spectrum,* pp. 76-81.
McPhail, T. L., & McPhail, B. M. (1986). *Telecom 2000: Canada's telecommunications future.* Calgary, Alberta: The University of Calgary Graduate Programme in Communications Studies.

Meade, N. (1984). The use of growth curves in forecasting market development—A review and appraisal. *Journal of Forecasting, 3,* 429-451.
Moyer, R. (1984). The futility of forecasting. *Long Range Planning, 17*(1), 65-72.
Naisbitt, J. (1982). *Megatrends: Ten new directions transforming our lives.* New York: Warner Books.
Nicholls, J. A. F., & Roslow, S. (1986). The "s-curve": An aid to strategic marketing. *The Journal of Consumer Marketing, 3*(2). 53-64.
Olshavsky, R. (1980). Time and the rate of adoption of innovations. *Journal of Consumer Research, 6,* 425-428.
Parente, J., Anderson, J. K., Myers, P., & O'Brien, T. (1984). An examination of factors contributing to Delphi accuracy. *Journal of Forecasting, 3,* 173-182.
Pool, I. de Sola. (1983). *Forecasting the telephone: A retrospective technology assessment.* Norwood, NJ: Ablex.
Renfro, W. L., & Morrison, J. L. (1983). The scanning process: Getting started. In J. L. Morrison, W. L. Renfro, & W. I. Boucher (Eds.), *Applying methods and techniques of futures research. New directions for institutional research* (Vol. 39, pp. 21-37). San Francisco: Jossey-Bass.
Rice, R. E., & Associates. (1984). *The new media: Communication, research, and technology.* Beverly Hills, CA: Sage.
Rice, R. E., & Rogers, E. M. (1984). New methods and data for the study of new media. In R. E. Rice & Associates. *The new media: Communication, research, and technology.* Beverly Hills, CA: Sage.
Rogers, E. M. (1983). *The diffusion of innovations.* New York: The Free Press.
Rogers, E. M. (1986). *Communication technology: The new media in society.* New York: The Free Press.
Sackman, H. (1975). *Delphi critique: Expert opinion, forecasting, and group process.* Lexington, MA: D. C. Heath.
Schnaars, S. P., & Berenson, C. (1986). Growth market forecasting revisited: A look back at a look forward. *California Management Review, 28*(4), 71-88.
Setzer, F. O., Franca, B. A., & Cornell, N. W. (1980). *Staff report on: policies for regulation of direct broadcast satellites.* Washington, DC: Federal Communications Commission.
Singleton. L. A. (1986). *Telecommunication in the information age* (2nd ed.). Cambridge, MA: Ballinger.
Svenning, L. L., & Ruchinskas, J. E. (1984). Organizational Teleconferencing. In R. E. Rice & Associates. *The new media: Communication, research, and technology* (pp. 217-248). Beverly Hills, CA: Sage.
Tigert, T., & Farivar, B. (1981). The Bass new product growth model: A sensitivity analysis for a high technology product. *Journal of Marketing, 45*(4), 81-90.
Tull, D. S. (1967). The relationship of actual and predicted sales and profits in new-product introductions. *The Journal of Business, 40*(3), 233-250.
Turoff, M. (1972). Delphi conferencing: Computer-based conferencing with anonymity. *Technological Forecasting and Social Change, 3,* 159-304.
Twiss, B. C. (1980). *Managing technological innovation* (2nd ed.). London: William Clowes & Sons.
Twiss, B. C. (1984). Forecasting market size and market growth rates for new products. *Journal of Product Innovation Management, 1,* 19-29.
Tydeman, J., Lipinski, H., Adler, R. P., Nyhan, M., & Zwimpfer, L. (1982). *Teletext and videotex in the United States.* New York: McGraw-Hill.
Von Hippel, E. (1986). Lead users: A source of novel product concepts. *Management Science, 32*(7), 791-805.
Waggoner, M. D., & Goldberg, A. G. (1986, June). A forecast for technology and education: The report of a computer conferencing Delphi. *Educational Technology,* (pp. 7-14).

Wheelwright, S. C., & Makridakis, S. (1985). *Forecasting methods for management* (4th ed.). New York: Wiley.
Wind, Y., Mahajan, V., & Cardozo, R. N. (1981). *New product forecasting: Models and applications*. Lexington, MA: D. C. Heath.
Wise, G. (1976). The accuracy of technological forecasts, 1890-1940. *Futures*, 8(5), 411-419.
Withington, F. G. (1985, July 1). Backcast. *Datamation*, pp. 125-134.

3

The Effects of New Technologies on Communication Policy

Christine L. Ogan
Indiana University

New technologies and methods of transmission of broadcast and film content have made possible dramatic increases in the amount of information that can be received in the home. Cable, satellites, master antenna television, low power television, pay-per-view television, videocassette recorders, and personal computers with modem attachments to telephone lines all help provide a wide range of choices to consumers in the 1980s. Adoption of these technologies differs from country to country. Communication policies throughout the world, which have been established and maintained over a long time to preserve the cultural heritage of nations as well as to protect local economic interests, are now undergoing changes in line with the new technological environment.

This chapter addresses the cultural, economic, and policy variables that determine diffusion patterns on an international level. The focus here is specifically on VCRs and broadcast satellite signals, with attention given to the phenomenon of piracy.

European countries newly involved in cable and satellite development are allowing more private ownership and permitting extended commercial broadcasting. In the United States, the Federal Communications Commission (FCC) has expanded the number of broadcast outlets that can be owned by a single individual or corporation, and regulations are evolving on new transmission technologies. In developing countries, where governments cannot afford to invest in cable, satellites—which are less expensive when transponders are leased—are a more useful technology. Developing nations will be able to reach remote areas with national signals and also with shared programs beamed from regional satellites. Policies on the use of satellite-delivered content are being developed in many Third World countries.

Although the literature on home adoption of the new media is extensive, few scholars have addressed two extremely pervasive communication phenomena of the 1980s: the use of the videocassette recorder (VCR), and the piracy of broadcast signals. And in revising communication policies to accommodate new media, governments have not done much better in taking these media into account.

VCRS: A POLITICAL ISSUE

The VCR, a private medium rather than a mass communication medium, has found a home in virtually every country of the world, including the U.S.S.R. and the People's Republic of China. VCRs are so popular, they are now crossing borders both legally and illegally. Much of the material played on VCRs is pirated. Ralston Coffin Jr., president of CBS/Fox International, estimates that 46% of all video transactions in the world involve illegal copies ("CBS/Fox International Restructures Markets," 1986). The Motion Picture Association of America (MPAA) claims that $750 million is lost annually to piracy (Zacks, 1986). In some markets, such as those of the Middle East, home video sales and rentals are said to be 100% pirated copies, ("Growth of Piracy," 1986), whereas other countries, such as Mexico and the United Kingdom, claim to have substantially reduced piracy. Instances of piracy and reports of raids netting substantial recovery of cassettes have come from all over the world—Canada, Greece, Brazil, Lebanon, Turkey, the Philippines, South Africa, and the Soviet Union, to name a few.

Officials in many countries have closed their eyes to the proliferation of illegally copied cassettes, even though many of the films recorded on the cassettes would be banned by the film censors of those countries were they to be imported for showing in public cinemas. And even in countries such as Colombia, where laws are said to be "theoretically sufficient" for dealing with piracy, officials generally do not take adequate action against pirates (Ehrman, 1986). Some officials in developing countries probably view the VCR popularity with a sense of relief, because the elites who own them (although ownership is certainly not confined to the upper classes in the Third World) no longer pressure the government for changes in national broadcast content.

In the United States, VCR owners use the technology as much for time shifting of over-the-air broadcast material as for viewing prerecorded films. Still, the MPAA has been concerned about pirated material and has lobbied Congress to pass legislation assessing a copyright royalty fee to both

3. NEW TECHNOLOGIES AND COMMUNICATION POLICY 45

recorders and cassettes, and more recently has requested that Congress require that all VCR manufacturers install an electronic antitaping chip in all machines. ("Hollywood takes Fight," 1986; Wharton, 1986). But although the film companies may have lost money from decreased box office sales, the industry has profited greatly from the legal sale of recorded films. In 1986, the MPAA expected 62 million videocassettes to be sold ("MPAA Reports First-Half B.O.," 1986).

The United States is a country of great media diversity. Although some people argue that the large number of cable and pay TV offerings only provides viewers with more of the same, critics of U.S. broadcast media would have to agree there is much more variety in the U.S. system than is offered in a one- or two-channel country. At least many people perceive that there is great diversity, and that may be the reason why VCR sales have, until recently, lagged behind that of European and Middle Eastern countries, as well as Canada and Japan. VCR penetration stood at 38% in mid-1986 ("Videocassette Penetration," 1986, p. 1), but was under 10% at the end of 1983, and was 17.6% at the end of 1984 ("MPAA Reports First-Half B.O.," 1986, p. 22). That compares with estimates of 75% in Japan, 45.9% in the United Kingdom and 50% in Australia.

According to early VCR research, Americans used VCRs more often to watch news, sports, and entertainment at a different time than broadcast, and to tape and watch home videos of their families than they did to watch films rented or purchased from a local video store. Ratings services in the United States are just beginning to distribute VCR-use diaries, and therefore have little data as yet on how much off-the-air versus prerecorded material is watched. An examination of video expenditures indicates that Americans are spending more time with prerecorded tapes than they did a few years ago (Bierbaum, 1986, p. 41). In 1985, video sales and rentals exceeded spending at the theatrical box office and was nearly double the box office take of 1984 (Bierbaum, 1986, p. 41).

In many countries, the VCR tends to be used for the showing of taped films rather than for time-shifting. One explanation is that there is less media diversity in those countries. Cable may not exist or be available to few households and the country may be broadcasting on only one or two channels.

In other countries, time-shifting may not be practiced at all. Video shop owners in Turkey claimed that VCR owners did not even know how to tape material off the air.

Recent reports from Britain and W. Germany have indicated a shift from watching prerecorded tapes to time-shifting ("8.6-Mil VCRs in Britain," 1986, p. 104; Kindred, 1986, p. 488). That change has come following new policies in both countries that have made additional television programming available through cable and the extension of program schedules. In other words, when there was little to watch on television, consumers watched more prerecorded films rented from the local video shop. And when television offered expanded viewing opportunities, people used their VCRs for maximizing television program choices.

Lack of diversity seems to be the key to the popularity and use of VCRs in most countries. In Eastern European countries with narrowly defined communication policies, people with money are buying VCRs on the open or black market and often apply innovative techniques to obtain and view films. "At the False Gelendzhik bar and restaurant on Soviet Georgia's Black Sea Coast, after-hours guests are screened at the door and allowed in for 50 rubles a head, the equivalent of $70 and 100 times the price of an average movie ticket. In the corner of the bar a television screen flickers with the forbidden offerings" (Schmemann, 1983, p. 1). "Rambo" is said to be one of the most popular of the blacklisted films in Moscow, where consumers buy copies for the equivalent of more than $300, often from tourists who bring cassettes into the country (Zacks, 1986).

Adoption patterns are more directly influenced by political variables in Communist countries, although even these countries have not been able to totally control the use of VCRs. The Soviet Union permits a legal trade in VCRs and cassettes. The government even manufactures VCRs, which sell for about $1,600 each, or about seven times a month's earnings (Tinsley, 1986, pp. G12–13). The Soviet-made machines are of inferior quality, however, and Japanese VCRs will now be imported at the rate of 10,000 per year (Melanson, 1986, pp. 1, 16). Rentals of mostly East European or U.S.S.R.-made tapes are available for about $2–$4 per night, but consumers prefer the black market films (Tinsley, 1986, p. G13).

Cultural variables influence adoption patterns in some Third World countries. A few years ago, when cassettes cost $30 or more to rent in Egypt (the current price is $1.50; Abboud, 1986, p. 30), families would serve food and drinks while the 10 or so guests divided up the rental cost of the tape. Egyptians are most interested in viewing films censored by their government, whereas people in other Arab countries want to view Egyptian-made products. Sometimes that presents an interesting problem, as cheap tapes made in Egypt will be reproduced abroad and smuggled back into Egypt to avoid copyright regulations or the censors. "The rule is to have such cassettes erased if and when they are seized" (Aboubakr, 1983, p. 48). Because there are so few theaters in Cairo (10 to serve 12 million people) and throughout Egypt (less than 200), home video is quite popular (Abboud, 1986, p. 30).

And in other countries, policy variables may influence the diffusion of prerecorded cassettes. Pornographic films, or blue movies, and horror films are more closely controlled in countries outside the United States and, as a result, these films have been very popular when sold in cassette form. Social workers in Bonn, FR Germany, make the rounds of local video shops regularly to make sure that pornography and horror films are not being sold or rented to juveniles. Restricted films may not be sold or rented except in adult-only (age 16 and over) shops (Pond, 1985, p. 30). The maximum fine for renting adult tapes to minors is $600,000 or 6 months in jail—and double that amount if the violation was "premeditated" (Pond, 1985, p. 30). However, one author noted that children get access to such films when their parents rent them—a legal activity (Grosskopff, 1984). A 1986 survey by the German Video Institute found that horror and softcore pornography each make up about 5% of the rental market (Kindred, 1986, p. 488).

In the U.K. there is also concern over what children watch. A Video Inquiry Parliamentary committee surveyed more than 7,000 children to determine the extent to which they viewed "video nasties," and found that 45% of the children questioned claimed to have seen such films. ("Videos for Little Neros," 1984, p. 37) A Video Recordings Bill that went into effect in Britain in 1985 forbids videos from children that deal with: "Human sexual activity or acts of force or restraint associated with such activity; mutilation, torture or other acts of gross violence; and human genital organs or human urinary or excretory functions" (Barker, 1984, p. 15).

In Canada, legislation has been introduced that would require cassette distribution to be licensed and cassettes to be subject to classification and censoring. Fines for sale of banned videos to minors may run as high as $2,000 (Devins, 1984, pp. 33-34). Fines and even threats of imprisonment have not deterred Filipino business owners who sell pornographic videos. The profits appear to be worth the risk (Giron, 1984, pp. 42-43).

Why Video is Ignored

Political variables influencing decisions and adoption of VCRs are often highly complex and involve economic factors. Countries often permit virtually unrestricted use of video even when it violates existing communication policies. One reason is that it takes the heat off governments without the means or inclination to improve existing broadcast programs. In Guyana, where it has been estimated that 15,000 VCRs and 500,000 cassettes exist, and where all cassettes contain imported material, other reasons have been offered:

> It is claimed that the exchange of the . . . cassettes in circulation, coupled with the craze for home video parties has the welcome potential of fostering cooperation and cementing friendships among a population of differing ethnic backgrounds, mainly African and East Indian. It is claimed too, that home video helps keep young people off the streets and thus reduces the local practice of "liming." Some say that it is the threat of the night video-burglar that

encourages couples to stay at home to "watchman" or guard their prized possessions.

And there is the humorous notion, rejected by Guyanese housewives, that video is there to keep the women at home while, even in isolated cases and places, the roving husbands enjoys his video shows in the second home of his so-called essential "deputy" wife. (Forsythe, 1983, p. 52)

But even in the face of such positive comment about the VCR, one wonders about the negative influence of "irrelevant and questionable North American life-style," the impact on the attitudes and behavior of youth and the increased rate of migration to North America mentioned as consequences of viewing (Forsythe, 1983, p. 52).

In some countries the importing of VCRs was out of control before the potential effects of the technology were realized. In both Nigeria and Denmark, color TV sets were purchased in tandem with VCRs. In Turkey, VCR owners and would-be owners are said to have pressured the government to have the national channel (now two channels) broadcast in color.

Nigeria's VCR explosion occurred in the late 1970s when oil brought prosperity to the country. At that time the broadcast industry was developing slowly and was not able to withstand the cassette competition. Now illegally produced cassettes are hawked along roadsides and on a black market that has survived repeated raids (Olusa, 1983, p. 64).

One rationale for the emergence of telecommunication policies has been the perceived scarcity of resource—of broadcast frequencies and of equipment (in poorer countries). Because the VCR is not a mass medium, it is likely that policy makers never considered it to be relevant to national communication policies. Initially, VCRs were seen as a gadget for the rich, but prices have fallen all over the world and they are now within the range of the middle class. Estimates on cost of a recorder vary from a low of around $250 in the United States to amounts exceeding $1,000 in many countries. Although it has taken a dramatic price drop in the United States to attract buyers, high prices have not deterred purchase in most other countries. Low-priced Korean-made units were imported in the United States at the beginning of 1985, and the U.S. penetration jumped from 17.6% to 38% in the year and a half following that event ("MPAA Reports First-Half B.O.," 1986, p. 22).

Accompanying the price of hardware has been a proliferation of video clubs around the world, where customers can rent cassettes, often for less than $1 per night. Some cities, like London, became so saturated with video rental shops that many have closed ("Euro Homevideo Market Grows," 1984, p. 34).

Now that cassette viewing has become so popular, it could be discussed in terms of abundance or scarcity of resources, as it has taken on some characteristics of a mass medium. As defined by one author of a mass com-

3. NEW TECHNOLOGIES AND COMMUNICATION POLICY 49

munication text, "media transmit information from one sender to many receivers; they require mechanical or electric intervention; and overt audience response is relatively light and slow in coming" (Murphy, 1977, p. 15). The VCR fits that description. Another sign that the VCR has become a mass medium is the use of advertising on recorded cassettes. In Saudi Arabia, advertisers have found the cassettes an ideal means of reaching a female audience. Chris Polley, an advertising sales person in Saudi Arabia, claimed that a given film will probably reach as much as 8.6% of the population ("Commercial Boom for Saudi Video," 1984, p. 18). If the VCR can be considered a mass medium, it should be taken into account in communication policy making as other mass media are.

Attempts to Control

Diffusion of VCRs and prerecorded cassettes is high even where there is a controlling factor. Ministries of culture and information in Third World countries have dispatched police to control the sale or rental of objectionable material, yet adoption continues. Kuwait, a country of strict policy on the moral, religious, and political elements of mass communication content, has been unsuccessful in its attempt to control illegal use. Eight out of every 10 households own at least one recorder. Ninety government licensed video shops serve the population of 2 million. The government attempts to enforce censorship laws by checking all entry points to the country for smuggled goods and conducting daily searches of video shops have been to no avail. An informal survey showed about half of the people obtain illegal materials from friends (Barakat, 1983, p. 61).

Where policy is especially strict relative to content, prerecorded cassettes have spread through more unconventional methods. Police in Turkey occasionally raid shops to control pornographic and censored films. In 1985, a list of 128 censored films was circulated to video distributors by the Security General Directorate. Most shop owners in Turkey claim not to rent pornographic films because it is too dangerous. But because such films bring two to three times the rental fees of other films, some shop dealers stock forbidden titles, and negotiate rentals on the streets, away from the shop itself.

When pornographic or censored films are found by the police, fines are assessed. One video shop owner said that the police are sometimes bought off, or the assessed fine is so low that it can be easily be paid. The same dealer said that his shop no longer rented pornographic films because one customer showed such a film in a coffee house. When the police were informed of the public showing, they discovered the name of the video shop on the side of the tape and thereafter closely monitored the activities at the shop.

The demand for VCR's and prerecorded content is so great that existing policies are often ignored. Third World countries, although taking a strong stand on the New World Information Order, and attacking the West for usurping local cultural values with imported media, have done little to control the more insidious cultural invasion through video cassettes. Although it is true that membership in the General Agreement on Tariffs and Trade (GATT) carries with it an obligation to maintain open markets, and that about two-thirds of GATT members are Third World countries, GATT regulations are often interpreted more flexibly for developing countries. Certainly, a case could be made for the need to at least postpone the importation of videocassette recorders in these countries. Yet, other than establishing quotas or restricting imports to families who have lived abroad and brought back VCRs as part of their household goods, I know of no country that has prevented VCR importation.

Among the West European countries, the loudest protest of cultural invasion has come from France—that is until the recent change of government, and therefore change in the position of minister of culture from Jack Lang to Francois Leotard. For a 6-month period in 1983, the French government forced all imported technology through the island of Poitiers, and also imposed an annual ownership tax on VCRs. These efforts resulted in a depression of the French video markets for a time. In 1983, only 9.7% of French homes were estimated to have VCRs. The dropping of the ownership tax and relaxing of import requirments means that more French homes now have VCRs—about 17.8% in 1985 and rapid increases in penetration were expected in 1986. Import quotas on films and the requirement of a 1-year window on release of films to video cassettes works against rapid development, however.

Threat to Other Communication Industries

Communication policies have not been established for cultural protection alone. A more important reason for the development of a policy has been to protect the nature of national communication industries. The increased adoption and use of video has been accompanied by decreased cinema attendance in many countries where video is in wide use. And this should be cause for some alarm to film industries no matter where the practice is found.

Some countries have tried to control the import of foreign material because of the damage—actual or potential—done to native film industries. In both India and Egypt, two countries with important film industries, there are laws to deal with film piracy, but the laws are not successfully enforced. The Indian film industry is said to be the world's largest; in 1986, about 1,000 films in 16 languages were expected to be produced. But pirated videos have caused a problem for this industry both at home and abroad. "Exports used to account for 15–17% of a film's earnings but they have become negligible. In 1979 there were 154 cinemas in Britain regularly screening films in Hindi; now there are three" ("A Mug's Game," 1986, p. 106).

It has been argued that cinema attendance only loses to VCR use in countries without strong film industries, but the examples of Egypt and India don't bear that out. In the U.K., a major film-producing country, home video business is three times the amount of box office receipts (Coopman, 1986, p. 51). Film attendance is also down in several other European film-producing countries.

Obviously, cassette sale and rental would suffer if film industries failed, so eventually the symbiotic relationship will have to be worked out to the benefit of both sides; rampant pirating of tapes serves no one in the long term.

Some people have speculated that the problem will go away when more countries initiate pay-TV channels delivered via cable or satellite. Pay-per-view and master antenna or pay cable schemes may have a detrimental effect on the video industry, but only if the cost of pay TV is cheaper, viewing times are at least as flexible as with cassettes and films are as up-to-date as those that can be obtained in a video shop. There is also something to be said for people wanting to get the most out of their investment in the VCR machine, as opposed to paying a potentially higher rate for the TV films. And what about the diversity of offerings? If consumers are interested in watching more foreign films and perhaps some pornographic films, which would not be acceptable according to existing restrictions on television programs, the effect may be the opposite—that is, video may prevent the success of pay TV.

It probably really depends on which technology gets a foothold first. In France, where video adotpion was depressed through a high value added tax on cassettes, video receiver taxes and control of VCR imports at a critical period, the new pay television channel, Canal Plus, has 1.2 million subscribers ("French H.V. Distribs' Hope," 1986, p. 51). But in other countries, such as the United Kingdom, where video has a high penetration rate, cable has been much slower to catch on.

In the early 1980s, when direct broadcast satellites (DBS) were expected to bring a great variety of programming to all European countries, there was little concern about the economic viability of the new transmission technology. Brian Wenham (1983), program director for the British Broadcasting Corporation, saw video and DBS as complementary services, rather than competitive. At the time, the BBC had plans to develop its own DBS services.

> In a nutshell, the answer to those who fear that the penetration of VCRs would automatically chop the legs off new services trying to get established on ca-

ble, or on satellite, or on both, is that there would seem to be little cause for fear. The VCR is a secondary tool. What it does best is to refashion what others put before it. A new film service, on cable or on satellite, would therefore be meat and drink to it, as would blocks of programming offering sport, film, classics, pop, opera and ballet. No video store can in the end match the determined program-provider either in range or in cost. To take the simplest example of the film service: you do not need to offer many attractive films in a package that might come out at 8-10 pounds a week to under-price the totted-up costs of all those trips to the video store. And you offer too great saving of bother. (p. 29)

Of course, Wenham was accurate in his assessment of the VCR's dependence on programming for its success, but he also described the basic reason for popularity of the VCR – to increase diversity. As the British viewer has been offered more of that through new cable and satellite services, there has been increased use of the VCR for time shifting, and fewer trips made to the video store, as Wenham suggested. The beginning of a fall off in video rentals occurred around mid-1984, when Sky Channel, with its high proportion of U.S. content claimed to have third place in the ratings (after ITV and BBC1) in 25 U.K. towns where it could be received ("Sky Channel Claims It's Gaining," 1984, p. 63).

The Malaysian government has followed the increased diversity theory. It has been trying to lure viewers who were turned off by the "dull programs on government-run channels" away from using VCRs through a new television channel – the first private one in the country. The new channel augments the two run by the information ministry; carries advertising; and has included soap operas, variety shows, Hong Kong movies, and Olympic coverage ("A Switch Off," 1983; "Clearing the Air," 1984).

SATELLITE PIRATING
AND COMMUNICATION POLICY

Video is not the only technology to circumvent national communication policies. In several countries (chiefly, but not exclusively developing countries), downlinks or earth stations have been installed for the reception of programming beamed to satellites. Most of the programs received in this way are initiated in the United States. And in many locations where these programs are received, a local entrepreneur has established a cable company and charges fees for the dissemination of the pirated signals.

Because the United States and Canada are two of the biggest users of communication satellites, reports of the pirating of signals come chiefly from the Western hemisphere, in areas where the footprint of the satellites is cleared. The MPAA and its counterparts for foreign distribution, the Motion Picture Export Association of America (MPEAA), which have gathered data on the practice of illegal reception of signals, claim that U.S. television signals have been retransmitted in Costa Rica, Honduras, Panama, the Bahamas, the Cayman Islands, the Dominican Republic, Haiti, Jamaica, and Belize (Kerr, 1983). And a Canadian communication researcher estimated that about 3,000 illegal stations existed in Canada in 1981 (McPhail & Judge, 1981, p. 18).

The importation of U.S. programs via satellite can wreak havoc on a national communication policy. The Canadian Broadcast Corporation's Northern Service, which included culturally appropriate and development-oriented programs in the native Inuit language, is received through direct broadcast satellite. An exhange on the topic of programming reception between a consultant doing work in a remote Northern Ontario village and government technicians from Canada's Department of Communication was reported to have gone as follows:

> Consultant: "Say, this Northern Service is all fine and well, but isn't it true that if you fellows made a slight adjustment on the dish we'd be able to pick up Ted Turner's Superstation, HBO and other American programming signals?"
>
> One of the technicians replied in a hurried, but hushed voice, "Don't ask that sort of question out loud around here. If the word got around that they'd be able to get Johnny Carson or Hawaii 5-O, that'd be the end of the native Northern Service." (McPhail & Judge, 1981, p. 1)

Canada has more than a passing interest in the development and maintenance of a communication policy appropriate to the technological advancements in the field and applicable to the Canadian situation. A 1983, Canadian Radio and Television Commission's policy statement regarding foreign content in television programming included the following:

> Canadian television programming must attract, engage and entertain. It must also inform, educate and enrich our cultural experience. For if Canadians do not use what is one of the world's most extensive and sophisticated communication systems to speak to themselves — if it serves only for the importation of foreign programs — there is a real and legitimate concern that the country will ultimately lose the means of expressing its identity. Developing a strong program production capability is no longer a matter of desirability but of necessity. (Hagelin & Janisch, 1983, p. 60)

Developing a strong program production capability is more easily accomplished in a country like Canada than in several of the Central American countries with less developed broadcast systems. In Belize, a country without a national television station, seven different U.S. television channels were being regularly received before the advent of scrambling of some U.S. signals. A U.S. communication researcher who was hired as a consultant to the Belize government to examine the possibility of establishing a national station said he was surprised to find that the citizens were avid Chicago Cub fans.

U.S. television stations and the MPEAA have expressed anger that they are not being reimbursed for rebroadcast of televised material, but the issue should be of greater concern to those countries in which the culture and values of an alien nation are being distributed indiscriminately. The owners and managers of some of the Caribbean and Central American stations have seen it differently. They have promoted this chapter's argument, that the lack of local diversity provides a rationale for importing foreign signals. "People living on our island have traditionally been isolated," said Walter Bussenius, the director of Tele Haiti, which had operated a cable television service in Haiti offering news and other U.S. cable television programs to 7,000 customers (Kerr, 1983, p. 21).

If the provisions of the Caribbean Basin Initiative are being upheld, Bussenius should now be out of business. Trade benefits were promised to the nations of the Caribbean on the condition that they provide copyright protection to U.S. program owners. And if those countries are not complying with the terms of the agreement, signal pirates in those nations and others are having to determine ways to unscramble HBO, CNN, and other signals that have since been encrypted to prevent theft.

Although it appears that satellite pirating is confined to the Western hemisphere, this practice will surely spread as more and more broadcast satellites are launched. In spite of the failures of the shuttle and of the French Arienne rocket, many communication satellites are scheduled for launch in the next few years. Many of these are European satellites and several are of the direct broadcast variety. Once off the ground, these satellites will cover most of the earth's surface and will make possible duplication of the Central American and Canadian practices throughout the world.

In anticipation of this possibility, communication policy makers could deal with this issue better than they have with cassette viewing. To their credit, a number of nations have recently discouraged piracy of cassettes through passage and enforcement of stricter copyright legislation. The most severe penalty meted out in the United Kingdom has been an 18-month jail term and a fine of $16,000 (Baker, 1986, p. 102). Jail sentences of up to 5 years and $A50,000 fines are the possible in a new Australian law ("Video Pirates in Australia," 1986, p. 71). Tougher piracy laws have also been enacted in the Phillipines, New Zealand, Turkey, Greece, and Mexico. Many countries tax the recorder and distribute the money to copyright holders—but France has recently rescinded that tax because it had the effect of reducing VCR sales. Other countries, like Finland and Sweden, tax all blank cassettes that come into the country. This practice applies only to legally imported cassettes, however.

3. NEW TECHNOLOGIES AND COMMUNICATION POLICY

The Europeans appear to be the most mindful of both the potential and the danger of DBS signals crossing borders. That was evidenced by the furor over the Coronet satellite that was to be launched by Luxembourg with U.S. financial backing. About 30 countries filed protests with the International Telecommunication Union against the Saloman Brothers' financed satellite that was to broadcast commercial television throughout Europe ("A Mouse that's Roaring," 1984, p. 55).

Although Coronet proved to be a financial failure before it could be launched, a new Luxembourg satellite, Astra, operated by the Societe Europeenne des Satellites (SES) was planned for launch in 1987. The reception market for Astra includes cable systems, apartment blocks, hotels, and condominiums — a potential market of 60 million receivers all across Europe (Hirsch, 1986, p. 31). According to de Tarle, when the Luxembourg satellite is launched, no national regulation will be able to be effective against it. "If cable networks are forbidden to transmit programs distributed by Astra, individuals will be tempted to buy their own antennas, jeopardising many countries' policies for the cable industry" (de Tarle, 1986, p. 80). He pointed to the examples of this practice in Belgium and Canada to illustrate his argument.

In expression of concern for both the potential good and harm to be done by the rapid increase of programs offered through satellite and cable, the EEC (1983) included the following statement in an interim report on the issue:

> All the initiatives and policies which are being developed for for DBS in the interest of the people of Europe, will have to take account of the fact that, because of the geography and population density of Europe, DBS will become a powerful unifying factor. Viewers in one country will be able to share television programs with viewers in other countries and will thus acquire a new feeling of belonging and involvement. This sharing of pictures and information will be the most effective means of increasing mutual understanding among the peoples of Europe, and will give them a greater sense of belonging to a common cultural and social entity. The development of a truly European spirit will therefore become possible in national audiences, who will still, of course, retain their full cultural identity.
> This European audience will develop new aspirations which cannot be fully satisfied by either national initiatives or initiatives by private commercial bodies, since both propose to use this European audience created by satellite television for their own ends.

More recently, the European countries have realized that in order to create this European spirit, local production of television programs and films must be increased. Otherwise it only draws Europe closer to the United States as cable companies use more and more U.S.-produced material to try to satisfy the insatiable appetite of the multiple channels offered by cable.

One French author predicts that DBS in Europe will be another Concorde and the European communications industry will receive no benefits from the new channels unless an adequate supply of European co-produced programs in several languages with themes stressing a common cultural heritage are developed. Otherwise he says that imports will increase and even receiver dishes might be imported from Asia (Wade, 1986, p. 77).

The European Parliament is applying EEC economic policies to audio-visual products in an attempt to create "television without frontiers" in Europe. The need for more programs to fill the increased time made available by cable and satellite channels has caused European countries to think of ways to finance European programs, rather than ones produced by individual nations (Monet, 1986; Young, 1986, p. 58). Co-production by European filmmakers is also more popular than it used to be. Jan Moito, of Beta/Taurus, a key pan-European production manager said, "The cost of productions has increased at a time when big, special projects are needed to establish a European presence in Europe and globally" (Werba, 1986, p. 42).

Policies, or lack of them, for satellite television (delivered via cable or directly to the home) and VCRs, appear to favor a market model over a public service model throughout the world. Without making any value judgments on whether this may be a good idea, it is certainly worth considering that once the public service feature of broadcasting is lost, it probably can never be regained. The heavy use of VCRs throughout the world—estimated at 100 million at the end of 1985—and the eager customers for pirated satellite programming in many developing countries only signal a need for more diversity. Diversity can be acquired through other means within the broadcasting system of a nation, but it requires thought and planning and probably a large economic investment.

This chapter includes only examples of satellite and VCR adoption and use. Other technologies—chiefly the computer—have also taken on a role that conflicts with national information policy. Rather than just sit back and watch what happens and then try to apply some makeshift post hoc policy, as some countries have done regarding broadcast TV, it is surely better to study the issue carefully now and draft some realistic guidelines for present and future use. There are signs that European countries are working in this direction, but it may already be too little and too late.

ACKNOWLEDGMENT

An earlier version of this chapter, "Media Diversity and Communications Policy: Impact of VCRs and Satellite TV," appeared in *Telecommunications Policy*, March 1985. The author prepared this chapter while she was a research fellow at the Gannett Center for Media Studies, Columbia University, New York.

REFERENCES

Abboud, M. B. (1966, July 9). Private investment policy blamed for decline of Egyptian cinema. *Variety*, p. 30.
Aboubakr, Y. (1983). Late arrivals. *Intermedia*, *11*(4/5), 48.
Baker, B. (1986, January 8). Britain goes after pirate sources to trim illegal home video mart; lotsa 'cottage industry' dupers. *Variety*, p. 102.
Barakat, S. (1983). Video land. *Intermedia*, *11*(4/5), 61.
Barker, M. (1984). Nasty politics or video nasties? In M. Barker (Ed.), *Video nasties* (pp. 7-38). London: Pluto Press.
Bierbaum, T. (1986, April 2). Showbiz wants copyright teeth in trade talks. *Variety*, pp. 1, 94.
CBS/Fox intl restructures markets to accommodate overseas growth. (1986, March 26). *Variety*, p. 45.
Clearing the air. (1984, September 8). *The Economist*, pp. 96-97.
Commercial boom for Saudi video. (1984, August). *TV World*, p. 18.
Coopman, J. (1986, October 15). *Variety*, pp. 51, 104.
de Tarle, A. (1986). Dream factories go international. *Intermedia*, *14*(4/5), 79-81.
Devins, S. (1984, June 6). Proposed Ontario law seeks cassette licensing censoring. *Variety*, pp. 33, 34.
EEC Commission. (1983, May 25). Interim report. Brussels: Author.
Ehrman, H. (1986, July 9). Cartagena hv seminar bids pols wise up to pirate tactics and tolls. *Variety*, p. 33.
8.6-mil VCRs in Britain mostly record from tube. (1986, January 8). *Variety*, p. 104.
Euro homevideo market grows: UK, Germany may be peaking. (1984, June 6). *Variety*, p. 34.
Forsythe, V. L. (1983). Video parties—fewer cars stolen. *Intermedia*, *11*(4/5), 52.
French h.v. distribs' hopes high now that that VCRs are sans $90 fee. (1986, October 15). *Variety*, p. 51.
Giron, M. V. (1984, June 6). Made-at-home porn steams Filipino biz. *Variety*, pp. 42-43.
Grosskopff, R. (1984, March 31). *Hannoversche Allgemeine*. Reprinted in *The German Tribune*. (1984, April 15), *1129*.
Growth of piracy in Mideast has MPEA, prods. seeing red; new laws on local books help. (1986, May 7). *Variety*, pp. 487, 494.
Hagelin, T., & Janisch, H. (1983). The border broadcasting dispute in context. In Canadian-US Conference on Communications policy, *Cultures in collision: The interaction of Canadian and US television broadcast policies* (pp. 40-99). New York: Praeger.
Hollywood takes fight against unauthorized videotaping to Congress. (1986, September 29). *Broadcasting*, p. 76.
Hirsch, M. (1986). Luxembourg: Big ambitions. *Intermedia*, *14*(4/5), 30-31.
Kerr, P. (1983, October 13). Foreign "piracy" of TV signals stirs concern. *The New York Times*, pp. 1, 21.
Kindred, J. (1986, October 15). Life's tougher for Germany's video pirates. *Variety*, pp. 47, 65.
McPhail, T. L., & Judge, S. (1981, November). *Direct broadcast satellites (DBS): The demise of public and commercial policy objectives.* Conference on Telecommunications in the Year 2000, New Brunswick, NJ.
Melanson, J. (1986, January 26). Soviets crack a window for U.S. homevideo, but flood of rubles unlikely. *Variety*, pp. 1, 16.

Monet, J. (1986, March 26). Europeans plan TV without frontiers. *Variety*, pp. 49, 84.
A mouse that's roaring in satellite TV. (1984, September 10). *Business Week*, p. 55.
MPAA reports first-half b.o. at lowest point in four years; vidcassette penetration balloons. (1986, August 13). *Variety*, pp. 3, 22.
A Mug's game. (1986, September 20). *The Economist*, pp. 104, 106.
Murphy, R. D. (1977). *Mass communication and human interaction*. Boston: Houghton Mifflin.
Olusa, C. S. (1983). The video shock. *Intermedia*, 11,4/5, 64.
Pond, E. (1985, May 3). Tougher West German law aims to shield youth from adult-only videos. *The Christian Science Monitor*, p. 30.
Schmemann, S. (1983, October 22). Video's forbidden offerings are alarming Moscow. *The New York Times*, p. 1.
Sky channel claims it's gaining in UK. (1984, August 15). *Variety*, p. 63.
A switch off. (1983, October 8). *The Economist*, pp. 77, 78.
Tinsley, E. (1986, April 21). Soviets open video shops. *Electronic Media*, G12, 13.
Video pirates in Australia saying "ouch!" (1986, October 15). *Variety*, p. 71.
Videocassette penetration at 38% of the market. (1986, October 8). *Variety*, pp. 1, 160.
Videos for little Neros. (1984, August 5). *The (London) Times*, p. 37.
Wade, P. (1986). The DBS challenge. *Intermedia*, *14*(4/5), 76–78.
Wenham, B. (1983). The broadcasters are learning to live with home video. *Intermedia 11*(4/5), 29.
Werba, H. (1986, September 24). Pan-European coprods on rise; b'casters look beyond borders for wider audiences, partners. *Variety*, pp. 42, 116.
Wharton, D. (1986, October 1). MPAA seeks copyright protection against homevideo duplicators. *Variety*, p. 48.
Young, D. (1986, October 8). Common market meet examines European audio-visual concerns. *Variety*, p. 58.
Zacks, R. (1986, January 19). That's not piracy, that's sacrilege. New York *Daily News*.

II

ADOPTING AND USING THE NEW COMMUNICATIONS MEDIA

4

A Framework and Agenda for Research on Computing in the Home

Charles W. Steinfield
Michigan State University

William H. Dutton
University of Southern California

Peter Kovaric
University of California, Los Angeles

The personal computer, perhaps more than any other modern commodity, symbolizes the growing availability and influence of new media in everyday life. It is virtually impossible to find a spokesperson for the position that computer technology in general, and personal computers in particular, will not become more prevalent in many areas of everyday life in most western societies. By the mid-1980s, fully one of every six U.S. households has acquired a personal computer. Moreover, personal computers are being used to an increasing extent and for more varied purposes in leisure and work situations (Anderson & Harris, 1984; Evans, 1979; Forester, 1980; Louis Harris, 1983; Nilles, 1980, 1982).

Nevertheless, there is uncertainty over the extent that personal computing has and will become integrated into everyday life in the home. Despite continually optimistic forecasts of adoption and evidence of steady computer sales, data are sparse concerning what actually happens after a family acquires a personal computer. Does it entertain in the living room, facilitate work in the study, or gather dust in the closest? This uncertainty is due largely to the difficulty of knowing what factors will contribute to different uses of personal computers. In this chapter, therefore, we present a framework to guide research on personal computing. It focuses attention on the ways in which a personal computer is used in the home, the major sets of variables that influence usage, and the implications that might flow from computer use in the household. As the personal computer enhances or is substituted for other technologies, ranging from the pencil and typewriter to the television set to the telephone, more and more of life in the household is becoming computer-mediated. Why is this occurring and with what effect upon technology and society?

The Diffusion of Home Computing

Nearly all the approximately 80 million households in the United States constitute a potential market for personal computers and because many families have already become multiple personal computer owners, the maximal size of the home market is huge indeed.

There is little doubt that the market is expanding. One 1980 estimate, based on a delphi study, suggested that there were over 4 million personal computers in homes, and that by 1990 there would probably be 20–30 million units, translating into a consumer market for personal computers that would exceed $3.5 billion per year (Nilles, 1980). More recent survey data indicate that even these estimates might be conservative (Dutton, Rogers, & Jun, 1987a).

A nationwide survey conducted by Louis Harris & Associates for Southern New England Telephone in the fall of 1983 estimated that about 10% of the general public already had a personal computer in their home (Louis Harris, 1983, p. 50). Another survey conducted in the fall of 1983 of persons 18 years of age and older in the seven-county metropolitan area of St. Paul and Minneapolis, estimated that 11% had a home computer, an increase of 83% for that region since 1982 (Anderson & Harris, 1984, p. 6). One year later, in the fall of 1984, a nationwide survey conducted by the Gordon S. Black Corporation for *USA Today* estimated that 16% of the public, nearly one in five, owned a home computer (Kolette, 1984, p. 1). A recent National Association of Broadcasters survey (NAB Technology Update, 1986) estimated home computer penetration to be 16%. Finally, Dutton et al., (1987a) in a meta-analysis of the diffusion of home computer studies settled on a 15% figure as an estimate of the proportion of households owning a personal computer in the mid-1980s. In short, various reputable surveys underscore the rapid pace at which this technology is being diffused among U.S. households. Given that home purchases might represent less than half (just over 40%) of the entire personal computer market (Yankee Group, 1982, p. 13), the overall diffusion of personal computers is remarkable indeed.

Adoption, however, does not necessarily lead to the successful adaptation and incorporation of the technology in the home setting (Rogers & Shoemaker, 1971; Yin, Heald, Vogel, Fleischauer, & Vladeck, 1976). Indeed, at any point in the process of integrating this (or any other) innovation into daily life, abandonment, rejection, or disuse of the technology can occur. Although there is little evidence to suggest that computers lie idle in households (Dutton et al., 1987a), adoption and use are not synonymous. Different adopters of home computing will use their devices for different purposes, having diverse implications for family life.

The Impacts of Home Computing

Identifying the factors that shape patterns of home computing can direct those studying its long-range social, psychological, and political implications. Before anticipating or forecasting the impacts of purchasing a personal computer, it is useful to focus on the more immediate issue of how people *use* this new and evolving technology.

The value of focusing on patterns of use can be illustrated by the widely divergent predictions that could be made about the impacts of home computing. Table 4.1 partitions the potential implications of computing into a number of distinct categories. These range from impacts on learning and education, family functioning, personal development, leisure activities, work at home, and household routines to impacts on privacy, civil liberties, and property rights (Table 4.1). Within any single area, it is not yet possible to provide compelling arguments for the magnitude, direction, or linearity of any given change. Within almost any domain of potential impact, diametrically opposed predictions of effects can be conceived, a characteristic of communication technologies that Pool (1977) labeled "dual effects." It can be hypothesized, for instance, that personal computers can improve or erode writing skills, enhance or invade privacy, or can increase or decrease family interaction. For example, as computers become increasingly affordable, there will be a tendency for each family member to own one, much like TV sets. As a result, family members may spend less time together and develop more divergent interests. Conversely, the multiple-user interactive capabilities of some applications might encourage group activities (e.g., games), minimally threatening avenues for conflict resolution (e.g., message systems), and ideal opportunities to observe other family members in the act of creative problem solving (e.g., programming or writing).

Preliminary studies of the impacts of home computing do little to resolve this dilemma of dual effects. Dutton et al. (1987a) reviewed the findings of studies focused on impacts, noting that these studies rely on user perceptions of impacts and attitudes rather than on actual patterns of use. The studies reviewed in this article showed some tendency for users to perceive educational benefits, particularly in the amount of time spent studying and in the level of interest in school work. Additionally, these studies found a decrease in time spent on various leisure activities such as TV viewing, reading, and use of other media. Although the use of computing in the home per se is associated with time spent in educational and leisure activities, Lieberman, Roberts, and Chaffee (1986) demonstrated that patterns of com-

TABLE 4.1
Some Areas That the Use of Personal Computers Might Impact[a]

Learning and Education

Organization of other educational activities at home
Attitudes toward "traditional" educational practices and content areas
Achievement on or skills at particular tasks or areas

Family Functioning

Organization of family interaction
Attitudes toward other family members or family relations in general
Development of new family rules concerning the personal computer
Prestige, status, and influence of family members

Personal Development

Organization of self-improvement activities
Attitudes about self in general and self vis-à-vis technology
Amount of physical activity and general health

Leisure Activities

Organization of leisure-time activities
Attitudes toward leisure activities in general and in relation to computing

Work From Home

Organization of work at home and away from home
Attitudes toward work in general and in relation to the personal computer
Productivity and worker evaluations

Household Routines

Organization of household routines
Attitudes toward household routines in general and in relation to computing
Skills required to maintain household

Privacy, Civil Liberties, and Property Rights

Organization of personal information and intellectual property
Attitudes toward violating copyright laws or the privacy of personal data
Skills required for maintaining security and privacy, and using a new means of expression

[a]Adapted from: Dutton, Kovaric, and Steinfield (1985).

puter usage were differentially related to school performance and media use. In a study of fourth-, fifth-, and eighth-grade students, those who used computers primarily for programming—called *reality* users—did conform to the general pattern. That is, they exhibited higher school achievement, less reading, and less television viewing. On the other hand, students who used the computer primarily for game playing exhibited lower school achievement, and higher television viewing.

The findings in the other impact areas are equally mixed according to Dutton et al.'s (1987a) meta-analysis. These findings underscore the need to identify patterns of computer usage, the extent to which usage will be

4. RESEARCH FOR HOME COMPUTING

integrated into family life, and the factors that influence usage, to explain the social, psychological, and other implications of this technological change.

Because the characteristics of computing in households are unique, there is little research on other media that applies directly to these concerns. However, social research on television in households and computing in organizations provides some important lessons for those interested in studying computing in the home. Most generally, it underscores the importance of studying patterns of utilization rather than simply the presence or absence of the technology.

Lessons from Research on Television

In recent decades, dramatic changes have occurred in family life, in terms of the way in which time is allocated (cf. Gershuny, 1983; Linder, 1970; Ogburn & Nimkoff, 1955; Robinson, 1977, 1981). The personal computer is a relatively recent addition to a growing array of communication technologies that are frequently identified as a symbol of and catalyst for these changes in family life. In this respect, the positive and negative implications forecast for the personal computer are remarkably reminiscent of early forecasts for television.

The multitude of television impacts with which social scientists have concerned themselves (see Pearl, Bouthilet, & Lazar, 1982, for summaries of some of these) are at least implicitly based on the integration of television into family life. As is virtually common knowledge by now, Nielson data indicate that the average amount of television viewing has consistently increased its introduction, with a leveling off to about 4 hours per day (Comstock, Chaffee, Katzman, McCombs, & Roberts, 1978).

In the few studies of individual use patterns immediately following television's introduction into a local society, rapid integration into the daily routine was observed (Brown, Cramond, & Wilde, 1974; Murray & Kippax, 1978; Williams & Handford, 1986). Additionally, studies in Australia, Great Britain, Israel, Japan, Scandinavia, and the United States have consistently reported that both children and adults use television for information, social guidance, and relaxation, and that it fulfills the functions ascribed to it quite well (Brown et al., 1974; von Feilitzen, 1976; Furu, 1971; Greenberg, 1974; Himmelweit, Oppenheim, & Vince, 1958; Katz, Gurevitch, & Haas, 1973; Kippax & Murray, 1980; Rubin, 1979). Although this integration of television into family life may not be desirable and its use may be less than optimal (e.g., Mander, 1978; Winn, 1977), nearly all the important impacts (of effects) attributed to television derive from such integration.

In the early years of television, there were few empirical attempts to identify the ways in which the medium would—or could—be used. Rather, discussion focused on speculations concerning the potential positive and negative social impacts. In the earliest conceptualizations, television was viewed as a hypodermic needle-like medium, capable of direct and powerful persuasion (cf. Katz, 1980 for a summary). This image spurred both hopes for an educational panacea, and fears of a political propaganda tool. The research that followed mostly dashed the hopes (see Chu & Schramm, 1967, for a review of television as an educational tool) and relieved the fears (Katz & Lazarsfeld, 1955; Klapper, 1960) as the findings suggested that media impacts were far more complex and less predictable than presented in the hypodermic needle approach. Yet out of these findings came suggestions that led to a reconceptualization of the effects process, focusing at least in part on the ways that audiences used the medium. This reconceptualization appears to have been typical for the study of other media in the twentieth century (Bryant & Zillmann, 1986; Reeves & Wartella, 1982).

More recently, it has been said that families of the industrialized nations are in the early stages of a new era again organized around communication technology. The symbol and catalyst of this era is the computer. In the 1980s, many forecasts about the American family, for example, view microelectronics and the personal computer as first enhancing and then replacing television as the major medium of communication in the home (Bowes, 1980; Nilles, 1982; Williams, 1982).

Not surprisingly, much of the early literature on personal computing focused on the impacts of this technology (Evans, 1979; Forester, 1980; Levy & Ferguson, 1983). As noted previously, the early empirical studies have found associations between the use of personal computing and other behaviors such as the viewing of television (Kolette, 1984; Rogers, 1985; Venkatesh & Vitalari, 1984; Vitalari, Venkatesh, & Gronhaug, 1985). Vitalari et al. (1985), in a survey of 282 personal computer owners in Orange County, also found personal computing to be associated with declines in family interaction and sleeping time, as well as with increased time being alone and doing homework. These findings, of course, are directly parallel to the findings that television, when initially introduced into households, displaced a number of activities (cf. Brown et al., 1974). However, when viewed from the historical perspective just noted, these and more subtle impacts of computing must be understood in terms of how this new medium is used and integrated into the home.

Moreover, the implications of computing, like those of television, are likely to be far more subtle and indirect (albeit no less powerful) than the direct effects forecast by the early proponents and critics of new technology. The more subtle implications of television on social modeling and agenda setting, for example, might have been overlooked, if researchers had limited their research to such commonly expected effects as increased aggression or improved learning and education.

Lessons from Research on Computing in Organizations

A conceptual approach that stresses how computers are used, in order to better anticipate impacts, can be derived also from prior research on computing in complex organizational settings, where most social research on computing has been anchored (Kling, 1980). Organizational analyses of computing bear some conceptual relationship to the study of personal computing in the home by virtue of similar, although generally not identical, technology. In contrast, research on television is dissimilar with regard to the technological focus, but valuable for its emphasis on the household as a social context. Each area thus contributes from a different perspective, yet both support the conclusion that a focus on uses is a proper starting point.

Research examining the impacts of computing in organizational settings demonstrates the importance of avoiding a technologically deterministic or entirely rational approach. Generally popular predictions of perfunctory increases in effectiveness and efficiency purely based on the attributes of any technological system are giving way to an understanding of computing as a malleable technology that is sensitive to the social dynamics of the organizational context (Danziger, Dutton, Kling, & Kraemer, 1982; Kling, 1980; Kraemer, Dutton, & Northrop, 1981). As Kling (1980) noted, "the consequences of computing are simply the consequences of lines of purposive action married to computing" (p. 100).

This approach to computing in organizations is rooted in the more general sociotechnical literature, which attempts to understand organizational outcomes of technological change by focusing on the social system and the environmental context as well as the technology. In this view, the social and technological systems are interrelated, if not overlapping. The task of research is to discover how people interact with and shape technology (and vice versa) under particular environmental conditions. For example, research on computer models has demonstrated how characteristics of the technology shape its use, but also how the interests of individuals and groups involved with the technology can influence the role models play in organizational decision making (Dutton & Kraemer, 1985). Research on the use of computer-mediated communication systems such as electronic mail has also focused on the influences of the social and organizational context in shaping usage patterns (Rafaeli, 1986). One study found that usage could be divided into two clearly distinct classes that were defined as task-related uses and socioemotional uses (Steinfield, 1985). Moreover, characteristics of the organizational context, individual users, and the electronic mail systems were found to predict the degree to which the systems were used for these different tasks (Steinfield, 1986),

Finally, an emerging conceptual framework in the organizational literature views the development of an individual's work-related attitudes and behaviors to be a function of information derived from the individual's social environment (Miller & Monge, 1985; Salancik & Pfeffer, 1978; Thomas & Griffin, 1983). Thus, the attitudes and behaviors of coworkers are considered critical influences on employees' perceptions of their jobs. Likewise, this social context might shape attitudes toward computing as well as behaviors (Fulk, Steinfield, Schmitz, & Power, 1987). Few academics have been immune from colleagues who enthusiastically endorse the benefits of particular word-processing software. Even faculty wedded to typewriters and cut-and-paste technology can be pushed out into the personal computer marketplace.

From these studies, research on personal computing in the home can draw several conclusions. First, overly rational or technologically deterministic approaches might fail to uncover characteristics of the social context and users that make any impacts contingent on those who control the use of technology within the home. Following from this, it appears that an intermediate step in understanding how personal computers might alter home life is to study the linkages between the social context of the home and applications of personal computing.

PERSPECTIVES ON COMPUTING IN THE HOME

Patterns of Personal Computing Use

Many forecasters assume, often implicitly, that personal computing will evolve in a natural progression from the limited use of few applications toward a heavier use of many applications (cf. Stone, 1982). Two major dimensions are thus presented as most critical in describing patterns of computer use: amount of time and variety of use (see Table 4.2, which provides a typology of computer utilization). The most common expectation regarding the evolution of personal computing would be characterized by a progression from Type I to Type IV in Table 4.2. For example, a person might begin personal computing in a limited way, using a few popular games, and progressively branch out into other games, graphics, instruction, communications, and programming. Moreover, this progression from games to a greater variety of applications is expected to correspond with the purchase of more sophisticated (and expensive) hardware and software.

Actual patterns of utilization are likely to be more variable. The few existing studies of home computer use provide only limited information regarding the amount of time devoted to use and the types of applications (see Dutton et al., 1987a, for a review). Generally, these studies suggest that most computers are used for a significant length of time (with estimates varying from 6 to 17 hours per week across surveys), although a large propor-

TABLE 4.2
Hypothetical Patterns of Personal Computing[a]

	Amount of Time	
	Light and Irregular	Heavy and Regular
Low	I Brief, sporadic use of a limited variety of applications (e.g., executive sporadically checking mail from home, weekend game players)	III Heavy, regular use of a limited variety of applications (e.g., writers using a personal computer for word processing, compulsive game players, hackers)
High	II Brief, sporadic use of a wide variety of applications (e.g., early users of a new system, people seeking to become computer literate)	IV Heavy, regular use of a wide variety of applications (e.g., computer consultants, officers of computer user groups)

(Row label: Diversity of Use)

[a]Adapted from: Dutton, Kovaric, and Steinfield (1985).

tion of survey respondents reported less use than expected. In addition, the usual distribution was that of a large number of light users and a small number of heavy users (Dutton et al., 1987a). Several studies did suggest that computer use increases over time, although some people might actually narrow their use of the personal computer over time as they discover applications that meet their specialized needs. For example, longitudinal studies of videotext usage have found that novelty and uncertainty lead to diverse use initially, but a gradual routinization to a narrower range of applications over time (Rice & Paisley, 1982). Studies of interactive cable television have arrived at similar longitudinal findings (Gonzales, 1986).

Several studies have attempted to identify applications of home computers (Dutton et al., 1987a). Types of uses varied widely across different studies, although generally such application areas as entertainment, education, word processing, and home budgeting and finance, working at home, and learning about computing were mentioned. Over time, there is some evidence of more specialized use as the use of personal computers for work-related applications appears to be growing, whereas entertainment uses appear to be declining proportionately (Dutton et al., 1987a).

Although the expense of upgrading a simple initial system to one that permits sophisticated applications is certainly a major constraint to increasing use and variety, it is just as surely not the only important factor. Anecdotes in the popular press depict a common scenario of use that may be more appropriately characterized as a move toward a "computer in every closet" rather than in every home. But most empirical evidence suggests that personal computers in the 1980s will not suffer the fate of the video telephone of the 1970s. They are unlikely to be relegated to the closet. Nevertheless, integration of the technology into family life is not predestined. How personal computing evolves in the home will be affected by characteristics of the technology as well as its users situated in social settings that more or less facilitate the adoption of personal computing and its use for different social purposes.

Factors Shaping the Use of Personal Computing

Based on the lessons from television and organizational research, as well as some preliminary research on home computing, we classified the determinants of personal computer usage into four sets of factors. First is the *social status* of the potential users, including their income, occupational, and educational backgrounds. Second, and most prominent in the literature on computing (and, for that matter, television), are features of the medium itself—what we call *technical features and human factors*. These include characteristics of the equipment, both hardware and software, sometimes thought of as technical features and content. Third, and somewhat less prominent in the literature on personal computing, is the *sociocultural setting*, that is, the social and cultural environment in which the medium is used. For personal computers, important sociocultural factors primarily are associated with networks of users linked in various ways as a function of their interest in computers. (For television, the sociocultural environment has most often been conceived as the viewer's family and, to a lesser extent, peers). Fourth, and least prominent for the study of computers (although somewhat more so for television), are the *personal attributes* of the user or viewer. These include the user's immediate needs, abilities, experience with, and attitudes toward computing technology, some of which might reflect the age and gender of users, factors which have been commonly linked to interest in computers (Fig. 4.1). Together, these classes of variables suggest a preliminary framework for studying the utilization and impacts of personal computing in the family setting (Fig. 4.1).

Social Status. The most basic level of usage for any technology is whether it is used at all. In the case of personal computing several social status variables—level of education, income, and occupation—are good predictors of adoption and use of personal computers at home (Anderson & Harris, 1984; Louis Harris, 1983; Rogers, 1985; Rogers, Daley, & Wu, 1982). For example, people who have already acquired a personal computer or who say they are likely to buy one tend to be more educated, have higher incomes, and be classified as professional managers or proprietors (Anderson & Harris, 1984, Table 1; Louis Harris, 1983, Table 4-7). The consistent

4. RESEARCH FOR HOME COMPUTING

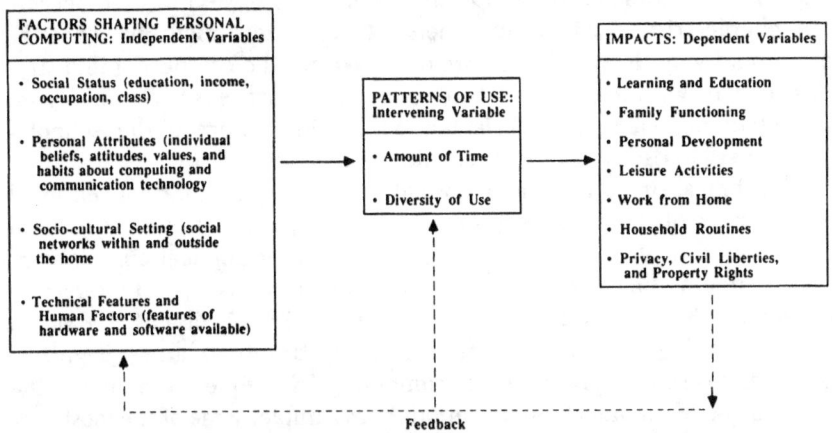

FIG. 4.1. Factors shaping the use and impacts of personal computing (adapted from Dutton, Kovaric, & Steinfield, 1985)

and strong association between social status factors and the adoption of personal computing is one major force behind rising policy concerns over equity across socioeconomic groups in society.

Social status might directly influence the use of computing by reducing economic constraints on access to the technology. However, it might also be more indirectly related to influencing social factors (the involvement of friends and coworkers with computing), and personal characteristics (the user's interests, needs, and abilities).

To some extent, these background characteristics influence the degree and kind of usage. Individuals from higher socioeconomic backgrounds might be more likely to view computing as an instrumental innovation as well as an enjoyable pastime. Likewise, social background might so constrain individual access to different kinds of computing technologies and social settings that patterns of computer utilization can be explained on that basis alone. For example, an affluent family in which one or more members is/are well educated and employed in a professional or managerial position is far more likely to provide more immediate as well as indirect social support to individual family members grappling with computing than a less affluent family in which no member is particularly well schooled or employed in work that involves computing (e.g., Anderson & Harris, 1984; Louis Harris, 1983; Rogers, 1985; Rogers et al, 1982).

Although social status variables—income, education, occupation, and class—are excellent predictors of entry into the world of personal computing, they are less robust predictors of utilization patterns that change over time or of more complex impacts. And, as the prices of personal computers continue to decline, a decline is also possible in the power of social status in predicting either adoption or use.

Technical Features and Human Factors. As has been argued for other media, characteristics or features of personal computers might influence the extent and ways in which they are used. Within the computing industry, this concern with technical features of computer systems is commonly labeled *human factors*, as it is oriented to matching features of the technology to characteristics of human cognitive processes.

A technical or human factors orientation underlies most conventional explanations of the attractions of personal computing as contrasted with older media, such as television. Personal computer applications are said, for example, to be more active, gamelike, textually based, and interactive (Malone, 1981; Paisley & Chen, 1982; Turkle, 1984; Williams, 1982). To some, matching these system features with constraints on human cognitive processing is said to give personal computing its unique place among the other media of human communication. For example, some of the most dramatic psychological implications of computing are based on the thesis that inherent features of personal computing systems make them a learning tool of nearly unparalleled importance in the contemporary world (Papert, 1980; Turkle, 1984). To others, characteristics of computer systems explain their *lack* of attraction. For instance, the complexity of computing compared to viewing television or dialing the telephone is often cited as a factor limiting its diffusion (Vallee, 1982).

Differences of system features across personal computing hardware and software might also explain variations in their use within the home (Anderson, 1980). Reviewing a wide range of text-oriented computer-based systems, Paisley and Chen (1982) concluded that certain hardware and software features are more likely to encourage use than others. For instance, hardware limitations such as uppercase-only lettering, slow display of characters, short line length (40 or fewer characters per line), few lines of text per screen (e.g., about 16), and poor character or graphics resolution were all found to inhibit use and satisfaction more than their opposites.

Somewhat more difficult to classify were software differences likely to influence usage. Within the general category of "educational" software, Paisley and Chen found a hierarchy in the kinds of programs available. "Drill-and-practice" software was the simplest, most repetitious, and most like traditional classroom assignments. "Tutorial" software, able to record a user's progress, could tailor individual response. "Simulation" software, usually relying on graphics displays that respond to user commands, allowed progression through complex visual development sequences. Finally, with "discovery" software, the user could employ a command language to explore "environments" rather than being pushed toward predetermined solutions. In general, this study asserted, the closer to the discovery model software, the more users will enjoy it and persist in using it.

According to Paisley and Chen, the features of these programs mainly matched the innate (and thus invariant) needs in children (and, presumably, adults) to explore and master the computing environment under as few constraints as possible. Analogous to this approach is that of Papert (1980), who has asserted that the *LOGO* language provides a computer environment configured to best match the developmental abilities of children, thus allowing them to acquire both system-specific and system-independent knowledge and skills.

Within this orientation, Malone (1981) and Carroll (1982) provide another approach. Both find that use of software is predicated on certain characteristics found in the more sophisticated computer games. Carroll identified a number of limitations of text systems, and suggested that the user's perception of being in control, plus the system's direct, immediate and unambiguous responsiveness, primarily determine the development of computing skill. In addition, Malone argued that, in system features, three factors ensure the successful use of computing: challenge, fantasy, and curiosity. These are the characteristics found in those computer games to which children (and possibly adults) repeatedly return after novelty effects dissipate.

The amount and variety of computer use might well be affected by access to more sophisticated games, powerful programming languages, "discovery" software, and fast, more colorful graphics and high-resolution displays. Because access to such systems remains costly, technical features and human factors are likely to be strongly associated with the social status of users, thus reinforcing concerns over equitable adoption. And because much of the research on children's use of computing is based on unusual samples of children (e.g., children of MIT faculty) its generalizability is a genuine issue.

Sociocultural Setting. Other authors have argued that primary responsibility for the ways and extent to which computers are used does not depend on technical features but on the user's sociocultural setting, the networks of friends, coworkers, and computer users both within and outside the home. For instance, Kling and Gerson's (1977) characterization of the social world of computing suggests that personal computing should be viewed as an array, system, or network of hobbyists (e.g., the "Apple Corps"), retailers, hardware and software vendors, users, and others linked through magazines, personal friendship, electronic mail, common interests, and shared ambitions. According to this conception, the users who become more integrated into this network will increasingly integrate the personal computer into their lives by employing it more frequently and regularly, and for different applications. On the other hand, this conception suggests that female entry into the social networks of computing in video arcades might be rare, not because of any lack of innate skills or interests, but because of the male culture that dominates the arcade environment (Kiesler, Sproull, & Eccles, 1983). Computer clubs might develop a similarly male dominated culture, albeit at a different age level.

Within this orientation, an alternative to the sociocultural setting derives from some research on television, which generally projects the viewers' immediate friends and family as important influences on how television is used. Messaris and Sarett (1981) and Corder-Bolz (1980) have found that parents, older siblings, and others who co-view with children influence what children take away from viewing television and how they will approach future viewing. Influences of this kind may operate equally, if not more powerfully, in the case of computing in the home setting. For television it is usually assumed that even a very young child's capabilities are sufficient to utilize at least some of the content in some way. This assumption may be no less valid with computers that have a variety of visual, tactile, and audio features that can interest young children. Nevertheless, because computer use requires at least some training or assistance, there might be greater opportunity for others to intervene directly and influence the way(s) that the computer is employed. In the case of personal computers, children might even influence their parents, rather than vice versa, as is usually assumed to be true with television.

Similar conclusions can be drawn from the social information-processing approach now popular in the study of organizational behavior (Salancik & Pfeffer, 1978). Social information communicated to individuals by coworkers and supervisors is thought to influence employees' perceptions and use of information technology. In particular, immediate coworkers are proposed to affect an individual's attitudes and use through (a) overt statements they might make expressing opinions of the technology, (b) comments that make one or more dimensions of information technology more or less salient, (c) their interpretations of events related to the use of technology, and (d) comments that call attention to a particular need that may or may not be fulfilled by use of the technology (Fulk et al., 1987).

Yet another way of representing sociocultural influences is the communication context in which the media are used. The ways that families structure the use of information in the home and their intolerance for diversity of expression have been shown to be important factors in the choice and use of media (Chaffee, McLeod, & Atkin, 1971; Roberts, 1973). Highly structured families that discourage diversity of expression might inhibit the development of more varied uses of a personal computer.

Some empirical support for the role of sociocultural factors is provided by general surveys of the adoption of computing. For example, owners of personal computers are more likely than others to use a computer at work and to share their household with a child using a computer at school (Louis Harris, 1983, Table 4-7). Computing is believed to migrate from work into the home and it might also migrate from school. Each source provides a network of friends or family that can support and reinforce the computer user.

The importance of all these ways of conceptualizing the sociocultural setting is suggested by a number of theories from social psychology, including social comparison, consensual validation, and social learning. Theoretical treatments of social comparison posit that individuals are powerfully influenced by the attitudes, beliefs, and behavior of the particular group with which they identify. Put simply, adults might purchase home computers for word processing because their colleagues at the office have done so. Children might pursue computing because their best friends have done so. Parents might purchase a system for their children after discussing the educational potentials of computing with parents and teachers at a school function. Likewise, theoretical treatments of consensual validation suggest that social definitions of reality (i.e., the belief among peers that personal computing will have educational benefits) will be more persuasive than other dynamics of persuasion, such as the pronouncements of an expert (DeFleur & Ball-Rokeach, 1982).

Social learning theory (Bandura, 1977a, 1986) argues that witnessing others' model attitudes and behavior will establish the observer's capacity to engage in those attitudes and behaviors, and increase the probability of their occurrence. Either the original model or others may then reinforce the attitudes and behaviors, which will contribute to the likelihood of their becoming a permanent part of the individual's attitudinal and behavioral repertoire. If these are central to the person's self-concept, then the consequences associated with their display might affect the person's self-concept, particularly feelings of personal efficacy (Bandura, 1977b, 1986). Applied to the use of personal computers in the home, this concept implies that family members (and peers) are likely to influence one another's use through modeling. Further, to the extent that activities associated with the consequences or outcomes of computing are central to the user's self-concept, successful or unsuccessful use might influence future use.

Personal Attributes. Independent of social status factors, technical features, and sociocultural factors, some investigators have asserted that the personal values, attitudes, beliefs, and habits of the individual user are the primary determinants of use. Working within the diffusion-of-innovations tradition, Rogers et al. (1982) found that those personal computer users who had greater experience and expertise with the technology tended to have fewer problems, show greater interest, and see more work applications for their computers than those with less experience and expertise. Experience was also associated with the adoption of computing in the Harris survey (Louis Harris, 1983, Table 4-7). Further, those who reported work-related reasons for owning a personal computer were less likely to report learning problems associated with their use. Pre-existing experience and expertise, and instrumental reasons or motives for use, have often been found in research on the use of television also, although usually labeled with such descriptors as abilities and needs (cf. Katz, Blumler, & Gurevitch, 1974).

The theoretical foundation for these expectations is largely drawn from research on the adoption and implementation of innovations (Roger & Shoemaker, 1971). Perceived attributes of innovations, including their relative advantage, complexity, and compatibility, are likely to be a function of an individual's experience and expertise, which in turn can be a function of social background, including age, gender, and socioeconomic status. But the relevance of individual's beliefs and attitudes will depend on the locus of decisional control within the family (Danzinger & Dutton, 1977; Danziger et al., 1982; Rogers & Shoemaker, 1971). The wishes of an enthusiastic child might be vetoed by an uninterested parent and vice versa.

However, research on the adoption and diffusion of innovations is difficult to classify unambiguously into any one of the categories of variables previously discussed (Dutton et al., 1987a, 1987b). Some researchers have noted the importance of social networks in understanding how an innovation diffuses through a social system (cf. Coleman, Katz, & Menzel, 1957), which we have grouped with sociocultural factors. More recently, Rogers et al., (1982) have examined interpersonal communications and the mass media as sources of information for both awareness and decision-making stages in the innovation process. Similarly, organizational innovation theorists note the importance of the sociocultural environment for generation, adoption, and implementation of innovations (Czepiel, 1975; Kraemer et al., 1981; Zaltman, Duncan, & Holbeck, 1973).

Other innovation theorists focus on subjective attributes of the innovation. Complexity, trialability, and observability have received much attention (Rogers & Shoemaker, 1971). These attributes might also be thought of as technical features. However, because all are often measured as subjective perceptions that vary across individuals, they can be conceptualized as personal factors—individual beliefs and attitudes about computing. Personal factors, then, remain an integral part of much innovation research. As such, these factors illustrate a set of variables that have been found to be important to the innovation process, and thus may further prove useful in explaining patterns of home computer use.

Another theoretical foundation for expecting personal factors to play a significant role in the use of personal computing can be constructed from research employing the uses-and-gratifications approach to media. This research tradition utilizes what can be characterized as a deficit-motivation model in which people have a set of needs that will, when gratification falls below a certain level, prompt activities to alleviate the deficit. It is further assumed that people are aware of such needs and can accurately report on them (Katz et al., 1974). Although media gratifications are typically measured as a reason for use rather than a representation of some internal need or process, it is still assumed that these reported reasons influence actual use (Kippax & Murray, 1980; Kovaric, Dorr, & Nicol, 1983). Thus, it is asserted that reasons reported for using personal computers will influence actual use independently of other factors.

An Integrated Model. Although the four sets of factors just outlined are conceptually independent, they are empirically intertwined. Moreover, in the real world of home computing, no set is individually powerful enough to predict adequately the amount and variety of usage. Rather, developing an adequate model of personal computer usage will require the simultaneous consideration of social status, technical features, sociocultural setting, and personal attributes, as suggested in Fig. 4.1. Each is likely to account for some variance in the evolution of personal computer use over time. Although exceptions to this generalization can readily be imagined (consider the iconoclast adolescent who can gain a sense of self-worth by overcoming system deficiencies and family and peer group hostility by the mastery of computing), it is expected that for most personal computer users all influences will operate together to shape the changes in level and diversity of computer utilization. That is, although each influence might be necessary, none is expected to be sufficient to account for the development of specific patterns of computer utilization. Thus, the existence of a favorable economic, social, and educational background, the existence (and increase) of particularly "friendly" system features, the existence and increase of both a broadly and narrowly conceived social environment that supports the development of computing use and skills, and the existence and increase of personal reasons for use, skill at use, and positive attitudes toward the technology are believed to operate together to shape the amount, regularity, and diversity of use over time.

Some social scientists have begun to focus increased attention on interactions between social status, technical features, individual needs, and sociocultural settings. Covvey and McAllister (1982) illustrate this approach simply by noting that any system with features that do not match the needs of the potential user(s) is likely to fall into disuse. From their perspective, it is the user's perceptions of the match between their needs and the system capabilities that are important, not some technical features per se. Taylor (1982) took an explicitly uses-and-gratifications approach in suggesting procedures for informational retrieval system design. Thus, for different kinds of users (identified primarily by the way they use their personal computer) different kinds of factors might be most critical in accounting for patterns of use. For example, for adults experienced with a single application such as word processing, the acquisition of more sophisticated software might account for variance in the amount and style of usage, although not affect the variety of ways in which computing is used. Alternatively, the novice child's usage might be primarily contingent on a facilitative sociocultural environment rather than strong personal reasons for use, but require the acquisition of more sophisticated "discovery-type" software to progress to more varied applications. Finally, disuse might be accounted for by the sudden elimination of facilitating factors among only one of the several clusters.

A primary motivation for considering a multifactor model of personal computer utilization is the likelihood that the numerous factors linked to personal computing are intricately interwoven. For example, the social status of individuals is systematically related to the nature of their personal attitudes and beliefs as well as their technological and social environments. Social status may act as both a filter, separating users from nonusers, and as a conditioning variable, influencing the relative importance of the other three classes of variables in predicting amount and kind of usage. Moreover, sociocultural variables, particularly the attitudes of a user's network of personal computing contacts, may serve to shape the user's personal attitudes and beliefs. Interrelationships among the various sets of factors are expected, then, rather than considering each as an empirically independent set of predictors.

TOWARD A RESEARCH AGENDA

Suggested by the foregoing discussion are four streams of research, including basic empirical research to (a) more fully develop a typology of use patterns (see Rubin & Bantz, this volume); (b) develop an integrated, yet reasonably parsimonious model by both isolating in each category those variables that best explain patterns of home computer use, as well as specifying the web of interrelationships between sets of factors; and (c) expand the model by examining the relationship between patterns of use and particular impacts. Another stream of research would involve (d) the conduct of quasi-experimental research aimed at informing social policy.

Typology Development

Existing typologies of personal computer users tend to be based on either stages of adoption, which distinguish, for example, early versus late adopters, or segments of the personal computing market, which distinguish, for example, hobbyists, elite consumers, mass consumers, and work-at-home users (Yankee Group, 1982). These typologies either ignore use or confuse use with the nature of the equipment. A typology based more on patterns

4. RESEARCH FOR HOME COMPUTING

of use, as suggested by this chapter, might be useful by moving speculation away from generic forecasts of the implications of home computing to explanations more contingent on patterns of use. Such a typology has been valuable to studies of computing in organizations which must also assess the implications of a highly malleable and general-purpose tool. Although we have suggested one approach to such a typology, based on level and diversity of use, a more functionally specific one might be derived from empirical research. One approach to a functional typology has categorized personal computing use among school children along reality and fantasy dimensions (Lieberman et al., 1986). Reality use involved instrumental applications such as programming, whereas fantasy use involved game playing. Users might be classified by the degree they focus on one, both, or neither kind of application. Such a derivation would be significant for studies of social impacts, as the implications of personal computing could be quite different for the compulsive programmer than for the child intrigued by computer games.

Taking as a starting point the set of categories ranging from low time commitments to high ones, as well as from narrow to diverse application patterns, descriptive research should be undertaken utilizing combined observational and interview methods. Following the work of Lieberman et al. (1986), usage styles might be more substantively differentiated into such categories as entertainment, education, and business. This approach, if repeated across heterogeneous populations of home computer users, is likely to yield an empirically grounded typology that conforms to more qualitative observation of home computer users. Multivariate techniques such as factor and cluster analyses could be used to isolate empirically dimensions of use that differ from those we have hypothesized.

Testing Independent Factors

Longitudinal field research, which is rare in this area (Dutton et al., 1987a), is suggested by the second stage of the research program. One option would employ a panel study to track a sample of users over time. An analytical strategy would involve categorizing users into groups characterized by similar patterns of use informed by the usage typology. Measures of the independent variables representing each of the perspectives could then be developed, the interrelationships among these factors could be identified, and their ability to discriminate among the various user groups could be assessed. In this fashion, the most critical variables affecting patterns of use and change over time could be isolated, and their relative causal ordering assessed. Moreover, the use of a panel design would enable researchers to explore the time lags between changes in the sociocultural environment or technical factors and changes in pattern of use.

Impact Analysis

Any discussion of home computer impacts should begin by examining uses. Once a model depicting the development of particular use patterns has been established, research on their impacts could be more effectively conducted. On the basis of usage patterns, a number of impacts can be theoretically derived from the model. For example, based on Liebermann et al. (1986), more pronounced improvements in educational achievement might be hypothesized among children who use their home computers on a more regular basis for more diversified applications than for children who primarily play video games.

Researchers have not studied many of the more subtle impacts that computing might have on such things as styles of writing, work-related stress, and the analytical approaches taken by researchers. Many other changes might be hypothesized to result from increasingly computer-mediated experiences at both work and play. Clearly, work remains to be done in conceptually and operationally defining areas of life that might be affected by more computer-mediated experiences. And there is no doubt that a great deal of qualitative research will need to be done before these conceptual and operational tasks can be successfully launched.

Finally, some impacts are more socially desirable than others, and insights into the path of influence from our independent factors to usage patterns and then to subsequent impacts might spur discussions aimed at promoting desirable outcomes to move beyond the common debate over the value of computers per se. This realization leads to the fourth stage of research.

Applied Research and Social Policy

Also suggested by this framework is the relevance of such basic research to more applied questions concerning social policy. Perhaps the most frequently raised social concern with regard to information technology in the home revolves around issues of equity (Anderson & Harris, 1984; Lautenberg, 1984). An uneven distribution of computing resources across income groups is implicit to the integrative model described previously, and well documented by early studies (Louis Harris, 1983). Clearly, policy makers feel that personal computers do provide a significant educational advantage to children (Lautenberg, 1984). Given this belief, if the subsidization for low-income families ever becomes feasible through taxing or spending programs, then we need to know much more about the factors other than income that are likely to affect the use of computing in the home. A simple formulation of available income affecting access might not allot significance to the array of factors that will facilitate the adoption and integration of computing into the household.

4. RESEARCH FOR HOME COMPUTING

Research rooted in the "knowledge gap" tradition underscores the more complex inequities associated with communication technology than are implied by issues of access (Titchenor, Donohue, & Olien, 1970). Even among lower socioeconomic groups who have equal access to home computers (say through subsidies), we might find that computing is less effectively integrated into home life than among higher socioeconomic groups. Subsidies might fail to narrow and might even widen the gap across social status groups. This is not an argument against subsidies, but only a possible scenario in which subsidies might require more consideration to be given to the process of implementing computing in the home.

Given the previous discussion, research might examine strategies for addressing such inequities. The analytical framework developed previously would suggest that a simplistic subsidy strategy would be inadequate in alleviating inequities. Rather, attention to the sociocultural environment, for example, might also support cost-reducing measures. These strategies might involve, for instance, the creation of clubs and other social networks of users and vendors of home computers. A field experiment might then compare the usage patterns among subsidized families against subsidized families who are linked into social networks as a condition of receiving hardware and software.

Important theoretical and social issues could be addressed by empirical research on the social dynamics of personal computing. Theoretically, an overview of the literature suggests the need for field research to examine a more integrated model of personal computing that is not limited to the users' social status, technical features, sociocultural environment, or personal beliefs and attitudes. Socially, the implications of personal computing might well be mixed. Although the potential benefits and concerns are the subject of daily personal testimonies, such benefits are disproportionately distributed and biased in favor of socially advantaged groups. Yet, the processes underlying this bias might be so fundamentally rooted in social dynamics that any quick economic fix would fail. If so, only knowledge of the factors that accentuate or mitigate these patterns can provide information useful to those who wish to alter this bias.

REFERENCES

Anderson, B. (1980). Programming in the home of the future. *International Journal of Man-Machine Studies, 12,* 341-365.

Anderson, R. E., & Harris, L. (1984). *Computer learning and the public need* (MCSR Rep. 84-3). Minneapolis: Minnesota Center for Social Research, University of Minnesota, MCSR Report 84-3.

Bandura, A. (1977a). Self-efficacy: Toward a unifying theory of behavioral change. *Psychological Review, 84,* 191-215.

Bandura, A. (1977b). *Social learning theory.* Englewood Cliffs, NJ: Prentice-Hall.

Bandura, A. (1986). *Social foundations of thought and action: A social cognitive theory*. Englewood Cliffs, NJ: Prentice-Hall.
Bowes, J. E. (1980). Mind vs. matter: Mass utilization of information technology. In B. Dervin & M. Voigt (Eds.), *Progress in communication sciences*. (Vol. 2, pp. 51-73). Norwood, NJ: Ablex.
Brown, J. R., Cramond, J. K., & Wilde, R. J. (1974). Displacement effects of television and the child's functional orientation to media. In J. G. Blumler & E. Katz (Eds.), *The uses of mass communications*. Beverly Hills, CA: Sage.
Bryant, J., & Zillmann, D. (Eds.). (1986). *Perspectives on media effects*. Hillsdale, NJ: Lawrence Erlbaum Associates.
Carroll, J. M. (1982, November). The adventure of getting to know a computer. *Computer*, pp. 49-58.
Chaffee, S. McLeod, J., & Atkin, C. (1971). Parental influences on adolescent media use. *American Behavioral Scientist*, *14*, 323-340.
Chu, G. C., & Schramm, W. (1967). *Learning from television: What the research says*. Washington, DC: National Association of Educational Broadcasters.
Coleman, J., Katz, E., & Menzel, H. (1957). The diffusion of an innovation among physicians. *Sociometry*, *20*, 253-270.
Comstock, G., Chaffee, S., Katzman, N., McCombs, M., & Roberts, D. (1978). *Television and human behavior*. New York: Columbia University Press.
Corder-Bolz, C. R. (1980). Mediation: The role of significant others. *Journal of Communication*, *30*(3), 106-118.
Covvey, H. D., & McAllister, N. H. (1982). *Computer choices*. Reading, MA: Addison-Wesley.
Czepiel, J. (1975). Patterns of interorganizational communications and the diffusion of a major technological innovation in a competitive industrial community. *Academy of Management Journal*, *18*, 6-24.
Danziger, J. N., & Dutton, W. H. (1977). Computers as an innovation in American local governments. *Communications of the ACM*, *20*(12), 945-956.
Danziger, J. N., Dutton, W. H., Kling, R., & Kraemer, K. L. (1982). *Computers and politics*. New York: Columbia University Press.
DeFleur, M., & Ball-Rokeach, S. (1982). *Theories of mass communication* (4th ed.). New York: Longman.
Dutton, W. H., Kovaric, P., & Steinfield, C. W. (1985). Computing in the home: A research paradigm. *Computers and the Social Sciences*, *1*(1), 5-17.
Dutton, W. H., & Kraemer, K. L. (1985). *Modeling as negotiating*. Norwood, NJ: Ablex.
Dutton, W. H., Rogers, E. M., & Jun, S. H. (1987a). Diffusion and social impacts of personal computers. *Communication Research*, *14*(2), 219-250.
Dutton, W. H., Rogers, E. M., & Jun, S. H. (1987b). The diffusion and impacts of information technology in households. *Oxford Surveys in Information Technology*, *4*, 133-193.
Evans, C. (1979). *The micro-millenium*. New York: Viking Press.
von Feilitzen, C. (1976). The functions served by the media: Report on a Swedish study. In R. Brown (Ed.), *Children and television*. Beverly Hills, CA: Sage.
Forester, T. (Ed.). (1980). *The microelectronics revolution*. Cambridge, MA: MIT Press.
Fulk, J., Steinfield, C. W., Schmitz, J., & Power, J. G. (1987). A social information processing model of media use in organizations. *Communication Research*, *14*(5), 529-552.
Furu, T. (1971). *The function of television for children and adolescents*. Tokyo: Sophia University Press.
Gershuny, J. (1978). *After industrial society: The emerging self-service economy*. Atlantic Highlands, NJ: Humanities Press.
Gonzales, I. (1986). *Utilization patterns of HI-OVIS Interactive Broadcasting System in Higashi-Ikoma, Japan*. Unpublished doctoral dissertation. Annenberg School of Communications, University of Southern California, Los Angeles.

Greenberg, B. S. (1974). Gratifications of television viewing and their correlates in British children. In J. Blumler & E. Katz (Eds.), *The uses of mass communications* (pp. 71-92). Beverly Hills, CA: Sage.
Himmelweit, H. T., Openheim, A. N., & Vince, P. (1958). *Television and the child.* London: Oxford University Press.
Katz, E. (1980). On conceptualizing media effects. *Studies in Communications, 1,* 119-141.
Katz, E., Blumler, J., & Gurevitch, M. (1974). Utilization of mass communication by the individual. In J. Blumler & E. Katz (Eds.), *The uses of mass communications* (pp. 19-32). Beverly Hills, CA: Sage.
Katz, E., Gurevitch, M., & Haas, H. (1973). On the use of the mass media for important things. *American Sociological Review, 38,* 164-181.
Katz, E. & Lazarsfeld, P. (1955). *Personal influence.* New York: The Free Press.
Kiesler, S., Sproull, L., & Eccles, J. S. (1983, March). Second-class citizens? *Psychology Today,* pp. 41-48.
Kippax, S., & Murray, J. P. (1980). Using the mass media: Need gratification and perceived utility. *Communication Research, 7,* 335-360.
Klapper, J. T. (1960). *The effects of mass communication.* New York: The Free Press.
Kling, R. (1980). Social analyses of computing. *Computing Surveys, 12*(1), 61-110.
Kling, R., & Gerson, E. M. (1977). The social dynamics of technical innovation in the computing world. *Symbolic Interaction,1*(11), 132-146.
Kollette, D. (1984, October 15). One in six buy computers. *USA Today,* p. 1, 10.
Kovaric, P., Dorr, A., & Nicol, J. (1983). *What's gratifying about different kinds of television programs.* Unpublished manuscript, Annenberg School of Communications, University of Southern California, Los Angeles.
Kraemer, K. L., Dutton, W. H., & Northrop, A. (1981). *The management of information systems.* New York: Columbia University Press.
Lautenberg, F. R. (1984, April). Equity in computer education. *The Computing Teacher,* pp. 13-14.
Levy, P., & Ferguson, B. J. (1983). *Microcomputers and children's learning.* Unpublished manuscript, Annenberg School of Communications, University of Southern California, Los Angeles.
Lieberman, D., Roberts, D., & Chaffee, S. (1986, May). *Reading, television, and computers: Relationships between children's media use and learning.* Paper presented to the International Communication Association, Chicago, IL.
Linder, S. B. (1970). *The harried leisure class.* New York: Columbia University Press.
Louis Harris & Associates. (1983). *The road after 1984: The impact of technology on society.* Report presented at the Eighth International Smithsonian Symposium, Harris Study No. 832033.
Malone, T. W. (1981). Toward a theory of intrinsically motivating instruction. *Cognitive Science, 4,* 333-369.
Mander, J. (1978). *Four arguments for the elimination of television.* New York: Morrow.
Messaris, P., & Sarett, C. (1981). On the consequences of television-related parent-child interaction. *Human Communication Research, 7,* 226-244.
Miller, K., & Monge, P. (1985). Social information and employee anxiety about organizational change. *Human Communication Research, 11,* 365-386.
Murray, J. P. & Kippax, S. (1978). Children's social behavior in three towns with differing television experience. *Journal of Communication, 28*(1), 19-29.
National Association of Broadcasters. (1986). *NAB technology update.* Washington, DC: Author.
Nilles, J. M. (1980). *A technology assessment of personal computers* (Vols. 1, 2, 3). Los Angeles, CA: Center for Futures Research, University of Southern California.

Nilles, J. M. (1982). *Exploring the world of the personal computer.* Englewood Cliffs, NJ: Prentice-Hall.

Ogburn, W. F., & Nimkoff, M. F. (1955). *Technology and the changing family.* Boston: Houghton Mifflin.

Paisley, W., & Chen, M. (1982). *Children and electronic text: Challenges and opportunities of the 'new literacy.'* Unpublished manuscript, Stanford University, Stanford, CA.

Papert, S. (1980). *Mindstorms: Children, computers, and powerful ideas.* New York: Basic Books.

Pearl, D., Bouthilet, L., & Lazar, J. (Eds.). (1982). *Television and behavior: Ten years of scientific progress and implications for the Eighties* (Vol. 2). Rockville, MD: National Institute of Mental Health.

Pool, I. (1977). *The social impact of the telephone.* Cambridge, MA: MIT Press.

Rafaeli, S. (1986). The electronic bulletin board: A computer-driven mass medium. *Computers and the Social Sciences, 2*(3), 123-136.

Reeves, B., & Wartella, E. (1982, May). *For some people under some conditions: A history of research on children and media.* Paper presented at the International Communication Association Meeting, Boston, MA.

Rice, R., & Paisley, W. (1982). The green thumb videotex equipment. *Telecommunications Policy, 6,* 223-235.

Roberts, D. (1973). Communication and children: A development approach. In I. de Sola Pool & W. Schramm (Eds.), *Handbook of communication.* Chicago: Rand McNally.

Robinson, J. (1977). *How Americans use time.* New York: Praeger.

Robinson, J. (1981). Television and leisure time: A new scenario. *Journal of Communication, 31*(1), 120-130.

Rogers, E. M. (1985). The diffusion of home computers among households in Silicon Valley. *Marriage and Family Review, 8,* 89-100.

Rogers, E. M., Daley, H., & Wu, T. (1982). *The diffusion of home computers: An exploratory study.* Unpublished manuscript, Institute for Communication Research, Stanford University, Stanford, CA.

Rogers, E. M., & Shoemaker, F. (1971). *Communication of innovations.* New York: The Free Press.

Rubin, A. M. (1979). Television use by children and adolescents. *Human Communication Research, 5,* 109-120.

Salancik, G. R., & Pfeffer, J. (1978). A social information approach to job attitudes and task design. *Administrative Science Quarterly, 23,* 224-252.

Steinfield, C. W. (1985). Dimensions of electronic mail use in organizations. In J. Pearce & R. Robinson (Eds.), *Proceedings of the Academy of Management* (pp. 239-243). Mississippi State, MS: Mississippi State University, Academy of Management.

Steinfield, C. W. (1986). Computer-mediated communication in an organizational setting: Explaining task-related and socioemotional uses. In M. McLaughlin (Ed.), *Communication Yearbook 9* (pp. 777-804). Beverly Hills, CA: Sage.

Stone, G. C. (1982, February). *New technology: Who will answer?* Paper presented at the meeting of the Association for Education in Journalism, Atlanta, GA.

Taylor, R. (1982). Value-added processes in the information life cycle. *Journal of the American Society for Information Science, 33*(5), 341-346.

Thomas, J., & Griffin, R. (1983). The social information model of task design: a review of the literature. *Academy of Management Review, 8,* 672-682.

Titchenor, P., Donohue, G., & Olien, C. (1970). Mass media flow and differential growth and knowledge. *Public Opinion Quarterly, 34,* 159-170.

Turkle, S. (1984). *The second self: Computers and the human spirit.* New York: Simon & Schuster.

Vallee, J. (1982). *The network revolution: Confessions of a computer scientist.* Berkeley, CA: And/Or Press.

Venkatesh, A., & Vitalari, N. (1984). Research at the Irvine campus shows family life changes when a computer enters the home. *University Bulletin, 32*(16), 57.

Vitalari, N., Venkatesh, A., & Gronhaug, K. (1985). Computing in the home: Shifts in the time allocation patterns of households. *Communications of the ACM, 28,* 512–522.

Williams, F. (1982). *The communications revolution.* Beverly Hills, CA: Sage.

Williams, T. M., & Handford, G. (1986). Television and participation in leisure activities. in T. M. Williams (Ed.), *The impact of television: A natural experiment involving three towns.* New York: Academic Press.

Winn, M. (1977). *The plug-in drug.* New York: Bantam.

Yankee Group. (1982). *Home of the future planning service: Personal computers in the home.* Boston: Author.

Yin, R. K., Heald, K. A., Vogel, M. E., Fleischauer, B. P., & Vladeck, B. C. (1976). *A review of case studies of technological innovations in state and local services.* Santa Monica, CA: Rand Corporation.

Zaltman, G., Duncan, R., & Holbeck, J. (1973). *Innovation and organizations.* New York: Wiley.

5

Teletext in the United Kingdom: Patterns, Attitudes, and Behaviors of Users

Bradley S. Greenberg
Michigan State University

INTRODUCTION

In 1986, the somewhat heralded efforts at teletext by CBS and NBC in the United States came to a crashing stop; transmissions seen by few except affiliate station engineers and convention goers were laid to rest, without being accessible to the general public.

In 1986, in England, Scotland, and Wales, the 10th anniversary of full government support for the British Broadcasting Corporation (BBC) and the Independent Broadcasting Authority (IBA) to begin nationwide public teletext services passed without special notice. In a nation fondly known for understatement, four largely separate teletext services were now available in nearly one of every five homes and expanding by thousands of sets per month. Furthermore, the Ceefax system, developed by the BBC, had been tried (and sometimes maintained) in Austrailia, Austria, Belgium, Finland, Holland, Sweden, and West Germany, among other nations, and was the system adopted by the Taft organization in Cincinnati, but not by the American networks. The IBA developed Oracle (Optional Reception of Announcements by Coded Line Electronics), transmitted it originally on the Independent Television channel, and than created a separate service on its newer Channel 4. BBC 1 and BBC 2 provide Ceefax (probably named from BBC-facts) with some overlap in content. Each home teletext set recevies all four services.

The origins of British teletext were within the BBC, attempting to deliver information to the hearing impaired on the vertical blanking interval (VBI) on the television screen. The VBI is the line that goes up and down when the television picture is unstable. The first notion was to send such information to a hard copy printer in the home; this was abandoned in favor of using computer semiconductor technology developed in the late 1960s. The end result was the display of characters on a television screen. At the same time, the independent television stations had been working on their own teletext system. In a combined committee, a single system standard was created in 1974, from which the Ceefax and Oracle systems were generated. Two years of field testing and very limited page transmission resulted in an upgraded set of specifications and final government approval on November 9, 1976. A critical parallel factor was that set manufacturers began to produce sets with internal teletext decoders, rather than external set-top converters. Throughout the mid-1970s, the system floundered with fewer than 500 teletext equipped sets; in 1979, the first year after teletext sets began being manufactured on a production line basis, there were 40,000 sets in use; this tripled the next year, doubled again in both 1981 and 1982 (Tydeman, Lipinski, Adler, Nyhan, & Zwimpfer, 1982; Vieth, 1983). At the time of this study (Greenberg, 1986) — in January and February, 1986 — industry estimates were that one in six or seven homes had teletext, and a year later, those estimates became one in five or six. Slow growth? Fast growth? Compared to what? One can say it was phenomenal growth compared to videotext development in either the United Kingdom or the United States. At the most conservative estimate — one in seven homes — 3 million households and 7.5 million residents had daily access to teletext in early 1986.

This off-air text system has its costs absorbed by the system operator; the user pays for the decoder built into the television set, either in the purchase price of the set or the rental price, in a country where nearly half the television sets are rented. The difference in rental price between a textless set and a teletext set is about $1.50 per month. It processes one page of text at a time and the user chooses pages by pressing numbers on a remote control device that also operates the television system. Any page has on it a maximum of 40 characters per row and a maximum of 24 visible rows. The "magazine" has 200 pages from which to select textual information and graphics; each service has pages of subtitling available for the hard-of-hearing; some of the services have telesoftware available by linkage to a personal home computer; the Oracle services have contained advertising since 1981. Oracle also contains regional teletext, whereby stations outside of London can insert their own pages into the nationally distributed service.

For the home user, accessing teletext requires first turning on the television set and choosing a television channel. For that channel, the related teletext service is accessed by pressing the TT button, which means that to access Oracle on ITV, you must first be on the ITV channel. From there,

5. TELETEXT IN THE UNITED KINGDOM

you may go wherever you wish among that system's teletext pages. If you know what the page number is for the section of interest to you, it is directly accessible by punching in that page number. If you are uncertain, you can go the main index (whose page number is displayed at the top of the screen), and then make your selection. There are main indexes, subindexes, and stories (or ads). When you have selected a page, you can watch the page numbers roll at the top of the screen to indicate you are on your way there. Average waiting time is 7 seconds, based on the 15 seconds it would take to cycle through the entire text. And of course, you can read teletext and watch television concurrently if you wish to have the teletext laid over the TV picture.

This chapter reports in detail on how and why teletext is used, and by whom. Perhaps a very brief personal description by one who experienced the systems for several months in 1985-1986 can be illustrative. For 13£/month or $20, we rented the largest possible teletext set, a 22-inch screen, with its splendid British color and picture resolution. Each morning, before the *London Times* was delivered, teletext was called up for the day's weather and the news headlines. Reading the headlines cued my newspaper reading—I knew what stories I wanted in more detail when the newspaper was delivered, or purchased at the subway stop. In the evening, with no afternoon paper, the process was repeated. On weekends, I determined what major civic events would be available in London, where, what time, and what mode of public transportation would get me there. Movie and play information were available: For movies, I could identify whether the movie was in a nearby cinema, rather than going to the West End. For the theater, there was the phone number to check ticket availability, and the opportunity to order tickets, against a credit card. The odds on the soccer matches were there for bettors; for me, it was to see if the local teams were playing at home or away. If it was a weekend of planned travel through the countryside, I identified highway construction projects, detours, and weather for the destination area. And for this long-term tourist, there was a special bonus; relatives' and friends' flights into Heathrow and Gatwick could be checked for delays, saving countless hours of waiting time. Teletext was convenient; it was informative; it was fast; it was helpful; it saved time, and probably money.

So, when invited to spend a sabbatical at the IBA and to identify projects of interest, we set out to examine what users were now doing with teletext, a question given little attention by the IBA or BBC in their decade of system development and sponsorship (Wober, 1985; Wober & Reardon, 1979).

METHODS

Interviewing was contracted to MARPLAN, Ltd. The sampling method used was quota sampling, using age, sex, and social class as criteria for contacting a representative sample of 7,056 adults in 63 randomly selected areas countrywide. That base number was used to reach 1,000 teletext households, if the 15% penetration rate were realized. Each person contacted in the quota sample was asked several screening questions, including whether there was a teletext (TT) set in their household. From this initial sample, 11% reported having TT sets; of that 11%, 3% refused to be interviewed, which resulted in a final sample of 574 teletext households and users. All interviewing was done in person; veteran interviewers trained by MARPLAN comprised the field staff for the 20-25 minute interview.

Primary sections of the questionnaire included these issues:

- who uses teletext
- what influenced the acquisition of teletext
- what is the context in which TT is used
- how is teletext typically accessed
- what amount of use is made of it
- what content sections are used among the different services
- what problems do users have with teletext
- how does each service compare with the others
- how does teletext compare with other mass media
- what use is made of advertising on teletext

RESULTS

Who Has Teletext?

As of early 1987, nearly one in five households in England had teletext, according to telecommunication industry estimates. At the time of this study conducted 12 months earlier, it was one in seven. As individuals have acquired new television receivers, there has been an increasing tendency to acquire one that is capable of providing the four teletext channels.

The sample of teletext users from TT households in the present study is distinctly upscale. Given the standard social class categories used in social surveys in England—A,B,C1,C2,D, and E[1]—25% of this sample was in the AB categories (more than twice their population proportion) and 33% were in the C1 category. Obviously, the more expensive television receivers

---

[1] A = higher management, administrative, or professional; B = intermediate management, administrative, or professional; C1 = supervisory, clerical, junior administrative; C2 = skilled manual workers; D = semiskilled or unskilled manual; E = the remainder.

5. TELETEXT IN THE UNITED KINGDOM

were more likely to be bought by those with higher incomes; only 11% of the sample were in the DE categories.

A subgroup of heavy users (daily use plus > 1 session per day) included more men than women; 41% of the sample and 49% of the heavy users were male. They also clustered in younger age categories; 56% of them were between the ages of 18-34, as contrasted with 46% of the entire sample.

What Influences the Acquisition of Teletext?

Asked how much they were influenced by five different sources in their decision to obtain a teletext set, two key influences emerged—a friend (or friends) who already had TT and advertisements they had read or seen. One third cited each of these as having at least a little influence. Given response categories of "much, some, a little, and no influence at all," friends were the strongest influence; 12% said friends were of much influence, compared to 4% for adverts. For other potential sources of influence asked about—the price, a salesperson, or stories they had read about TT—one in six thought these were at least a little influential.

Heavy TT users were even more likely to attribute the purchase source influence to friends, and then to advertising. A separate question asked how helpful (very, fairly, not very, not at all) the salesperson was in explaining TT at the shop where the set was chosen. Although the average response was fairly helpful, one in five judged them as not helpful at the point of purchase (or rental).

An open-ended question asked if there were any other influences. One in five spontaneously responded that they obtained TT because it was good for news and sports, 1 in 10 that it just happened to be part of the new TV they bought, and 1 in 10 just wanted it. A final question thought to bear on the influence process was what they expected of teletext; of course it would be more informative if parallel responses existed from nonteletext households, as well. Nevertheless, respondents were asked what they thought TT was better for: information, entertainment, or both equally? The responses were 2-1 for information over both equally, and a paltry 2% said TT was better for entertainment.

What Is the Context of Use?

The TT television set was the only television set among one third of the sampled households, although 45% of the homes had two sets, 16% had three, and 6% more than three. Given the higher average cost of a television set in England (at least twice what a comparable set would cost in the U.S.), this is further indication of the upward income bias among the TT households. The primary television set is located in 99% of the lounges (living room), in 45% of a first bedroom, in 20% of a second bedroom, in 11% of the kitchens and 11% of the dining rooms, in 8% of a third bedroom, and in 9% of other rooms. But the TT set itself is located in the lounge, 97% of them.

Unlike the American situation, the British TV environment is characterized by TV rental. At the time of this study, nearly half the TT receivers (46%) were rented units — for only 1£ more per month than rental of a nonteletext unit. So, the major set in the home, normally in the lounge, is as often as not a rented unit, and likely more often than not in nonteletext households. For the multiple set households, all but the first set are owned; in this sample, 95% of all sets other than the one in the lounge were purchased.

Time of use is another context characteristic. Respondents were asked when they usually use teletext, with these results:

	Sample	Heavy Users
8 a.m.–noon	31%	43%
Noon–4 p.m.	34	41
4–7 p.m.	48	58
7–10 p.m.	63	73
After 10 p.m.	26	35

From this, it is clear that TT is likely in use in all dayparts by at least one fourth of the TT households, except for pre-8 a.m. The heavy user group were heavier users in each of the day parts examined; for each time block, about 10% more of the heavier users said they were regular users than was identified across the entire sample of users.

When asked if teletext was being used at different times from when they watched television or in conjunction with TV watching, slightly more than half the sample (56%) said they usually used teletext at the same time as they watched TV. So, teletext is as often a complementary activity as it is a competitive one.

Because the home has but a single teletext set, and only one person at a time can control it, other potential users form part of the context for TT use. In this study, we did not determine how many total people there were in the household; nevertheless, 42% of the sample indicated that one other person in the home also used the teletext, and 46% said that more than one other person did so. Although most of these other users were adults (18 or over), in one third of the homes, at least one of the other users was under 18. Clearly, then, TT sets are more likely to be in multiple person households, and the other members of the households also are likely to be TT users.

5. TELETEXT IN THE UNITED KINGDOM

Finally, teletext use is done far more often in the context of seeking some specific information, rather than merely browsing through what is available. Two thirds of the time, users said they were seeking something specifically, whereas browsing occurred one fourth of the time.

How Is Teletext Accessed?

Once the viewer has decided to use teletext (either by having it displayed by itself on the television screen, or displaying it on top of the television image being watched), there are four basic modes of entering or accessing teletext sections. Each requires knowledge of the page(s) where something is located—the main index, a subindex, the A–Z index, or some specific page where the same information (e.g., weather, travel information) is placed each day. Two thirds of the respondents indicated that they "almost always" or "often" started with the main index, one half said they went directly to a specific page they wanted and remembered, one fourth began with a subindex, and only 14% referred to the A–Z master index of all entries. However, three fourths of the heavy TT users typically began with the specific page they wanted to examine. Heavy use of the main index persisted, as half the sample indicated that it returned to the main index two or more times during each teletext session.

What Use Is Made of Teletext in Terms of Services?

Recognizing that there are four channels containing teletext services, we wished to determine knowledge about each of the services and the preferred services. The most important finding is that there is considerable overlap in service use; about 90% of the sample said they used both Ceefax on BBC1 and Oracle on ITV, and 66% said they used both Ceefax on BBC2 and Oracle on Ch. 4. Those indexed as heavy TT users used more of all four services.

Because this question merely probed if they used each of the services, a more precise estimate was obtained by asking each respondent what percentage of the time they spent looking at (Ceefax on BBC1, Oracle on ITV, . . .) when they looked at teletext. The time apportionments indicated a standoff among the main channel competitors: 35% of the time was reported to be spent with BBC1's teletext service, 31% with ITV, 10% with BBC2, and 11% with Ch. 4. These add to less than 100%, but much of the remainder were nonuser respondents in these households.

In a further analysis, we compared use of competitive services by dividing the sample into three parts—those who spent more than half their teletext time with Ceefax (BBC1 + BBC2), those who spent more than half their time with Oracle (ITV + Ch. 4), and those who divided their time 50-50 with the two. On average, those who spent a majority of their time with one or the other pairs of services still made substantial use of the second pair. Oracle fans (more than 50% use of Oracle) apportioned 19% of their teletext time to BBC1 and 10% to BBC2; Ceefax fans attributed identical portions to Oracle on ITV and Ch. 4 respectively.

As an aside, we asked early in the interview on what channels these services could be obtained. Just about 10% of the sample mislocated each of the four services, saying that Oracle could be found on BBC1 (12%) and BBC2 (10%), or that Ceefax could be found on ITV (12%) or on Ch. 4 (9%).

What is the Amount of Teletext Use?

Amount of use was assessed in several ways: use yesterday; number of days used in the last 7 days; number of times used each day (sessions); typical minutes in any one session, number of topic sections examined in a session, and number of pages looked at per session. Table 5.1 presents a summary of these results.

Three-fifths of the respondents had used teletext yesterday, they claimed. This included the heavy users, who by definition had used it each day in the last 7. Nearly the same proportion had used it each day in the last 7 days, with a fairly even distribution of the remainder of the sample across the lesser daily use categories. Then, among those who had used TT yesterday, they typically used it one (32%) or two (25%) times, with a lesser bulge of fans who used it more than five times (14%). Of course, the heavy users had more sessions—25% of them had used TT more than five times each day.

The raw time scores indicate an average teletext session of a little more than 9 minutes, reflected in the finding that 79% of the sessions were reported as ranging from 1-10 minutes, with the bulk of them estimated at 10 minutes. This means that the majority of TT users were spending 10-20 minutes each day with teletext, and the heaviest users were spending just under an hour with it.

As to number of different topic sections, the proportion who said one, two, or three sections were 23%, 31%, and 26% respectively. As for total pages per session, the overall average was 6.7 pages, evident from the long rectangular distribution in Table 5.1. Heavy users averaged one more page per session. Thus, heavy users, originally defined by the number of days of use, and the number of sessions, are heavy users by all of the usage measures explored here.

One additional measure of use has been created for exploratory purposes. It is not tabled here, but consists of an index wherein the number of days

5. TELETEXT IN THE UNITED KINGDOM

Table 5.1
Amount of Use of Teletext

	Sample
1. Watched yesterday (%Yes)	59%
2. Number of days in last 7	
0	13%
1-2	15
3-4	10
5-6	5
7	55
3. Number of sessions per day	
1	32%
2	25
3	16
4-5	12
6+	14
4. Number of minutes per sessions	
1-10	79%
11-20	11
21+	10
5. No. of topic sections examined	
1	23%
2	31
3	26
4+	17
6. No. of pages examined/session	
1	9%
2	14
3	14
4	15
5	9
6-9	13
10	10
11+	12

of use (in the last 7) was multiplied by the number of sessions per day. This yields an interesting pattern of use, with 15% of the sample at scores of 0, 35% with scores of 1-7 (10% at 7), 17% with scores of 8-14 (10% at 14), 13% with scores of 15-21 (12% at 21), 6% from 22-28 (all at 28), 4% from 29-35 (4% at 35), and 11% (true fans with 6 sessions per day for seven days) with scores of 42. The bulk of the users are at the low end of the distribution, but there is a substantial bulge at the far end.

What Content is Used?

For each topic section in the main index of each channel's teletext service, respondents who made any use of the service were asked whether they used that section "almost always," "often," "not very often," or "not at all." Here, we identify proportions who used the content sections "almost always" or "often," for each of the services, and then make comparisons across the services.

Use of Oracle on ITV (users were 88% of the entire sample) had the following patterns:

- a majority of its users made that frequency of response to the weather/travel section (55%) and the television guide (61%)
- a near majority cited news (47%) and sports (45%)
- one-fourth regularly used the "What's On" section, a listing of major London events
- from 8%–16% of the Oracle on ITV users cited the advertising, TV Plus (an expanded set of information on television shows), the subtitling, and a feature section called "Breaktime," consisting of horoscopes, crosswords, quizzes, and puzzles.
- Across all the sections, Oracle users averaged 3.12 of the 9 sections "almost always" or "often" each time they used the system.

Use of Ceefax on BBC1 (by 91% of the sample) consisted of:

- a majority who cited the weather/travel section (64%), the television and radio guides (62%), news (53%) and sports (50%).
- 16% who regularly checked the finance section, and 10% who used the subtitling available.
- the typical user of this service averaged 2.69 sections of the six available "almost always" or "often" each time they used the service.

Use of Oracle on Ch. 4 (64% of the sample) featured:

- one-fourth who looked at the holidays (vacations) section, and the news headlines
- one-fifth who looked regularly at the children's content section
- from 3%–13% who looked "almost always" or "often" at the remaining nine content sections in this teletext service—racing; classified ads; blue suede views (the pop music charts); your money; advertising; subtitles; the home file; time off; and 4-Tel (a special set of pages containing television program listings, mini-magazines, educational information, and other features)
- The typical user averaged 2.28 of the 12 sections almost always or often.

5. TELETEXT IN THE UNITED KINGDOM

Use of Ceefax on BBCC2 (also 64% of the sample) featured:

- 37% who regularly looked at the television and radio information
- 31% who checked the sports, 27% for the news, 23% for features, and 21% for the fun section
- 8% who looked at the finance section and 4% who used the subtitling
- Typically, users looked at 2.23 of the sections almost always or often.

The interests across these services are common ones—first in teletext's function as a television (and radio) guide and as a weather/travel expert, second for the information conveyed in its general news and sports news sections, and tertiary interest in all other content areas. This is buttressed by a question asked as to what specific pages were used each time they used the service. The page numbers cited primarily were determined subsequently to be those of news, sports, and football (soccer) headlines, and weather and television listings for Oracle on ITV, the television listing on Oracle on Ch. 4, the news headlines, news index, weather map and television listings on BBC1's Ceefax, and news headlines, sports, television listings and Top 10 albums on BBC2's Ceefax.

What Problems Do Users Have?

From pretesting, prior research and a log of user complaints, 10 potential problems became the core set asked about. With response options of "big problem," "medium problem," "small problem," and "no problem," the large majority of users had "no problem" with the large majority of potential problems.

From 64% to 87% had no problem at all with finding what they wanted, punching the right numbers, the size of the text, the clarity of the graphs, the indexes, either too little or too much news, and the variety of content.

Two problems with teletext were identified—the waiting time to get where you want to go, and finding yourself in the middle pages of the item you want when you get there. As for waiting time, 23% found it a big problem, and 27%, 21%, and 26% found it a problem in descending order of response categories. Waiting time was not differentiated in the questionnaire as to whether it meant waiting for the requested section to appear, or for a subsequent page to appear in a multipage sequence. The problem of finding yourself midstream in the desired content area was major for 24%, and the remaining response categories were cited by 21%, 24%, and 28% respectively.

An index constructed across all the potential problem areas simultaneously, ranging from a score of 1 (all are big problems) to 4 (all are no problem) yielded an average score of 3.51, which offers a summary index indicating that the users generally find no problems of the kind examined.

All teletext systems are operated by a remote control device that is the television channel changer as well as the teletext page selector. This device is capable of handling certain factors that might otherwise be considered problems (or larger problems) in the use of teletext. It is also the device for which new options are being planned (e.g., microchips to hold in storage preselected pages for more rapid access). But the device in use in 1986 contained seven features that were assessed for their frequency of use—"often," "sometimes," or "never."

Most "often" used were the sound mute feature (47%) and the hold button (held the page on the screen until released—46%). Next most often used were the clock (real time) recall (36%) and the option of concurrently watching television and teletext (23%). The final features were the page enlarger (took one-half a page of text and filled the screen with it—17%), the subtitles (4%), and the alarm clock (3%). Heavy users were more likely to use each of these features more often than lighter users. Another analysis of this set of items indicated that the teletext user, on average, used 4.2 of these remote features often or sometimes.

Which Service Is Favored?

Direct comparisons between Oracle and Ceefax were requested from the respondents. As indicated earlier, there was similar overall use of the two services across the sample, and there was widespread use of both services by all within the sample. A dozen different attributes were assessed, ranging from which service was more up-to-date to whose graphics were better. The most general finding is that for each of the characteristics, more than a majority and usually a large majority said that the two services were equal. Differences perceived between the services, then, are relative differences, held by the minority who believed they exist.

Oracle was judged to be better than Ceefax on four attributes (the percentage in parenthesis is the margin of difference between the two services): its regional information (23%); faster to go where you want (13%), more variety of information (12%), and its page-changing speed (10%). Ceefax was judged stronger than Oracle on no characteristics; at best its main sections and its information were judged better by a slim 5% margin. When the data are examined from the individual respondent's perspective, Oracle was judged better on an average 3.1 features, and Ceefax on 3.2.

Heavy TT users were even more intense about Oracle's superiority in terms of speed (the margin was 20%), variety (19%), and regional information (36%) but equally ambivalent about Ceefax's lack of specific strengths. Attributes of no difference included the ease of finding something, reading ease, ease of understanding, the indexes, graphics, and the currentness of the information.

How Does Teletext Compare with Other Media?

Teletext exists in an environment of competitive media. Having just compared it with itself, as constructed by a competitor, we next compared it with the traditional media— newspapers, radio, and television. Sixteen content and credence characteristics were assessed, and the findings are in Table 5.2. We asked "whether you think the newspaper, television, teletext, or radio is best for each of these things?"

Even though this is from a sample of teletext households, the number of areas of perceived superiority for teletext over all the other media is striking. Teletext was judged best for travel information, as a television guide, for its current information, and for product, financial, feature, and household information—in all, 7 of the 16 areas. The average teletext respondent judged TT better in 6.02 areas.

Teletext users acknowledged that television was best for entertainment, children's content, weather, sports, reliability, and accuracy, although the final four of these were victories for television by only a few percentage points (2-9) over teletext.

Newspapers were considered best for classified advertisements, gossip, and regional news. Radio was considered best for none of these.

Heavy users of teletext were even stronger in their preference for TT,

TABLE 5.2
Comparisons between Teletext and Other Media
(percentage choosing each medium as best)

	TT	TV	Radio	Paper	DK
a. Travel information	61	11	13	4	10
b. TV guide	50	6	0	42	2
c. Weather	44	46	6	2	2
d. Current information	40	30	9	20	1
e. Product information	40	14	1	27	17
f. Financial information	40	5	1	28	26
g. Features	37	29	2	25	8
h. Sports	34	37	2	14	12
i. Accuracy	32	34	7	7	21
j. Household information	31	16	5	21	28
k. Reliability	30	39	10	6	15
l. Regional information	22	19	17	36	7
m. Classified ads	22	7	0	55	16
n. Children's content	22	55	1	2	20
o. Entertainment	11	77	3	5	5
p. Gossip	7	16	11	49	17

as one might anticipate, and for each of the content areas, but especially for television guidance (61%), current information (55%), weather (53%), sports (43%), accuracy (42%), and reliability (40%).

One other facet of media comparisons was created by asking, "Since you have had teletext, compared with before that, have you been (reading newspapers, listening to radio, watching television, reading books) more, about the same or less?" For the sample, 19% reported less newspaper reading (27% among the heavy TT users), 12% less radio listening, 8% less book reading, and 5% less television watching. As for the possibility of more use, it was trivial (2%–5%) for all media save television for which 13% of the sample said they were using TV more now than preteletext.

What About Advertising on Teletext?

For the two commercial channels containing teletext (Oracle on ITV and Ch. 4), the possibility of self-support, let alone profit-making, has led to the introduction of teletext commercials. They come in three forms — whole page, bottom of page, and classified advertising. The study probed access, attentiveness, attitudes, and potential and actual sales.

Access to adverts occurs primarily by accident; one appears on a page you have selected, or on your way to that page, an occurrence reported "almost always" or "often" by 29% of the sample. An additional 18% reported that they came to advertising that frequently by reference (from another page), 13% by specific seeking of an advertisement, and 10% from using the ad index to find something. So, if the first of these methods is happenstance and the latter three more product oriented, the sum of the latter three indicates a goodly portion of ad selection; even a conservative statement would be that there is at least as much ad seeking as ad serendipity.

How often are the ads read when appearing on a selected page — not as much as the exposure access pattern would suggest. One third were read "almost always" or "often," 38% "not very often," and 28% "not at all." On the other hand, most media advertising departments would be quite pleased with a one third rate of reading across all their ads, following initial exposure. When users were asked specifically about their readership of full page TT ads, 22% said they generally read it, 40% said they glance at it in part, and 28% said they just wait for the next page of text without reading it. Heavy TT users were no more or less prone to examine the advertising than the lighter users.

How useful is the advertising? One in six users characterized the ads — asked separately for full page, bottom of page, and classified — as useful, with 44–47% saying not useful, and the remainder indicating "it depends" or they didn't know (or care).

As for teletext ad quality, it was generally characterized as of moderate

5. TELETEXT IN THE UNITED KINGDOM

quality (42%), although 22% rated it high or very high, 6% as low or very low, and the remainder did not know; graphics quality on the other hand was much more favorably evaluated, with 39% rating it high or very high, 30% moderate, 7% low or very low, and 24% saying they did not know.

A constructed index of advertising satisfaction, across the five items just described, put the average teletext user response at the midpoint of the index — satisfaction neither high nor low, but moderate.

As for direct purchase behavior, only 5% said, "Yes," they had tried to purchase something found in the classified ad section in Oracle; 6% said they had actually bought something seen in a teletext advert. The most promising finding for advertisers came in response to asking if the user had ever thought about or discussed booking a holiday (vacation) from the holiday advert section — one in five had done so. At the time of this study, advertising on Oracle was 5 years old, but had been newly urged to make the service self-sustaining.

CONCLUSIONS

This chapter has described the state of affairs and the state of the art with teletext in the environment where it has been more successful than anywhere else, and with the longest history. Subsequent analyses will permit us to build models predicting usage patterns, but for those without TT, perhaps the basic information is the best beginning.

Why there and why not here? Certain key differences loom large. First, there was government endorsement and government financial support, probably inclusive of pressure on set manufacturers to produce internally driven decoders, and a single standard adopted. And the entire system continues to be subsidized by the broadcast television system, either through the BBC budget for Ceefax or subsidies by the IBA and independent television stations for Oracle. They have decided that it is a good thing to have, or at least not to kill it.

Want a new set? Why not get one with teletext; there's no unsightly extra piece of gear, just a large, bright TV set that happens to have another feature as part of the same package that brings you the wonderful world of British television.

So, growth creeps along. Perhaps one in five homes is the "critical mass" beyond which normal set replacement will require what may be acquiring the value of a modest status symbol. The prognosis is for continuing growth, but no particular reason to expect a sudden leap forward. There is time and patience to permit television nature to run its course; at the same time, there are rumblings at the IBA for Oracle to become more self-supporting, to increase its advertising — not at the expense of television advertising, but perhaps through print advertisements. And the BBC, with its constant struggles for increases in the license fee and its recent debate over alternative means of fiscal support, might re-examine its investment and its return.

Those with teletext use it, are pleased with it, perceive few problems and thereby become excellent spokespersons for adoption by others. These data contain a variety of findings to suggest to the system providers what might be done to improve satisfaction and thereby increase takers, what content is popular and which is not, how the services compare to each other, and so on.

Were I able to create the ideal study of teletext users, these survey data would be accompanied by electronic measurement of actual use of services, sections, and pages, rather than any form of recall techniques. How well do people gauge time estimates, sessions, dedication to one service, let alone four of them? Not precisely, but hopefully with some accuracy. Equipment that can make such measures has been demonstrated in London, but the motivation has not yet been found to support that kind of audience research studies; AGB is too busy at the moment trying to compete with Nielsen for the U.S. television ratings market, among others. Clearly, such an effort is worthwhile, especially if Oracle wishes to pursue its advertising capabilities.

Why four services, though? Pride, I think, in large measure; if the competition has it, we must also to hold our heads up. Perhaps a less selfish motive is the belief that the amount of pages available at any one time is too few on a single channel; that more is needed to maximize audience interest and adoption. Because this study indicates that one tends to use the teletext on the channel one happens to be watching at the time, there may be some merit in multiple services. But only the argument that more text is needed competes with the notion that the best 100 or 200 pages could be identified and run on two channels, rather than largely or entirely separate texts.

The most interesting and provocative findings may be the impact on other media when teletext has been added to the home. The findings here argue that newspaper use suffers, that radio suffers and that television prospers. Long-term implications of that, if replicated and elaborated, are meaningful in a nation whose newspapers are already extraordinary (and where two or three additional daily newspapers have started up in the last 18 months) and whose radio is of such historic proportions.

Finally, the extensive use of teletext in all four services as a meta-medium should be noted. Although the primary content choices reflect an orientation to news (across a broad set of news categories), teletext is used heavily to find out about television, essentially an on-screen radio and television guide. Perhaps that is idiosyncratic in a country where you cannot buy a single television guide that covers all channels for a week's period of time (you have to buy two such guides, one for the BBC programs and one for

5. TELETEXT IN THE UNITED KINGDOM   103

the ITV shows). Nevertheless, it may be a genuine symbiotic relationship that can be used to nourish current users and attract the 80% who have yet to make a positive decision about teletext.

ACKNOWLEDGMENTS

The research on which this chapter is based was made possible through funding by the Independent Broadcasting Authority in London. From September 1986, through February, 1987, Dr. Greenberg was on sabbatical leave and located in the IBA's research department. Considerable assistance in the conception and conduct of this project came from Dr. Robert Towler, then head of the IBA's research department, Dr. Mallory Wober, deputy head, and Dr. Barrie Gunter, current department head. In the U.S., Carolyn Lin provided assistance in the data analysis for this chapter.

REFERENCES

Greenberg, B. S. (1986). *Patterns of teletext use.* London: Independent Broadcasting Authority.
Tydeman, J. H., Lipinski, R., Adler, M. N., Nyhan, M., & Zwimpfer, L. (1982). *Teletext and videotex in the United States.* New York: McGraw Hill.
Vieth, R. H. (1983). *Television's teletext.* New York: North-Holland.
Wober, M. (1985). *Screens and speakers: Ownership, use and ideas on payment for electronic devices for entertainment and information.* London: Independent Broadcasting Authority.
Wober, M., & Reardon, G. (1979). *Teletext services and devices: A study of London viewers' knowledge about them.* London: Independent Broadcasting Authority.

6

Interactive Electronic Text in the United States: Can Videotex Ever Go Home Again?

James S. Ettema
Northwestern University

VIDEOTEX AT VALLEY FORGE

One winter day in 1986 while reorganizing address files, I discarded the business cards of three people whose organizations no longer existed. But then, struck by the irony of the situation, I retrieved them. One card was from an employee of "Keyfax," the Centel/Honeywell/Field venture into consumer videotex. Another was from an employee of "Gateway," the Times Mirror Company's venture. Surely you can guess the third. It was, of course, from an employee of Knight-Ridder's "Viewtron." Suddenly these cards seemed somehow valuable as momentos of people who had been there, people whose careers had, perhaps, suffered frost bite at what would someday be seen as the Valley Forge of the Information Revolution. I kept the cards.

If it really is a revolution, casualties are to be expected, I suppose. Even so, the demise of these highly touted consumer videotex services was a rather cold and dark period in the history of The Information Society. After all, interactive electronic text of which consumer-oriented videotex was one form, had inspired entreprenuerial visions of new information businesses — electronic newspapers, teleshopping, home banking. But more than that, the technology had become entwined with moral visions of a new means for the conduct of public affairs — information utilities. "Mass information utilities, linked to real-time information bases in the public domain," wrote Harold Sackman (1971) the most eloquent of the information utility theorists, "could conceivably provide the leading instrumentality for the public to scan the social scene, identify problems, contribute to social control and provide corrective feedback on the interplay of pluralistic social experimentation" (p. 257). Videotex services, whether delivered by television cable or telephone line, did for a time seem like a step toward development of an information system that, as Sackman hoped, could facilitate the transformation of the public from "passive impotent spectators to active constructive participants over an expanding spectrum of social affairs" (p. 261). The demise of these consumer-oriented services was, then, tinged not only with the regrets of entrepreneurs for a failed business venture but also with the regrets of visionaries for a lost social opportunity.

Like the Continental Army's winter at Valley Forge, the fate of consumer videotex was a symbol of larger events. The demise of these services was emblematic of the emerging realities of information technology in the 1980s—the tightening control of cable television by the entertainment industry (Capuzzi, 1987), the scramble among businesses to "hook up or lose out" (Clemons & McFarlan, 1986), the realization that high tech was not high on jobs ("America rushes to high tech for growth," 1983). In the particular case of interactive electronic text, it became clear that the technology would not suddenly revolutionize the life of the consumer and citizen but would continue to reorganize the life of the information worker. This trend was neatly captured in a number of articles with titles like "Videotex leaves home" (Wallace, 1984) and "Will videotex find a home at the office?" (Finn & Stewart, 1985). Videotex was no longer seen as the means to a universally accessible information utility but rather as a means of corporate communication with employees and/or customers that could create or enhance a competitive advantage ("Information power," 1985; McFarlan, 1984; Porter & Millar, 1985).

It also became clear that the new media would not sweep away the old but rather seek specialized niches of their own to serve. Interactive electronic text in the form of videotex did not replace general-interest newspapers as some had prophesied, but interactive text in the form of online databases grew rapidly in the 1980s as commercial information vendors joined government and nonprofit agencies in the production and marketing of highly specialized electronic information services directed toward business, science, and the professions. The number of such databases doubled from 300 to 600 between 1975 and 1980 and then quadrupled to more than 2,400 by 1984 (Neufeld & Cornog, 1986). Thus, although fears about consumers' abandonment of print for electronic newspapers abated, concerns about libraries' "migration" from print to electronic abstracts and indexes remained.

These developments did not necessarily mean the end of interactive electronic text for public affairs and consumer-oriented use in the United States, although expectations about its widespread adoption and use had certainly diminished by the mid-1980s. By one estimate (Arlen, 1987), about 20 video-

6. INTERACTIVE ELECTRONIC TEXT IN THE U.S. 107

tex services of one sort or another were used by 1 million people in 1986. About 60% of these were users of "Dow Jones News/Retrieval" (250,000), "CompuServe" (280,00), and "The Source" (70,000). Despite the business and professional orientation particularly of "Dow Jones News/Retrieval" and "CompuServe," these services probably had the most potential for consumer and citizenship-oriented use of interactive electronic text in this period (Falk, 1984; O'Leary, 1985). Indeed, "CompuServe" and "The Source" made claim to the title of "information utility" by offering a variety of services including access to news wire copy as well as a number of business and general interest periodicals, teleshopping, computer conferencing, and electronic mail all accessible through modem-equipped microcomputers rather than dedicated videotex terminals as a number of the doomed services had employed. Also in this period, several database vendors began to make selected subsets of their professional and business-oriented databases more accessible to consumers through reduced rates for off-peak periods and more user-friendly search procedures. These vendors included Dialog ("Knowledge Index") and BSR ("BSR/After Dark").

And finally, several videotex projects involving major players in banking, retailing, and telecommunications were slowly moving from drawing board to marketplace at that time. These included "Trintex" a joint venture of Sears and IBM and "CNR Partners" formed by Citicorp, NYNEX, and RCA. Nevertheless, as *Business Week* ("Information Business," 1986, p. 90) concluded, it was at that time "too soon to tell if videotex will ever really take off . . . But niche players with properly focused markets are already making big money. And as technology improves and the work habits of both businesses and individuals change, it could turn into a major industry—just later than the optimistics predicted." (See Aumente, 1987, for a useful overview of these and other electronic text developments in these years.)

The mid-1980s were, then, a period in which the socioeconomic definition of the interactive electronic text technology was revised somewhat. The definition of the technology as the consumer-oriented mass medium of videotex faultered in the marketplace, whereas the definition of essentially the same technology as the specialized, business-oriented medium of electronic publishing was beginning to succeed. In light of these developments, this chapter considers some of the lessons learned and some of the issues still to be addressed in the adoption and use of interactive electronic text.

SOME LESSONS FROM THE VENTURES IN VIDEOTEX

Perhaps the first and most basic lesson to be learned from recent ventures in videotex concerns the limits of the information business. Consumer videotex turned out to be a technology with considerable marketer push rather less market pull—or as sometimes said, a solution in search of a problem. The push was provided in part by financial institutions and retailers seeking to reduce transaction costs and reliance on brick and mortar facilities by bringing banking and shopping into the home electronically. Home banking "must happen," wrote an executive of Banc One Corporation, a joint venture of seven banks that experimented with videotex. "We will not be able to afford the kinds of services the marketplace demands otherwise" (Fisher, 1985, p. 144).

The push was also provided by newspapers seeking to reduce production and delivery costs. The logic of newspaper publishers' interest in the technology as the 1980s dawned was probably most neatly captured by television entrepreneur Ted Turner:

> There's nothing more inefficient than going out and chopping down trees that we're going to need for firewood and making them into paper and printing the damn paper everyday. And then, with oil supplies drying up, driving them all over town and sticking those bulky things in everybody's mailbox. And then we have to send the garbage trucks to pick them up. (quoted in Neustadt, 1982, p. 6)

Interest in the technology on the part of newspaper firms, however, was probably more defensive than offensive. Newspaper publishers sought to push news into the home electronically before other information businesses—telephone companies, for example—could do so. The failures of videotex ventures were, then, at worst a mixed blessing for the newspaper industry as made clear in the statement by James H. Holley, president of Times Mirror's videotex venture upon the abandonment of "Gateway":

> We reached the point where we learned enough to know that [videotex] was not a threat to our newspapers or our cable companies or our magazines which is what drove us into this project in the first place. (quoted in Goldberg 1986, p. 26)

The banks, retailers, and newspapers pushing videotex had, of course, hoped for some customer "pull" but from the earliest videotex field trials, entreprenuerial enthusiasm had been mixed with persistent doubts about consumer response to the technology. The transactional services were sometimes seen as the "core" services that could "trigger" or motivate adoption at least among the typically upscale "early adopters" (Hooper, 1985; "Window on the world," 1981). At the same time, however, market researchers were wondering if consumers really were ready for the information age. Ledingham (1984), for example, found that 66% of the San Diego residents he surveyed were uninterested in teleshopping, with many saying that shopping was a social as well as an instrumental activity. Those who regularly made purchases by direct mail (about half of the respondents) were no more likely to be interested in teleshopping than those who did not. Similarly, 55% of the respondents were uninterested in home banking with many saying that they saw no advantage in it or that they preferred personal contact with bank personnel. Those who used automatic teller machines (43%) and those who banked by phone (10%) were, however, more likely to be interested in home banking than those who did not.

The results of numerous videotex field trials suggested that consumers were, in fact, not ready. Because nearly all of the information generated by these trails remained proprietary, it was difficult to know how consumers actually responded to the transactional services though occasionally a telling fact or two slipped through the public relations machinery. For example, according to the "Viewtron Newsletter" (cited in Veith, 1983) 68% of the 200 households involved in the original test of "Viewtron" purchased at least one item through the system. On the other hand, fewer than 1,000 items were purchased in the 14-month trial.

There was also a mixture of enthusiasm and doubt about the response of consumers to videotex as an information medium. The information delivery potential of videotex was, of course, what captured the interest of both newspaper publishers and social visionaries but there was also doubt about the ability of consumer-oriented applications to exploit the vast capabilities of the technology—at least at a price consumers were willing to pay. Interactive electronic text technology is, for example, capable of extremely rapid distribution of information—once the information has been entered into the host computer it is immediately available to all users. The medium is, then, ideal for time-sensitive information requiring constant updates. Stock and commodity price quotation services such as "Quotron" exploit this capability of the technology (Sieck, 1984) but there seem to be few consumer applications that demand the capability. The operators of "Prestel," for example, concluded that "the mass market did not require information updated more quickly than every few hours" (Hooper, 1985, p. 190).

The interactive electronic text technology is also capable of storing and retrieving vast quantities of information—computer storage is essentially unlimited. The medium is then ideal for storage and retrieval of reference material. The bibliographic and full-text database services such "Lexis" and "Medlars" exploit this capability but, again, it is not clear that there are many consumer applications that demand the capability. By one estimate (Neuman, 1985), for example, about 20% of the population does consult the telephone book once a day but only about 5% consults an encyclopedia once every 6 months. The average daily time spent with such information resources: 35 seconds. The most commonly used information resource: other people. The operators of Time Video Information Services concluded that even if consumers did not require updates more than every few hours, "the thing that drives the service is not (as we once thought) encyclopedic masses of data, but items that are different every time you return to the screen. . . . People do not place much value on 300,000 pages that never change" (McCarthy, 1985, p. 166.).

Consumer videotex greatly simplified retrieval procedures by employing hierarchical menus and user-friendly keyword search operations, but, even so, retrieval remained cumbersome compared to competitive print media—newspapers and magazines. As Dozier and Rice (1984) argued, hierarchically structured databases, even with user-friendly menus and keywords, are better suited for retrieval of predetermined items of information than browsing for unspecified items. However, consumer information gathering—particularly newspaper and magazine reading—is less often purposive information seeking than recreational browsing. In addition, electronic text is much less portable than its printed counterpart. Altogether, then, electronic text seems more amenible to information work than communication play and, more generally, to business-oriented than consumer-oriented applications.

Of course, any such conclusions about the appropriate application of the technology must be viewed within the context of cost. The educated and upscale consumers upon whom the systems were typically tested probably were not entirely unappreciative of the capabilities of the technology, but even these consumers were unwilling to pay enough to make the systems economically viable. For example, Time Video Information Services concluded from its test that the service was very price sensitive with the pricepoint at only about $5 to $8 a month in 1983. And even at this price, videotex would not be a mass medium; it would "not have an audience like Monday Night Football but like *Time* [4.75 million readers] or *People* [2.5 million]" (McCarthy, 1985, p. 166).

These conclusions about cost, in turn, must be viewed in the context of what, in fact, was offered to the consumer for the price. Price is important, concluded Prestel's Richard Hooper (1985), but not the biggest problem:

> Media analysts of Prestel's early take-off problems claimed that customers were not buying because of price. This was at best a half truth. Prestel research demonstrated that customers did not want the service *at any price* because they did not find it useful enough. If over the same period, 25% of all British homes were acquiring video cassette recorders for $600, price could not be the central reason for Prestel's sluggish sales. The problem was the product. (p. 191)

The problem with the systems tested in United States was also the product. The services that had seemed to hold so much potential, in fact, emerged as little more than an alternative delivery mode for a few of the traditional products of banks, retailers, and the media. For example, the potential for consumer databases that could facilitate comparison shopping (Biehal, 1983; Jones, 1984; Pemberton, 1982) and, in turn, perhaps, help to rationalize the consumer marketplace were realized largely as just more movie and restaurant reviews and, of course, advertising—although obviously not enough of the latter to make the systems financially viable. Similarly, the potential for a new electronic journalism (e.g., Smith, 1980) was realized largely as edited wire copy with, perhaps, a snappy computer graphic or two (cf. Overduin, 1986; Weaver, 1983). A content analysis of "Viewtron," "Gateway," and "Keyfax" by Brown and Atwater (1986), for example, found that a majority of stories came from the wire services and most of the rest from the local paper owned by the system's parent firm. Although electronic news may have been available sooner than its printed counterpart, it was no more comprehensive, contextualized or process-centered that any other form of news. At its best, electronic news did rise above "rip-and-read" radio for the eyes. Graphics were often clever and occasionally informative renderings of how, for example, space shuttles or nuclear reactors worked or failed to do so. Stories were sometimes told with "sidebars" which developed angles in more detail. Even at its best, however, electronic news did not rise above conventional big-city and wire service journalism because at is best it *was* conventional journalism which had sustained only minimal damage in editing.

All in all, consumer-oriented videotex fell far short of both the entreprenuerial and social visions that it had inspired. However, the key to its market failure is not that is fell short of the ideal information utility but that it never became anything other than more expensive and often less convenient substitutes for services—news, advertising, catalog shopping, and phone banking—already easily and cheaply accessible to consumers. We can only speculate on what might have been if these services had solved the "chicken/egg problem"—too few users to support innovative services and no innovative services to attract users—in a way that produced a truly new informational and transactional medium.

"FIRSTHAND": AN EXAMPLE OF THE PERILS OF THE INFORMATION BUSINESS

A number of the problems in bringing interactive electronic text to market are illustrated by the field trail of "FirstHand," a system that included several consumer and business-oriented information services and thus provided an opportunity for the side-by-side comparison of these applications (Ettema,

1984a, 1984b, 1985). This system was conceived in the executive suite of First Bank System, a Minneapolis-based bank holding company that, like other financial institutions, faced the increasing cost of paper records and brick-and-mortar facilities as well as the changing organizational environment created by the Monetary Deregulation and Control Act of 1980. Preliminary market research had convinced management that home banking would be of interest to many bank customers. However, a viable service would require more than banking and would have to be designed around a specific market segment to serve these nonbanking needs. A number of segments including small business operators, farm operators, middle and upper income consumers were all considered. Farmer operators were chosen as the test market in part because this segment overlapped each of the others and in part because of the efforts of a senior manager responsible for that segment. Thus, it came to pass that another marketer began its technological push.

The extent to which the market pulled was guaged by a survey of adopters (i.e., farm operators who agreed to participate in the field trial) and by nonadopters (i.e., operators who were invited but declined to participate) conducted near the end of the 9-month filed trial. In an attempt to specify information needs and interests that could motivate adoption, these farm operators were asked to rate the importance of various sorts of information as well as satisfaction with existing sources of that information.

TABLE 6.1
Information Needs of Adopters and Nonadopters

Information Needs	Adopter Mean (n = 225)	Nonadopter Mean (n = 104)
Farm Market Information		
Importance of information[a]	4.47	4.03[c]
Satisfaction with sources[b]	2.82	3.05
Farm Production Information		
Importance of Information	3.35	3.38
Satisfaction with sources	2.95	3.19
General News		
Importance of news	3.14	3.62[c]
Satisfaction with sources	3.54	3.62
Family and Home Information		
Importance of Information	2.28	2.57[c]
Satisfaction with sources	2.86	2.91

[a] Importance scale is: 1 = not at all important to, 5 = extremely important.
[b] Satisfaction scale range is: 1 = not at all satisfied, 5 = extremely satisfied.
[c] Comparison of adopters and nonadopters is statistically significant at $\leq .05$.

Among the information needs, as shown in Table 6.1 both adopters and nonadopters rated the time-sensitive farm commodities market information as much more important to them than the less time-sensitive farm production information, general news, or home and family information. On the other hand, both adopters and nonadopters reported much greater satisfaction with existing sources of general news than with existing sources of any other sort of information.

Market data was, then, highly valued by both adopters and nonadopters. Indeed, nearly all farmers mentioned timing of commodity sales as one of the most important business decisions they must make. Even so, the ratings of the importance attached to various kinds of information differentiated adopters from nonadopters — the adopters rated market data as more important to them than did the nonadopters, but they rated general news as less important than did the nonadopters. On the other hand, satisfaction with existing sources of information did not distinguish between adopters and nonadopters — adopters were *not* less satisfied with existing sources than nonadopters.

The adopters were also distinguished from the nonadopters by a number of now-familiar demographic variables (e.g., Rogers, 1986). Adopters were significantly younger and better educated than nonadopters. They read one more farm publication per month and spent about 6 minutes a day *less* reading newspapers but otherwise differed little from nonadopters in their media use. Their farm revenues, but not their family incomes, were also significantly larger than those of nonadopters. The most powerful discriminator between adopters and nonadopters, however, was the number of innovative farming and management techniques employed — adoption of this innovation was best predicted by adoption of other innovations (Ettema, 1984a).

To further probe the adoption process, the farm operators were asked about the factors that influenced their adoption decision. As shown in Table 6.2 adopters rated access to the market data as a far more important factor in the decision to adopt than access to any other informational or transactional service. Moreover, when asked about particular features of the market information service, adopters rated the opportunity to receive "up-to-the-minute" commodity reports as the single most desirable feature of the entire "FirstHand" system. Nonadopters, on the other hand, anticipated difficulties with the system and lack of benefits given their farm size or proximity to retirement.

And so, First Bank System began to learn the lessons of the information business. It had indeed found a market segment with an information need that could be well served by interactive electronic text. This information need, however, turned out to be highly differentiated. The importance assigned to various kinds of information varied considerably, and, more importantly some kinds of information were more valued by adopters, whereas

TABLE 6.2
Decision-Criteria of Adopters and Nonadopters

	Adopter Mean	Nonadopter Mean
Desired Information and Transactional Services		
Farm Market Information[a]	4.2	3.2[b]
General News	2.5	2.8
Other Information Services	2.7	2.4
Home Banking Service	2.6	2.1[b]
Farm Accounting Service	2.9	2.4[b]
Home Shopping Service	1.9	1.9
Perceived Drawbacks		
Would cost too much to keep when experiment ended	3.1	3.1
Wouldn't provide information wanted	2.9	3.2
Would be difficult to learn to use	1.8	2.5[b]
Farm is too small to take advantage	2.2	3.0[b]
Too close to retirement to take advantage	1.7	2.7[b]

[a]Decision criteria scale range is: 1 = not at all important in your decision, 5 = extremely important in your decision.
[b]Comparison of adopters and nonadopters is statistically significant at $\leq .05$.

other kinds were more valued by nonadopters. Satisfaction with existing sources of information also varied. Thus, although a generalized innovativeness may have facilitated adoption, there was no corresponding generalized information interest—a conclusion supported by the finding that "adopters were not, on the whole, heavier consumers of other informational media.

What these farm operators wanted, despite their relative isolation on prairie farmsteads, was not technologically up-to-date catalogue shopping or banking; at least, not as much as the bank had hoped. Nor did they want technologically up-to-date newspapers and cookbooks. Rather they wanted a technologically up-to-date stock and commodity "ticker"—something that was, for them, really new and useful. There was, then, a "trigger" service that this market wanted, although a highly specialized one and not the one the bank would have preferred.

At the end of the field trial, bank management decided not to pursue the project. Its decision was based not simply on the lukewarm response to home banking but rather on projections of the cost and complexity of

6. INTERACTIVE ELECTRONIC TEXT IN THE U.S.

developing a system with enough informational and transactional triggers to appeal to a broad range of bank customers. After discussions with several companies including AT&T and IBM, First Bank System sold "FirstHand" to J.C. Penney. After an attempt to assemble a consortium of retailers and banks to participate in a consumer videotex service, this system was returned to the drawing board; although a few years later Penney was experimenting with "Telaction," a shopping service that employed cable television for display and touchtone telephone service for upline interaction.

Although the bank had seen enough, there is more to be learned from "FirstHand" about the degree of match between the possible applications and the capabilities of the technology, the "content/format fit" that adds value to the information provided (Urban, 1985, p. 50). Analyses of user response to the farm market and general news services reveal that these services were actually used by the farmer operators about the same amount (in terms of time spent) but the market service was rated as slightly more satisfactory than other sources of market information, whereas the news service was rated as significantly less satisfactory than other sources of news. Furthermore, when the market and news services were compared to each other, the market service was rated as a significantly more valuable service and as a significantly more efficient method to obtain information. Users also said that they came to depend more on the market than news service (Ettema, 1985).

Even more tellingly, the correlation between users' ratings of the value of a service and the efficiency of that service was much stronger for the market service ($r = .55$) than for the news service ($r = .19$). The value of a service was, then, more intimately related to the efficiency of information retrieval for market information than for news. Further, the correlation between users' ratings of the value of a service and their dependence on that service was stronger for the market service ($r = .60$) than for the news service ($r = .34$). Those who valued the market service were more likely to come to depend on that service than those who valued the news service were to depend on it. Videotex, it seems, was a better substitute for farm market media than general news media.

"FirstHand" was more successful as a stock and commodities ticker than a newspaper, but even as a ticker it was not without problems. The most common complaint was that stock and commodities information was not updated fast enough—more evidence about where users' interests really lay. Other problems rated as most troublesome included: (a) connecting with the host computer, (b) tying up the phone during system use, and (c) finding the desired information in the databases. All of these problems, particularly finding desired information, were negatively related both to use of the system and to the ratings of the value of the system. Other problems such as the small keyboard and the absence of a printer were rated as less troublesome and were *positively* related to use and value of the system. Some problems may then, have been hinderances to beneficial use of the system, whereas others may have been merely nuisances to those who did use and find benefits in the system.

A number of other variables were correlates of use and benefit as well. Among the significant zero-order correlates of use were age, family income, and newspaper use (all *negative* correlates) and the importance of agricultural information (a positive correlate). Among the correlates of farm-related benefits were age, family income, and newspaper use (again, all negative correlates) as well as the importance of information, innovations previously adopted and education (all positive correlates). Use itself (as recorded by the host computer) was the strongest correlate of benefit. If these results are viewed within the context of the demographic correlates of adoption (reviewed previously) there is cause for concern about information equity although that concern is tempered somewhat by these results from Ettema (1984a):

> (1) innovativeness and the ability to see the importance of the information offered by the system rather than socio-economic status were the best predictors of adoption; (2) ability to see the importance of the information was positively related to system use while family income was negatively related; (3) use itself was, in turn, the most strongly related to reported benefit though information needs and other factors may have facilitated the translation of use to benefit. Such findings suggest that the rewards of this information system accrued not simply to those with resources such as good educations and large farms but to those who were willing and able to direct their resources—including information resources—toward productive applications. This conclusion does not dismiss equity concerns. Rather it suggests a tension between the two socially desirable goals of equity and productivity. Given the possibility of such a tension, it is important to monitor the balance struck between these two goals by particular information systems . . . and by the new and emerging information technologies in general. (pp. 394-395)

FURTHER EXPLORATIONS IN ELECTRONIC TEXT

As the 1980s rush to a close, most observers have come to believe that the potential audience for all forms of electronic publishing "is not the 90 million TV households in the country or the 80% who still predominantly watch network television," as Walter Baer of the Times Mirror Company concluded (1985, p. 121). "It is a 10% sector: business users, professional users and the high end of the consumer market." Opportunities for widespread use of interactive electronic text by individuals in their roles as citizens and consumers remain limited and are likely to continue to be so in the immediate future. As communication researchers interested in the adoption, use and, in turn, social impact of this technology we are now in much the same position as those writing about the technology well more than a decade ago (e.g., Parker & Dunn, 1972; Sackman, 1971; Sackman & Nie, 1970. The social possibilities of widespread use are no less tantalizing now than in the past but we are still left to speculate on what firms in a position to develop the technology might do in the future and how consumers might use the technology. Our primary advantage over earlier observers is, perhaps, a keener sense of what will not work.

Our speculation on what players in the information business might do can safely assume that the forces behind the marketer push—increasing labor and real estate costs, decreasing computer hardware costs—will continue to be felt by the banks, retailers, and, perhaps, newspapers. Transactional services particularly banking are, then, likely to be the core of any systems seeking a mass market. And, indeed, banks remain major players in most of the planned or operating systems such as Covidea, a venture of Bank of America, Chemical Bank, and AT&T.

The departure of publishers such as Knight-Ridder and Times Mirror has, perhaps, "left the door ajar for telephone companies to try to enter" (Arlen, 1987, p. 87). Although publishers enlisted the aid of Congress and the courts to help stall the entry of AT&T and the Bell Operating Companies into the information business, the phone companies have not lost interest. One example is Pacific Bell's "Project Victoria" test in California that employed digital technology to provide two-voice and five data circuits carrying electronic mail and banking as well as information and educational services (Arlen, 1987). Another example is BellSouth's testing of the "TranstexT Universal Gateway" that provides simplified access to a variety of electronic databases and other services. As these activities suggest, the technical infrastructure—the telecommunications grid and personal computers in offices and homes—continues to develop. Another mass market push, perhaps triggered by further change in the regulatory environment of telecommunications, by the rapid deployment of integrated services (i.e., voice, video, data) digital networks (ISDN) or by the next energy crisis, is not unimaginable.

Our speculations on what consumers would want from interactive electronic text can begin with the assumption that the technology, as Prestel concluded, "will not sell itself" (Hooper, 1985, p. 185). Transactional rather than informational services may provide the core, but services that are merely costly and cumbersome alternatives to those easily available in other forms will not sell the technology either. Our speculations about consumers can also assume that "early adopters" will be younger, higher in socioeconomic status, and have access to, and experience with, microcomputers. Beyond these conclusions, a decade of research and field trials offers little insight into "the formula to bring this long-ballyhooed technology into every home" (Arlen, 1987, p. 86).

The attempt to learn what it is that people want is, of course, hindered by their inability to predict their response to goods or services that they have not used. The history of market research is littered with disasterous projections of consumer response to imaginary products and the research on videotex has contributed it own debacles to this history. For example, research by Time Video Information Services found adults projecting more than 2 hours a day of videotex use, teenage boys more than 3 hours, and teenage girls more than 4 hours. The actual use during the field trial by those households that used the service at all averaged 1.6 accesses a day with about 25 minutes spent per access. Only 60% of the participating households used the service at all, and 40% discontinued use after the first few weeks. The service, as McCarthy (1985, p. 166) concluded, did not live up to the expectations of either the users or the vendor. Indeed!

With this in mind, surveys of consumer response to the general concept of videotex (e.g., Butler & Kent, 1983) or to hypothetical systems (e.g., Garramone, Harris, & Pizante; 1986) should be analyzed with a healthy skepticism. Such studies are probably most credible when, like the one by Ledingham (1984) cited previously, they probe the barriers and limits to consumer adoption of the technology. Butler and Kent, for example, found that older and better educated respondents (i.e., those who are more likely to actually read a newspaper) were quite unwilling to give up printed for electronic text. Similarly, Garramone et al. (1986) found that those least interested in the hypothetical political information system were the older and less-educated respondents. Even when cost was not an explicit consideration, the issue of information equity emerges. Perhaps the interpretive principle here is simply that bad news is more credible than good!

Even so, it is not easy to know what to make of bad news. For example, the apparent indifference to "Teleshopping" found by Ledingham is called into question by the apparent success of television shopping programs that now threaten to turn cable and independent broadcasting into "a giant flea market" (Storch, 1986, p. 1). According to data collected in late 1986, only about 6% of cable subscribers had made purchases, but of those, 64% made purchases one or more times per month and, 71% spent more than $20 per purchase. One estimate of the potential for television shopping projected an increase in revenues from $250 million in 1986 to $3 billion in 1990 (Motavalli, 1987). Even if qualified as "optimistic," these numbers invite consideration of whether it was consumer resistance to home shopping itself or to the cost and format of videotex that was encountered by videotex shopping services. Perhaps, then, *computerized* purchasing is the province of information workers such as travel agents who make airline reservations though American Airline's "Sabre" system ("Information power," 1985; McFarlan, 1984). *Televised* purchasing, however, may yet find a place at home.

The alternative to research on user response to imaginary systems (i.e., user response to actual systems) is also problematic if the goal is to understand the possibilities and problems of widespread consumer and citizenship-oriented use of interactive electronic text. As noted previously, most systems now in operation are specialized, business-oriented database services often accessed by trained database "searchers" in the employ of managerial, professional, and technical "end users." And even the do-it-yourselfers— "end-user searchers"—are typically information workers or students who are, of course, at least minimally computer literate (Janke, 1984; Kupferberg, 1986; Ojala, 1986). Nevertheless, as Ojala (1986, p. 198) noted, searches are conducted from homes as well as offices with, perhaps, the home end-user searchers "more analogous to public library users than are the office end-users who more closely resemble clients of corporate libraries." Analyses of what users do with the more general interest systems such as "The Source," "Compuserve," "Dow Jones News/Retrieval," and "Knowledge Index" may, then, tell us something useful about the information-gathering behavior of those on the front lines of the Information Revolution.

Research attention to these users is sometimes justified as research on "early adopters," but it may well be more accurate to characterize it as research on people who are, in one way or another, the information elite. Their information needs are not likely to be everybody's information needs. Furthermore, they are using information resources that have not been designed to serve everyone's information needs. Thus, for example, following the performance of personal investments by downloading market data from "Dow Jones News Retrieval" and analyzing it with Dow Jones software may qualify as a consumer-oriented use of the technology but, of course, the information needs of those who must manage an investment portfolio are not the same as those who must manage on a welfare check. This invites attention to questions not only of what "early adopters" are able to learn through access to databases but what the rest of us are *not* able to learn because we do not have access to appropriate information resources (e.g., Jurgensmeyer & Bishop, 1985). This perspective also invites attention to the means for creation of new information resources as well as the privatization of information resources that have formerly been public (e.g., Schiller, 1981).

Information elites are, of course, worthy of study in their own right but they are not always easy to find. For some (typically experimental) studies, "users" have been created by the researchers. For example Edwardson, Kent, and McConnell (1985) brought equipment into a sample of homes to compare user recall of videotex news stories with recall of stories presented by a "talking head." Access to "real" users, however, is often difficult. Client lists needed for proper sampling from the relatively small universe of users are almost always jealously guarded as proprietary information. Occasionally this problem has been overcome by a close relationship between the information system operator and the researchers. The research on "First-Hand," for example, was possible only because of a collegial relationship between a bank executive and a university faculty member. The problem has also been overcome for highly specialized systems by choosing a universe with a relatively large proportion of users and for which a list is available. Research on perceptions of legal research systems by Barnett and Siegel (1985), for example, sampled from published lists of lawyers, judges and accountants. Similarly, Williams (1985) sampled business firms, government agencies, legal and medical institutions, libraries, universities, and other nonprofit organizations that use online databases to compile estimates of the size and character of the electronic database industry.

Williams' studies of organizational users provide a useful reminder at this point that information technology is more rapidly changing the life of the worker—or at least some workers—than that of the citizen and consumer. This is not to say, of course, that such changes will have no effect on the individual citizen/consumer but these effects may be broadly social, mediated by organizations that, in turn, structure the lives of individuals. For example, few individuals may now use electronic text services as their daily news media but the news media themselves are using services such as "Dow Jones News/Retrieval" and Knight Ridder's "VU-Text" for newsgathering purposes (Aumente, 1987; Miller, 1983). Electronic text may increasingly come *in* the paper rather than instead of it. Communication researchers must, then, confront the fact that productive knowledge is an attribute less of individuals than integrated systems (Neale, 1984). Similarly, researchers must recognize that the empowerment of the "information poor" is not simply a matter of more information but of information in the service of more organization. The technology may well have its greatest impact on the citizen and consumer—whether for good or ill—by assisting organizations in the pursuit of their goals—whether empowerment or exploitation.

With this in mind, the public affairs and consumer-oriented use of interactive electronic text made by the various organizations surveyed by Williams (1985) emerges as an issue (perhaps *the* issue) central to any understanding of the social implications of this technology. Interactive electronic text seems unlikely to develop into a mass medium in the next few years, perhaps even decades. It is, however, a powerful organizational tool *now*. Nevertheless, an interest in the possibilities of the technology as a mass informational medium ought not be abandoned, It would be worthwhile to keep alive the moral vision that inspired the utility theorist to see in the technology possibilities for greater equity of information access, enhanced participation in public affairs and, most generally, a renewed sense of community. Such a vision may be even less realistic now than a few years ago but it is no less ethically compelling.

REFERENCES

America rushes to high tech for growth. (1983, March 28). *Business Week*, pp. 84-90.
Arlen, G. (1987). Videotex: High rollers with high hopes. *Channels '87 Field Guide*, pp. 86-87.
Aumente, J. (1987). *New electronic pathways: Videotex, teletext, and online databases.* Newbury Park, CA: Sage.
Baer, W. S. (1985). Defining a new business. In M. Greenberger (ed.), *Electronic publishing plus* (pp. 121-124). White Plains, NY: Knowledge Industry Publications.
Barnett, G. A., & Siegel G. (1985, May). *The diffusion of computer assisted legal research systems.* Paper presented at the International Communication Association Annual Convention, Honolulu, HA.
Biehal, G. (1983). Implication of consumer information processing research for the design of consumer information systems. *Journal of Consumer Affairs, 17,* 107-122.
Brown, N. A., & Atwater, T. (1986, Autumn). Videotex news: A content analysis of three videotex services and their companion newspapers. *Journalism Quarterly, 63,* 554-561. munication Association Annual Convention, Denver, CO.
Capuzzi, C. (1987). Wall Street's affair with the wire. *Channels '87 Field Guide*, pp. 68-70.
Butler, J. M., & Kent, K. E. M. (1983). The potential impact of videotext on newspapers. *Newspaper Research Journal, 5,* 3-12.
Clemons, E. K., & McFarlan, F. W. (1986, July-August). Telecom: Hook up or lose out. *Harvard Business Review*, pp. 91-97.
Dozier, D. M., & Rice, R. E. (1984). Rival theories of electronic newsreading. In R. E. Rice & Associates, *The new media: Communication, research and technology* (pp. 103-127). Beverly Hills, CA: Sage.
Edwardson, M., Kent, K., & McConnell, M. (1985). Television news information gain: Videotex versus a talking head. *Journal of Broadcasting and Electronic Media, 29,* 367-378.
Ettema, J. S. (1984a). Three phases in the creation of information inequities: An empirical assessment of a prototype videotex system. *Journal of Broadcasting, 28,* 383-395.
Ettema, J. S. (1984b). Videotex for market information: A survey of prototype users. In J. Johnston (Ed.), *Evaluating the new information technologies* (pp. 5-21). San Francisco: Jossey-Bass.
Ettema, J. S. (1985). Videotex for news and business data: Comparison of user response to two information retrieval applications. *Telecommunications Policy, 9,* 41-48.
Falk, H. (1984). The Source vs. CompuServe. *Online Review, 8,* 214-224.
Finn, T. A., & Stewart, C. M. (1985). From consumer to organizational videotex applications: Will videotex find a home at the office? In M. McLaughlin (Ed.), *Communication yearbook, 9,* (pp. 805-826). Beverly Hills, CA: Sage.
Fisher, J. F. (1985). Video transaction services. In M. Greenberger (Ed.), *Electronic publishing plus* (pp. 141-147). White Plains, NY: Knowledge Industry Publications.
Garramone, G. M., Harris, A. C., & Pizante, G. (1986). Predictors of motivation to use computer-mediated political communication systems. *Journal of Broadcasting and Electronic Media, 30,* 445-457.
Goldberg, L. (1986, March 10). L.A. videotex outlet not profitable enough. *Electronic Media*, pp. 26, 48.

Hooper, R. (1985). Lessons from overseas: The British experience. In M. Greenberger (Ed.), *Electronic publishing plus* (pp. 181-199). White Plains, NY: Knowledge Industry Publications.

The information business. (1986, August 25). *Business Week*, pp. 82-90.

Information power. (1985, October 14). *Business Week*, pp. 108-114.

Janke, R. V. (1984, November). Online after six: End-user searching comes of age. *Online*, pp. 15-29.

Jones, M. G. (1984). Videotex systems: The issues for consumers and consumer behavior specialists. In T. C. Kinnear (Ed.), *Advances in consumer research* (Vol. 11, pp. 514-518). Provo, UT: Association for Consumer Research.

Jurgensmeyer, J. E., & Bishop S. G. (1985). Access to information: The dream and the reality. *Journal of the American Society for Information Science, 36*, 383-388.

Kupferberg, N. (1986, March). End-users: How are they doing? A librarian interviews six 'do-it-yourself' searchers. *Online*, pp. 24-28.

Ledingham, J. A. (1984). Are consumers ready for the information age? *Journal of Advertising Research, 24*, 31-37.

McCarthy, S. J. (1985). What Time Inc. learned. In M. Greenberger (Ed.), *Electronic publishing plus* (pp. 163-167). White Plains, NY: Knowledge Industry Publications.

McFarlan, F. W. (1984, May-June). Information technology changes the way you compete. *Harvard Business Review*, pp. 98-103.

Miller, T. (1983, September). Information, please, and fast. *Washington Journalism Review*, pp. 51-53.

Motavalli, J. (1987). Home shopping network: Home is where the mart is. *Channels '87 Field Guide*, pp. 77-78.

Neale, W. C. (1984). Technology as social process: A commentary on knowledge and human capital. *Journal of Economic Issues, 18*, 573-580.

Neufeld, M. L., & Cornog, M. (1986). Database history: From dinosaurs to compact discs. *Journal of the American Society for Information Science, 37*, 183-190.

Neuman, W. R. (1985). The media habit. In M. Greenberger (Ed.), *Electronic publishing plus* (pp. 5-12). White Plains, NY: Knowledge Industry Publications.

Neustadt, R. M. (1982). *The birth of electronic publishing*. White Plains, NY: Knowledge Industry Publications.

Ojala, M. (1986). Views on end-user searching. *Journal of the American Society for Information Science, 37*, 197-203.

O'Leary, M. (1985, June). CompuServe and The Source: Databanks for the end-user. *Database*, pp. 100-106.

Overduin, H. (1986). News judgement and the community connection in the technological limbo of videotex. *Communication, 9*, 229-246.

Parker, E. B., & Dunn, D. A. (1972). Information technology: Its social potential. *Science, 176*, 1392-1399.

Pemberton, J. (1982, July). The inverted file: How the information utilities changed us by '92. *Online*, pp. 6-7.

Porter, M. E., & Millar, V. E. (1985, July-August). How information gives you competitive advantage. *Harvard Business Review*, pp. 149-160.

Rogers, E. M. (1986). *Communication technology*. New York: The Free Press.

Sackman, H. (1971). *Mass information utilities and social excellence*. Princeton, NJ: Auerback Publishers.

Sackman, H., & Nie, N. (Eds.). (1970). *The information utility and social choice*. Montvale, NJ: AFIPS Press.

Schiller, H. I. (1981). *Who knows: Information in the age of the Fortune 500*. Norwood, NJ: Ablex.

Sieck, S. K. (1984). Business information systems and databases. In M. E. Williams (Ed.), *Annual review of information science and technology* (Vol. 19, pp. 311–327). White Plains, NY: Knowledge Industry Publications.

Smith, A. (1980). *Goodbye Gutenberg.* New York: Oxford University Press.

Storch, C. (1986, December, 14). TV, phone, plastic . . . bonanza: Christmas year-around for shop-at-home services. *Chicago Tribune*, Section 7, pp. 1, 5.

Urban, C. D. (1985). The competitive advantage of new publishing formats. In M. Greenberger (Ed.), *Electronic publishing plus* (pp. 41–56). White Plains, NY: Knowledge Industry Publications.

Veith, R. H. (1983). Videotex and teletext. In M. E. Williams (Ed.), *Annual review of information science and technology* (Vol. 18, pp. 3–28). White Plains, NY: Knowledge Industry Publications.

Wallace, B. (1984, August 1). Videotex leaves home. *Computerworld on Communications*, pp. 14–16.

Weaver, D. A. (1983). *Videotex journalism: Teletext, viewdata and the news.* Hillsdale, NJ: Lawrence Erlbaum Associates.

Williams, M. E. (1985). Usage and revenue data for the online database industry. *Online Review, 9*, 205–210.

Window on the world: The home information revolution. (1981, June 29). *Business Week*, pp. 74–75.

7
A Quantitative Analysis of the Reasons for VCR Penetration Worldwide

Joseph D. Straubhaar
Michigan State University

Carolyn Lin
Southern Illinois University at Carbondale

One of the more striking phenomena in recent times in the area of electronic media and telecommunication is the rapid spread of the videocassette recorder (VCR). Unlike many other new technologies, VCRs have found an almost immediate acceptance by audiences or consumers in many nations. VCRs have diffused rapidly throughout the world, penetrating societies closed and open, rich and poor. VCR penetration ranges from 90% of households in Kuwait, to 40% in Great Britain, to under 1% in a number of African countries.

The effects of VCRs are also becoming a major policy issue in many countries. In the United States, the impact of VCRs has primarily been a commercial issue. Media industries, such as broadcast TV, cable TV, or film distribution compete intensively with the VCR for audiences. Similar issues exist in many other countries, such as India, where a thriving film industry now finds its revenue base in theatrical distribution threatened by pirate distribution via VCRs. In many societies, the policy implications are even broader. The impact of VCRs is greatly feared by political leaders, development planners, and civic and religious leaders.

The reasons for much of this concern are inherent in the nature of the new medium. Rather than being a mass medium, VCRs place control over viewing with the individual. They loosen or even destroy the considerable control over audiences exercised by various authorities through the selection of broadcast or film content. The VCR user may choose to record a broadcast for playback at a more convenient time (*time-shifting*). While taping, the user can pause to avoid unwanted materials such as advertisements, public service announcements, political propaganda, and so on (i.e., *zapping*). Moreover, during playback, the user can fast forward through any undesirable materials recorded as well (i.e., *zipping*). Even more threatening to broadcasters and other authorities, the user may also play a prerecorded tape (*playback*), which amounts to the "substitution" of prerecorded material for a period of time that might otherwise have been spent watching a broadcast.

Substituting prerecorded materials for regular broadcast programs has multiple implications. In most cases, VCR users substitute prerecorded entertainment materials for broadcast programs such as news, educational, political, or religious materials. Other commonly replaced programs may include public service announcements and development service messages (Boyd & Straubhaar, 1985; Lent, 1984; Straubhaar & Boyd, this volume). Less common, but more directly threatening to authorities, are cases where the material substituted is itself politically or socially controversial (Boyd & Straubhaar, 1985). For instance, despite government efforts to restrict its broadcast abroad, videos of "Death of a Princess" were very popular in Saudi Arabia (Boyd & Straubhaar, 1985). The recent campaign by Corazon Aquino to depose then-President Marcos in the Philippines made use of videotapes of foreign newscasts about the Aquino assassination and Marcos' corruption, and so on. Tapes were smuggled in, copied, and passed by the Aquino campaign, shown in homes and even around the edges of political rallies (M. de Jesus, personal communication, March 10, 1986).

With the addition of a camera and other production equipment, individuals or groups can record their own videos of news, commentary, ceremony, and the like and circulate them in communication networks that completely bypass the existing media structures. This kind of usage is fairly infrequent as yet. A tentative effort in this direction is the Catholic Church's sponsorship of video production and exchange between parish-related community groups ("base communities") in Venezuela and Brazil (M. Bisbal, personal communication, June 14, 1985; Santoro, 1986). Such video productions would be inherently political in their efforts to discuss community problems and potential solutions on a grassroots level. As a consequence, they could challenge authorities' control of communication channels and political mobilization.

REASONS FOR VCR PENETRATION

VCRs are not being diffused and adopted evenly throughout the globe. A large number of potential factors predict and explain this variation in VCR diffusion. To determine which factors or conditions critically affect VCR

7. REASONS FOR VCR PENETRATION WORLDWIDE

penetration, a study was conducted in which a number of indicators (both quantitative and categorical) were examined. Following is a literature review that discusses each of these indicators and builds to specific hypotheses. These hypotheses are tested by analysis of 81 countries, for which data were available for most indicators.

Income and VCR Penetration

VCRs tend to penetrate first those nations and socioeconomic groups that can best afford them. But VCRs do not show up to the same extent in all nations with high levels of GNP per capita. They also have remarkable diffusion in some nations that have less national wealth. Nevertheless, the income available to purchase equipment such as VCRs will affect the ability of individuals and groups to acquire them. Therefore, our first hypothesis concerns the connection between the average income per capita (GNP per capita) and VCR penetration in countries.

H1 – GNP per capita will be positively correlated with VCR penetration.

Work on development shows that aggregate figures such as GNP per capita can be deceptive, particularly in the Third World (World Bank, 1985). If income is highly concentrated in the hands of a fairly small proportion of the population, then average GNP may not indicate the true purchasing power of the average individual. Therefore this study looks also at the relationship between VCR penetration and the proportion of income held by the richest 10% and 20% of the population.

H2 – A less concentrated distribution of national income will be positively correlated with VCR penetration.

The relationship is complex, however, and actually greatly depends on the relative wealth of a country and the kind of economy and social structure it has. In the relatively wealthy, industrialized countries, where mass consumption of fairly expensive equipment such as VCRs is common, more even income distribution should be positively related to VCR penetration. The same should be true of Third World countries where a mass consumption middle class is being created either by industrialization – as in the case of "newly industrializing countries" (NICs) such as Brazil or South Korea – or by oil wealth – as in the case of OPEC nations such as the Arab Gulf states or Venezuela.

H2(a) – Among industrialized and oil-rich nations (or middle- and high-income nations), a lower concentration of national income will be correlated with greater VCR penetration.

In the poorest countries, the relationship may be somewhat different. Income concentration does create a small elite that can afford expensive purchases, such as VCRs.

> H2(b) — Among economically underdeveloped nations (or low-income nations), a greater concentration of national income will be correlated with greater VCR penetration.

Prices and VCR Diffusion

The price of VCRs is also an important predictor of their diffusion. In general, VCR prices have dropped rapidly in many nations, enabling VCRs to become a mass consumption electronic medium. Prices still vary, however, and affect VCR penetration.

> H3 — Higher VCR prices will be negatively correlated to VCR penetration.

A price-related factor is individual government restrictions on VCR imports (Straubhaar & Boyd, this volume; *Variety*, various). Many governments consider VCRs luxuries and tax them heavily. Others place import restrictions on VCRs or even prohibit their importation. All of these measures raise prices, even though many VCRs come through the black market to avoid restrictions (Ganley & Ganley, 1986; "Video around the world," 1983). This has caused a widely varied global price range for VCRs, from less than $300 to upwards of $3,000.

> H4 — The degree of import restrictions on VCRs will be negatively correlated with VCR penetration.

Prices and import restrictions may limit the number of VCRs sold, but other factors tend to motivate individuals to want a VCR, that is to create demand. The literature on VCRs, although still scant in many areas, indicates several key factors: familiarity with other media or sophistication in using media, the felt need to increase television viewing options by using a VCR for either time-shifting or program substitution, and access to VCR equipment and videotapes as facilitated by urban living (Boyd & Straubhaar, 1985; Boyd, Straubhaar, & Lent, 1988; "Video around the world," 1983).

Other Media and VCR Penetration

The penetration of different media is related to the state of adoption and to use of other media, to cultural patterns and to economic development. Cultural patterns are too complex to explore adequately for the present type of quantitative approach, but interrelationships of media penetration are readily observable. Access to other media should tend to enhance VCR penetration by making potential users aware of the media options available and increasing their perceived leisure needs to use different media. Media also develop in a certain general pattern related to economic development (Lerner, 1958).

Radio is the most widespread mass medium around the world. Even in remote areas of developing nations, low cost and portability has made radio an easily accessible medium for many people (Katz & Wedell, 1977). Radio penetration is, therefore, probably not as strongly related to VCRs as are some other mass media. Newspapers, for instance, are an urban medium in most nations (Lerner, 1958) and also demand literacy and purchasing power more characteristic of a wealthier, more complex economy. Therefore newspaper use may show a stronger relation to VCR use, which is also more common in wealthier societies and in elite communities. Use of VCRs is most clearly connected to broadcast television, which is available at least in urban areas in all but two of the countries examined in this study. (In several smaller African and Caribbean countries, all video viewing is done via VCRs.) Because telephones require both relative sophistication to use and, in most of the countries studied, considerable socioeconomic status to obtain, telephone penetration is also an important indicator. Moviegoing will probably have a negative connection with VCR penetration because VCR users tend to use them to substitute for movie-going as well as television viewing.

- H5 – Television set penetration will be positively correlated with VCR penetration.
- H6 – Radio set penetration will be positively but weakly correlated with VCR penetration.
- H7 – Telephone receiver penetration will be positively correlated with VCR penetration.
- H8 – Newspaper penetration will be positively correlated with VCR penetration.
- H9 – Movie-viewing frequency will be negatively correlated with VCR penetration.

Another factor related to media-user sophistication (i.e., the users' degree of familiarity with various electronic media) is the degree of urbanization found in different nations. Early work on media and development by Lerner (1958) and others (e.g., Frey, 1972) has connected urbanization with the development of media use, particularly print media. More current research also notes the connection between urbanization and use of more complex electronic media, such as telephones (Hudson, 1984). Certainly, the literature to date on VCRs in the Third World shows a correlation between access to both hardware and software and urban living situations (Boyd & Straubhaar, 1985).

> H10—Degree of urbanization will be positively correlated with VCR penetration.

Television Programming Diversity and VCR Penetration

For those countries with relatively complex media development and sophisticated audiences, the felt need to add diversity to what is already available may not be high. If audiences are satisfied with available programs on broadcast television or other media, the extra expense of a VCR may limit demand. For instance, VCR penetration is higher in some countries, such as Colombia, than in geographically and culturally comparable countries, such as Brazil, where average incomes are higher (Straubhaar, in press). Part of the explanation for such differences in VCR penetration, based on the case studies available on India, Malaysia, Kuwait, Saudi Arabia, Brazil, Columbia, and other countries (Boyd & Straubhaar, 1985; Lent, 1984; Straubhaar, in press) seems to lie in the diversity of broadcast television options.

Definition of diversity can be difficult. It implies at least some range of different choices to the viewer in television programming. A review of the literature on broadcasting content indicated that the main program categories encountered are information, education, culture, sports, and entertainment (Katz & Wedell, 1977; UNESCO, 1985). These are frequently dichotomized into programming that is primarily informational or educational and that which is primarily entertainment. Another possible measure of diversity is the number of television channels available to the viewer, including cable TV channels in some countries.

Detailed information on programming was not available for most of the countries in this study. To measure diversity, countries are categorized by whether they had television channels whose content was primarily education/information, entertainment, or mixed. Judgments about the orientation of channels were collected from reference works such as the *UNESCO Statistical Yearbook, World Press Encyclopedia* (Kurian, 1982), the series of Area Handbooks issued by the U.S. government, various academic articles, and the like. We also interviewed "experts": academic specialists, visiting scholars and graduate students from the countries in question. We only used characterizations that were consistent between all the available sources and based on at least two sources.

7. REASONS FOR VCR PENETRATION WORLDWIDE

To facilitate correlational analysis, a five-step ordinal scale was created. Given the control exercised by governments over information/education channels in many countries, particularly Eastern bloc (Paulu, 1974) or Third World (Katz & Wedell, 1977), the least diverse systems were defined as those that had predominantly information/education channels. Next least diverse were systems with channels with predominantly entertainment. The next were systems with more evenly mixed content. Next were systems that had channels of two types. More diverse were systems with channels of all three types.

> H11 — Diversity of broadcast television, as measured by number of channels with different orientations (information/education, entertainment and mixed), will be, overall, negatively related to VCR penetration.

Diversity is probably negatively related to VCR penetration because VCRs are often used to add nonbroadcast programs to what is available to the viewer. If adequate diversity is available on broadcast television, as in Brazil with four commercial entertainment channels and one government educational channel, then VCRs may not be perceived as necessary.

However, diversity has a potentially more complex relationship with VCR penetration. That is, VCRs are used not only for substitution of new content but also used for time-shifting. Therefore, diversity of TV channels will be:

> H11(a) — negatively correlated with use of VCRs for playing prerecorded programs
>
> H11(b) — positively related with use of VCRs for time-shifting

This relationship should be qualified even further. Review of the cases available suggests that time-shifting is more widespread in industrialized countries than in the Third World. Research in the United States (Levy & Fink, 1984) and the United Kingdom (Gunter & Levy, 1987) suggests that VCRs diffuse there both for playback and because the diversity of broadcast/cable television encourages VCR use for time-shifting. In both, however, acquisition of a VCR does not demand the resource commitment that it would in most Third World countries, so a convenience use, like time-shifting, may be an adequate reason for buying a VCR. In contrast, research to date suggests that VCRs diffuse rapidly in some Third World countries because substitution of prerecorded programs for existing broadcast content is more necessary, given much lower diversity. In middle or lower income countries, the expenditure required to acquire a VCR primarily for time-shifting may not be considered worthwhile, although substitution of desired content is (M. Bisbal, personal communication, June 14, 1985; Santoro, 1986).

H12 — Effects of diversity on VCR penetration will vary by the typical use of VCRs and the income level of the country such that:

H12(a) — in industrialized or oil-rich countries, diversity of content will be more positively correlated with use of VCRs for time-shifting than for playback;

H12(b) — in middle-income or lower income nations, lack of diversity will be more correlated with use of VCRs for content substitution/playback than time-shifting.

The number of channels of broadcast television, is also another measure of diversity. Most countries studied here have only one television channel, which automatically limits the diversity available. In nations where there is more than one television channel, the content of these channels tend to be more diversified (Katz & Wedell, 1977). For instance, if a nation has two channels, one of them can be devoted to public service or educational purposes whereas the other channel can be geared toward entertainment purposes. This measure thus supplements the diversity measure just given.

H13 — The number of channels of broadcast television will be:

H13(a) — negatively correlated to use of VCRs primarily for playback, and

H13(b) — positively correlated to use of VCRs primarily for time-shifting.

Cable television is another significant means of adding diversity to what is available to the viewer. Most cable systems in Western Europe, North America, and Japan add channels for movies, music, news, and sports, as well as repeats of broadcast series, and so forth.

H14 — Availability of cable television, as measured by the proportion of homes with cable TV, will be:

H14(a) — negatively related to the use of VCRs for playing prerecorded programs

H14(b) — positively related to the use of VCRs for time-shifting

This study recognizes the importance of government controls or restrictions on broadcast content as well as restrictions on importation and distribution of certain kinds of prerecorded tapes as negative indicators of diversity. However, sufficient reliable, current data on broadcast controls to permit the use of these indicators were not available. As a substitute index of control, an indicator of programming freedom in the television systems of various nations was created through classifying type of ownership of broadcast media. Government-owned systems are lowest on the scale, "public" systems next (many public systems are highly controlled—Boyd, 1982; Head, 1985; Lent, 1978) and commercial and/or mixed systems were rated most open. This scale is admittedly flawed, but seems the best representation of such aggregated information about complex systems.

H15—More tightly controlled broadcasting systems will be positively correlated with VCR penetration.

More complete data were available on restrictions and controls on the importation of prerecorded tapes. In many cases, government restrictions have been aimed at importation of pornographic videos (Lent, 1984; "Video market free-for-all," 1984). In a few others, restrictions also exist for ethnic, religious, ideological, or political reasons. For example, Pakistan restricts the importation of Indian films to theaters and now attempts to restrict their importation on videotape as well. Smuggling and reproduction of tapes is so easy—and increasingly, so well organized by international networks of tape pirates—that most such restrictions are widely circumvented. Nevertheless, attempted restrictions do still indicate a governmental intention to limit diversity.

H16—Suppression of certain kinds of imported pre-recorded video programs will be positively related to VCR penetration.

METHODS

Data Selection

An elaborated search was conducted for any relevant information on the uses of VCRs, import restrictions on VCRs and market conditions of VCRs. Data for 81 nations were collected from a number of journal articles, newspapers (particularly the weekly *Variety*, which had a number of related articles), industry reports from the Motion Picture Export Association (MPEA) and the Electronic Equipment Exporters Association, government records (particularly media studies by the U.S. Information Agency and Radio Free Europe/Radio Liberty), the *World Radio/TV Handbook* (1985), and statistical yearbooks of international institutions (e.g., the World Bank and UNESCO). For a number of African and Asian countries where data were particularly difficult to obtain from written sources, a number of graduate students from those countries as well as country experts were asked to make estimates. Those estimates that approximated the data obtained from the literature and achieved close inter-interviewee reliability were used (i.e., multiple interviewees' responses for one nation were compared and when at least two were no more than 1%-2% apart, an average of their estimates was used).

Because of the difficulty in finding some data, a number of particular indicators are missing for various countries. For this reason, the number of cases involved is reported in the text whenever correlations are cited in all tables.

Definitions and Measurement

VCR penetration ratios are defined as the VCR sets available per 1,000 inhabitants of a population. VCR penetration ratios among TV households were not used in this study because households with television often reflect a very small, concentrated, relatively wealthy segment of the population in most developing nations. As such, in some cases, VCR penetration by TV households is relatively large but population penetration quite small. *VCR prices* are recorded directly from the secondary sources compiled. If a price range is obtained, the average (mean) of the prices is adopted as the measure.

Time-shifting, defined as recording TV programs for later viewing, is measured at three levels. The first level is when there is no time-shifting activity. The second level is when time-shifting is not the main use of VCRs. The third level is when time-shifting is the major use of VCRs. *Prerecorded tape playback* is also measured at three levels. The first level is when no playback activity is reported. The second level is when playback is not the main use of VCRs. The third level is when playback is the primary use of VCRs. (These data are taken, where available, from sample surveys of user behavior. If not, industry or expert assessments are used.)

Content control on videotape imports was measured by the presence or absence of censorship on video content and program types of imported prerecorded tapes (e.g., pornography or politically or socially sensitive content). *Import control on VCRs* is classified into three categories based on the degree of restrictions placed on the imported sets. The first category, the least restrained type, includes control devices such as licenses or taxes. The second category, either a VCR import ban or import quota, is regarded to be within a medium level of restraint. The third category, the most restrained class, involves combinations of the other two categories and/or whether the nation is a VCR manufacturer (or assembler).

Variables related to a nation's overall TV programming content are described later. *TV system*, an indicator of a nation's TV system programming freedom, is defined according to structural characteristics. Government-owned systems, public service systems, and commercial and/or mixed systems (combinations of two or more systems) are considered to have the lowest, the intermediate, and the highest degree of programming freedom,

7. REASONS FOR VCR PENETRATION WORLDWIDE

respectively. *TV channel repertoire*, an indicator of the viewing options for a nation's TV viewers, is defined as the number of TV channels available in a nation's TV system. *Programming diversity* is determined by the types of programming available to a nation's TV system. Program types are classified into information, mixed (mixture between informational and entertainment), and entertainment. If only informational programs are available, the TV system is coded as the first class (or the least diversified system). The second class is coded when only entertainment programs are available. The third class is coded when mixed information and entertainment programs are available. If two types of programs or all three types of programs are available, the system is coded as the fourth or the fifth class (the most diversified system), in that order.

Variables forming the overall pervasiveness of the media culture of a nation are defined as follows. *TV penetration ratios*, measured by the number of TV sets owned per 1,000 inhabitants of a population, indicates the spread of video culture. *Radio penetration ratios*, measured by the number of radio receivers owned per 1,000 inhabitants of a population, illustrates the degree of adoption of the most basic form of mass media culture. *Newspaper penetration ratios*, measured by the estimated circulation per 1,000 inhabitants of a population, depicts the extent of media culture relative to literacy rates. *Movie attendance frequency*, measured by the annual attendance per inhabitant of a population, represents the popularity of non-TV film culture. *Cable penetration ratios*, the proportion of homes with cable TV, based on available data, is regarded as the indicator of the expansion of TV programming content to a nation.

GNP per capita, an indicator of a nation's overall wealth, is considered to be directly related to a nation's VCR buying ability. *Urbanization ratios*, a measure of the proportion of a population living in urban areas, reflects the extent of modern life and the degree of likely access to electronic media of a population. *Concentration or distribution of income*, measured by the percentage of national household income held by the top 10% and 20% high-income population, is relevant to whether an expensive product like VCRs can affect the market across various socioeconomic classes of a population. High concentration of income in the upper 10% indicates a very skewed distribution favoring a relatively small elite. Less concentration in the upper 10% and relatively more in the upper 20% indicates skewed income distribution but the beginnings of distribution among an middle or upper middle class. *Income Category* as defined in the *World Development Report* (World Bank, 1985) is reclassified into three categories based on GNP per capita. The high-income category includes "industrial market economies" and "high-income oil exporters." The middle-income category is the combination of "upper middle" and "East European nonmarket" economies. The low-income category is composed of the "low-income" and "lower middle" income economies. (See the Appendix for a list of countries in each category.)

Data Analysis

All the data collected were statistically analyzed. Specifically, a Pearson Correlations test was used to produce simple correlation coefficients to demonstrate the relationships between VCR penetration ratios and all other variables. This was done across all nations and for nations within each separate income separate income category. Correlation coefficients were also computed for the relationships between VCR use variables (time-shifting vs. playback) and program diversity variables (program diversity, number of TV channels, and cable TV penetration ratios) across all nations and within income categories. This procedure was used to examine how television diversity and income categories may affect VCR penetration in a nation. Diversity effects are reported in Tables 7.3 and 7.4. The mean values for each variable studied were tabulated across all nations and within each income category. These are reported in 7.1 and 7.2 respectively.

The general standard for determining statistical significance employed in this chapter is $p \leq .05$. To facilitate interpretation, not only correlation coefficients are reported, but also the size of the group or subsample (represented by "n") in which both qualities were found. (In the tables, group size is reported in parentheses, not as "$n = x$".)

RESULTS

The results of this study emphasize the degree of relationship between three kinds of variables and VCR penetration. These three groups of variables are income- and price-related variables, media-related variables, and television content diversity-related variables. The relationship between some of these variables and VCR penetration is strongly related to whether VCRs are primarily used for time-shifting or playback in a particular country.

The single strongest correlation with VCR penetration was shown by GNP per capita ($r = +.54$, $n = 74$). The correlation was significant at the $p \leq .00$ level. Clearly, as can be seen by an examination of Table 7.1, the average wealth of a nation is relevant to individuals' ability to acquire VCRs, supporting Hypothesis 1.

Income distribution also plays a considerable role. Overall, for all 46 countries for which information was available, VCR penetration was negatively and significantly correlated to skewed or concentrated distribution (as can also be seen in Table 7.2). This was true for both concentration of income in the upper 10% ($r = -.26$, $p \leq .05$), which reflects primarily

TABLE 7.1.
Correlations Between VCR Penetration and All Variables

	VCR penetration by population/1,000			
	r	p	$\bar{X}$	
VCRs/1,000			38	(81)
GNP per capita	.54 (74)	.00*	4,697	(74)
Income distribution				
Top 10% income	−.26 (46)	.04*	32.3%	(46)
Top 20% income	−.39 (46)	.00*	46.7%	(46)
TV/1,000	.37 (77)	.00*	174	(77)
Radios/1,000	.23 (75)	.02*	353.1	(75)
Telephones/1,000	.62 (33)	.00*	291.1	(33)
Newspapers/1,000	.21 (41)	.09	188.1	(41)
Movie average/person	−.04 (55)	.40	7.6	(55)
Program diversity	.11 (81)	.16	2.9	(81)
Playback	−.18 (75)	.06	1.9	(75)
Time-shifting	.13 (71)	.15	1.1	(71)
Cable/TV households	.08 (21)	.36	25.1%	(21)
TV systems	.13 (81)	.13	1.6	(81)
Content control	−.05 (52)	.37	.8	(52)
Urbanization	.43 (80)	.00*	55.1%	(80)
VCR prices	−.34 (55)	.00*	1,037	(55)
VCR import control	−.23 (37)	.09	1.1	(37)
TV channels	−.06 (80)	.30	2.5	(80)

Note: Figures in parentheses represent number of cases.
*Statistical significance at $p \leq .05$

the economic elite, and in the upper 20%, which in many countries includes the upper middle class ($r = -.39$, $p \leq .00$). This provides support for Hypothesis 2.

The specific relationship expected between concentration of income, VCR penetration, and country income level did not emerge, as can be seen in Table 7.2. High concentration was not positively correlated with VCR penetration in those countries defined as having low per capita income. Lower concentration of income was not correlated with VCR penetration in high-income or middle-income countries, so Hypotheses 2a and 2b were not supported. The subsamples seem to have been too small, because income distribution information is quite limited (47 out of 81 countries).

Prices of VCRs are also significantly related to their penetration among nations. Confirming Hypothesis 3, higher VCR prices are negatively related to VCR penetration ($r = -.34$, $n = 55$, $p = p \leq .00$). Price shows a strong relationship in the upper income countries ($r = -.45$, $n = 21$, $p \leq .02$) and lower income countries ($r = -.36$, $n = 19$, $p \leq .07$). Although statistically significant at only the $p \leq .10$ level, the next measure shows that policies that raise VCR prices, such as import duties, limits, or bans,

TABLE 7.2
Correlations Between VCR Penetration and All Variables by Income Categories
VCR Penetration by Population/1,000

	Low Income			Middle Income			High Income		
	r	p	X̄	r	p	X̄	r	p	X̄
VCRs/1,000			13.3 (28)			26 (27)			77.1 (26)
GNP per capita	.10(27)	.32	627 (27)	.21(22)	.18	2,760 (22)	.29(25)	.08	10,798 (25)
Income Distribution									
Top 10% income	−.07(15)	.40	38.2% (15)	−.04(14)	.45	32.7% (14)	.28(17)	.14	26.8% (17)
Top 20% income	−.13(15)	.32	51.8% (15)	−.01(14)	.49	49% (14)	−.12(17)	.32	40.3% (17)
TVs/1,000	−.03(27)	.45	53.0 (27)	.02(24)	.46	166.3 (24)	.17(26)	.20	306.8 (26)
Radio/1,000	−.04(26)	.43	151.4 (26)	.05(25)	.41	329 (25)	−.09(24)	.34	596.9 (24)
Telephones/1,000	.14(7)	.39	21.0 (7)	.52(11)	.05*	169.6 (11)	.29(15)	.15	506.2 (15)
Newspapers/1,000	−.14(13)	.33	34.5 (13)	.50(9)	.09	177 (9)	−.15(19)	.27	298.5 (19)
Movie average/person	−.14(15)	.31	14.2 (15)	−.20(19)	.21	4 (19)	.21(21)	.18	6.1 (21)
Program diversity	.23(28)	.12	2.3 (28)	.06(27)	.37	3.2 (27)	−.27(26)	.09	3.3 (26)
Playback	.03(25)	.44	2.0 (25)	**	**	2.0 (25)	.03(25)	.44	1.6 (25)
Time-shifting	.14(24)	.26	.9 (24)	.23(23)	.15	1.0 (33)	−.24(24)	.13	1.4 (24)
Cable/TV households	−.11(4)	.45	13.5% (4)	−.96(3)	.10	25% (3)	.03(14)	.46	28.5% (14)
TV systems	.09(28)	.33	1.4 (28)	−.44(27)	.01*	1.5 (27)	.32(26)	.05*	1.7 (26)
Content control	−.01(21)	.49	.8 (21)	−.32(16)	.11	.8 (16)	.25(15)	.18	.7 (15)
Urbanization	.08(28)	.34	33.4% (28)	.15(27)	.23	62.7% (27)	.38(25)	.08*	71.1% (25)
VCR prices	−.36(19)	.07	1,346 (19)	−.28(15)	.16	1,257 (15)	−.45(21)	.02*	601 (21)
VCR import control	−.28(15)	.16	1.1 (15)	.07(10)	.42	1.5 (10)	−.24(12)	.23	.7 (12)
TV channels	−.12(28)	.28	2.1 (28)	.29(26)	.08	2.8 (26)	−.29(26)	.08	2.7 (26)

Note: Figures in parenthesis represent number of cases.
*Statistical significance at $p \leq .05$.
**Uncomputable
Note: Figures in parentheses represent number of cases.

7. REASONS FOR VCR PENETRATION WORLDWIDE

are somewhat weakly and negatively correlated with VCR penetration ($r = -.23$, $n = 37$, $p \le .09$). Thus, Hypothesis 4 is also partially supported (see Tables 7.1 and 7.2).

One of the next most significantly correlated factors related to VCR penetration was the proportion of the population living in urban areas ($r = +.43$, $n = 80$, $p \le .00$). This result substantiates support for Hypothesis 10. Related media availability variables also correlated quite highly with VCR penetration. As suggested by the results in Table 7.1, telephone receiver penetration ($r = +.62$, $n = 33$, $p \le .00$) yielded the largest single correlation coefficient, supporting Hypothesis 7. Of all the media variables, telephone penetration also indicated the only significant variation in correlation with VCRs due to country income level. The correlation was strongest for the middle income countries ($r = +.52$, $n = 11$, $p \le .05$) (see Table 7.2). That is probably because a number of middle-income developing countries are increasing telephone penetration, due to its demonstrated connection to economic growth (Hudson, 1984). In particular, telephone penetration seems to be expanding in the same population sectors, the urban middle class and upper middle class, where most VCR penetration is taking place in places such as Brazil, Columbia, and Venezuela (Straubhaar, in press).

Television set penetration ($r = +.37$, $n = 77$, $p \le .00$), and radio set penetration ($r = +.23$, $n = 75$, $p \le .05$) also were significantly and positively correlated with VCR penetration, providing statistical support for both Hypotheses 5 and 6. Newspaper circulation per 1,000 showed a positive correlation with VCR penetration ($r = +.21$, $n = 41$), which is significant at the $p \le = .10$ level but not $p \le =.05$, weakly supporting Hypothesis 8. The results indicate a very strong role for the various aspects of media availability and media sophistication among various nations' audiences in the acceptance and use of VCRs. The only media variable not strongly correlated with VCR penetration was average movie attendance, which did not show the expected negative correlation predicted in Hypothesis 9 ($r = -.04$, $n = 55$) (see Table 7.1).

By itself, diversity of content on broadcast television is not significantly correlated with VCR penetration. The scale of content diversity used here ranges from nations with only information/education channels to those with information, entertainment and mixed channels. As revealed in Table 4.1, there is no indication of a negative relationship between content diversity and VCR penetration ($r = .11$, $n = 81$) as predicted in Hypothesis 11 (see Table 7.1). Overall, this measure of diversity also does not correlate very strongly with either VCR use for time-shifting ($r = +.10$, $n = 71$) or playback ($r = +.12$, $n = 75$). This fails to support Hypotheses 11a and 11b (see Table 7.3).

The correlation between diversity of TV content and VCR penetration comes closer to significance when countries are separated by income groups.

TABLE 7.3
Correlations Between VCR Predictor Variables and VCR Use

	Playback		Time-Shifting	
	r	p	r	p
Program diversity	.12(75)	.15	.11(71)	.19
TV channels	.06(75)	.31	.19(71)	.05*
Cable/TV households	−.51(20)	.01*	.39(20)	.04*

Note: Figures in parentheses represent number of cases.
*Statistical significance at $\leq .05$.

It seems that there may be a positive relationship between content diversity and VCR penetration in low-income countries ($r = +.23$, $n = 28$, $p \leq .12$), whereas in high income countries, a negative relationship seems to exist ($r = -.27$, $n = 26$, $p \leq .10$). Furthermore, use of VCRs for time-shifting shows a strong and significant positive correlation with diversity in low-income countries ($r = +54$, $n = 24$, $p \leq .00$), which is the reverse of what was expected in Hypothesis 12b. Similarly, VCR playback use correlates strongly with diversity in high-income countries ($r = +.2$, $n = 25$, $p \leq .05$), whereas time-shifting shows little correlation with diversity ($r = -.1$, $n = 24$) reversing the expectation set in Hypothesis 12a (see Table 7.4). This indicates the necessity for more work in developing measures on the issue of diversity in content.

The next measure of diversity, the number of broadcast television channels available showed little relationship ($r = .06$) to VCR penetration, overall, thus not supporting the main Hypothesis 13. This is probably due to the large number of low-income countries with only one channel ($n = 28$) (see Table 7.1). The number of channels shows much stronger correlations with VCR penetration in both middle-income ($r = +.29$, $n = 26$) and upper income countries ($r = -.29$, $n = 26$), both significant at the $p \leq .10$ level (see Table 7.2). This does tend to imply the expected relationship between measures of diversity and VCR penetration. However, this needs to be understood in the context of VCR use (whether primarily for time-shifting or playback), because that seems to act as an intervening variable, as anticipated in Hypotheses 11a and 11b.

In general, when countries are separated by predominant use of VCRs for either time-shifting or playback/substitution, these two uses show more significant relationships with some of the indirect measures of TV content diversity. For example, overall, the number of TV channels available is significantly and positively correlated with use of VCRs for time-shifting ($r = +.19$, $n = 71$, $p \leq .05$), supporting Hypothesis 13b. However, playback use does not result in negative correlation with the number of TV channels ($r = +.06$, $n = 75$), thus failing to support Hypothesis 13a (Table 7.3).

TABLE 7.4
Breakdown of Correlations Between VCR Predictors and VCR Use
by Country Income Categories

	Low Income				Middle Income				High Income			
	Playback		Time-Shifting		Playback		Time-Shifting		Playback		Time-Shifting	
	r	p	r	p	r	p	r	p	r	p	r	p
Program diversity	.21(25)	.17	.54(24)	.00**	**	**	−.17(23)	.22	.33(25)	.05*	−.13(24)	.28
TV channels	.09(25)	.33	.27(24)	.10	**	**	−.42(23)	.02	.12(25)	.28	.38(24)	.03*
Cable/TV households	**	**	.37(4)	.32	**	**	−.60(3)	.30	−.57(13)	.02*	.42(13)	.07

Note: Figures in parentheses represent number of cases.
*Statistical significance at ≤ .05.
**Uncomputable

This relationship between TV channels, VCR penetration, and VCR use is clearer when analyzed by country income category. Middle-income countries show a clear and significant negative correlation between use of VCRs for time-shifting and the number of TV channels available ($r = -.42$, $n = 26$, $p \leq .05$). Upper income countries show a reversed pattern, the number of TV channels correlated significantly with time-shifting ($r = +.38$, $n = 24$, $p \leq .05$) but not with playback ($r = +.12$, $n = 25$). This measure does support the differences between upper income and other countries stated in Hypotheses 12a and 12b (see Table 7.4). It may be that the number of channels is a better indicator of diversity than the scale above which was constructed around channel program orientations.

Another measure of television diversity, cable TV availability, shows little overall correlation with VCR penetration ($r = .08$, $n = 20$) (see Table 7.1). However, the availability of cable TV is positively correlated with VCR penetration ($r = +.39$, $n = 20$, $p \leq .05$) in countries where time-shifting is a major VCR use, supporting Hypothesis 14b. Cable TV availability is also negatively correlated with predominant use for playback ($r = -.51$, $n = 20$, $p \leq .05$), supporting Hypothesis 14a (see Table 7.3). Both relationships are significant. Because few countries outside the upper income level have cable TV, these relationships were even clearer when confined to upper income countries. In that group, VCR use for playback had a strong and significant negative correlation with cable TV availability ($r = -.57$, $n = 13$, $p \leq .05$), and VCR use for time-shifting had a strong but not clearly significant positive correlation ($r = +42$, $n = 13$, $p \leq .10$) (see Table 7.4). It appears that, as measures of diversity, both number of broadcast channels and cable TV penetration indicate the expected negative correlation with VCR use for playback and positive correlation with use for time-shifting, which our overall approach to diversity suggested.

An indirect measure of content diversity comes from the type or orientation of the countries' television systems. Overall, the nature of the television system structure showed little correlation with VCR penetration ($r = +.13$, $n = 81$) (see Table 7.1). Some significant differences emerged between middle- and upper income countries, however. In middle-income countries, VCR penetration showed a significant negative correlation with more open systems ($r = -.44$, $n = 27$, $p \leq .05$). In upper income countries, VCR penetration showed a significant positive correlation with open systems ($r = +.32$, $n = 26$, $p \leq .05$) (see Table 7.2). This indicates a need for refinement in Hypothesis 15, investigating the reasons for such income-level differences, or a refinement in measure. A last negative measure of television content diversity was whether countries suppressed certain kinds of prerecorded video programs. That showed essentially no correlation with VCR penetration ($r = -.05$, $n = 52$, $p \leq .37$), thus failing to support Hypothesis 16 (see Table 7.1).

CONCLUSIONS

Most of the anticipated predictors of VCR penetration specified in this study's hypotheses were supported as being significantly correlated with VCR diffusion. These indicators were related to (a) income and price, (b) other media and urbanization, and (c) television content diversity.

The most obvious of these, income per capita, income distribution, VCR prices, and price-related controls, were in fact among the most significantly related to VCR penetration. Next in strength, generally, were measures of media sophistication and development, and the related increase in urbanization. In the third group, the most abstract measures of diversity, such as programming emphasis of different channels, show little relationship with VCR penetration. More concrete indicators, such as the number of channels or cable TV availability, did show significant correlations wtih VCR penetration, particularly with specific kinds of VCR usage. These also showed a tendency to be varied effects in countries at different income levels. More refinement is needed in both measures and hypotheses about the effects of television content diversity on VCR penetration.

Two kinds of variables showed a tendency, frequently a significant one, to affect the correlations between other predictors and VCR penetration. Those were the income level of the country in question, which directly reflects the most significant predictor, GNP per capita, and whether VCRs were primarily used for time-shifting or playback in the country.

The use of VCRs is a particularly interesting variable because it tended to be related to the content diversity variables. With two measures of diversity, number of TV channels and cable TV penetration, a fairly strong relationship was shown between VCR use for time-shifting and content diversity, whereas VCR playback showed a negative relationship with diversity. This leads us to postulate two fairly separate models of VCR penetration. There is one in which VCRs diffuse fairly widely, associated with diverse broadcast content and relatively high country income level, because they are used for time-shifting to enable a fairly affluent group of consumers to take better advantage of diverse broadcast or cable offerings, as well as to playback prerecorded tapes. There seems to be a second "path," more typical for less wealthy societies, where VCR penetration is associated with less diverse television content, because VCRs are used as much or more for playback or program substitution than they are for time shifting. The connection with lower GNP and lower country income category is interesting because it does indicate that lower diversity is associated with less developed systems and tends to create a demand for means to add diversity to viewing through VCRs that is much stronger than in upper income countries.

There are interesting implications of these two quite different models for VCR diffusion. The most significant is the concern addressed in the introduction to this chapter, the concern in Third World countries about the effects of people using VCRs to substitute prerecorded programs for those that are broadcast on television. This study verifies that VCR penetration in lower and middle-income countries, largely Third World, is, in fact, quite clearly related to the tendency to use the machines for playback/program substitution. Although measures of diversity used in this chapter were not as consistent in their relationships as might be desired, lower diversity of television content, which is frequently characteristic of Third World as well as some industrialized and socialist countries, also seems to correlate with VCR acquisition and VCR use for playback/substitution. These two related phenomena suggest that increased broadcast television diversity may mitigate a movement toward using VCRs to substitute for watching broadcast television. This should be of interest to nations concerned about losing their TV audience.

REFERENCES

Boyd, D. A. (1982). *Broadcasting in the Arab World*. Philadelphia: Temple University Press.
Boyd, D. A., & Straubhaar, J. D. (1985). Developmental impact of the home video cassette recorder on Third World countries. *Journal of Broadcasting and Electronic Media, 29*(1), 5–21.
Boyd, D. A., Straubhaar, J. D., & Lent, J. (1988). *VCRs in the Third World*. White Plains, NY: Longman.
Frey, F. W. (1972). Communication and development. In I. S. Pool, F. W. Frey, W. Schramm, N. Maccoby, & E. Parker (Eds.), *Handbook of communication*. Chicago: Rand McNally.
Ganley, G. D., and Ganley, O. H. (1986). *The policy implications of the global spread of videocassette recorders and videocassette programming*. Cambridge: Harvard University Center for Information Policy Research.
Gunter, B., & Levy, M. R. (1987). Social contexts of video use. In M. Levy (Ed.), *The VCR age*, (An issue of *American Behavioral Scientist, 30*(5), 486–494.)
Head, S. W. (1985). *World broadcasting systems*. Belmont, CA: Wadsworth.
Hudson, H. E. (1984). *When telephones reach the village*. Norwood, NJ: Ablex.
Katz, E., & Wedell, G. (1977). *Broadcasting in the Third World*. Cambridge: Harvard Press.
Kurian, G. T. (Ed.). (1982). *World press encyclopedia*. New York: Facts on File.
Lent, J. (1978). *Broadcasting in Asia and the Pacific*. Philadelphia: Temple University Press.
Lent, J. (1984). A revolt against a revolution: the fight against illegal video. *Media Asia, 11*(1), 25–30.
Lerner, D. (1958). *The passing of traditional society*. Glencoe, IL: The Free Press.
Levy, M. R., & Fink, E. L. (1984). The use of home video recording and the transience of television broadcasts. *Journal of Communication, 34*(2), 56–71.
Paulu, B. (1974). *Radio and television broadcasting in Eastern Europe*. Minneapolis: University of Minnesota Press.
Santoro, L. (1986) *Video in Brazil*. Unpublished manuscript, Universidade de Sao Paulo, Escola de Comunicacoes e Artes, Sao Paulo, Brazil.
Straubhaar, J. D. (in press). The impact of VCRs on television broadcasting in Brazil, Columbia, The Dominican Republic, and Venezuela. *Studies in Latin American Popular Culture*.

7. REASONS FOR VCR PENETRATION WORLDWIDE

United Nations Educational, Scientific and Cultural Organization. (1985). *UNESCO Statistical Yearbook*. Paris: UNESCO.
Video around the world. (1983). [Special issue]. *Intermedia, 11(9-5)*.
Video market free-for-all. (1984, March). *TV World*, pp. 12-13.
World Bank. (1985). *The world development report*. Washington, DC: World Bank.
The World Radio/TV Handbook. (1985). New York: Billboard Publications.

APPENDIX

A. LOW-INCOME CATEGORY

Low-Income Economies
Ethiopia	India
Sri Lanka	Pakistan
China	Tanzania
Kenya	Ghana
Bangladesh	Zaire
Sudan	Mali

Middle-Income Economies
Nigeria	Philippines
Lebanon	Egypt
Jamaica	Indonesia
Peru	Columbia
Thailand	Dominican Republic
Zambia	Zimbabwe
Cameroon	Liberia
Syria	El Salvador
Honduras	

B. MIDDLE-INCOME CATEGORY

Upper Middle-Income Economies
Malaysia	Chile
Mexico	Panama
Brazil	Jordan
Iran	Iraq
South Africa	Venezuela
Barbados	Fiji
Israel	Argentina
Algeria	Puerto Rico
South Korea	Greece
Portugal	Uruguay
Taiwan	Yugoslavia
Ireland	Spain

B. MIDDLE-INCOME CATEGORY

East European Nonmarket Economies
Soviet Union	Poland
Romania	Hungary
East Germany	Bulgaria
Czechoslovakia	

C. HIGH-INCOME CATEGORY

High-Income Oil Exporters
United Arab Emirates	
Oman	Kuwait
Saudi Arabia	Qatar
Libya	Bahrain

Industrial Market Economies
Hong Kong	Singapore
Trinidad	Japan
Switzerland	Sweden
Netherlands	Italy
West Germany	France
Finland	Denmark
Belgium	Canada
United States	Australia
New Zealand	Austria
United Kingdom	

8

Uses and Impacts of Home Computers in Canada: A Process of Reappropriation

André H. Caron
Luc Giroux
Sylvie Douzou
Université de Montréal

Of all recent technology innovations, few have inspired as much awe as the computer. Whether this information technology will indeed have a radical and determining effect on the direction of social evolution is still an open question. What appears undeniable, however, is that people clearly believe it will. This is reflected in the fact that *Time* magazine, in a significant gesture that culminated a period of enormous expansion in computer-related media material, crowned the computer "Man of the Year" in 1983.

Information technology and the many innovations it has fostered have become a central element of the social, political, and economic discourse of the 1980s. Governments encourage the use and development of these technologies as the key element in our future economic health. The large amount of funds now being devoted to the introduction of computers into our educational systems testify to a widely held belief that understanding this technology constitutes a high social priority.

In the academic arena, where the so-called "information-processing" paradigm has invaded many different disciplines (biology, communication sciences, psychology, and management sciences, to name but a few), the impact of these techologies is already so visible as to be undeniable. Bolter (1984) argued that the computer has become the defining technology in western culture, a cultural metaphor comparable to the clock that suggested a mechanistic universe to the philosophers of the 17th century, or to the steam engine in the 19th century. Rice (1984), pointing to the interactive nature of these new technologies, underlined the related emergence of wholly new communication behaviors. Gumpert and Cathcart (1982) suggested that these new "media" may change our perception of our physical and social environment, further underscoring the importance and power bestowed on information technology in its many forms.

For some social "forecasters," the advent of an accessible personal computer has reinforced their predictions of a movement toward an "information society" in which information technology takes on a determining and defining role. From this perspective, personal computers have been presented as indispensable to modern living and have come to symbolize the democratization of information technology—an innovation whose accessibility would allow for the ordinary family to reap the benefits of a rapidly expanding science in the context of their daily lives. In light of the already tangible presence of the technology, many have predicted that home computers would soon become as endemic to modern society as the telephone. When one examines the rate at which this particular innovation is penetrating into the general public, reaching 13% of the population of United States in 1985 (*USA Today*, 1985), 17% in Great Britian (EMNID-Institut, 1985), and rising from 4% to 13% in the short span of 3 years in Canada (CROP, 1985), it would be tempting to accept this contention, were it not for its technological bias.

One can argue, indeed, that technological progress is not the only force at play in the relationship between the technical and social spheres. Social pressures and individual attitudes also intervene in the process. People have an active role not only in choosing to adopt or not to adopt a technological innovation but in its very definition and development. Rogers' (1983) suggested that the diffusion process includes a stage where an innovation may be *redefined* by its users. Pool's (1978) work demonstrated how one notable innovation, the telephone, was largely redefined as the result of pressures emanating from the social context surrounding its emergence. Flichy (1980) also stressed this point in his political and historical analysis of European and American innovations. Christian (1973) argued that many predictions related to new technologies have failed because of their technology-oriented biases. This author stated that innovations are largely influenced by the social structure in which they are introduced, and that there may be a wide gap between their potential and effective uses.

This theoretical perspective seems remarkedly well developed by Mercier, Plassard, and Scardigli (1984), who claim that the integration of technology in a given social environment results from a dynamic interaction between what they call the "socio-trade" sphere (e.g., the industrial market) and the sphere of social practices. A technology may indeed have an impact on people's attitudes and behavior, but people are not merely passive recipients; their perceptions and motivations will determine their reactions toward the innovation, and in turn modify its fate. Mercier et al. (1984)

identify this process as one of *potential reappropriation* of the innovation by its end-users.

This perspective suggests an investigation of the initial contact between the technology and its users, particularly when the innovation in question offers a wide variety of potential uses. In the following study, we have focused on the case of the home microcomputer in an attempt to demonstrate that its ill-defined nature and its symbolic value as an innovation renders it an object of active reappropriation by its adopters. Therefore, one cannot speak of its impact without taking into account how it is perceived by its various adopters.

THE HOME COMPUTER AS INNOVATION

The Diffusion Perspective

Since the beginning of the 1980s, a number of studies have been conducted on the diffusion of personal computers (Dutton, Kavaric, & Steinfield, 1983; Rogers, Daley, & Wu, 1982; Venkatesh, Vitalari, & Gronhaug, 1983) in which particular attention is paid to the characteristics of the adopters. In general, these studies have been conducted so as to describe how this innovation is diffusing into the social fabric, reaching different segments of the population as the diffusion process continues. Among others, Dickerson and Gentry (1983); Rogers et al. (1982); and Day, Barnett, Kim, and Miller (1983) show that in general, adopters of this technology tend to be professional males, aged 30 to 35, and earning above-average salaries. These adopters are, in general, in search of new options and resources and resemble those that Rogers (1983) identified as "early adopters." When compared to adopters studied by Muller (1977), 40% of whom were either programmers or electronic engineers and who overwhelmingly (74%) used their computers in a professional capacity, we begin to perceive a penetration into a larger and more diversified portion of society.

This perspective has been a fertile source of research that provides insight into who is adopting this innovation and why. It does not take into account, however, certain features of the personal computer that makes it a very peculiar innovation, and thus make a wider focus of analysis necessary.

Characteristics of the Home Computer

The "potential reappropriation" perspective is particularly relevant to the case of home computers in that it underlines the relationship of the impact of an innovation to the context of use and highlights three of the computer's traits that distinguish it from virtually all other innovations. First and foremost, the computer is an object without a fixed or predefined function. It is the substantiation of Turing's (1936) machine, a device theoretically capable of emulating any computable process. Depending on how the home computer is used, it may take the form of a work tool, a calculator, a toy, a learning tool, or the object of learning itself, as in the case of mastering the science of programming. For each function, one can assume the impact will vary accordingly.

Another distinction, related to the first, is that a significant appropriation of the computer into one's daily routine can require a continuing and substantial investment on the part of the user, not only in terms of financial investment, but perhaps more significantly in terms of time and energy. The investment can vary a great deal as a function of the intended use, and inevitably, the user himself must constantly re-evaluate the costs and the benefits of his investment.

Third, and perhaps most importantly, is that the innovation itself is in a state of constant and rapid evolution; prices continue to fall, and we continue to bear witness to fantastic, exponential gains in terms of performance and sophistication, as well as in the quality of the interface between the user and the computer.

The home computer's unique character as an innovation renders our vision of this integration process considerably more complex. As a multifaceted object in constant evolution, and thus susceptible to change of both form and function, the *process* of its integration invites closer scrutiny. The computer has the character of a powerfully symbolic innovation. The importance of its probable impact as well as its metaphorical nature makes it imperative to investigate in detail the process of integration of the home computer into the household.

METHOD

In 1983, the educational television network in Québec began broadcasting a series of programs designed to sensitize and initiate *the general public* to home computing. The response to this series titled "Octo-Puce" (the English version of this series was entitled "Bits and Bytes") attracted the attention of a large number of viewers. Access to these participants provided an opportunity to study the home computing "phenomenon" from the perspective of a relatively nonspecialized group of people. The sample drawn from the Octo-Puce viewers was not meant to be representative of the population in general, but of the segment actively engaged in the discovery or

8. HOME COMPUTERS IN CANADA

exploration of the innovation. We are aware that these viewers only represent a part of that segment of the population. Our aim, however, was to identify and describe different trends among these people, not to ascribe a precise distribution to those trends.

The methodology chosen was intended to reveal both the quantitative and qualitative features of the computer's integration. A mail questionnaire comprised of 75 closed and open-ended questions, requiring some 45 minutes to complete, was sent out to a random sample of 4,300 French Canadian viewers of "Octo-Puce" in November of 1983. The response rate was over 50%, for a sample of 2,157 respondents. Of the sample, 1,157 respondents did not own a home computer, 120 had been using one for over a year, and another 880 were recent adopters, having purchased a home computer in the preceding year.

In November 1985 a follow-up questionnaire was sent to those who had been classified as recent adopters ($n = 880$), of these almost half ($n = 403$) were returned. A series of in-depth interviews were conducted in eighteen households chosen from this group, including 32 adults and 28 children, each of whom were each questionned separately. The variables selected for study included (a) sociodemographic, (b) media consumption, (c) motivations and perceptions, (d) technological antecedents, (e) information sources, (f) decision-making, (g) personal use, (h) interpersonal environment, (i) impact, and (j) perception of technology and society. This chapter draws on the results of our study of the original 880 respondents, the follow-up questionnaire, and the 18 families interviewed.

RESULTS

Although the purpose of this chapter is to present an overview of our results, detailed longitudinal data is referred to in order to illustrate the more tangible features therein. The reader might want to consult other reports (Caron, Giroux, & Douzou, 1985, 1987) and an article (Caron, Giroux, & Douzou, 1986) for more detailed statistical data.

The sociodemographic profile of our respondents concords in general with the results of other studies. On the whole, the adopters in our sample are somewhat better educated and slightly above the average population in income, although less so than the adopters in earlier studies. In contrast to other studies, we found our original sample contained a greater variety of occupations, including professional and education-related employments (primarily grade-school teachers) and both skilled and nonskilled workers. Our sample also contained a higher proportion of women among adopters (one in three) than reported in earlier studies. The results appear to indicate that this technology is no longer the exclusive object of innovators or early adopters and that computers as innovations have begun their diffusion into the first strata of what Rogers has termed the "early majority."

Motivations and Information Sources

Various dimensions of the decision to purchase the computer were explored, such as who bought it, and under what circumstances was the purchase made? Similarly, we wanted to know what motivated the purchase, was it the result of careful deliberation and related to some prior initial contact with the technology? On the whole, less than 25% of our sample reported having prior experience with computers. Typically, we found that it was the elder male (68%) of the household who actually purchased the computer, although in many of the adopting households, the decision to purchase seems to have been encouraged by a widely held conviction about the technology's importance by the whole family.

For many of our respondents, a desire to learn the basics of the technology, how it works, and how to use it appears to have taken on the dimensions of a sort of obligation, a necessary concession to "keeping up with trends" in a rapidly evolving society. This sentiment was even more striking in those households with children. Many parents voiced a concern that their children should be "prepared for the future" and, if possible, "ahead of the others." Not surprisingly then, a large proportion of respondents purchased their computer in order to acquire a certain computer "literacy."

When questioned about the principal application foreseen prior to purchase, learning to program and word processing were cited by about one third and one fifth of our respondents respectively (see Fig. 8.1). Use of children's educational software was also mentioned, along with games and entertainment, although by only a very small portion. This, as we shall see, was in sharp contrast with the patterns of use observed later on.

In addition to seeking a profile characteristics of adopters and nonadopters and motivations surrounding the initial purchase of the computer, we were equally concerned with measuring the effect of other variables, such as the role of interpersonal and media sources of information about computers.

Interpersonal and Media Sources

In 1983, our respondents reported a wide variety of sources of computer information, the most prominent of which were the media. This was not surprising given few could identify friends, family, or colleagues at work on whom they could rely for such information. Prior exposure to computers in the workplace for example was reported by only one fourth of

8. HOME COMPUTERS IN CANADA

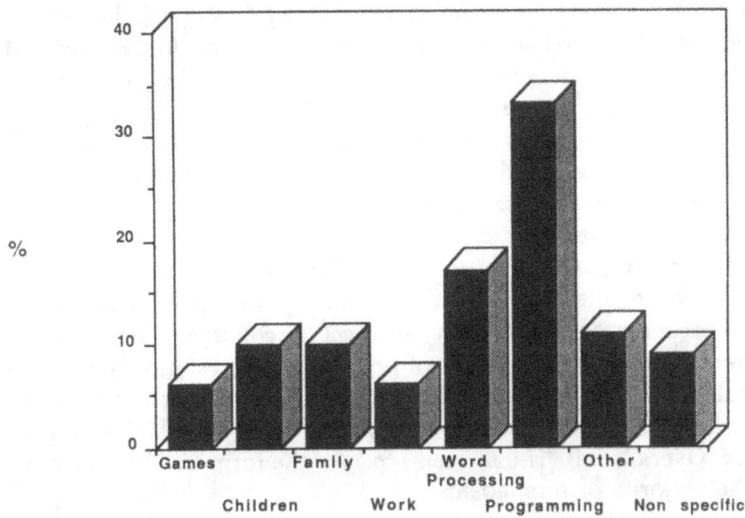

FIG. 8.1. Main anticipated uses of the homecomputer before purchase

our respondents and no longer appeared to be the main source of influence and information cited in some earlier studies. One should also take into account that at that time the media were highly promoting homecomputers.

Buying Informed, Buying Naive: Predominant factors

Given the wide variety of variables that can be used to delineate the purchase and adoption/rejection process, it is difficult to describe tendencies in absolute terms. Notwithstanding these difficulties, it is nevertheless possible to distinguish between two types of buyers, one that could be qualified as "informed," and the other "naive." The naive adopters are distinguishable by their relative inexperience and lack of contact with the technology, by their predominant dependence on the media for information about the technology, by a higher tendency towards the purchase of less sophisticated (Vic-20, Timex/Sinclair) machines, and a lower incidence of reported specific applications prior to purchase.

Conversely, the informed adopters were more likely to have had prior contact with the technology (typically at work), to have purchased what was at the time somewhat more sophisticated computer models (TRS-80, Commodore 64), to have reported a higher incidence of interpersonal sources of information, and a higher incidence of specific, predetermined applications prior to purchase.

A Ritual of Discovery

If there was one consistent feature among all the households we queried, it would be what we have labeled the *ritual of discovery*. This term refers to the highly charged enthusiasm for the new arrival in the house. Most, if not all of our respondents reported some or all of the features of this "ritual." The most tangible was a prolonged and intense "usage" of the machine during the first few weeks of its introduction. Other features of the ritual include a certain amount of competition among family members for time on the machine, and other similar tensions arising from one or more member's excessive control. In some cases, this ritual preceded a rise of tensions dividing spouses, and parents and their children. Although fervent interest in the new computer was particularly manifest where the head of the household was concerned, it also seemed to affect the children — for some of whom the new computer was a source of pride and added status. In some cases, the rules aimed at regulating the usage of the computer were established following what seems to have been perceived as the children's abuse of games. Overall, this "ritual" seems to take the form of a "rite of passage" for the majority of respondents.

Seeing the Computer in a New Light

The "ritual" of discovery, experienced by so many of our respondents, is an indicator of the symbolic, almost mythical importance typically bestowed upon the computer. We were curious to determine, however, how long lasting the computer's symbolic importance would be. In our analysis, then, we probed for evidence of a "reappropriation" or "redefinition" of the innovation.

In the most general terms, we found three patterns of subsequent behavior with respect to the computer, based on the original 1983 sample of owners: A first group of households (almost one fifth) had completely stopped using their computer, whereas a second group, the majority (three in five), had maintained use of their original computer. Finally, a third group (about one in five) bought a second personal computer (PC). Once again, one must be cautious in interpreting the preceding proportions. Considering the nature of our sample, these findings are more significant of the trends than of their distribution in the total population of home computer adopters. Of the group that had abandoned their computer, we found a significantly higher incidence of those buyers we had previously qualified as "naive." Indeed, the combination of high expectations, unsophisticated computers, and a naive approach to the purchase seemed to be the most telling attributes of this group. Our respondents cited dissatisfactions related to a variety of causes, most prominent being the lack of practical uses, technical limitations of their system, and the unavailability of software, cost of servicing, and other market-related complaints.

Of those who had purchased a second, we found that a substantial portion (almost half) of these second computers were intended for one person's exclusive use, rather than uses including other members of the family. In this group, we found an even distribution of makes and models ranging from the medium-powered Commodore 64 and TRS-80; to the more powerful IBM and Apple models. For many, the second investment was made in an effort to improve on the technical weaknesses of their previous system, to gain access to a greater choice of software, and to open up the possibility of doing some of their work at home.

One of the more interesting features that characterize the "second PC" group was that the majority paid much more personal attention to the second purchase than to their previous purchase decision. A substantial majority of these respondents report having had prior experience or a demonstration of their second choice before the purchase, as compared to the relatively small proportion (23%) who had had similar exposure prior to their first purchase in 1983. With respect to sources of information, we found that the influence of the media was much higher in 1983 (64%) than the proportion in 1985 (14%). Congruently, a much higher proportion of this "second PC" group cited having consulted a friend or colleague in 1985 (64%), compared with 1983 (27%). In summary, then, the decision for this group appears as a considerably more "personal" one, based on a higher degree of individual choice and learning, and in which one's interpersonal contacts play an increasingly pivotal role.

Telling Variables

In comparing these three groups, we found that for the most part a person's sociodemographic characteristics were not good variables in terms of predicting eventual outcome. Indeed the only significant variable among the ones we tested (education, income, employment, etc.), was the gender of our respondents, with women being found in significantly higher numbers among the group that had stopped using their computer. Although prior exposure to computers at work was not a significant variable in terms of predicting outcome in 1983, we found two concomitant trends in 1985 that point to exposure at work as a growing, if not yet significant factor. In general, a higher proportion of our 1983 respondents who would subsequently continue using their computer, or buy a second, reported having used computers at work in the original survey.

Patterns of Use and Family Dynamics

The three groups distinguish themselves most clearly in terms of the total time spent on the home computer. Figure 8.2 clearly indicates that even in 1983, a seriation of these groups was observable. The most active use was observed in the "second PC" group, followed by the "original PC" and "abandoned" groups in consecutive order. In 1985, the total amount of time spent using the computer increased slightly for the "second PC" group, whereas decreasing slightly for the "original PC" group.

An examination of the types of use by these three groups is equally revealing (Fig. 8.3). In 1983, the group that was to eventually cease using their computer reported games and learning the technology as their most frequent types of use (80%), whereas work-related uses were noticeably less present (6%). In contrast, the other two groups reported a similar exploitation of games and time spent learning the computer, but a much higher frequency of work-related uses (14% for the "original PC" and 20% for the "second PC" groups).

Between 1983 and 1985, the evolution of uses reported by the latter two groups reveals that entertainment and learning activities were to decrease as a function of the increase in work-related applications. A significant increase in work-related applications was particularly visible in the "second PC" group, eventually comprising more than 50% of the total time spent on the computer. Family and household applications such as budgeting and calendaring were reported with marginal, although similar, frequency by the two groups.

Finally, it is important to underline the heterogenous nature of this "original PC" group. One third of this group purchased additional equipment for their original computer, and a subsequent comparative analysis shows

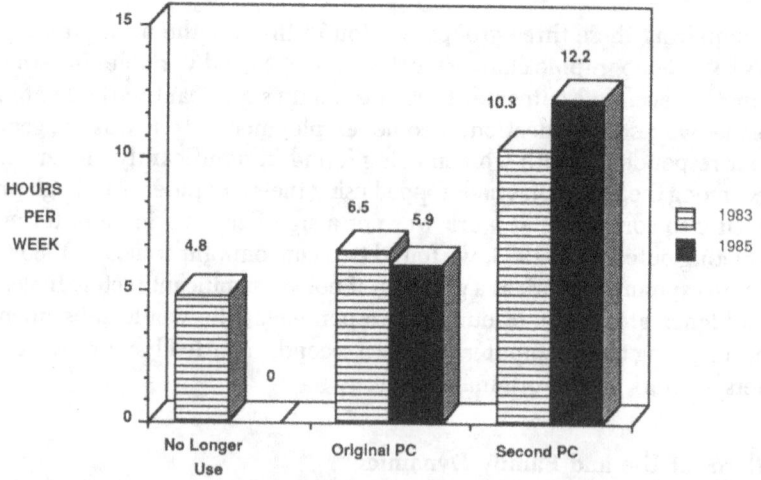

FIG. 8.2. Change over time of the weekly use of the home computer by different various types of adopters

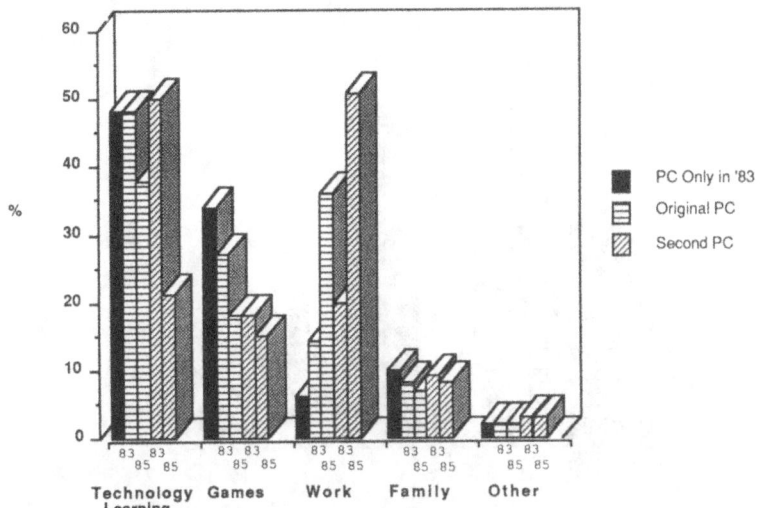

FIG. 8.3. Change over time in terms of the different types of uses by different types of adopters

that they are similar to the rest of their group in every respect except in terms of their more frequent work-related applications. It would appear, then, that the possibility of applying the computer to one's occupation is a determining factor in the appropriation process. Indeed, the presence of computers at work is a telling variable; in the "original PC" group, the proportion of owners using a computer at work increased from 14% to 24% between 1983 and 1985 and increased more sharply (from 15% to 44%) in the same period for the "second PC" group.

In 1983, we noted that the spouse in the household spent significantly less time on the computer than the person who actually purchased it, the same holding true for both those who would continue using their computer, and those households where a second computer would eventually be purchased. In 1985, however, a comparison of the total amount of time spent on the computer by the spouses in these two groups reveal a divergent evolution: although the spouses in the "second PC" group report spending a total of almost 4 hours a week on the computer, those of the "original PC" group spent only 2 hours a week. The evolution in specific types of uses by the spouses, however, follows patterns very similar to those reported by the main users: that is, decrease over time in learning the technology and games, and concomitant increases in work-related uses. The only divergence between these two groups was that those with a second computer attached significantly greater importance to family uses (Fig. 8.4).

We were also interested to examine the use of the computer by our respondents' children to see if there were any tangible differences between groups

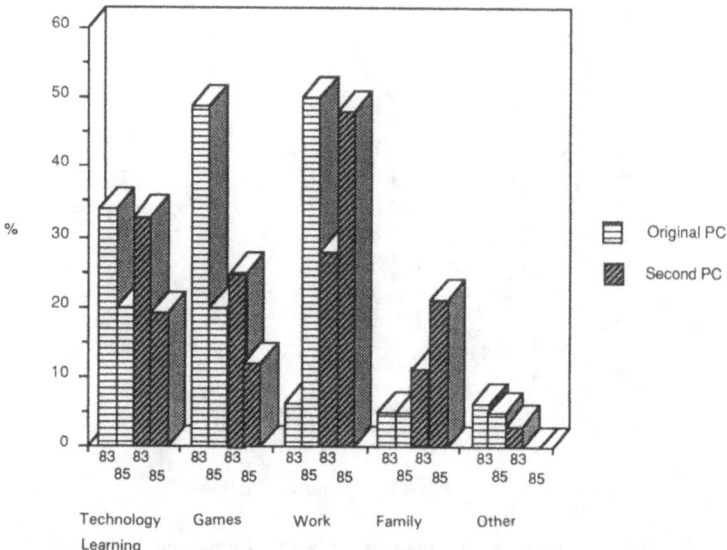

FIG. 8.4. Change over time of the different types of uses by the spouse

in terms of their children's orientation. In 1983, we discovered that the children in those households destined to maintain use of their systems devoted slightly more time (3.7 hours) in a week to the computer than those who lived in households that were to purchase a second (3.1 hours).

In 1985, however, those children of the "second PC" group spent more time (4.8 hours) in a week on the computer than those in the other group (3.7 hours). Similarly to their parents, the children in both groups report an increase of time spent on work-related uses, and a decrease in games. The only divergence reported with their parents' patterns of use was that children in both groups indicated an increase over this 2-year period in time spent learning the technology.

Attitudes Toward Information Technology

We were also interested in following the evolution of attitudes toward computers in terms of our respondents' assessment of the potential impact on their personal lives, and in terms of their assessment of its importance for society at large. It is interesting to note that whatever their profile, our respondents seem to have generally favorable attitudes toward this technology. Indeed, enthusiasm for the technology appears to be directly related to the extent to which a respondent has invested in his or her own computer. Thus, the "second PC" group are practically unanimous in the high degree of personal satisfaction they feel about their system (98%) in contrast to the two other groups (original PC 86% and "no longer use" groups 63%). The "second PC" group also felt considerably more at ease (94%) with their computer than the other two groups (73% and 48% respectively). Congruently, those who had invested further were also more likely to believe that the technology was going to be a learning tool, a source of entertainment, and a complement to their work. It is interesting to note that in 1983, those that were to become members of the groups that continued to use their personal computer were, at the time, also more favorable in their assessment of the technology than those who were destined to cease using their computers.

In terms of defining and identifying any tangible "impact" on those adopting households, we discovered, as in other studies, that in the final analysis, it is preponderantly those media-related activities that were most likely to be affected by the presence and continuing use of the personal computer. The tendency toward a decrease in time spent reading and listening to the radio, first reported following the introduction of the computer into the home, seemed to maintain itself over this 2-year period we studied. The time spent watching television, continued its decline — even more for those who purchased a second computer. Other nonmedia activities did not appear to be significantly affected. In 1985, those that continued an active use of their computer noticed changes as a result of their adoption of the technology. In general, the changes reported seem to be related to the development of what can be identified as a new pastime, substituting more traditional ones such as watching television, collecting stamps, and so on.

We were intrigued by those respondents who felt that the presence of the computer had structured not only their own way of thinking but also that of their children. This reported change appeared mainly in our qualitative data, and is a fascinating and potentially important yet unexplored dimension of the computer's ultimate impact.

CONCLUSION

In light of this more complex vision of the integration process, our analysis of the home computer appears to confirm the innovation's symbolic importance. For a significant proportion of our respondents, integrating this technology into their lives would appear to be originally motivated more by a sense of obligation than by a genuine and individual interest. Investing in this technology, then, is perceived as a necessary concession to keeping up with a society in transition and, in a certain sense, indexes both a tacit acknowledgment and a legitimization of the projected importance of the computer. Three features of our findings illustrate this.

First, the most tangible motivation cited by our respondents at the time of their initial purchase was simply to facilitate the acquisition of what can be called computer *literacy*. Indeed, many of our respondents feel that this new literacy will be as indispensable to life in the future as reading and writing are today.

Second, our analysis of the applications cited by our respondents prior to their first purchase reveals that a large majority foresaw no specific application for their new acquisition. The computer's symbolic importance, and perhaps the concomitant importance of the new literacy appear to have been established in the minds of many of our respondents prior to any tangible experience with the technology on their part.

Third, the decision to purchase a computer is only rarely taken by an individual independently of the other members of the household. Although it would be misleading to state that the decision is uniformly consensual, it is nonetheless apparent that the purchase of a home computer is often motivated by the family's collective perception of the technology's importance.

In the light of this finding, we were not surprised then to discover that 2 years later, certain families had lost all interest in their computer, although this loss of interest is by not means indicative of a dominant reaction (18%). A much more significant proportion (64%) are still using their computer with more or less the same frequency. In contrast, for the third group (18%), the computer took on a sufficiently important role to warrant the purchase of a second. For these respondents, their motivations are most often directly related to their occupation. The importance of the "potential reappropriation" (Mercier et al., 1984) of the innovation would appear to be verified in light of our findings; those respondents who eventually succeeded in integrating the computer into their daily lives did so as a result of an on-going process of exploration and reappraisal.

It would be mistaken, in our opinion, to describe this redefinition process as either well-articulated or deliberate. As some authors have argued, this integration process is more tactical than strategic (Proulx & Bordeleau, 1986), resembling more an improvised response to a dynamic situation than a premeditated or planned process. Integrating this technology reveals itself to be largely dictated by trial and error, and highly affected by the idiosyncratic experiences of the particular user. In summary, then, the diffusion/adoption process is largely affected by the social context surrounding its emergence, a context that intervenes forcibly, albeit in a subtle and unstructured fashion.

From this perspective, we are inclined to argue against the essentially deterministic perspective of other studies in which the technology develops autonomously, yet paradoxically catalyses dramatic social changes. However untenable this latter view, the more neutral perspective that would subordinate the technology and its influence to the uses made of it does not fully account for the phenomenon either. Both of these theoretical perspectives suggest a causal interpretative model. More than a response to social change, the process of integrating this technology is visibly driven by the discourse surrounding its emergence. The symbolic image of the computer is one powerful enough that it can initially provoke a substantial commitment (purchase). Subsequently, it is the user that must rearticulate the technology's original function in terms of one's own motivations and needs if this commitment is to persist. In summary, technology behaves as a social product, conceived in one manner and subsequently altered as it diffuses into the social context.

ACKNOWLEDGMENTS

The authors would like to express their gratitude to Dr. James R. Taylor for his comments on preliminary drafts of this chapter. They would also like to thank John Patterson, graduate student, for his contribution to this study. The research reported therein was funded by Communications-Canada, under the French Language Centers of Excellence Development and Promotion Program.

REFERENCES

Bolter, J. D. (1984). *Turing's man: Western culture in the computer age.* Chapel Hill, NC: University of North Carolina Press.

Caron, A. H., Giroux, L., & Douzou, S. (1985). *Analyse de la diffusion des micro-ordinateurs domestiques et de leur intégration à nos modes de vie* (The diffusion of home microcomputers and their integration into our daily life). Département de communication, Université de Montréal, Canada.

Caron, A. H., Giroux, L., & Douzou, S. (1986). Diffusion et adoption des nouvelles technologies: le micro-ordinateur domestique (Diffusion and adoption of new technologies: The home microcomputer). *Canadian Journal of Communication, 11*(4), 369-389.

Caron, A. H., Giroux, L., & Douzou, S. (1987). *L'appropriation du "virage technologique"; le cas du micro-ordinateur.* (Adapting to the challenge of technology: the case of the home microcomputer). Département de communication, Université de Montréal, Canada.

Christian, C. (1973). Home video systems: a revolution? *Journal of Broadcasting, 17*(2), 223-234.

CROP, Bulletin CROP (1985). *Sondage omnibus.* (Omnibus Survey) Rapport statistique sur les médias québécois, Montréal, Canada.

Day, K., Barnett, G., Kim, K., & Miller, D. (1983). *The diffusion of home computers: Differences between adopters, planners and non-adopters.* Buffalo, NY: Department of Communication, State University of New York at Buffalo.

De Certeau, M. (1980). *L'invention du quotidien: les arts de faire* (Defining everyday life). Paris: UGE, collection 10/12.

Dickerson, M. D. & Gentry, J. W. (1983). Characteristics of adopters and non-adopters of home computers. *Journal of consumer research, 10,* 225-234.

Dutton, W. H., Kovaric, P., & Steinfield, C. (1983). *The social dynamics of personal computing: The use of computing in the home.* Unpublished paper in Information Program Division for Information and Technology of the National Science Foundation. Los Angeles: Annenberg School of Communications, University of Southern California.

Emnid-Institut Gmbh & Co. (1985). *Einstellungen zum Microcomputer: 6 Lander im Vergleich.* (Integration of Microcomputer: comparison of six countries). Frankfurt.

Flichy, P. (1980). *Les industries de l'imaginaire pour une analyse économique des media.* (The image industries. An Economic Analysis of Media). Presses universitaires de Grenoble, Institut national de l'audio-visuel.

Gumpert, G., & Cathcart, R. (1982). *Intermedia (interpersonal communication in a media world.)* (2nd ed.). Oxford, England: Oxford University Press.

Mercier, P. A., Plassard, F., & Scardigli, V. (1984). *La société digitale-les nouvelles technologies au futur quotidien.* (Digital society-new technology for our future lives). Paris: Editions du seuil.

Muller, D. (1977). Personal computers in home and business applications. *Computers and People*, December, 12–20.

Pool, I. de Sola. (1978). *The social impact of the telephone* (2nd ed.). Cambridge, MA; MIT Press.

Proulx, S., & Bordeleau, P., (1986). *Stratégies d'appropriation de la culture informatique dans une societe d'information.* (Appropriation strategies of the computer culture). Congrès international d'éducation et de technologie, Vancouver.

Rice, R. (1984). *The new media: communication, research and technology.* Berkeley, CA: Sage.

Rogers, E. (1983). *Diffusion of innovations* (3rd ed.). New York: The Free Press.

Rogers, E., Daley, H., & Wu, T. (1982). *The diffusion of home computers.* Stanford, CA: Institute for communication research, Stanford University.

Turing, A. M. (1936). On computable numbers, with an application to the Entscheidung problem. *Proceedings of the London Mathematics Society* Series 2, 42, 230–265.

USA-Today (1985). High-Tech equipment at home, *USA Today, October 21,* 1.

Venkatesh, A., Vitalari, N., & Gronhaug, K. (1983). *Household Product Adoption and Changes in Allocation of time: the case of home computers.* Bergen, Norway: Graduate school of management (Irvine), Norwegian school of economics.

9

Adoption and Use of Videocassette Recorders in the Third World

Joseph D. Straubhaar
Michigan State University

Douglas A. Boyd
University of Kentucky

Videocassette recorders (VCRs) are undergoing an explosive growth or diffusion in a number of Third World countries, throughout Africa, Asia, the Middle East, the Caribbean, and Latin America. At least two Arab nations, Saudi Arabia and Kuwait, at 80%-90% household penetration of VCRs, far surpass even the United Kingdom and the United States in the number of VCRs owned. In some Third World countries, such as the Arabian Gulf States, many people are wealthy enough that acquisition of VCRs is not surprising. When it is considered that a number of less wealthy countries also have high numbers of VCRs, it becomes clear that the reasons for VCR adoption are broader than purchasing power.

This chapter explores two interacting levels of causation or explanation for Third World VCR diffusion. First are systemic reasons, such as government tariff policies that make VCRs more expensive, and broadcast policy and media structures that produce certain types of media content and limit others. Second are aggregated interests of individuals in controlling and diversifying their media comsumption. Among the reasons for VCR diffusion that will be explored are the audiences' desire to add diversity to "television" viewing, particularly in entertainment; the desire to circumvent system/government controls on content; and the general desire for greater personal control over the variety of possible informational and entertainment viewing. Such viewer needs will be contrasted with VCR costs (largely determined by government tariff policy) against income or purchasing power to consider the marginal utility of VCRs to Third World viewers, who have other pressing needs to be met.

VCR CONTEXT: ELECTRONIC MEDIA IN THE THIRD WORLD

As the media most likely to reach remote and often illiterate mass audiences, first radio and then television have been invested with considerable hopes and fears in most Third World nations. There even more than in most industrialized countries, electronic media have been seen both as "magic multipliers" of educational/developmental information and as instruments of political mobilization and control.

Mass media in the Third World have often been overemphasized in development planning. Lerner (1958) emphasized the role of media in creating empathy and awareness of the outside world and breaking into and changing traditional ways. Rogers (1983) emphasized the media's ability to communicate innovations or new ideas essential to change. Others, such as Schramm (1964), and Pool (1961), also emphasized the value of media in development.

However, beginning in the late 1960s and early 1970s, a number of researchers began to criticize this "dominant paradigm." Beltran (1978), Rogers (1978), and others criticized simple receiver-oriented diffusion paradigms and highlighted the need to look at the structure and context of diffused messages. In some contexts, development messages came to be seen as irrelevant or even counterproductive and anticipated effects shifted from rising expectations to rising frustrations (Rogers, 1978).

Western influence on Third World communication contexts came in for further criticism. Pasquali (1976) and Dorfman and Mattelart (1975) looked at the role of imported media structures and media content in maintaining capitalist systems, international relations of dependency, and "First World" ideological elements, such as consumerism, racism, and sex roles (Beltran, 1978) considered inappropriate for many Third World nations. Some in the United States such as Schiller (1969) and Wells (1972), began directly to criticize the U.S. role in exporting media products, advertising and, technology to Third World nations. Nordenstreng and Varis (1973) documented the flow and criticized the role of imported media products, particularly television programs, and wire-service news was examined by Boyd-Barrett (1980) and others.

Another wave of research looked at the influence of imported broadcasting models on the Third World, particularly the British (BBC public service license fee-based systems), the American (tending to commercial finance and a mix of libertarian and social responsibility ethics), and French (more state control and mixed government–commercial financing). Such studies were done by Tunstall (1977), Read (1976), Katz and Wedell (1977), and Lee (1980).

It was also clear that in many cases, models from abroad were modified

9. VCR IN THE THIRD WORLD

substantially, as in the case of the American model in Brazil, for example (Mattos, 1984; Straubhaar, 1984). Other models were copied less extensively (U.S.S.R. influence on Eastern Europe and some Third World nations; Nasserite "mobilization" systems in the Arab world, etc.). In all, a number of diverging systems appeared. Third World systems can now be found to fit all of the "four theories of the press" (Siebert, Schramm, & Peterson, 1956) as well as the more recent "development journalism" model (McPhail, 1981; Rosenblum, 1979). Several of these Third World broadcasting tendencies are particularly significant for VCR diffusion. Those include the issues of centralized versus individual control over content, education versus entertainment in content, and national content promotion versus desires for free flow of content across borders. Each of these issues has system/structure, policy, and audience demand aspects, which we try to relate to VCR diffusion.

Why VCRs Are Being Adopted at a Rapid Rate

The spread of VCRs is still a recent phenomenon, albeit an explosive and rapid one. Preliminary empirical research identifies several factors involved in VCR diffusion: price, variations in price due to government restrictions, income and income distribution, the content of broadcast television, the diversity of entertainment media available, and, for minority cultures, the degree to which audiences' languages and cultures are represented in the broadcast system (Boyd & Straubhaar, 1985).

The first three variables are linked. If prices are low, broader and lower income groups are more likely to be able to purchase a VCR. This is increasingly the case, as VCR prices have continued to decline. Price reduction and available discretionary income are behind the explosive growth of VCRs and have made them a "mass medium" (in that large audiences see the same nonbroadcast material using VCRs) in a number of countries. Where prices remain high, it is usually due to attempts by governments to discourage VCR acquisition by imposing tariffs or import barriers. Where national policy dictates that VCRs be locally manufactured, as in Brazil, prices increase as much as 200% or 300%. Such barriers are widely violated by smuggling, but barriers increase the price and restrict access to VCRs (Ganley & Ganley, 1986; Heeter, 1984). In several countries a significant proportion of VCRs are smuggled (Ganley & Ganley, 1986). In Brazil, roughly 66% of existing VCRs are estimated to have been brought in from outside, primarily by smugglers (*Veja*, 1986). Even where VCRs are manufactured, as in Brazil, local supplies may not meet demand.

Even when prices have not been artificially increased by tariffs or barriers, the marginal cost of a VCR is still very high for an individual, family, or even a village in most Third World countries. That is, a much larger proportion of income will be required to buy a VCR than in nations with higher per capita incomes. Therefore, the marginal utility of the VCR must also be correspondingly higher. The prospective VCR owner in most Third World areas has little discretionary income and therefore the machine must offer something sufficient to make it prized above competing goods, like washing machines, refrigerators, vehicles, and so on. One of the most impressive aspects of the VCR boom is that the video machines do surpass these alternatives for many. For that to happen, the VCR must be in a position to add greatly to the gratification, status, or quality of life of the viewer.

According to correlational studies carried out by Heeter (1984) and Straubhaar and Lin (this volume), one of the variables most significantly associated with worldwide VCR penetration is the diversity of what is available on broadcast or cable television. Both the number of channels, per se, and more content-oriented measures of diversity tend to be negatively correlated with VCR penetration in poorer Third World countries where VCRs are primarily used for playing nonbroadcast materials to add diversity to television viewing.

In the Third World, as well as in industrialized nations, VCR penetration must be put into the larger perspective of video media competition (Lhoest, 1983; Noam, 1985). In some wealthier countries, such as the United States or Britain, or in a few of the more media-rich developing countries, VCRs seem to be used primarily for time-shifting. In wealthier countries, VCR penetration is positively correlated with measures of broadcast diversity, number of TV channels, and cable-TV availability (Straubhaar & Lin, this volume). However, in most Third World countries, VCRs are diffused most rapidly where television viewers feel they are not well served by what is broadcast, in short, where the "marginal utility" of VCRs for adding diversity is high. In poorer countries, VCR use is negatively correlated with measures of TV diversity (Straubhaar & Lin, this volume). The explanation seems to be that in those countries where resources must be more carefully guarded, the marginal utility of VCRs is lower, given a more adequate diversity of content available on broadcast television.

In either case, VCRs offer greater personal control over what is watched. VCRs enable owners to personalize their video viewing and better meet their own perceived needs or interests. To some degree, this is simply a Third World manifestation of what has long been predicted in communication research, a more active audience that seeks to gratify its own needs with selective media exposure (Rosengren, Wenner, & Palmgreen, 1985).

Personalization or individuation of video consumption via VCRs enables wider variety or diversity among the programs that an individual, family, or larger group may choose to watch. Still, some patterns do emerge. Above all, VCRs seem to be predominantly used to add entertainment material where relatively little entertainment is available on broadcast television or where certain kinds of entertainment are not broadcast. In analyzing why audiences seek entertainment Atkin (1985) noted that there are both positive drives for content that is enjoyable and negative selection to avoid or compensate for tension/relaxation, boredom/killing time, loneliness/companionship, and escape from problems.

This research-based profile of VCR diffusion patterns matches us relatively well with the pattern and context of Third World media use. Some major relationships between VCR diffusion and media patterns deserve further discussion, however.

Centralization, Broadcasting, and VCRs

At least until recently, in most approaches developmental use of the electronic mass media was seen as properly or perhaps inevitably centralized. Ambitious experiments, such as India's Satellite Instructional Television Experiment (SITE), tended to rely on centralized production and distribution of messages (Mody, 1979). Although evaluations showed that one of the more successful parts of the overall SITE project was a regional production and broadcast operation in Kheda, that part was also the most politically and bureaucratically problematic, and has, in fact, been aborted (Chiruvolu, 1986). The great political advantage of SITE was, it seems, the opportunity offered to national leaders to communicate more directly with remote parts of the country not previously reached by mass communication.

As with the Kheda project, newer theoretical research and field work carried out in development communication shows that decentralized media have greater effectiveness in reaching and holding the audience (Chiruvolu, 1986). Other work with community radio stations in the Caribbean, Latin America, and Africa indicates that Third World audiences react very favorably to media that offer the possibility of greater local feedback or interaction (Jamison & McAnany, 1978; White, 1976). Nevertheless, the temptation for Third World leaders to centralize and control broadcasting is very strong. A recent overview by Head (1985) placed most Third World systems in the general category of "authoritarian" (taken from Siebert, Schramm, & Peterson's, 1956, four theories of the press) or simply government-dominated. Few national systems exhibit the kind of "totalitarian" control exercised by the U.S.S.R., but relatively few are willing to entrust the media themselves with final responsibility for content as the "libertarian" or "social responsibility" models might prescribe.

The detailed study of Third World broacasting conducted by Katz and Wedell (1977) indicates that despite an initial tendency to copy American, British, or French broadcast models, modifications had been widespread, particularly in the area of political control. In particular, they noted that the British ideal of BBC-style independent corporations had not fared well in the often unstable politics of many former British colonies. Even such relatively democratic states as Nigeria and India had moved broadcasting either into government ministries or under much closer control. Similarly, Latin American countries that had used the U.S. model of private commercial systems often showed far more assertion of government control over content, both reactively in terms of censorship and proactively in terms of guiding content (Alisky, 1983).

One of the effects VCRs may have is to challenge the prevailing system of government controls on television. (Audio cassette recorders are doing much the same thing in radio broadcasting.) VCRs circumvent both development use and political control of television by bringing de facto media decentralization. They put the control of programming in the hands of the audience. What VCR owners choose to watch (and what is most available to them) seems likely to circumvent and frustrate both development programs' intentions to educate them and leaders' desires to control the information content available to them.

VCRs and Broadcast Content Diversity

Centralized broadcasting systems seem to create structural conditions that lead to a desire for greater individual control via VCRs or other means. A related issue is the direction or control of content inherent in mass media, but more explicit and clear in many Third World countries. In most Third World states outside of Latin America, broadcast media systems were created with goals consistent with the British public service concept, the French notion of cultural nationalism and political control, the "development journalism" concept of cooperation with development programs, or Soviet- or Chinese-style total involvement with government programs. All of these goals exclude certain kinds of content that viewers might desire. In particular, few of these systems and patterns of media goals include strong emphasis on entertainment.

Because VCRs provide a wider variety of programs that an individual, family, or larger group may choose to watch, it is not surprising that they are popular in societies that traditionally control broadcasting. In Indonesia and Malaysia, for example, "the public seeks video because of the limited fare of the state television service" (Lent, 1985, p. 8). VCRs seem to be used to add entertainment material where relatively little is available on broadcast television or where certain kinds of entertainment are not broadcast (Straubhaar & Lin, this volume).

In places such as Saudi Arabia, where television has been highly didactic, stressing religion, education, cultural improvement, or political persuasion, almost any type of entertainment programming is snapped up for

9. VCR IN THE THIRD WORLD

VCR consumption. What tends to be most readily adopted are feature films, followed by television series taped off air (Boyd, 1985a; Lent, 1985; Ogan, 1985; Straubhaar, 1986). Most often these are from America, followed by Europe, then local or regional productions (cf. Varis, 1984).

Even in more entertainment-oriented broadcast systems, specific kinds of entertainment are frequently downplayed or prohibited. Perhaps the most visible and controversial example is pornography. Pornography, or even less explicit sexual content, is particularly worrisome to authorities in Islamic countries such as those in Asia and the Arab world (Boyd, 1985b; Lent, 1985). Various case studies show that pornography frequently dominates VCR viewing, particularly while it is still a new phenomenon in a given country or area. Even so, the novelty effect tends to wear off and the frequency of pornography viewing often declines (*Intermedia*, 1983), particularly if there is evidence that children are watching when parents are not at home.

Another controversial type of programming is news or political information on videotape. A study by Ganley and Ganley (1986) focused on the potential of VCRs for allowing politically challenging or subversive material to bypass national censorship and counter national points of view or propaganda. They found the political potential of VCRs to be considerable. The main case to date is the Ayatollah Khomeini's use of audio cassettes to spread opposition to the Shah of Iran and to create support for his Islamic revolution. The Philippine opposition movement, led by Corazon Aquino, also used videotapes of foreign coverage of her husband's asassination to accentuate indignation about the slaying and opposition to Ferdinand Marcos (Lent, 1985). Marcos' supporters later disseminated from his exile in Hawaii a videotape showing him "physically fit" in connection with an apparent coup attempt.

Other less controversial genres of material are also sometimes limited by broadcast policy. A number of countries limit showings of some "Rambo"-type American adventure films and series that are considered too violent, but that remain popular with sizeable parts of the audience. Indian movies are similarly popular but proscribed in Pakistan because of conflict between the two nations and, in some cases, because of sexual content (Lent, 1985).

VCRs also play a visible role in supplying programs wanted by minority audiences (e.g., interest groups, such as martial artists or bird watchers, who want specialized material). Perhaps more significantly in the Third World, VCRs can help ethnic or linguistic minorities find material in their languages, catering to their cultures. For example, the Chinese community in several Southeast Asian nations is not directly served by broadcast television, which as a matter of national policy tends to emphasize the dominant language of the nation. In Malaysia, for example, the broadcast authorities acknowledge that they are losing the Chinese audience but are reluctant to modify their language policy and goals (Lent, 1985). English-speaking travelers are often catered to in hotels by in-house cable systems fed by VCRs with videotapes flown in from the United States or the United Kingdom, whereas a number of ethnic groups in those two countries use VCRs to watch television programs and recent movies from home (Dobrow, 1986).

Film/TV Program Flow and VCRs

A great deal of controversy in international debate has centered on the flow of films, recorded music, news agency reports, television programs, and other cultural products from country to country. In many cases, the impact of imported media on national/regional/local culture has been shown to be at least somewhat worrisome (Beltran, 1978; Boyd, 1985a; Straubhaar, 1984). One of the goals of broadcast policy is a number of countries has been to limit the inflow of foreign culture on film, music, and video, and to promote national production instead (McBride Commission, 1980). Even in Great Britain and Canada, imported material is limited to a certain proportion of broadcast time. However, as with the previous examples, this may pit government policy against the interests of individual viewers, who might prefer to watch imported material.

This conflict is accentuated as VCRs give individuals or ethnic minorities the ability selectively to import television programs, music videos, or films from other countries. As just noted, the importation of Chinese films into Malaysia and Indian films into Pakistan has already reached sufficiently significant levels to concern authorities there (Lent, 1985). Similar regional video flow is likely to increase from countries such as Egypt to more conservative Arabic-speaking nations (Boyd, 1985a).

Of most concern, however, is the likelihood that VCRs will add to the already pronounced flow of Anglo-American film, television, and music video material in English to Third World countries. Surveys of video rental shops by the authors in several countries in Latin America and the Middle East show that American movies (and television shows in the Middle East) dominate much of what is available for rent or exchange in shops or clubs. Several reasons for this phenomenon fit into the pattern of VCR diffusion. First, from the early days of cinema, American movies have tended to set a pattern for what is considered entertaining in many countries (Guback & Varis, 1984; Read, 1976; Tunstall, 1977). Second, relatedly, the stock of available films for either legal or pirated distribution via the VCR is highly dominated by American products, following years of avid U.S. exportation. Thus, when individuals look for entertainment to supplement viewing, the main option they may find, because of existing film and television distribution patterns, are American films and series recorded off air.

Third, the fact that many Third World countries are trying actively to reduce American and other media imports may repress an existing demand that has built up over the years.

VCRs and Third World Government Economic Measures

A last major area of Third World development policies related to VCR diffusion is government policy that affects prices of imports. Except in South Korea and more recently Brazil and India, VCRs are imported in the Third World. As Table 9.1 shows, as of 1984, VCR prices in a number of countries averaged about $400. That seems to have been the natural market price, except where extremely difficult trade conditions or government import policies raised prices.

Some governments deliberately set high taxes or tariffs on VCRs to restrict their importation. Means and motives are varied but they center on economic and political policies.

A number of governments, including non-Third World nations, such as the Soviet Union and France, have tried to restrict VCR imports out of fear of the kinds of cultural and political effects previously mentioned. However, flat prohibitions or restricted quotas have not worked very well in restricting VCRs. In many countries, VCRs are smuggled in in massive quantities (Ganley & Ganley, 1986). Such measures do raise prices, however, because the smuggled goods are usually more expensive. In some countries, such as India, governments have eventually stopped trying to keep VCRs out for political or cultural reasons and have moved to economic concerns about reducing imports.

Some countries, such as Brazil, India, and Egypt, want to create domestic VCR-producing industries in order to reduce imports. This follows from a general tendency, particularly among the larger Third World nations, to follow a policy of import substitution industrialization. This economics-based policy largely does not object to the consumption of goods per se. Rather, the objective is to avoid foreign exchange problems, create employment, and develop industry/technology bases in their own countries by substituting nationally manufactured goods for imports. In any case, this type of policy tends to raise prices. Cheaper imports are either blocked or heavily taxed, whereas locally manufactured goods, protected by such policies, tend to be more expensive.

For many smaller countries, the idea of producing or even assembling VCRs from "kits" of imported parts may not be feasible. Still, many of these countries see VCRs as luxury consumer items and tax them accordingly. This policy also raises prices.

Running against either import-substitution or tariff policies on VCRs is the overwhelming demand for them in a number of countries. Still, as we

TABLE 9.1.
VCR Penetration in 1984

Country	VCR Percentage of TV Houses[a]	VCR Percentage of Total[b]	No. TV Channels	Av. VCR Price
Algeria	*	*	1	–
Argentina	5***	1***	4	$ 850
Bahrain	79***	–	2	400
Bangladesh	1	*	1	1,000
Barbados	2	*	1	–
Brazil	11***	2***	5	1,000
Cameroon	–	*	0	2,300
Chile	4	1	5	800
China (PRC)	*	*	1	1,900
Colombia	25	2	2	1,950
Dominican Rep.	–	*	5	800
El Salvador	2	*	5	500
Egypt	4***	*	2	2,500
Ethiopia	8	*	1	1,100
Fiji	–	6	0	450
Ghana	8	*	1	700
Honduras	3	*	2	500
Hong Kong	27	8	4	400
India	29	*	1	800
Indonesia	6	*	1	–
Iran	13	1	1	–
Iraq	24	1	1	–
Israel	56	9	2	–
Jamaica	8	1	1	2,450
Jordan	30***	3***	2	2,100
Kenya	10	2	1	1,500
Kuwait	88***	55***	2	350
Lebanon	14	1	2	450
Liberia	5	*	1	1,000
Libya	84**	6**	2	–
Malaysia	30	3	3	400
Mali	*	*	0	–
Mexico	5	1	4	550
Nigeria	2	*	½	1,000
Oman	75	55	1	400
Pakistan	15	*	1	–
Panama	10	1	5	400
Peru	11	1	5	–
Philippines	14	1	3	400
Qatar	77***	25***	1	400
Saudi Arabia	75	–	2	400
Singapore	25	14	1	400
South Africa	20	2	1	–
South Korea	7**	1**	4	400

(Continued)

TABLE 9.1.
(Continued)

Country	VCR Percentage of TV Houses[a]	VCR Percentage of Total[b]	No. TV Channels	Av. VCR Price
Sri Lanka	5	*	2	
Sudan	*	*	2	2,000
Syria	10***	1	1	–
Tanzania	*	*	0	2,000
Taiwan	19	8	3	700
Thailand	9	*	4	–
Trinidad	47	9	1	500
United Arab E.	80	7	2	400
Uruguay	–	–	4	1,000
Venezuela	14	2	3	500
Yemen (North)	25***	3	1	650
Zaire	50+	1	2	1,000
Zambia	*	*	1	–

[a]This column shows the proportion of households with TV and VCRs.
[b]This column shows the proportion of VCRs to the total population of the country.
*Indicates less than one-half of 1%
**These data are from 1983.
***These data are from 1986. (All others are from 1984.)

have seen, demand for VCRs is not inflexible and largely depends on how satisfied audiences are with other media. If demand is not, in fact, extremely strong, then restrictions that raise prices can have the effect of reducing VCR diffusion considerably. In Brazil, for example, despite a higher GNP per capita than Colombia, VCR penetration is much lower (Table 9.1). This is partially due to greater diversity and "quality" of what is available on broadcast television, according to interviews by one of the authors (Straubhaar, this volume). However, to give economic factors their due, it seems that a revived economy in Brazil is leading to a greatly increased purchase of VCRs in 1986, not so much to substitute for broadcasting as to let owners create new content with cameras or to meet special interests in sports, health, or art films that are not released in the country (*Veja*, 1986).

This review of literature shows several phenomena, largely related to Third World media structures and media or economic policies, that create the conditions that in some cases lead to rapid adoption and use of VCRs. What has been written matches up reasonably well with the quantitative studies of VCR acquisition and diffusion that have been done to date. (See Straubhaar & Lin, this volume.)

VCR Ownership and Viewing Patterns

There are a variety of reasons why VCRs are popular in Third World countries. Although VCR ownership/access information is problematic, it is clear that VCRs are not spreading evenly in all countries or income groups.

Information about ownership of or access to VCRs is still incomplete. Governments are inefficient in collecting import and sales data. Even manufacturers' sales data are often misleading. Part of the problem is the widespread purchase of smuggled or black market VCRs. Ganley and Ganley (1986) reported both the importance of the black market to many economies and the particularly extensive sales of VCRs on the black market in countries as diverse as Burma, the People's Republic of China, Mexico, Nigeria, and the Soviet Union. If, for example, manufacturers' sales figures were accurate for Panama, a major smuggling point, almost all residents there would have a VCR (Ganley & Ganley, 1986). In the Arabian Gulf as much as 50% of imported machines are taken home by expatriate workers or smuggled by sea or land to other countries.

In some countries, market surveys have estimated VCR ownership on the basis of samples. In most other Third World countries, expert estimates are probably more accurate than official government or sales data.

VCR Penetration

Table 9.1 gives VCR penetration levels, as of 1984, the last year for which broadly comparable data were available. Newer data were used when available. Because VCR penetration seems to be inversely related to the number of television channels available and to the price of VCRs, these data are also supplied for comparison.

MECHANISMS OF VCR DIFFUSION

Software Sales

Given the demand, a number of new businesses have started to supply videotapes to very diverse audiences. Most tapes—75%–80% in many countries (*Variety*, various)—are pirated (i.e., copied illegally without compensation to copyright holders). Therefore, copying and sale of these tapes has become an underground cottage industry in the Third World. Even countries like the Soviet Union or France have been unable to stop illegal importation of VCRs, much less tapes of undesirable or illegally pirated material, which can be easily carried in a coat pocket (Lhoest, 1983; Smale, 1983). Even the most authoritarian or totalitarian developing-country governments have not been successful in controlling programs deemed contrary to national interests.

Most VCR software piracy is cross-border, typically involving bringing entertainment programming in from other countries (Ganley & Ganley,

1986; *Intermedia*, 1983). The Motion Picture Export Association of America (MPEAA) estimated in 1985 that its members had lost $700 million in potential theater ticket receipts because potential viewers in a number of countries watched U.S. movies on videotape instead of in movie houses. In just one country, Venezuela, where VCR penetration of households is 18%-20%, losses by MPEAA distributors were estimated at $20 million in 1981 alone (" 'Legal' homevid in Latino orbit," 1985). Depending on price, availability, and controls over what films are theatrically released, the option to see pirated films is a significant incentive to VCR adoption.

However, there are several Third World countries that have major film or television industries that produce video entertainment. In those countries, piracy via VCRs can be threatening to national film industries. In India and Egypt, for example, VCRs are a serious challenge to the national film industry. "Video parlors" show pirated films at cheaper prices than movie houses. The Indian parlors frequently show films before they are released in rural or suburban areas (Ninan & Singh, 1983).

Alternative Content

In some countries, significant use of VCRs is being made to create and view alternative material (i.e., material not previously shown in film or broadcast form). In some cases, as in Brazil, this tends to be programs on sports, how-to information, and custom-made programs about families, childbirths, and weddings (*Veja*, 1986). This seems to be spawning a second wave of VCR adoption, at least in Brazil. There, VCR adoption remained limited when the primary use was only for rental of pirated films, but it has grown enormously in the last year as other uses have been publicized (*Veja*, 1986).

In Brazil and elsewhere in Latin America, where most broadcasting is already entertainment-oriented, VCRs are also being used by community groups, unions, and political parties; in Central America, they are utilized by guerilla groups to spread alternative political and social messages. The extent of such use is difficult to gauge, hence its significance in VCR adoption is somewhat unclear, except that it creates a completely new set of uses for the equipment, with a substantially new set of users (Karen Rannucci, personal communication, October, 1986).

CONCLUSION

This chapter has examined VCR diffusion in the Third World. There, as elsewhere, VCR acquisition and use is largely an individual or household decision, although some are acquired through village or communal decisions or government programs. VCR diffusion then represents, as with the classic diffusion of innovations, a series of "individual" adoptions (Rogers, 1983). However, as the general critique of diffusion research has shown, there are a series of structural and systemic factors that condition and influence these decisions (Rogers, 1976).

Even at world market prices (around $400 in 1984), VCRs are an expensive acquisition for any but Third World elites. Furthermore, in many countries, government tariff policies make VCRs even more expensive. The marginal utility or informational-entertainment utility of purchases must therefore be high for VCR purchase to take precedence over other competing goods. This utility also seems related to systemic limits on information and entertainment, although there may be more individual factors that have not yet emerged in research.

There are a series of interacting systemic reasons why individuals in many Third World countries might feel a need to supplement existing broadcast or film fare. Centralized broadcast structures work against individual, ethnic, and regional variety in audience interests. Didactic propagandistic or educational system goals frequently limit access to content, particularly entertainment, that audiences may desire. In particular, increasing restrictions on trans-border program flow limits some kinds of individual, linguistic, and ethnic interests.

REFERENCES

Alisky, M. (1983). *Censorship or guidance.* Iowa City, IA: University of Iowa Press.
Atkin, C. K. (1985). Informational utility and selective exposure to entertainment media. In D. E. Zillmann, & J. Bryant (Eds.), *Selective exposure to communication* (pp. 63-91). Hillsdale, NJ: Lawrence Erlbaum Associates.
Beltran, L. R. (1978). TV etchings on the mind of Latin Americans, *Gazette 24*, 61-85.
Blumler, J. G., & Katz, E. (Eds.). (1974). *The uses of mass communications: Current perspectives on gratifications research.* Beverly Hills: Sage.
Boyd, D. A. (1985a). VCRs in developing countries: An Arab case study. *Media Development, 32*(1), 5-7.
Boyd, D. A. (1985b). The Janus effect? Imported television entertainment programming in developing countries. *Critical Studies in Mass Communication, 1*(4), 379-391.
Boyd, D. A., & Straubhaar, J. D. (1985). The developmental impact of the home videocassette recorder in the third world. *Journal of Broadcasting and Electronic Media, 29*(1), 5-21.
Boyd-Barrett, O. (1980). *The international news agencies.* Beverly Hills: Sage.
Chiruvolu, P. (1986). *Mass media and participatory development: A study of Kheda.* Unpublished masters thesis, Department of Telecommunication, Michigan State University, East Lansing, MI.
Dobrow, J. A. (1986). *The social and cultural implications of the VCR: How VCR use concentrates and diversifies viewing.* Unpublished doctoral dissertation, Annenberg School of Communication, University of Pennsylvania, Philadelphia, PA.
Dorfman, A., & Mattelart, A. (1975). *How to read Donald Duck: Imperialist ideology in*

9. VCR IN THE THIRD WORLD

the Disney comic (D. Kunzle, Trans.). New York: International General. Originally published, 1971)

Ganley, G. D., & Ganley, O. H. (1986). *The political implications of the global spread of videocassette recorders and videocassette programming.* Program on Information Resources Policy, Harvard University, P-86-3.

Guback, T., & Varis, T. (1984). Transnational communication and cultural industries. *Reports and Papers on Mass Communication,* 92. Paris: UNESCO.

Head, S. W. (1985). *World broadcasting systems.* Belmont, CA: Wadsworth.

Heeter, C. J. (1984). *Explaining the video boom: Factors related to national VCR penetration.* Unpublished manuscript, Michigan State University, Department of Telecommunication, East Lansing, MI.

Jamison, D., & McAnany, E. (1978). *Radio for education and development.* Beverly Hills: Sage.

Katz, E., & Wedell, G. (1977). *Broadcasting in the Third World.* Cambridge: Harvard University Press.

'Legal' homevid in Latino orbit. (1985, March 20). *Variety,* p 1.

Lee, C. (1980). *Media imperialism reconsidered: The homogenizing of television culture.* Beverly Hills: Sage.

Lent, J. A. (1985). Video in Asia: Frivolity, frustration, futility, *Media Development,* 32(1), 8-10.

Lerner, D. (1958). *The passing of traditional society.* New York: The Free Press.

Lhoest, H. (1983). The interdependence of the media. *Council of Europe mass media files,* no. 4. Strasbourg, France: Council of Europe.

Mattos, S. (1984). Advertising and government influence on Brazilian television. *Communication Research,* 11(2), 203-220.

McBride Commission. (1980). *One world, many voices.* Paris: UNESCO.

McPhail, J. C. (1981). *Electronic colonialism: The future of international broadcasting and communication.* Beverly Hills: Sage.

Mody, B. (1979). Programming for SITE. *Journal of Communication,* 29(4), 90-98.

Ninan, T. N., & Singh, C. U. (1983, September). India's entertainment revolution. *World Press Review,* 58-59.

Noam, E. N. (Ed.). (1985). *Video media competition.* New York: Columbia University Press.

Nordenstreng, K., & Varis, T. (1973). Television traffic: A one-way street? *UNESCO Reports and Papers on Mass Communication* (No. 71). Paris: UNESCO.

Ogan, C. L. (1985). Media diversity and communication policy: Impact of VCRs and satellite TV. *Telecommunication Policy,* 9(1), 63-73.

Pasquali, A. (1976). *Comunicacion y cultura de masas* [Mass communication and culture]. Caracas: Monte Avila.

Pool, I. de S. (1961). Mass media and politics in the modernization process. In L. W. Pye (Ed.), *Communications and political development* (pp. 234-253). Princeton, NJ: Princeton University Press.

Read, W. H. (1976). *America's mass media merchants.* Baltimore: Johns Hopkins University Press.

Rogers, E. M. (1976). *Communication and change: A critical review.* Beverly Hills: Sage.

Rogers, E. M. (1978). The rise and fall of the dominant paradigm. *Journal of Communication,* 28(1), 4-69.

Rogers, E. M. (1983). *Diffusion of innovations* (3rd ed.). New York: The Free Press.

Rosenblum, M. (1979). *Coups and earthquakes: Reporting the world for America.* New York: Harper.

Rosengren, K. E., Wenner, L. A., & Palmgreen, P. (1985). *Media gratifications research: Current perspectives.* Beverly Hills: Sage.

Schiller, H. I. (1969). *Mass communication and American empire.* New York: Augustus Kelley.
Schramm, W. (1964). *Mass media and national development.* Stanford: Stanford University Press.
Siebert, F. S., Schramm, W., & Peterson, T. (1956). *Four theories of the press.* Urbana: University of Illinois Press.
Smale, A. (1983, April 10). Soviets battle black market in western movie cassettes. *Philadelphia Inquirer,* 5-I.
Straubhaar, J. D. (1984). Brazilian television: The decline of American influence. *Communication Research, 11*(4), 221-240.
Straubhaar, J. D. (1986). *The impact of VCR on broadcasting in Argentina, Brazil, Dominican Republic, and Venezuela.* Paper presented at the conference on Popular Culture in Latin America, Tulane University, New Orleans, LA.
Tunstall, J. (1977). *The media are American.* New York: Columbia University Press.
Varis, T. (1984). The international flow of television programs. *Journal of communication, 34*(1), 143-152.
Veja. (1986, December 24). Videocassette no Brasil: a maquina do ano., pp. 54-61.
Video cassette recorders: National figures. (1983). *InterMedia, 11,* 39.
Wells, A. (1972). *Picture tube imperialism?: The impact of U.S. television on Latin America.* Maryknoll, NY: Orbis Books.
White, R. (1976). An alternative pattern of basic education: Radio Santa Maria, *Experiments and Innovations in Education 30.* Paris: UNESCO.

III

EMERGING MODELS OF MEDIA USE IN THE INFORMATION AGE

10

Uses and Gratifications of Videocassette Recorders

Alan M. Rubin
Kent State University

Charles R. Bantz
Arizona State University

Although more than three decades old, the videocassette recorder (VCR) has become a socially significant communication technology as it has moved from the workplace of the professional to the home of the consumer in the 1980s. In this investigation, we employed uses-and-gratifications theory to examine the videocassette recorder. A uses-and-gratifications perspective is especially appropriate for studying new communication technologies because it is based on the concept of an active audience.[1]

The individual communicator is considered central to the study of media effects in uses-and-gratifications theory. In contrast to more direct effects explanations of new and traditional media, it is thought that a person must typically have some use for a medium or message in order for that medium or message to have the potential to influence (Katz, 1959). Therefore, understanding one's motives to use communication media, such as the videocassette recorder, enhances explanation of media effects. Consistent with the psychological communication perspective, uses-and-gratifications researchers seek to explain media effects "in terms of the purposes, functions or uses (that is, uses and gratifications) as controlled by the choice patterns of receivers" (Fisher, 1978, p. 159).

Uses and gratifications has been detailed extensively by several writers (e.g., Katz, Blumler, & Gurevitch, 1974; Palmgreen, 1984; Palmgreen,

---

[1]Some portions of this chapter are adapted with the permission of Sage Publications, Inc. from: Alan M. Rubin and Charles R. Bantz, Utility of videocassette recorders, *American Behavioral Scientist*, May/June 1987, 30, 471-485.

Rosengren, & Wenner, 1985; Rubin, 1985, 1986). Therefore, we provide only a brief outline in this essay. Principal elements of uses-and-gratifications models include: a person's social and psychological environment, an individual's needs or motives to communicate, functional alternatives to media selection, communication behavior, and the consequences or effects of such behavior.

Uses-and-gratifications theory rests on several basic assumptions, which underscore the belief that audience activity mediates communication effects (see e.g., Katz et al., 1974; Palmgreen, 1984; Rubin, 1985, 1986). First, people are motivated and purposive in their communication behavior. Second, people take the initiative to select and use communication media and messages to satisfy felt needs or wants. Third, individuals are influenced by social and psychological factors when seeking to communicate and selecting among communication alternatives. Fourth, the media compete with other forms of communication for attention, selection, and use. Fifth, individuals are able to articulate their reasons for using media.

Uses and gratifications, then, assumes audience activeness in media selection and use. According to Blumler (1979), the concept of the "active audience," however, has a range of meanings including: *utility*, or the uses people have for communication; *intentionality*, or prior motivation directs communication behavior; *selectivity*, or prior interests and desires affect communication choices; and *imperviousness to influence*, or the obstinate audience (Bauer, 1964). Blumler astutely argued that audience activity should be thought of as a variable. Not all communicators are equally active at any given time or in any given situation; "some media might invite more, or less, audience activity than others" (Blumler, 1979, p. 13). The VCR is one medium that invites greater audience activity. VCRs entice heightened utility, intentionality, and selectivity.

Empirical research has supported the variable nature of audience activity. Levy and Windahl (1984), for example, identified an activity sequence for Swedish television viewers: previewing, during viewing, and postviewing activity. They noted different links between activity and viewing motives. Although preactivity and entertainment motives were weakly related, preactivity and surveillance motives were strongly related. Levy and Windahl argued that those in their sample actively selected news to gain information about their worlds, but did not actively seek diversion.

This finding is similar to the results of other studies (Rubin, 1981b, 1983, 1984; Rubin & Rubin, 1982). Degree of audience activity varied when media use motives were treated as interrelated structures, instead of independent factors. This research located a range from instrumental to ritualized media use. Instrumental media use reflects greater audience utility, intentionality, and selectivity, as compared to ritualized media use. In general, instrumental media use means seeking certain media content for information or other goal-directed reasons, whereas ritualized television use translates to using the medium more habitually, to fill time and for diversionary purposes.

Such variations in audience activity have important implications for media influence. Windahl (1981), for example, argued that using a medium instrumentally or ritualistically will produce different effects or consequences. Windahl saw effects as the outcome of using media content and consequences as the outcome of media use. This argument has been supported in recent studies of parasocial interaction with television newscasters (Rubin, Perse, & Powell, 1985), audience activity and soap opera involvement (Rubin & Perse, 1987a), and audience activity and news viewing (Rubin & Perse, 1987b). The latter investigation proposed a model of more instrumental media use that flowed from media use motives through attitudes, such as perceived realism and affinity, to media intention, selection, attention, and involvement. Individual motivation or utility was at the heart of this uses and effects model.

The utility dimension of audience activity is of particular interest to the study of VCRs. Utility refers to the actual or anticipated use of a communication medium for social or psychological purposes (Levy & Windahl, 1985, p. 112). An analysis of communication utility asks what purposes motivate specific uses of a medium or its content. Thus, the researcher identifies the variety of uses for a medium and the motives for those uses. Consistent with uses-and-gratifications assumptions, those uses and their attendant motives can be identified by asking individuals who use the medium.

Uses and gratifications is congruent with much of our current understanding of VCRs. The VCR is an evolving technology that enables people to be more active communicators. VCRs provide alternative communication content and contexts, and complement and extend other modes of communication. In contrast to more traditional media, which provide a person with a constrained range of options, VCR technology provides a plethora of content options and allows greater communicative choice, participation, and control. The VCR is a "permissive medium [that] can be used and managed in different ways, transmit different messages, satisfy different needs and achieve different purposes" (Wang, 1986, p. 378).

The increased ability of audience members to exercise choice among a host of options has generated concern in the broadcast, cable, and satellite industries. This is so because VCR owners time-shift and take "programming into their own hands" by recording programs for viewing at their own convenience (Mahoney, 1984, p. 42). The impact of VCRs in "changing the way consumers perceive TV" (Trost, 1986, p. 14) centers on the ability to choose what programming to view and when to view it.

In particular, trade-press writings over the last several years show concern about the active choice-making nature of VCR use, especially the avoidance of commercials. Yorke and Kitchen (1985), for example, found that VCR users in their British sample typically fast forwarded past commercials when watching programs (i.e., *zipping*) or paused their recorders when taping (i.e., *zapping*). In addition to zipping through programs and zapping commercials, Harvey and Rothe (1985/1986) argued VCR use affected commercial message viewing because VCR users time-shift, exercise greater control over children's viewing, and watch more noncommercial video. They also noted that VCR use increases audience fragmentation.

The few scholarly studies on VCRs that were done in the early 1980s lend support for this view of active consumers. Summarizing early industry studies, Agostino, Terry, and Johnson (1980) noted that the primary use of VCRs was to shift time. Interestingly, these authors concluded that VCR use seemed "unimaginative and conditioned" by traditional broadcasting viewing habits (p. 35). Levy (1980a, 1981) observed that through time-shifting, VCRs make television watching easier and more convenient. Levy (1980b) found that VCR households exhibit "strong patterns of program preference" and that VCR users specialize in the programs they select. Levy (1981) concluded that early adopters used VCRs to complement and not to replace regular viewing patterns. Research indicates, then, that individuals are active media consumers who often use VCRs to facilitate program selection through time-shifting of broadcast programming.

In this volume, Straubhaar and Lin and Straubhaar and Boyd, argue that VCR adoption reflects that the purchaser weighs the range of available programming in relation to VCR cost. These analyses suggest that VCRs are seen from the time of purchase as facilitators of programming choice. The authors report, for example, that in equally poor countries VCR penetration is greater in countries with less diversity of television outlets. Their argument suggests that those who seek more choice in content buy VCRs to aid that choice.

The extant research, then, suggests a level of audience activity that makes VCR use well-suited for uses-and-gratifications analysis. VCR use emphasizes selective and intentional audience choice behavior. The exact nature of VCR utility, however, requires closer scrutiny.

In this study we considered the motivated character of VCR use. We expected to find patterns to (a) preferences in what VCR users record and watch, (b) instrumental VCR user motivations that reflect more than just habit or filling time, and (c) indications that VCR use complements traditional media behavior, such as television viewing, and interpersonal communication. Given our assumption that VCR use evolves from other communication behavior, we expected to find relationships among user demographic traits, selected media experiences, and motivations similar to such patterns for traditional media (e.g., Rubin, 1981a).

METHOD

Questionnaire Development

It was necessary to identify the variety of motives people have for using VCRs in order to develop the questionnaire. Because of the paucity of VCR research, we treated this study as exploratory. We attempted to develop an exhaustive array of VCR uses and motivations.

Six interviewers purposefully sought respondents of widely diverse demographics in different size communities.[2] There were several primary groups of VCR users surveyed: low to modest income young workers (25 to 35 years old) in a remote area on the West coast; young professionals (20 to 45 years old) in a metropolitan area; upper income established professionals (over 50 years old and earning more than $100,000 annually) in an upscale metropolitan suburb; minority customers of a large video store in a lower middle class metropolitan neighborhood; college students and professors at a small midwestern college in a modest-sized community; and children in a metropolitan area.

Respondents were asked to detail 10 ways in which they use their VCRs and to provide reasons for those uses. These reasons were first collected individually, then collated and reviewed. The procedure resulted in a master list of categories of VCR use and specific statements of motives for each category.

A questionnaire was developed from this master list and divided into several sections: one section for each way the VCR could be used (e.g., time-shifting, building a library of programs, playing rented movies) with a set of motive statements for each section. Respondents were first asked to state how frequently they use their VCRs for that purpose. They then evaluated the importance of several statements of motivation for that purpose. The questionnaire was pilot tested with students at the University of Minnesota. The order and phrasing of items were revised.

The final questionnaire included sections about the frequency of 11 types of VCR uses and 95 statements of motivation for these 11 a priori uses. The last section included demographic, media experience, and technology equipment ownership items. The present analysis considered the associations among VCR motives and the frequency of VCR use, amount of television and VCR use, and demographic traits.

The Sample

Data were gathered between Spring 1985 and Winter 1986 from several groups mostly in the Minneapolis–St. Paul area. Some responses were gathered in northern California and northern Minnesota. Only those with

---

[2]We are grateful for the invaluable assistance of Robbin Crabtree, Tom Endres, Ted Larson, Liz Paisner, Sammi Reist, and Gayle Statman in developing the questionnaire and gathering the data.

regular access to a VCR were asked to respond to the questionnaire. The nonprobability sample produced 424 usable questionnaires.[3]

The respondents were diverse. They ranged in age from 13 to 62 years ($M = 29.0$). Most (56.5%) were male (0 = male, 1 = female). The household income distribution indicated steadily increasing percentages: 6.1% reported less than $10,000 per year; 12.7% from $10,000 to $19,999; 16.4% from $20,000 to $29,999; 22.0% from $30,000 to $39,999; and 42.8% over $40,000. About one third of the respondents were students (36.6%); 17.3% were professionals, 10.1% in service occupations, 6.0% each in sales and clerical jobs, 5.5% in education, 4.3% were managers; the rest were spread through technical, homemaker, labor, transportation, farm, and other occupations, with 0.5% being unemployed.

Data Reduction of VCR Motives

The sample consisted of 424 respondents who were asked to specify their perceived importance of 95 reasons for using VCRs for 11 different purposes (i.e., categories of use). The 11 categories were: (a) recording programs to watch within the next week (7 motivation items); (b) recording programs for future viewing, more than a week after recording (8 items); (c) building a permanent library of programs (17 items); (d) recording a program when watching it (5 items); (e) watching rented movies (27 items); (f) using the VCR for professional reasons (4 items); (g) viewing recorded music videos (10 items); (h) using the VCR for instructional reasons (3 items); (i) viewing exercise tapes (5 items); (j) using the VCR for home projects (2 items); and (k) 7 items that did not fit cleanly into the other categories (e.g., using the VCR because it is an exciting technology).

We attempted to provide broad coverage of VCR utility with the 95 statements of motives across the 11 categories of use. We used a multistage analysis to examine the structure of motivations to use VCRs. We sought to identify meaningful factors of VCR user motivation by deleting unreliable statements or those that were unimportant to respondents.

First, mean scores for the 95 motivation items (5 = very important, 1 = not at all important) were examined. Items with means of "not very important" to "not at all important" ($M < 2.00$) were eliminated from subse-

---

[3]Because our major goals were to provide a broad categorization of VCR utility useful for future research and to examine relationships among variables without intending to generalize, a probability sample was not essential or desirable. The extensive questionnaire that was developed to meet these objectives was not suitable for an economical mail or telephone survey. In addition, given the 95 motivation and 37 other items contained in the instrument, the response rate for a random administration would have been jeopardized severely, weakening the representativeness of any random sample. A large sample was needed to analyze statistically responses to many items. Therefore, we chose to use personal contacts to select individuals purposely from diverse groups with regular access to VCRs.

quent analyses. This deleted 21 motivation items, including all professional and instructional motives, and most home project motives.

Second, principal axis factoring (PAF) with iterations and oblimin rotation was used with the remaining 74 items. This resulted in 16 factors (11 with eigenvalues > 1.0) that explained 59.6% of the total variance. By using a retention rule of at least two items with .50 minimum primary loadings and no secondary loadings of .30 or greater on retained factors, 25 motivation items were eliminated.

Third, this PAF procedure was repeated with these 49 motivation items and then, using the same .50 − .30 factor retention rule, on five subsequent PAF analyses of 44, 41, 39, 37, and 35 items. The final analysis retained 8 factors (6 with eigenvalues > 1.0) that explained 66.8% of the total variance. Given the exploratory nature of the study, and because the final two factors were conceptually meaningful, all 8 factors were interpreted. Factor scores produced via the regression method (SPSS, 1986) were used to compute the VCR motives (i.e., utility variables).

Media Experience Variables

Responses to the frequency of VCR use (5 = very frequently, 1 = never) were averaged to produce a VCR Frequency index. This was done across 7 of the 11 original purposes that were represented in the VCR motives that remained after the final PAF analysis: time-shifting, future viewing, building a library of programs, recording when watching another program, and watching rented movies, music videos, and exercise tapes. Because of the variety of possible uses, we did not expect a high degree of internal consistency. The VCR Frequency index ($M = 2.72$) had a .60 Cronbach alpha.

Respondents also were asked to estimate, on the average, how many hours of television they watched each day and how many hours they used their VCRs each day. Daily television viewing averaged 2.59 hours, and daily VCR use averaged 1.46 hours.

Statistical Analysis

Pearson correlations were computed to consider the relationships among the eight VCR motives that remained after the factor analyses. The multivariate relationships between the set of eight VCR motives and the set of six demographic and media experience variables were examined with canonical correlation analysis.[4]

---

[4]The frequencies of use and motive statements for some variables (e.g., music video and exercise tape) had more missing data than did other variables. Therefore, a listwise deletion of missing data was used for the factor analyses and all subsequent analyses. This resulted in an N of 346 for the final factor analysis and the Pearson correlation analysis, and an N of 263 for the canonical correlation analysis.

RESULTS

As just mentioned, the final PAF analysis explained 66.8% of the total variance. The analysis identified eight VCR utility factors that are summarized here.[5]

Factor 1, *library storage*, had an eigenvalue of 8.92 and explained 14.2% of the total variance after rotation. These nine items reflected a desire to retain copies of tapes and to use VCRs as a convenient alternative to regularly scheduled programs. Statements included using the VCR for library storage because: "I like to have movies and shows that can be viewed many times," "it is entertaining," "I like to have the ability to view programs anytime," "I like to have tapes on hand," "it provides options to regularly scheduled TV programs," "I like to watch special programming when the mood hits me," "I like to have special programs on hand," "I want to keep a permanent copy of the program," and "I like to save tapes for repeated viewings."

Factor 2, *music videos*, had an eigenvalue of 4.42 and accounted for 16.9% of the variance after rotation. These eight items connoted available, entertaining, and economical VCR use that centered on music videos and performers. Statements included using the VCR for music videos because: "it's entertaining," "I can see and hear my favorite songs on video anytime," "video tape adds the visual dimension to music," "I can watch my favorite musicians," "it doesn't cost much money," "it's like having a record or cassette," "I like to see what the musicians look like," and "I can use music videos for parties."

Factor 3, *exercise tapes*, had an eigenvalue of 3.63 and explained 10.5% of the variance after rotation. These four items indicated convenient use of exercise tapes in one's home. Statements included using the VCR for exercise tapes because: "it is convenient," "I can exercise at any time," "I don't have to join an exercise class," and "someone is directing the exercise."

Factor 4, *movie rental*, had an eigenvalue of 2.18 and accounted for 6.2% of the variance after rotation. These four items reflected the convenient and easy selection of rental movies in the home. Statements included using the VCR for movie rental because: "renting movies is more convenient," "renting gives you more choice over what to watch," "renting movies is easy," and "renting movies provides a better selection than movie theaters."

Factor 5, *child viewing*, had an eigenvalue of 1.31 and explained 4.5% of the variance after rotation. These two items focused on having movies available for children to watch. Statements included using the VCR for child viewing because: "I like to have movies available for the kids" and "I rent movies for children to watch."

Factor 6, *time-shifting*, had an eigenvalue of 1.28 and accounted for 4.9%

---

[5] See Rubin and Bantz (1987) for the complete factor matrix.

of the variance after rotation. These four items reflected convenience and choice in program viewing, and the ability to eliminate commercials. Statements included using the VCR for time-shifting because: "I like the freedom to set my own schedule," "I want the convenience of recording programs and watching them later," "when I view later I can skip through the commercials," and "I am busy doing something at home when a show is on the air."

Factor 7, *socializing*, had an eigenvalue of 0.86 and explained 3.7% of the variance after rotation. These two items indicated a desire to entertain others. Statements included using the VCR for socializing because: "I rent movies for parties" and "I want to entertain people who come over."

Factor 8, *critical viewing*, had an eigenvalue of 0.76 and accounted for 3.2% of the variance after rotation. These two items focused on the ability to review and study critically a taped program or a rented movie. Statements included using the VCR for critical viewing because: "I want to rewatch the program and review it critically" and "renting a movie allows me to study the movie."

According to the mean scores of the primary loadings of these eight VCR utility factors, the most important VCR uses were movie rental (3.68), time-shifting (3.24), library storage (3.15), and socializing (2.92). The least important VCR uses were child viewing (2.14), exercise tapes (2.24), critical viewing (2.43), and music videos (2.44).

Communication motives are interrelated structures (Rubin & Rubin, 1985). Therefore, the eight VCR motives were intercorrelated to assess these associations. The VCR motive correlation matrix is presented in Table 10.1.

Several VCR use motives were related. The strongest associations were among three logically related utility variables: library storage, critical viewing, and time-shifting. Programs must be stored and retrieved so that tapes can be analyzed and time-shifted. Two other logical and salient associa-

TABLE 10.1
Correlation Matrix of VCR Motives

	LIBR	MUSC	EXER	MOVI	CHLD	TIME	SOCL	CRIT
Library storage	.92							
Music videos	.31*	.96						
Exercise tapes	.02	.16	.98					
Movie rental	.19*	.17*	.09	.81				
Child viewing	.11	.08	.29*	.17	.86			
Time-shifting	.41*	.07	.02	.24*	.15	.75		
Socializing	.25*	.36*	.20*	.37*	.09	.07	.75	
Critical viewing	.52*	.23*	−.05	.13	.01	.35*	.12	.68

Note: Cronbach alpha coefficients are listed in the diagonal.
*$p < .001$.

tions were between socializing and both movie rental and music videos. Movies and music videos can be used to entertain others.

The multivariate relationships among the set of demographic and media experience variables and the set of VCR utility variables were examined with canonical correlation. This analysis is summarized in Table 10.2, which includes canonical loadings (i.e., structure coefficients) and redundancy coefficients. As compared to canonical weights, canonical loadings or structure coefficients are mostly free of the effects of multicollinearity (Lambert & Durand, 1975). Redundancy coefficients reflect the variance of one set shared by the canonical variate of the other set (Levine, 1977). Three significant canonical roots were identified. Because loadings below .30 may be unstable (Lambert & Durand, 1975), interpretation focused on the canonical loadings of .30 or greater.

The first canonical root ($R_c = .75$, $p < .001$) explained 56.8% of the common variance between the canonical variates. The primary relationship in set one was a negative association between age and VCR frequen-

TABLE 10.2
Canonical Correlation: VCR Motives x Demographics and Media Experiences

	ROOT 1	ROOT 2	ROOT 3
	Canonical Loading	Canonical Loading	Canonical Loading
SET 1: DEMOGRAPHICS & MEDIA EXPERIENCES			
Age	-.49	-.57	.60
Gender	.27	-.81	-.40
Income	.00	-.34	-.41
TV viewing hours	-.02	-.05	.08
VCR viewing hours	.17	.00	.27
VCR frequency	.93	-.10	.33
Redundancy	[.11]	[.06]	[.03]
SET 2: VCR MOTIVES			
Library storage	.72	.04	.51
Music videos	.71	.28	.00
Exercise tapes	.48	-.69	-.37
Movie rental	.40	-.17	-.17
Child viewing	.18	-.53	.02
Time-shifting	.32	-.06	.68
Socializing	.63	.32	-.52
Critical viewing	.47	.22	.30
Redundancy	[.15]	[.04]	[.03]

Note: Root 1: $R_c = .75$, $R_c^2 = .57$, $F(48, 1229) = 9.14$, $p < .001$
Root 2: $R_c = .55$, $R_c^2 = .30$, $F(35, 1054) = 5.14$, $p < .001$
Root 3: $R_c = .45$, $R_c^2 = .21$, $F(24, 877) = 3.28$, $p < .001$

cy. Set two included positive associations among library storage, music videos, socializing, exercise tapes, movie rental, critical viewing, and time-shifting. Across the two sets, younger persons more frequently used VCRs and they did so to store and retrieve music videos, exercise tapes, and movies, and to use these videocassettes to socialize, time-shift, and view critically.

The second canonical root ($R_c = .55$, $p < .001$) explained 30.4% of the common variance between the canonical variates. The dominant relationship in set one was between age and gender; there also were positive links between these variables and income. Set two included a positive association between exercise tapes and child viewing, and a negative link between these motives and socializing. Across the two sets, as compared to younger males from lower income households, older females from higher income households were more likely to use VCRs to view exercise tapes or to have children watch movies or programs; they are less likely to use VCRs to socialize.

The third canonical root ($R_c = .45$, $p < .001$) explained 20.7% of the common variance between the canonical variates. Set one contained positive associations among age and VCR frequency, and negative relationships between these variables and both income and gender. Set two had positive correlations among time-shifting, library storage, and critical viewing, and negative associations between these motives and both socializing and exercise tapes. Across the two sets, as compared to younger women from higher income households, older males from lower income households used their VCRs more frequently to store and retrieve programs, to shift time, and to view programs more critically, but not to socialize or to watch exercise tapes. The low redundancy coefficients, however, advise caution in interpreting across the sets.

DISCUSSION

In this investigation *utility* was defined in terms of eight identified motives for using the VCR. Univariate and multivariate analyses found many of these motives to be interrelated. In addition, there were clear patterns of association between these VCR utility motives and audience demographics and media experiences.

We began the study by anticipating that uses and gratifications would be invaluable for explaining VCR use because such communication behavior is active. The results indicate that VCR use is indeed active behavior. VCR users make choices based on the utility of those choices for them. The findings reflect that television viewing is controlled by the consumer through selective and intentional use of the VCR, which complements personal and mediated communication.

In four ways, the findings demonstrate that VCR use is active communication behavior. First, our investigation, similar to earlier VCR studies, indicates that time-shifting and convenience are two important uses of the VCR. The concepts of time-shifting and convenience directly reflect the more instrumental manner in which VCRs are used. For example, convenience and time-shifting connote arranging the availability at home of certain programs and movies, not currently on television or in theaters, by prior taping or renting. Convenience here does not mean simply having a television to turn on at will, but being able to view, intentionally and selectively, what one wants when one wants to do so. This suggests that VCR technology facilitates the exercise of choice behavior. The consumer makes programming decisions.

Second, the results provide additional evidence that media consumers are more active than portrayed in more direct effects modes of inquiry. VCR users are differentiated groups of individuals who are motivated and intentional in their behavior. They select what content to tape or rent and when to view it. We found that using VCRs for specific purposes is related to age, gender, and income. Different audience groups use VCRs for different content and different purposes. To understand a new technology, then, requires an understanding of the differentiation among users based on social and psychological circumstances of the members of the group and the types of choices made.

Third, the users of VCRs demonstrate the active participation in communication that is evident in interpersonal communication. Using VCRs provides active interpersonal communication links (e.g., sharing tapes, social entertainment, being with children), as well as mass communication links (e.g., off-air taping, movie availability). In fact, time-shifting illustrates the ability to meet both mass and interpersonal communication needs and desires. For example, not only can the scheduling of a television program be shifted to a more convenient time, but also to a time when other family members also can watch. Active VCR use parallels active interpersonal communication, providing additional evidence in support of the argument that uses and gratifications is not just a mass communication perspective, but a communication perspective (Rubin & Rubin, 1985). This parallel further suggests that an understanding of new communication technology needs to be located within a general understanding of communicative behavior.

Lastly, active VCR use is also illustrated by how VCRs complement and extend traditional media such as television. Comparing our findings to uses and gratifications examinations of television use helps to clarify this point. Motives for using television can be placed roughly into several categories: surveillance or seeking information, diversion or seeking entertainment, social utility or seeking interpersonal connection, and habit or viewing out of ritual to fill time or to relieve boredom (Bantz, 1980; Blumler, 1979; Rubin, 1981a, 1983). The structure of VCR motives seems similar to television use, yet even more goal directed. For example, VCR use reflects intentional selection of preferred programs or content (e.g., movies, music videos, exercise tapes). Also, there are more instrumental than ritualistic components to using VCRs. Libraries of tapes are built for future viewing. Individuals shift their usual television schedules and add rental materials to be their own programmers. Tapes are used to aid and to complement interpersonal interaction.

VCRs, then, allow the viewer more control over the time, place, and type of programs viewed on his or her video screen. This increased control highlights the need to differentiate empirically communication media from the user's perspective. Such comparative analysis allows the contribution of the new communication medium to be situated in the variety of communication media available in contemporary society.

A uses-and-gratifications analysis extends our understanding of videocassette recorders beyond the role of the VCR as a new communication technology. It enables us to consider how using a VCR complements other communication behavior. When we examine the VCR we are clearly studying, not just mass communication, but mediated communication. Both mass and interpersonal communication can be mediated to varying degrees. The telephone, of course, is a prime example of mediated interpersonal communication. Talk radio is an example of mediated mass and interpersonal communication. Our investigation demonstrates that VCRs also mediate mass and interpersonal communication. This duality and differentiation in how VCRs are used illustrate the contribution an understanding of audience activity makes to assaying the nature, role, and impact of new communication technologies.

REFERENCES

Agostino, D. E., Terry, H. A., & Johnson, R. C. (1980). Home video recorders: Rights and ratings. *Journal of Communication, 30*(4), 28-35.

Bantz, C. R. (1980). Exploring uses and gratifications: A comparison of reported uses of television and reported uses of favorite program type. *Communication Research, 9*, 352-379.

Bauer, R. A. (1964). The obstinate audience: The influence process from the point of view of social communication. *American Psychologist, 19*, 319-328.

Blumler, J. G. (1979). The role of theory in uses and gratifications studies. *Communication Research, 6*, 9-36.

Fisher, B. A. (1978). *Perspectives on human communication.* New York: Macmillan.

Harvey, M. G., & Rothe, J. T. (1985/1986). Video cassette recorders: Their impact on viewers and advertisers. *Journal of Advertising Research, 25*(6), 19-27.

Katz, E. (1959). Mass communication research and the study of popular culture. *Studies in Public Communication, 2*, 1-6.

Katz, E., Blumler, J. G., & Gurevitch, M. (1974). Utilization of mass communication by the individual. In J. G. Blumler & E. Katz (Eds.), *The uses of mass communications: Current perspectives on gratifications research* (pp. 19-32). Beverly Hills: Sage.

Lambert, Z. V., & Durand, R. M. (1975). Some precautions in using canonical analysis. *Journal of Marketing Research, 12,* 468-475.

Levine, M. S. (1977). *Canonical analysis and factor comparison.* Beverly Hills: Sage.

Levy, M. R. (1980a). Home video recorders: A user survey. *Journal of Communication, 30*(4), 23-27.

Levy, M. R. (1980b). Program playback preferences in VCR households. *Journal of Broadcasting, 24,* 327-336.

Levy, M. R. (1981). Home video recorders and time shifting. *Journalism Quarterly, 58,* 401-405.

Levy, M. R., & Windahl, S. (1984). Audience activity and gratifications: A conceptual clarification and exploration. *Communication Research, 11,* 51-78.

Levy, M. R., & Windahl, S. (1985). The concept of audience activity. In K. E. Rosengren, L. A. Wenner, & P. Palmgreen (Eds.), *Media gratifications research: Current perspectives* (pp. 109-122). Beverly Hills: Sage.

Mahoney, W. (1984, May 31). Home tapers tapping cable programming. *Advertising Age,* pp. 40, 42.

Palmgreen, P. (1984). Uses and gratifications: A theoretical perspective. In R. N. Bostrom (Ed.), *Communication yearbook 8* (pp. 20-55). Beverly Hills: Sage.

Palmgreen, P., Rosengren, K. E., & Wenner, L. A. (1985). Uses and gratifications research: The past ten years. In K. E. Rosengren, L. A. Wenner, & P. Palmgreen (Eds.), *Media gratifications research: Current perspectives* (pp. 11-37). Beverly Hills: Sage.

Rubin, A. M. (1981a). An examination of television viewing motivations. *Communication Research, 8,* 141-165.

Rubin, A. M. (1981b). A multivariate analysis of "60 Minutes" viewing motivations. *Journalism Quarterly, 58,* 529-534.

Rubin, A. M. (1983). Television uses and gratifications: The interactions of viewing patterns and motivations. *Journal of Broadcasting, 27,* 37-51.

Rubin, A. M. (1984) Ritualized and instrumental television viewing. *Journal of Communication, 34*(3), 67-77.

Rubin, A. M. (1985). Uses and gratifications: Quasi-functional analysis. In J. R. Dominick & J. E. Fletcher (Eds.), *Broadcasting research methods* (pp. 202-220). Boston: Allyn & Bacon.

Rubin, A. M. (1986). Uses, gratifications, and media effects research. In J. Bryant & D. Zillmann (Eds.), *Perspectives on media effects* (pp. 281-301). Hillsdale, NJ: Lawrence Erlbaum Associates.

Rubin, A. M., & Bantz, C. R. (1987). Utility of videocassette recorders. *American Behavioral Scientist, 30,* 471-485.

Rubin, A. M., & Perse, E. M. (1987a). Audience activity and soap opera involvement: A uses and effects investigation. *Human Communication Research, 14,* 246-268.

Rubin, A. M., & Perse, E. M. (1987b). Audience activity and television news gratifications. *Communication Research, 14,* 58-84.

Rubin, A. M., Perse, E. M., & Powell, R. A. (1985). Loneliness, parasocial interaction, and local television news viewing. *Human Communication Research, 12,* 155-180.

Rubin, A. M., & Rubin, R. B. (1982). Older persons' TV viewing patterns and motivations. *Communication Research, 9,* 287-313.

Rubin, A. M., & Rubin, R. B. (1985). Interface of personal and mediated communication: A research agenda. *Critical Studies in Mass Communication, 2,* 36-53.

SPSS, Inc. (1986). *SPSSX user's guide* (2nd ed.). New York: McGraw-Hill.
Trost, M. (1986, January 9). VCR sales explosion shakes up the industry. *Advertising Age*, p. 14.
Wang, G. (1986). Video boom in Taiwan: Blessings or curse? *The Third Channel*, 2, 365-379.
Windahl, S. (1981). Uses and gratifications at the crossroads. In G. C. Wilhoit & H. de Bock (Eds.), *Mass communication review yearbook* (Vol. 2, pp. 174-185). Beverly Hills: Sage.
Yorke, D. A., & Kitchen, P. J. (1985). Channel flickers and video speeders. *Journal of Advertising Research*, 25(2), 21-25.

11

Television Audience Behavior: Patterns of Exposure in the New Media Environment

James G. Webster
Northwestern University

Nowhere has the emergence of the new media been more keenly felt than among those who study television audiences. Broadcasters fear that newer technologies may rob them of viewers and, in turn, of their profits. Policy makers promote new media in the belief that this will open the electronic marketplace, encourage diversity, and allow the audience to realize television's fullest benefits. Social scientists and media critics wonder whether changing technology may force changes in their models of media effects and social influence. In many ways, our ability to shed light on these concerns depends on understanding how the audience will respond to the changing environment.

This chapter examines television audience behavior in the new media environment. It first identifies critical conceptual differences between traditional and newer forms of television. It then discusses two features of audience behavior that occur in response to that changed environment. Finally, it explores some implications of these new patterns of audience behavior for work on media effects and policy making.

CHANGES IN THE MEDIA ENVIRONMENT

Within the last decade there have emerged a variety of new technologies that promise to change both the quantity and quality of television programming available to the viewer. Although these new media may not be quite what visionaries had imagined, more than a few have taken hold, and they are in some ways quite different from the media to which we have grown accustomed.

At the same time, much contemporary research and theory on the media operates as if no changes were taking place. Instead, television is conceptualized in a traditional, and increasingly inadequate, form. The first step toward understanding changing patterns of exposure, then, is recognizing certain significant shifts in the audience's media environment.

Specifically, there appear to be three dimensions or attributes along which old and new media differ. The characteristics of each media environment are described here in somewhat oversimplified and extreme versions. For purposes of definition, *new media* include all those technologies that have the net effect of opening the television distribution system to potentially unlimited channel capacities (e.g., cable television, satellite networks, VCRs, etc.). Conversely, *old media* are traditional broadcast distribution systems that use a relatively small number of channels to deliver content on a fixed timetable.

Characteristics of Old Media

Television Programming is Uniform. One of the most prevalent characterizations of television has been that its content is, for all intents and purposes, homogeneous. Programming, it is often argued, displays an excessive sameness that caters to socially prevalent values and paints a uniform, if distorted, picture of social reality. Such representations of television are not only consistent with arguments made by social critics who view the medium as an instrument of social control and class domination, they are also commonplace in the work of many theorists inclined toward a more "liberal-pluralist" view of mass media.

Television's homogeneous quality is usually attributed to the fact that programming is conceived, produced, and broadcast in an effort to attract as many viewers as possible. Given this overriding concern with maximizing audiences, programmers are loath to present anything that might offend or alienate even a modest portion of the audience. Rather, they resort to formulas and themes that can easily be accepted by the broadest possible audience.

This characterization of American media is hardly new. Klapper (1960) noted the argument was popular as early as the late 1940s and concluded that, despite occasional exceptions, "the economic character of commercial media in a free enterprise society is such that they appear destined forever to play to, and thus reinforce, socially prevalent attitudes" (p. 42). Nor has this line of reasoning lost much of its appeal in the intervening years. In fact, a number of contemporary analysts have portrayed commercial television as a medium inexorably commited to the production of standarized, homogeneous programming (e.g., Bagdikian, 1985; Gerbner & Gross, 1976; Murdock & Golding, 1977; Neuman, 1982).

Television Programming Is Uncorrelated With Channels. If all television programming caters to the same mass audience, it would be impossible, or at least imprudent, for one channel to offer content of a type that was systematically different from the channels with which it competed. In the American context, this has meant no significant difference in what a viewer could see on ABC, or CBS, or NBC. Indeed, this condition is consistent with the predictions of formal models of network behavior. Owen, Beebe, and Manning (1974) have noted such duplication of program content "occurs because there is a tendency for a decentralized system of broadcasting, with limited channel capacity, to produce rivalry for large blocks of the audience with programs that are, if not identical, at least close substitutes. There is a tendency, in our case, for the three networks to produce the same kind of programming" (p. 101).

As a practical matter, characterizing television in this way has allowed theorists to treat it as a single, undifferentiated medium. Nowhere is this strategy more evident than in the work of Gerbner and Gross (1976) who have argued that "the 'world' of television is an organic system of stories and images" (p. 180). Only the absolute rate of exposure to "television" is needed, or for that matter appropriate, as an independent variable. Even among researchers who might not adopt cultivation analysis as a theoretical framework, television, as a cause of social or psychological effects, has often been "considered globally" (Cook, Kendzierski, & Thomas, 1983, p. 164).

Television Is Universally Available. If television programming does not vary across channels, then in principle, to own a set capable of receiving one signal is to have access to all the medium can offer. Throughout the United States and much of the industrialized world television is, by this definition, universally available. Unlike many forms of media, television "penetrates every home in the land" (Gerbner & Gross, 1976, p. 175).

Represented as such a uniform, inescapable presence, the only relevant feature of audience behavior would seem to be how much of the medium is actually consumed. Descriptions of television's omnipresent quality, therefore, are quite often accompanied by statistical summaries of the enormous amount of time people spend watching (e.g., Gerbner, Gross, Morgan, & Signorielli, 1986; Neuman, 1982). Once it is documented that exposure occurs in "massive doses," many social theorists have been inclined to regard further questions of audience behavior as trivial.

Right or wrong, such characterizations of the medium and its audience have had significant implications for theorizing about the medium's social impact. Indeed, the assertion that television presents a homogenous system of messages, so pervasive and uniform as to override mechanisms of selectivity, is at the heart of the arguments urging a return to the concept of powerful media effects (e.g., Noelle-Neumann, 1973; Signorielli, 1986).

Characteristics of New Media

Television Programming Is Diverse. One of the more hotly contested attributes of new media is their ability to promote diversity. At the center of this debate is the realization that *diversity* means different things to different people. Several writers have commented on the meaning of diversity (e.g., Glasser, 1984; Jacklin, 1978; Levin, 1980; Meehan, 1984; Wildman & Owen, 1985). To some, diversity means little more than increasing the number of choices that a viewer has at any point in time. Certainly to the extent that technologies such as cable and VCRs increase the people's access to vast libraries of programming that already exist, there is a practical increase in the diversity of their options. What is less clear is whether changes in the structural features of the industry will contribute to the creation of newer and more diverse forms of expression.

Despite the arguments reviewed earlier, a good case can be made that the competitive character of television does not inevitably lead to the production of uniform program content catering only to the broadest possible audience (Hirsch, 1982). To be sure, the owners of media seek to maximize long-run profits, but the strategies for achieving that end may change as the competitive environment changes. In the case of the major broadcast networks, the limited number of channels has predetermined the strategy of audience maximization just outlined. Economic models of audience behavior, however, suggest that this is not a necessary result if the number of channels, and hence competing services, is unconstrained (e.g., Owen et al., 1974).

Under an assumption of unlimited channels, alternative profit-making strategies emerge. Specifically, it may now be desirable, and profitable, to produce programming that caters to smaller, more specialized audiences. In the process of doing so, it is possible, perhaps even necessary, to offend large portions of the public. Further, if one considers technologies where the intensity of viewer preferences can be reflected in direct payments (e.g., pay TV or VCRs) it is feasible to produce genuine esoterica for very small segments of the audience.

The factor that opens the door for such possibilities is an increase in the channel capacity of the delivery system. Virtually all new media contribute to that general expansion. In the United States, the most important of these has been cable television. As recently as 1972, 69% of all households received eight or fewer television signals. In 1986, with the inclusion of cable, 85% of all homes could receive nine or more channels (A.C. Nielsen, 1987). With cable subscribers now constituting half of all households, and with VCRs having eclipsed that level of household penetration, it is apparent that the nature of television's delivery system has undergone rapid and dramatic change. Nor is this structural change unique to American media (McCain, 1986).

The availability of increased channel capacity does not, of course, guarantee that diverse programming will be produced. Nevertheless, given the relative youth of most new media, increasingly heterogeneous content has begun to appear. Perhaps the most significant is programming that caters to ethnic and racial minorities. Wilson and Gutierrez (1985) have gone so far as to argue that the growth of minority media foretells the end of "mass communication." Additionally, there is increased variety in news and information, sports, children's programming, religious media, and, of course, entertainment. None of this differentiation would have been feasible under the old delivery system. How far it will go depends on a complex interplay of factors including the attractiveness of audience subsets to advertisers (Owen et al., 1974), the range and intensity of viewer preferences (Barwise & Ehrenberg, 1984; Owen et al., 1974; Waterman, 1986), the ability of viewers to pay directly for programming (Poltrack, 1983; Wildman & Owen, 1985), the cost of producing various program forms, (Barwise & Ehrenberg, 1984; Hirsch, 1982; Waterman, 1986), and a variety of structural and regulatory reforms (Wildman & Owen, 1985).

Television Programming Is Correlated With Channels. As the medium's programming becomes more varied, new questions about how that content will be organized and delivered emerge. Will the owners and programmers of this increased number of channels continue to offer content that is indistinguishable from their competitors, or will some channels position themselves as purveyors of relatively specialized programming designed for subsets of the mass audience? The answer is almost certainly the latter.

It is one of the principle assumptions of both economic models of audience choice and "uses-and-gratifications" theory that viewers have relatively consistent differential preferences for program types (Webster & Wakshlag, 1983). Similarly, it is one of the principle strategies of television programmers to retain audiences within a channel by scheduling a succession of programs with similar appeal (Tiedge & Ksobiech, 1986; Webster, 1985). Both the theory and practice of managing audience flow, then, suggest organizing content by types into channels. This, in combination with organizational factors that make it more efficient for a firm to specialize in acquisition and production of one type of programming (e.g., news, sports, etc.), should promote a correlation between channels and content.

A brief survey of how the new media have begun to organize and market themselves confirms this expectation. The National Cable Television Association (1985) has reported that there are 45 video services or networks being distributed to cable systems via satellite. These include services specializing in the arts, news, sports, movies, weather, science, public affairs, financial and business information, country music, rock music, Spanish-language programming, "Christian" programming, "Black" programming, "family" programming, "women's" programming, "children's" programming, and "adult" programming.

Not all cable networks, of course, are designed to offer content of one type. A few channels have opted for a strategy that mimicks the broadcast networks, and even some of the specialized services find it advantageous to maintain a degree of variation in their programming. Nevertheless, the tendency for most, if not all, new channels to telecast relatively specialized content seems well established.

The use of a VCR, if conceptualized as a "channel" that is programmed by its owner, is entirely consistent with this characterization of new media. Levy and Fink (1984), for example, have reported that videorecorder users tend to specialize in a type of content. Assuming that the user has access to a relatively diverse program library, the content of that channel will be of a type defined by the viewer's preference. In fact, such a "viewer-defined" typology is, theoretically, a very appealing way to establish program types (Greenberg & Barnett, 1971; Owen et al., 1974; Webster & Wakshlag, 1983).

Channels Are Differentially Available. As the new media emerge, the assumption of television's universal availability will become increasingly hollow. To be sure, set ownership may continue to provide access to some common realm of programming, but that will constitute only a portion of what is consumed by the public. Much of what is viewed will be delivered through channels that are differentially available across the audience.

This phenomenon of differential availability occurs as a result of technological, economic, and regulatory factors. Consider the case of cable television. The economics of cabling are such that it is unprofitable to wire areas that are sparsely populated. Even if the potential subscribers could pay the going rate for service, there are too few of them for cable companies to recover the costs of constructing the distribution system. Barring direct government subsidies, or a kind of utility regulation that allows cross-subsidization, people in these areas will have to resort to extraordinary means to gain access to the channels available to cable subscribers.

Even in areas that are cabled, the differential availability of channels is, at least in the short term, a fact of life. Cable systems have varying channel capacities and may therefore be unable to carry all the cable networks that viewers desire. Systems wth no practical limit in capacity, often "bundle" channels into levels or tiers service, making classes of channels available only for a premium (Wildman & Owen, 1985). Finally, of course, households that are passed by a cable may, for reasons of cost or preference, simply decline to subscribe.

Although alternative delivery systems, such as satellite reception dishes, multipoint distribution systems, and VCRs do not exhibit the same limiting factors as cable, they carry their own technical limitations and impose their own sets of costs. It appears, then, that the net effect of the new technologies will be to make channels, and the kinds of content they carry, differentially available to the public.

Far from being the uniform and inescapable presence so often portrayed, the new media seem capable of recreating what we think of as television in a different form. It seems reasonable to expect that the medium will offer increasingly diverse programming, that this material will tend to be organized in channels specializing in relatively homogeneous forms of content, and that these channels will be available to some, but not all members of the public. Further, it is worth noting that this evolution does not assume any changes in the motivations of either media owners or their audiences. Quite the contrary, change occurs because entrepreneurs continue to seek profits, and viewers continue to seek programming.

AUDIENCE BEHAVIOR IN THE NEW MEDIA ENVIRONMENT

How these new media might alter the social impact of television or the need for various public policies, will, in large part, depend on how the audience responds to the changing environment. Will people distribute their viewing widely across diverse program options, continue to view only mass appeal programming, or consume relatively heavy doses of specialized content? To begin answering these questions, we turn our attention to two features of audience behavior that are especially sensitive to the changing character of television just described. The first, audience fragmentation, has to do with how the total audience is distributed across available channels. The second, audience polarization, addresses the intensity with which individuals or audience subsets use specific classes of programs.

Audience Fragmentation

The most widely anticipated and well-documented effect of new media on audience behavior is audience fragmentation. Increased channel capacity has allowed new program services to enter the marketplace and to compete for the viewers' attention. Each service has, in turn, laid claim to some portion of the time people spend watching television. The total television audience that once distributed its viewing across four or five channels may now spread its viewing across dozens. In the aggregate, then, the audience is said to have become increasingly fragmented.

Indirect evidence of audience fragmentation has been apparent for some time through year-to-year comparisons of the combined audience share of the broadcast networks. In 1972, the three major networks commanded 97% of all the time the audience spent watching prime-time television. By 1984, that combined share had gradually dropped to 80% (Beville, 1985). The missing 20% was presumably spread across independents, public stations, and cable services, all of which grew in number and strength in the intervening years. During other dayparts, losses in audience share were even more pronounced (CAB, 1988).

A clearer picture audience fragmentation can be seen in a side-by-side comparison of noncable and cable households. Problems of self-selection aside, these reception types embody many of the qualities of old and new media, respectively. Table 11.1 summarizes how the total national audience in each reception type distributed its weekly viewing in the 1986/1987 tele-

TABLE 11.1
Audience Fragmentation:
Weekly Channel Shares in U.S. Television Households by Reception Type

	Reception Type		
Channel	Total TVHH	Noncable TVHH	Cable TVHH
Local Channels			
ABC affiliates	19%	23%	16%
CBS affiliates	22	26	18
NBC affiliates	22	27	18
Independents	14	18	10
Public	4	5	3
Total	81	99	65
Cable Channels			
Basic networks	13	—	23
Pay cable networks	6	—	10
Superstations	4	4	4
Total	23	4	37

Source: 1986/1987 A.C. Nielsen data developed by Cabletelevision Advertising Bureau. Totals may exceed 100% due to rounding and multiset usage. (A.C. Nielsen figures reprinted from "1988 Cable TV Facts, copyright Cabletelevision Advertising Bureau")

vision season. Not surprisingly, noncable households allocated virtually all their viewing to local, over-the-air, channels. Among cable households, the picture was different. Over one-third of all the time cable households spent watching television was devoted to cable channels of one sort or another.

What is not entirely clear is whether the use of cable channels has reduced the amount of time viewers spend watching local stations or, simply represents new viewing time added to the audience's daily diet of television. If broadcasters are, in effect, getting a smaller piece of a bigger pie, then much of their concern about audience erosion may be overblown. Although it is known that cable and, especially, pay cable homes watch more television than other households (A.C. Nielsen, 1984; Webster, 1983), such descriptive data make unequivocal causal inference impossible. A fairly substantial body of research and theory suggests, however, that total television use is not determined by the combined drawing power of available content (e.g., Barwise, Ehrenberg, & Goodhardt, 1982; Gensch & Shaman, 1980; Webster & Wakshlag, 1983). In that event, the pie has not gotten substantially bigger, but is simply being divided into more pieces. Fragmentation may, as a result, pose some threat to conventional broadcasters, though the economic consequences of this erosion are far from obvious (e.g., Wirth & Bloch, 1985).

Generally speaking, the phenomenon of fragmentation is a function of the number and strength of channel options available to viewers. For example, pay cable subscribers are known to distribute their viewing more widely than are basic cable subscribers (Webster, 1983). Across the entire audience, then, as more independent stations go on the air, as more people subscribe to cable, as the systems to which people already subscribe expand their services, fragmentation is likely to increase. Further, although good data are currently hard to come by, it seems probable that rapid growth in VCR equipped households will facilitate the general trend toward fragmentation.

It is also clear, however, that not all channels contribute equally to the fragmentation of an audience. Introducing a third broadcast network signal into a market that previously had two will certainly have a more dramatic effect on how the local audience distributes its viewing than adding a 35th new cable network to the local CATV system. Although this is intuitively obvious, it is worth considering why it is so.

The broadcast network signal will, excepting vagaries in local geography, be available to virtually all homes. Conversely, the impact of a new cable network is confined to those households that are in the cable system's franchise area and have subscribed to a bundle of services that include that network. Moreover, the limited reach of the cable network will diminish its appeal to advertisers, and so deny it the resources it needs to attract viewers. The differential availability of channels, therefore, circumscribes their potential for fragmenting the total audience. Because of these, and other factors any one cable network is unlikely to have a dramatic impact on total audience fragmentation. Nevertheless, the total of audiences diverted from old media by cable, VCRs, and other new media may be substantial indeed.

Audience fragmentation, then, is a feature of aggregate audience behavior that occurs in response to the increased availability of channels. It has important implications for the viability of new media and the economic well-being of older broadcast media. Further, to the degree that attendance to new media curtails the ability of the broadcast networks to command vast heterogeneous audiences at any point in time, fragmentation may also have larger social implications. Certainly the ability of television to provide society with some common ground, a core of shared experiences, has been an important aspect of the medium's presumed power (Gerbner & Gross, 1976; Hirsch, 1982).

As Heeter and Greenberg (1985) have noted, however, evidence of total audience fragmentation reveals little about how intensively individual channels are used. For example, does an overall market share of 5 result from everyone spending about 5% of their time watching a channel, or does it result from some subset of the audience devoting larger portions of time to the channel? To more fully understand the impact of new media, we must consider a less well-understood feature of audience behavior, audience polarization.

Audience Polarization

Audience polarization is the tendency of viewers to move to the extremes of either watching or not watching some class of programs. Such classes of programs might be defined by similarities in content, the channel on which they are telecast, or whatever dimensions are theoretically relevant. To the extent that one subset of the audience comes to use that class of programs while other viewers tend not to use it, the audience can be said to have polarized. The amorphous, universally available quality of the old media has, for the most part, made audience polarization a moot point. The characteristics of new media, however, could produce substantial levels of polarization. Broadly speaking, two factors are associated with the emergence of this phenomenon: program content and the structures through which content is delivered.

The availability of relatively diverse program content will, in principle, facilitate audience polarization. As noted earlier, both uses-and-gratifications theories and economic models of program choice (e.g., Webster & Wakshlag, 1983) assume viewers have consistent preferences for programs of a type. Similarly, most theories of selective exposure to communication predict that choice will be systematically related to content characteristics (e.g., Zillmann & Bryant, 1985). All other things being equal, as programming content diversifies it should be easier for viewers to find content that more closely conforms to their preferences and avoid content that does not. As a practical matter, this could mean an increased tendency for people to watch programs that portray social reality in accordance with their own world views, a systematic avoidance of what they consider irrelevant or irreverent, and, certainly, differential consumption of programming with distinct ethnic appeals. All of which bespeaks greater audience polarization.

It should be noted at this point that, theoretical expectations aside, the actual tendency of audiences to systematically watch or not watch content of a type is far from overwhelming. In fact, Goodhardt, Ehrenberg, and Collins (1987) have reported that there is no special tendency for people who watch one program to also watch different programs of the same genre. Other researchers, however, have found evidence of program type effects (e.g., Headen, Klompmaker & Rust, 1979; Tiedge & Ksobiech, 1986; Webster, 1985; Webster & Wakshlag, 1982). It appears that program type effects are limited by a number of variables including structural factors that are characteristic of conventional broadcast television (Webster & Wakshlag, 1983). There is some indication that content-based polarization is likely to be more pronounced in new media environments (Webster, 1986).

A second factor that has been associated with audience polarization is the structures through which program content is delivered. Channel loyalty, sometimes called a *network effect* (Bruno, 1973), is a common feature television audience behavior. It is "the tendency of programs on the same channel to have a disproportionately large duplicated audience" (Webster & Wakshlag, 1983, p. 434). So, for example, Goodhardt et al. (1987) have reported that the audience for one network program is about 60% more likely than the general population to watch another program on the same network on a different night. In other words, audiences are known to polarize around programs defined by the channel on which they are telecast. Why this happens is not entirely clear. During a single viewing session, it may result from several factors including a kind of "attentional inertia" (Anderson & Lorch, 1983; Webster, 1985). On a day-to-day basis, Darmon (1976) has speculated that such loyalty may, in fact, be a function program content. Goodhardt et al. (1987), however, suggest that it is independent of program type.

In any event, the very label of channel loyalty implies that a segment of the audience affirmatively seeks out a channel. It seems likely that a similar result would occur if some subset of the audience systematically avoided a channel. To the extent that new media channels are differentially available to substantial segments of the audience, the potential for a kind of *de facto* polarization is considerable. That is, audiences would move to the extremes of channel use and nonuse, not for reasons of preference, but because they are physically precluded from membership in the channel's audience. Such a potentially powerful determinant of polarization has not been contemplated by most audience analysts because television channels have been so routinely conceptualized as universally available.

Although either factor alone (i.e., content or structure) could produce audience polarization, in new media environments content and channels tend to be correlated. This is a situation ripe with possibilities for moving channel audiences to the extremes of use and nonuse. It also raises interesting questions about the patterns of audience behavior that may underlie the audience fragmentation described in the previous section. For example, do such overall patterns imply that each individual's viewing time is similarly distributed, or do they mask considerable variation from person to person?

Table 11.2 presents data that allows us to explore such questions. Arbitron television diaries, collected in a large southwestern market in 1982, were analyzed to reveal how intensely various audience subsets used different channels (Webster, 1986). The market had a typical complement of five broadcast stations, including an independent that offered Spanish-language

TABLE 11.2
Audience Polarization:
Weekly Channel Shares Across All Viewers
versus Those Who Actually Watch the Channel

	Channel's Share Across All Viewers	Percent Who Watch	Channel's Share Among Those Who Watch
Local Channels			
ABC affiliate	27%	84%	30%
CBS affiliate	30	86	32
NBC affiliate	19	79	22
Spanish independent	6	16	38
Public	2	20	7
Cable Channels			
Pay movie channel	4%	17%	19%
Superstation 1	3	20	12
Superstation 2	2	15	11
Superstation 3	1	8	6
Music video channel	<1	2	14
Sports channel	<1	3	8
News channel	<1	2	8
Religious channel	<1	1	8

Source: Adapted from Webster (1986).

programming. The left-hand column of numbers is the weekly share of viewing that each channel received across all individuals in the sample. These are much like the shares reported in the left-hand column of Table 11.1. The middle column reports the percentage of the sample that actually watched each channel at least once in a week. Such numbers are sometimes called a station's cume rating or circulation. The right-hand column is the share of viewing each channel received among only those people who watched the channel at least once in that week. This is an unusual share calculation based on subsamples of varying size depending, in each case, on a station's circulation.

Each of the local affiliates was watched at some point in the week by the overwhelming majority of the market population. The ABC station, for example, was seen by 84% of the sample, and across the entire market commanded a 27% share of audience. Further, among those who watched the station at all, it occupied 30% of their viewing time. The other affiliates exhibited the same general pattern, with overall market shares and audience subset shares being almost identical. Once we get beyond these traditional purveyors of mass appeal programming, however, the patterns of audience behavior begin to change.

The Spanish independent station had, overall, a 6% share of audience. However, it was viewed by only 16% of the sample and among those people it achieved a 38% share. For this subset of the audience then, the Spanish station was a more substantial presence than any one of the network affiliates. Such intensity of use is not apparent in conventional market shares. In this case, polarization appears to have been a function of preference for content because, as a broadcast signal, structural barriers to station use were minimal. A similar, although less dramatic, pattern existed for the public station.

The audience for cable channels also shows signs of polarization, although here causes are more difficult to clearly identify. Certainly, overall shares and circulation were limited by subscription to cable. Nevertheless, the differential availability of channels cannot completely explain the audience shares of all these channels. In the case of more specialized services, it appears that some special affection for or revulsion from content also drives polarization (Webster, 1986). In any event, among each group who used a given cable channel, it was a substantial item in their diet of television programming. In fact, research on music videos indicates very intense use of such services among their otherwise limited audiences (Sun & Lull, 1986).

Underlying the broad patterns of audience fragmentation described in the preceding section are various subpatterns of audience polarization. Although the total audience is more widely distributed than ever before, that apparently does not mean that individual viewers spread their viewing across an equally wide range of sources. Indeed, Heeter and Greenberg

(1985) have argued that even cable subscribers limit their viewing to a relative handful, or repertoire, of preferred channels. It seems likely that VCRs will only increase the tendency to watch or avoid classes of programs (Levy & Fink, 1984). As television becomes more diverse and structurally complex, then, people have created, sometimes by default, media environments that can be quite different from their neighbors. In the aggregate, this manifests itself as both audience fragmentation and polarization.

What extremes these emerging features of audience behavior will take remains to be seen. Although this section of the chapter has represented audience behavior as a simple result of the changing characteristics of the medium, in reality it is both cause and effect. If, for example, individuals demonstrate an appetite for continuous doses of relatively specialized kinds of content, then the industry is likely to oblige them and increased levels of polarization will result. If, as Ehrenberg (1986) has argued, viewers have a "demand for range" in programming, then more modest levels of polarization, probably attributable to structural factors, will occur. Finally, of course, if the consumption of new media threatens to produce undesirable social or economic effects, governments might set in place various policies that would affect the course of their development.

IMPLICATIONS OF EMERGING PATTERNS OF EXPOSURE

It is apparent that changes in the nature of television (i.e., increased diversity, a correlation of content and channels, and a differential availability of channels across the audience) bring with them increased levels of audience fragmentation and polarization. It is also apparent from the currently available data that traditional, mass appeal, network television still dominates the viewing habits of the American people. Nevertheless, changes in patterns of exposure to the medium need not be dramatic to be of real significance. As Gerbner et al. (1986) have pointed out, a "slight but pervasive shift" (p. 21) in the audience's experience with the medium may have far-reaching cultural implications. Offered here are some thoughts on what these emerging features of audience behavior may imply for media effects, media policy, and the study of television itself.

Media Effects

It has been a central tenent of much contemporary research and theory on the effects of television that the medium is a pervasive and uniform presence in the lives of all members of society. Represented as such a monolithic entity, television has been readily conceptualized as the source of many significant social effects. Among these are the medium's ability to promote social integration and cultural uniformity (Neuman, 1982), cultivate political moderation (Gerbner, Gross, Morgan, & Signorielli, 1984) and distorted perceptions of social reality (Gerbner et al., 1986), facilitate a "spiral of silence" in the formation of public opinion (Noelle-Neumann, 1973; cf. Katz, 1983), set broad societal agendas (McCombs & Shaw, 1972), and, more generally to maintain a scheme of class stratification (Murdock & Golding, 1977).

The audience's response to the new media raises questions about theories that blindly assume television is a uniform presence in the lives of all people. Not only are the new media themselves more diverse, but individual audience members seem to exploit that diversity to create increasingly unique media environments for themselves.

Audience fragmentation suggests that there is a decreasing probability that any two people will have seen the same program on television on a given evening. This might in some way alter the social utility of the medium as a common "coin of exchange." Conversely, this same phenomenon raises the possibility that advertising messages, which span the entire medium, might take on added salience as topics of conversation and definers of popular culture.

More importantly, the trend toward audience polarization suggests that there may be long-term, systematic differences in the kinds of content to which different segments of the population are exposed. Traditional forms of television enforced a certain breath of exposure on viewers. Ironically, it is only in more diverse media environments that individuals can consume relatively narrow regimens of content. Might such polarization in the consumption of television content ultimately produce an analogous kind of social polarization?

Even if the use of specialized channels or content does not dominate an individual's viewing time, it is conceivable that it may wield a disproportionate influence on the viewer. Minority language programming, for example, may be especially effective in forming perceptions of social reality, setting agendas, or maintaining the cultural identity of those who watch it. Such possibilities warrant further investigation by effects researchers.

Media Policy

Audience fragmentation, as noted earlier, can pose an economic threat to traditional broadcast media by eroding their audiences. Fears of "economic injury" to broadcasters have, in fact, been used as a regulatory rationale for limiting the growth of new media such as cable (e.g., Botein, 1985). Although new media may reduce the profitability of old media, at present, it seems unlikely that broadcasters will be driven from the air. Broadcasters and their networks enjoy near universal coverage of any given market area. In that sense, they are unique among televised media, and may constitute a "must buy" for advertisers (Wirth & Bloch, 1985). As long as broadcasters maintain that preferred position, broadcast television is likely to remain substantially unchanged.

Although ordinary "economic injury" has fallen into disfavor as a cause of government action, the FCC has noted a possible caveat. The commission has stated that if cable policies resulted in substantial diversion of audiences from local news and public affairs, some regulatory remedy might be called for (Webster, 1984). Such diversion is thought to pose a special threat to a participatory democracy by causing the electorate to be less well informed on issues of public importance. That the government would identify some preferred class of speech is certainly not unusual. That it might further devise a means to encourage exposure to that speech is more problematic. As a practical matter, it is hard to imagine how such a result could be achieved (Webster, 1984). It does, however, raise the possibility that audience behavior could be an aspect of policy making even if questions of economic injury are not at issue.

Perhaps the new media's tendency to polarize television audiences will pose the most difficult questions for policy makers. The growth of new media has long been encouraged as a way to increase television's diversity. But, as we have seen, increasing the medium's diversity does not necessarily increase the range of content to which any one individual is exposed. In fact, just the opposite is possible. If people systematically avoid entire classes of content that are thought to be "good for them" (e.g., news), or consume a steady diet of content that is "bad for them," might the government be compelled to act?

Traditionally, the government has relied on the existence of spectrum scarcity to justify regulations that imposed certain standards of fairness and balance on broadcasters. This was true even though the old media's economic motivations led them to present broad, socially acceptable programming anyway. The new media environment, with its profusion of channels, appears to be immune from content regulations other than those imposed by franchising agreements. If balance and diversity are to be imposed on a new media channel, then some alternative regulatory standard would have to be developed. Benno Schmidt (1978) has, in fact, raised the possibility that such a new standard could be framed in terms of audience behavior. Anticipating the possibility of extreme levels of audience polarization, Schmidt suggested that a "scarcity of viewer preferences and habit" (p. 215) might be used to justify government regulation. Such an approach, unlikely as it may be, would place audience behavior at the heart of communications policy.

Media Studies

Our relatively brief, and often humbling, experience with foretelling the future of communications media should, of course, temper pronouncements that great changes are afoot. Nevertheless, the long-term implications of the new media are so profound that we should be equally suspect of cynics who charge that television will never change. At present, the study of new media might proceed on two fronts.

First, we should be more deliberate in monitoring the media environment. Simple assertions that television is both uniform and ubiquitous are no longer tenable. How these new media evolve, and the structural characteristics they exhibit, will have important consequences for patterns of audience use and, in turn, our understanding of the media's impact. Of central importance to this exercise will be careful consideration of how diversity is to be defined and measured. Despite considerable lip service paid to the benefits of diversity, we are far from any consensus as to what, exactly, it means.

As the new media create possibilities for increasingly varied and complex television viewing environments, then our second task is to develop a fuller appreciation of how and why people are exposed to the various forms of television. What factors determine the options that confront different segments of the audience? How do viewers make choices among those options? How does the audience respond to, and in turn shape, is media environment?

Traditional communications scholars have devoted surprisingly little attention to audience behavior, perhaps because it has always seemed trivial, or even irrelevant, when addressing "larger" questions of the medium's influence or cultural significance. As a result, much contemporary work on media theory would have us focus almost exclusively on the system of messages television presents and/or how those messages are decoded (e.g., Blumler, Gurevitch, & Katz, 1985; Gerbner et al., 1986; Newcomb & Hirsch, 1984; Neuman, 1982). Although those remain important questions, to understand the role of media in modern societies, they should not be asked in isolation. Not only should we concern ourselves with the message and its interpretation, we must also ask, as never before, who in the audience sees to the message and how did they come to watch it.

ACKNOWLEDGMENT

Portions of this chapter appeared in, Webster, J. (1986). Audience behavior in the new media environment. *Journal of Communication, 36*(3), 77–91.

REFERENCES

A. C. Nielsen. (1984). *Nielsen report on television*. Northbrook, IL: Author.
A. C. Nielsen. (1987). *Nielsen report on television*. Northbrook, IL: Author.
Anderson, D. R., & Lorch, E. P. (1983). Looking at television: Action or reaction? In J. Bryant & D. Anderson (Eds.), *Children's understanding of television* (pp. 1-33). New York: Academic Press.
Barwise, T. P., & Ehrenberg, A. S. C. (1984). The reach of TV channels. *International Journal of Research in Marketing, 1*, 34-49.
Barwise, T. P., Ehrenberg, A. S. C., & Goodhardt, G. J. (1982). Glued to the box?: Patterns of TV repeat-viewing. *Journal of Communication, 32*(4), 22-29.
Bagdikian, B. H. (1985). The U.S. media: Supermarket or assembly line? *Journal of Communication, 35*(3), 97-109.
Beville, H. M., Jr. (1985). *Audience ratings: Radio, television, cable*. Hillsdale, NJ: Lawrence Erlbaum Associates.
Blumler, J. G., Gurevitch, M., & Katz, E. (1985). Reaching out: A future for gratifications research. In K. Rosengren, L. Wenner, & P. Palmgreen (Eds.), *Media gratifications research: Current perspectives* (pp. 255-273). Beverly Hills: Sage.
Botein, M. (1985). The FCC's regulation of the new video technologies: Backing and filling on the level playing field. In E. Noam (Ed.), *Video media competition: Regulation, economics, and technology* (pp. 311-329). New York: Columbia University Press.
Bruno, A. V. (1973). The network factor in TV viewing. *Journal of Advertising Research, 13*, 33-39.
Cabletelevision Advertising Bureau (1988). *Cable TV facts*. New York: Author.
Cook, T. D., Kendzierski, D. A., & Thomas, S. V. (1983). The implicit assumptions of television research: An analysis of the 1982 NIMH report on television and behavior. *Public Opinion Quartely, 47*, 161-201.
Darmon, R. (1976). Determinants of TV viewing. *Journal of Advertising Research, 16*, 17-20.
Ehrenberg, A. S. C. (1986, February). Advertisers or viewers paying? *ADMAP Monograph*.
Gensch, D. H., & Shaman, P. (1980). Models of competitive ratings. *Journal of Marketing Research, 17*, 307-315.
Gerbner, G., & Gross, L. (1976). Living with television: The violence profile. *Journal of Communication, 26*, 173-199.
Gerbner, G., Gross, L., Morgan, M., & Signorielli, N. (1984). Political correlates of television viewing. *Public Opinion Quarterly, 48*, 283-300.
Gerbner, G., Gross, L., Morgan, M., & Signorielli, N. (1986). Living with television: The dynamics of the cultivation process. In J. Bryant & D. Zillmann (Eds.), *Perspectives on media effects* (pp. 17-40). Hillsdale, NJ: Lawrence Erlbaum Associates.
Glasser, T. L. (1984). Competition and diversity among radio formats: Legal and structural issues. *Journal of Broadcasting, 28*, 127-142.
Goodhardt, G. J., Ehrenberg, A. S. C., Collins, M. A. (1987). *The television audience: Patterns of viewing*. (2nd ed.). Westmead, UK: Gower.
Greenberg, E., & Barnett, H. J. (1971). TV program diversity: New evidence and old theories. *American Economic Review, 61*, 89-93.
Headen, R. S., Klompmaker, J., & Rust, R. T. (1979). The duplication of viewing law and television media schedule evaluation. *Journal of Marketing Research, 16*, 333-340.
Heeter, C., & Greenberg, B. (1985). Cable and program choice. In D. Zillmann & J. Bryant (Eds.), *Selective exposure to communication* (pp. 203-224). Hillsdale, NJ: Lawrence Erlbaum Associates.
Hirsch, P. M. (1982). The role of television and popular culture in contemporary society.

11. TELEVISION AUDIENCE BEHAVIOR

In H. Newcomb (Ed.) *Television: The critical view* (3rd ed., pp 280-310). New York: Oxford University Press.

Jacklin, P. (1978). Representative diversity. *Journal of Communication, 28*(2), 85-88.

Katz, E. (1983). Publicity and pluralistic ignorance: Notes on the "spirial of silence." In E. Wartella & C. Whitney (Eds.) *Mass communication review yearbook* (Vol. 4, pp. 89-99). Beverly Hills: Sage.

Klapper, J. T. (1960). *The effects of mass communication.* Glencoe, IL: The Free Press.

Levin, H. J. (1980). *Fact and fancy in television regulation: An economic study of policy alternatives.* New York: Russell Sage Foundation.

Levy, M. R., & Fink, E. L. (1984). Home video recorders and the transience of television broadcasts. *Journal of Communication, 34*(2), 56-71.

McCain, T. (1986). Patterns of media use in europe: Identifying country clusters. *European Journal of Communication, 1,* 231-250.

McCombs, M. E., & Shaw, D. (1972). The agenda-setting function of mass media. *Public Opinion Quarterly, 36,* 176-187.

Meehan, E. R. (1984). Towards a third vision of an information society. *Media, Culture and Society, 6,* 257-271.

Murdock, G., & Golding, P. (1977). Capitalism, communication and class relations. In J. Curran, M. Gurevitch, & J. Woollacott (Eds.), *Mass communication and society* (pp. 12-43). Beverly Hills: Sage.

National Cable Television Association. (1985). *NCTA satellite services report.* Washington, DC: Author.

Neuman, W. R. (1982). Television and american culture: The mass medium and the pluralist audience. *Public Opinion Quarterly, 46,* 471-487.

Newcomb, H. M., & Hirsch, P. M. (1984). Television as a cultural forum: Implications for research. In W. Rowland & B. Watkins (Eds.), *Interpreting television* (pp. 58-73). Beverly Hills: Sage.

Noelle-Neumann, E. (1973). Return to the concept of powerful mass media. In H. Eguchi & K. Sata (Eds.), *Studies of broadcasting* (pp. 67-112). Tokyo: NHK.

Owen, B. M., Beebe, J. H., & Manning, W. G. (1974). *Television economics.* Lexington, MA: Lexington Books.

Poltrack, D. F. (1983). *Television marketing: Network, local, and cable.* New York: McGraw-Hill.

Signorielli, N. (1986). Selective television viewing: A limited possibility. *Journal of Communication, 36*(3), 64-76.

Schmidt, B. C. (1978). Pluralistic programming and regulation of mass communications media. In G. Robinson (Ed.), *Communication for tomorrow: Policy perspectives for the 1980s* (pp. 191-228). New York: Praeger.

Sun, S. W., & Lull, J. (1986). The adolescent audience for music videos and why they watch. *Journal of Communication, 36*(1), 115-125.

Tiedge, J. T., & Ksobiech, K. J. (1986). The "lead-in" strategy for prime-time TV: Does it increase the audience? *Journal of Communication, 36*(3), 51-63.

Waterman, D. (1986). The failure of cultural programming on cable TV: An economic interpretation. *Journal of Communications, 36*(3), 92-107.

Webster, J. G. (1983). The impact of cable and pay cable television on local station audiences. *Journal of Broadcasting, 27,* 119-126.

Webster, J. G. (1984). Cable television's impact on audience for local news. *Journalism Quarterly, 61,* 419-422.

Webster, J. G. (1985). Program audience duplication: A study of television inheritance effects. *Journal of Broadcasting and Electronic Media, 29,* 121-133.

Webster, J. G. (1986). Audience behavior in the new media environment. *Journal of Communication, 36*(3), 77-91.

Webster, J. G., & Wakshlag, J. J. (1982). The impact of group viewing on patterns of television program choice. *Journal of Broadcasting, 26*, 445-455.

Webster, J. G., & Wakshlag, J. J. (1983). A theory of television program choice. *Communication Research, 10*, 430-446.

Wildman, S. S., & Owen, B. M. (1985). Program competition, diversity, and multichannel bundling in the new video industry. In E. Noam (Ed.) *Video media competition: Regulation, economics, and technology* (pp. 244-273). New York: Columbia University Press.

Wilson, C. C., & Gutierrez, F. (1985). *Minorities and media: Diversity and the end of mass communication.* Beverly Hills: Sage.

Wirth, M. O., & Bloch, H. (1985). The broadcasters: The future role of local stations and the three networks. In E. Noam (Ed.), *Video media competition: Regulation, economics, and technology* (pp. 121-137). New York: Columbia University Press.

Zillmann, D., & Bryant, J. (Eds.). (1985). *Selective exposure to communication.* Hillsdale, NJ: Lawrence Erlbaum Associates.

12

Implications of New Interactive Technologies for Conceptualizing Communication

Carrie Heeter
Michigan State University

Communication scholars widely recognize a need to reconceptualize communication, in part because of changes brought about by new telecomunication technologies. Rogers and Chaffee (1983) argue that "scholars are going to have to shift toward models that accommodate the interactivity of most of the new communication technologies. New paradigms are needed, based on new intellectual terminology" (p. 25). Rice and Williams (1984) concur, adding that "new media may, in fact, necessitate a considerable reassessment of communication research. Intellectual changes must occur to match the growing changes in communication behavior" (p. 80).

Developments in telecommunication technologies continue to alter the ways in which we can communicate. Broadband cable, fiber optics, and various other transmission media provide wider bandwidth to carry more (and more complex) signals simultaneously. Systems that combine telecommunication and computer technologies allow diverse configurations for user involvement and services. What has traditionally been considered mass communication is complicated with many new "media" and different kinds of "masses" than before. The ability to engage in mediated interpersonal communication becomes increasingly available in a variety of manners.

These technological developments illuminate inadequacies in and issues relevant to traditional conceptualizations of communication, particularly mass communication. Few if any of the problems or solutions are unique to new telecommunication technologies; they have been raised by communication scholars in many areas. But for those studying new technologies, the need to address such issues is more immediate because many of the anomalies of the old models are physical realities as well as conceptual concerns. (For example, interpersonal scholars have suggested that receivers should be conceived of as playing a more active role in the communication process, whereas new technology researchers are studying computer-based electronic text news services such as videotex and teletext where "receivers" must play an active role, selecting each page of specific content they wish to view.) This chapter briefly reviews traditional conceptualization of mass communication. Properties of new technologies that may necessitate changes in those traditional conceptualizations are outlined and used to organize criticisms of existing models and propositions for a new model.

REVIEW OF TRADITIONAL CONCEPTUALIZATIONS

Mass communication was originally modeled as the one-way transmission of a message from source to receiver. Shannon and Weaver's (1949) mathematical theory of communication defines a communication system as an information source that produces messages to be communicated, a transmitter that operates on the message to produce a transmittable signal, a channel or medium to carry the signal to a receiver (the opposite of a transmitter), and a destination (the person or thing for whom the message is intended). Noise on the channel interferes with accurate transmission (Fig. 12.1). Although their model was developed to help engineers describe transmission of an electrical signal from one machine to another, it was widely adopted by communication researchers as a model for human communication. Osgood (1954) added the idea of human "encoding" and "decoding" of messages, referring to the translation of thought into expression, or the

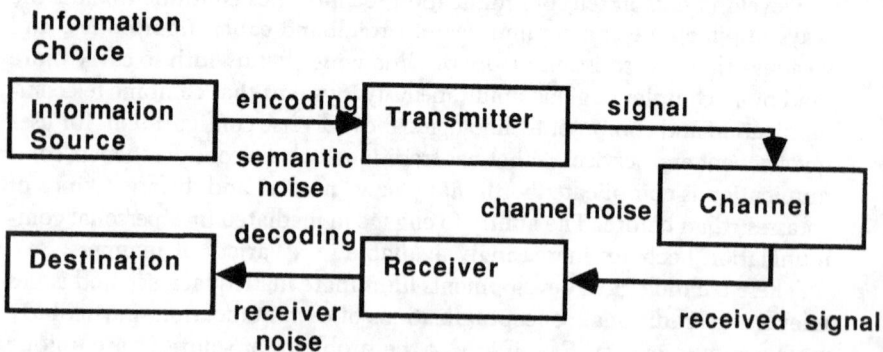

FIG. 12.1. Shannon and Weaver's model of communication

interpretation of expression as thought. The mechanics of encoding and decoding were not articulated in Osgood's model; he merely noted that the processes occurred.

Shannon and Weaver (1949) outlined three levels of communication problems their model was designed to address: (a) technical problems: How accurately can communication symbols be transmitted?; (b) semantic problems: How precisely do the transmitted symbols convey the desired meaning?; and (c) effectiveness problems: How effectively does the received meaning affect conduct in the desired way?. Their model is mechanistic, resembling a technical system. It also assumes that communication is purposive: that there is a desired impact. Early mass media research focused on purposive communication. Finally, it was a static rather than process model.

Following World War I, the "magic bullet" or "hypodermic needle" theory of mass media effects emerged: a belief that media propoganda had power to influence public opinion (DeFleur & Ball-Rokeach, 1982). Instinct psychology predominated, proposing uniformity of human nature and therefore uniformity of mass media effects. "The basic idea behind these [theories] is that media messages are received in a uniform way by every member of the audience and that immediate and direct responses are triggered by such stimuli" (DeFleur & Ball-Rokeach, 1982, p. 161).

When research findings failed to provide dramatic proof of uniform media effects, new perspectives emerged. The "two-step flow" model of media effects recognized that some people consume more mass media than others. Thus, information transmitted by the media may reach relatively well informed individuals (opinion leaders) who frequently attend to mass communication. The information is then passed on to those with less direct media exposure, through interpersonal communication. DeFleur and Ball-Rokeach (1982) label this the "social relations" perspective of media effects because it accounts for the influence of informal social relationships. In this one-way flow of information, a media message is sent to opinion leader receivers who transmit it in person to low media users.

Alternatively, the "social categories" perspective assumes that people with similar locations in society will relate their orientation and behavior to "such phenomena as the mass media in a fairly uniform manner" (DeFleur & Ball-Rokeach, 1982, p. 189). Individuals may not respond uniformly to mass media, but members of the same social group do. Sex, age, and education remain among the best predictors of media use habits. They serve as the primary intervening variables in this adaptation of the magic bullet theory (mediating direct, uniform effects), as do opinion leaders in the social relations perspective.

A third major perspective is that of individual differences. "The logical structure of the individual differences view of media effects is also a "cause (intervening process)-effects" structure, just as was the magic bullet theory before it" (DeFleur & Ball-Rokeach, 1982, p. 189). Here however, the intervening processes are variations in personal-psychological orientation, due to both biological and learning experiences.

"*The principal of selective attention and perception* was formulated as a fundamental proposition regarding the way ordinary people confronted the content of the mass media" (DeFleur & Ball-Rokeach, 1982, p. 187). Selective attention and perception suggest that individuals selectively attend to media messages, noticing some and ignoring others. Selective perception results in different impacts of the same message. An example of selective attention and perception (which presumably act together during media exposure) is the differential effects found for "All in the Family," a television sitcom portraying a bigoted character in a humorous manner. Those viewers who were initially prejudiced perceived Archie Bunker to be credible, whereas those who reported low prejudice found him pathetic or laughable (Surlin & Tate, 1976).

Westley and MacLean (1957) proposed a model that included features particularly pertinent to mass communication (Fig. 12.2). They introduced the concept of a gatekeeper, "C," (for example, a newspaper editor or TV news editor) who selects messages about external stimuli to which a receiver, "B," is not otherwise exposed, and transmits those messages to receivers. An original source, "A," may also exist (for example, a government official holding a press conference). The importance of gatekeepers is their role in selecting the information to which receivers can be exposed.

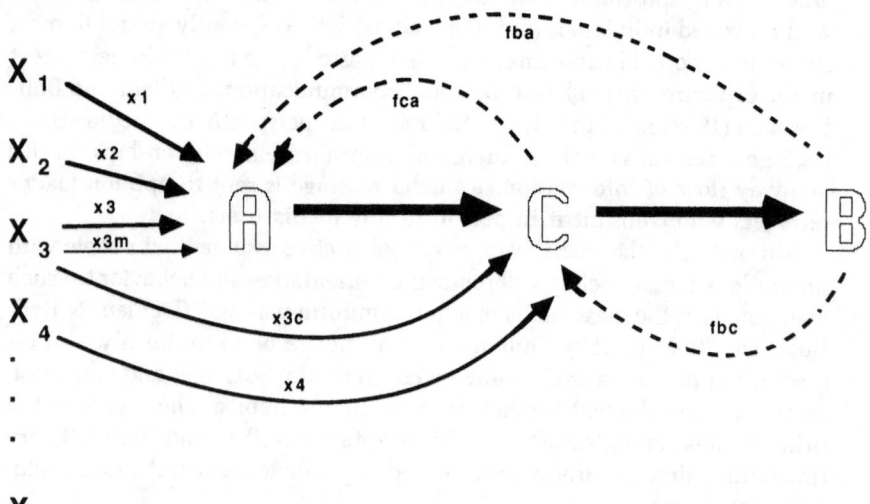

FIG. 12.2 Westley and MacLean's model

12. IMPLICATIONS OF NEW TECHNOLOGIES

Westley and MacLean also introduced the concept of feedback: responses from the receiver to the source, in reaction to receiving a message. In traditional mass media, feedback takes such forms as letters to an editor or phone calls to a TV or radio station, or purchasing an advertised product. The majority of mass media receivers do not engage in feedback for the majority of messages.

Westly and MacLean's (1957) addition of the concept of feedback moved away from a one-way flow of information, but not to the extent of considering the receiver as a full-fledged deliverer of messages. Even in interpersonal communication, where in practice there has been a two-way flow of messages all along, all receiver responses to a source's messages are considered feedback, rather than messages in their own right. Responses to an original message were somehow given second class treatment, perhaps due to the orientation toward purposive communication.

All of these perspectives basically maintain a one-way flow view of mass media, as do other models of communication that have been developed. Lasswell's (1948) verbal model, "who says what to whom in what channels with what effects," further exemplifies an overall concern with media effects. Berlo (1960) and Schramm and Roberts (1971) offer similar models differentiating source, message, channel, and receiver.

DIMENSIONS OF INTERACTIVITY

Most of the newer technologies feature increased interactivity. Rice (1984, p. 35) defined new media as communication technologies "that allow or facilitate interactivity among users or between users and information." Rafaeli (1985, p. 6) suggested that "studying interactivity is the special intellectual niche for communication researchers" in the realm of computers. *Interactivity* often is cited as a primary distinction of new technologies, but the term is rarely defined. When it is, a different range of meanings emerge. This chapter proposes that interactivity as it relates to communication technologies is a multidimensional concept. Six dimensions of interactivity are defined. This set of dimensions is a beginning, not intended to be exhaustive, but covering many of the major ways the term is used.

Dimension 1: Complexity of Choice Available

Rice (1984) approached interactivity in terms of the amount of choice provided to users. He selected this definition because more user choice makes it difficult to define a particular mass using a specified content of a given medium at a particular time. When more choice of content is available, the audience for any particular content at a given time is smaller. Broadcast television initially provided users almost exclusively with the three major network channels. Broadcast television is a mass medium in the traditional sense, reaching large mass audiences with the same program content at the same time. Cable television carries many channels, and the handful of subscribers choosing to use a public access program resembles a specialized audience fragment more than a mass audience. Even more disparate from the original concept of mass audience are media such as videotex. The group of subscribers accessing a particular page of videotex from the hundreds or millions of pages available at the same moment is minute. When users are provided with a choice, they must interact with a medium in the sense that they must make a choice. This dimension of interactivity, also referred to as "selectivity," concerns *the extent to which users are provided with a choice of available information.* (Information in this context includes any sort of media content, be it entertaining, persuasive or educational.)

Dimension 2: Effort Users Must Exert

Researchers have also defined interactivity as the amount of effort a user of a media system must exert to access information. Paisley (1983, p. 155), in his work with the videotex system Green Thumb, defined interactivity mathematically as "the ratio of user activity to system activity." At one extreme is cabletext (alphanumeric cable channels that provide a repeating cycle of text information). Cabletext has a zero ratio of user-to-system activity. Once tuned to the cabletext channel, users exert no effort beyond watching and reading the text information which the cable operator provides on that channel. At the other extreme is The Source (an alphanumeric computer network that provides news retrieval and other interactive services to subscribers). Paisley considered The Source to be near parity (a one-to-one ratio of user and system activity). In accessing news stories on The Source, users select each page they view, sending a message to the central computer asking to display the requested page. Diverging from Paisley's mathematical ratio but maintaining the focus on user effort, this concept can be broadened. For example, videocassette recorder users must exert more effort traveling to a rental store to pick up a tape than broadcast viewers do sitting down to watch television. A second dimension of interactivity is *the amount of effort users must exert to access information.*

Dimension 3: Responsiveness to the User

Rafaeli (1985) defined interactivity as a continuous variable measuring how "actively responsive" a medium is to users. He focused on interactivity from a user's perspective. Responsiveness is defined as conversationality, or the

12. IMPLICATIONS OF NEW TECHNOLOGIES

degree to which a communication exchange resembles human discourse. Some degree of "intelligence" is necessary in both the user and the medium of interaction. Rafaeli does not define intelligence other than to clarify that it could be artificial or natural. Technologically, intelligence might reside in a computer processor, either micro- or mainframe that is capable of recognizing and responding to information. The sophistication with which a processor is capable of responding to information varies widely. The microprocessor in a microwave oven is programmed to store and react to input about time and temperature. The central processor in a mainframe computer can be programmed to run all manner of software, for a variety of tasks. Rafaeli considered the sophistication of a processor from a user's perspective. Humanlike responsiveness is the highest level of sophistication. Thus, "ultimate interactivity is achieved when communication roles [of human and machine] are interchangeable and any third exchange in a series of communication transmissions is predicated on the bearings of the second exchange on the first" (p. 13). Rafaeli pointed out that ultimate interactivity is currently difficult or impossible for media systems to achieve. (Human communication also does not always achieve that ideal in conversationality.) However, media systems can begin to electronically approach human discourse standards of responsiveness. Artificial intelligence research is an attempt to do just that. Teletext and videotex programmers may achieve lesser levels of responsiveness by programming instructions, help pages, and error messages. Teaching machines and computer-aided instruction offer programmed interactive instruction that requires responses from and provides feedback to learners, to improve performance (Pressey, 1964). The third dimension of interactivity is *the degree to which a medium can react responsively to a user.* (Media systems can also interpose a human who responds to user queries, for example, the telephone operator. Thus media systems can be technologically or humanly responsive to users.)

Dimension 4: Monitoring Information Use

New technologies are changing the nature of feedback. With traditional media such as television, radio, and newspapers feedback refers primarily to media users calling or writing to the station management or editors. Newspapers conduct occasional reader surveys. For commercial TV and radio, audience rating services provide station operators and advertisers with data on what programs different types of people consume. A small sample of the audience is measured, usually by telephone survey, to generalize to overall viewing and listening habits. Stations drop programming that appeals to too small an audience and search for more popular content.

With some of the new technologies, user selection of information can be monitored on a continuous basis, across the entire population of users.

Videotex central computers can track every screen of information each user accesses. Similarly, videocassette rental outfits can monitor use of their film library. Two-way cable television systems can monitor viewership. The potential for continuous monitoring of system use has implications for billing and for programming system content to meet user interests. The fourth dimension of interactivity is the *potential to monitor system use*.

Dimension 5: Ease of Adding Information

With some new technologies, users actually act as an information source, providing information that is carried on a media system to other users. Broadcast television carries virtually no user-programmed content (with the occasional exception of an editorial comment). Electronic bulletin boards, on the other hand, are computer-based systems that link users by telephone to public message databases comprised almost entirely of user-generated content. Similarly, when cable television franchises provide public access channels, they offer a means for users to act as information providers. Some videotex systems permit users to add pages of information directly to the system's central database information collection. When a user can act as a source of information that is communicated to a mass audience, the traditional user role is substantially changed. A fifth dimension of interactivity is *the degree to which users can add information to the system that a mass, undifferentiated audience can access*.

Dimension 6: Facilitation of Interpersonal Communication

The dimensions of interactivity articulated up to this point apply primarily to mass communication, in which information is provided to many users. But interpersonal communication (not intended as synonymous for face-to-face communication, but communication between two people or among a small group of people, in which each participant can send and receive messages with each other participant) is also increasingly possible over technical systems. Media systems impose limitations on interpersonal communication that are not present in face to face interpersonal communication. Teleconferences can be configured to simulate face to face communication to varying degrees. Some teleconferences offer no possibility for interaction between source and receiver, involving merely the transmission of a television signal to a specific group or groups of receivers. Other configurations allow the receivers to ask questions of the teleconference originators by telephone. More fully interactive teleconferences provide full motion video origination capability to all participants. The degree of interpersonal

12. IMPLICATIONS OF NEW TECHNOLOGIES

communication possible is still limited by the choice of camera shots transmitted at any given time, and with the traditional channel limitations of video and audio resolution of television.

In computer conferencing, interpersonal communication can also exist, limited to an alphanumeric text channel for communication but varying in time limitations. Some computer conferences are asynchronous, with users responding to messages at different points in time during a day or week. Others are synchronous, with all conference participants participating concurrently. The computer conference most similar to face to face communication would allow any participant to communicate with any other participant, simultaneously. The time element of communication has rarely been discussed by communication scholars other than to say that communication by mail involves a delay. Technologies now permit machines to process faster than humans can, with data transfers occurring at fractions of a second. On the other extreme, during asynchronous computer conferences, the system may "wait" for a minute or a week for the user to finish typing a sentence. Time, channel, and various other elements may facilitate or inhibit interpersonal communication. A sixth dimension of interactivity is the *degree to which a media system facilitates interpersonal communication between specific users*. (Many technologies such as broadcast television allow for no interpersonal communication.)

IMPLICATIONS OF INTERACTIVITY

These six dimensions of interactivity are used to focus a synthesis of conceptual communication issues raised by developing technologies. Propositions about mass communication related to the six dimensions of interactivity will be derived, for use in developing a new model of communication. In some cases implications relate to more than one dimension of interactivity and the dimensions are discussed together.

Complexity and Amount of User Choice

> Broadcast television is like the passenger railroad, taking people to scheduled places at scheduled times. Cable television has the potential of becoming like a highway network, permitting people to use their television sets in the way they use their personal automobile; they may be able to select information, education and entertainment at times and places of their own choosing. (Parker & Dunn, 1972, p. 1395)

New technologies frequently offer users more choice of content than traditional technologies. The minimal level of user choice might be the captive audience—for example, a videotape being shown in a classroom (or, for that matter, an in-person lecture). The student can ignore the message, but selectivity operates most often in selective attention, perception, and retention. Somewhat more choice is offered to the home viewer in a community with a single broadcast television station. A watch—don't watch option is available in addition to the option of whether to pay attention once the set is on. Cable television provides users with more choice: numerous watch—don't watch options at any given time. Rental of videocassettes for home use affords even more choice at any point in time, so much so that users *must* (rather than can) actively seek content. Unlike cable, where the only effort needed is to turn on the set, the VCR rental user must go out, select a tape, bring it home, and choose a time to watch (and return it the next day). Many of the new technologies increase user choice as well as the amount of effort a user must exert to receive content. Some technologies (for example, videotex or VCRs) only provide information that is requested or sought. If the user seeks no information, none is transmitted. At this level, the physical process of communication is quite different from a one-way flow. The connection from source to receiver is activated by receiver actions. In other cases like cable television, engaging in active selection is an option available to the user.

Chen (1984) claimed that "we begin to see that passivity and interactivity are qualities of individuals making use of media, not the media themselves" (p. 284). That passivity is a user trait is most true for situations where user activity is optional. Active use characterizes both individuals and media systems. Chaffee pointed out that we are "already beginning to see theories in which the activation agent is the person, or a social system, in place of linear effects models that assume a message is the stimulus to action" (Rogers & Chaffee, 1983, p. 26). Chaffee's perspective moves the research focus to the user as an activator—a major departure from traditional models.

A move to consider receivers as active participants in the communication process is not unique to new technologies. Miller (1983), taking stock of the communication discipline, also observes a movement toward recognition of receivers as active participants. "Among communication researchers, a respect for the role of human volition has replaced the law-governed, deterministic paradigm of communication behavior" (p. 21). Further, quoting Reichenbach (1951, pp. 59-60), Miller (1983) added that humans actively exercise influence over their environment, rather than passively reacting to it. "Humans can *choose* among alternative courses of action in the pursuit of their goals" (p. 31).

White (1983) proposed a receiver-centered paradigm.

> Initially communication was conceived in terms of a relatively simple paradigm as a direct transfer of a message from the source to the receiver.

It was assumed that the completion of the transfer depends largely on the ability of the source to make the receiver accept and implement the message as the source intends. The paradigm was tested largely by measuring particular effects on attitudes or behavior such as imitative violence, sexual deviance, and voting. Virtually every attempt to test some version of this paradigm revealed "anomalies" which suggested that *the activity of the receiver and the sociocultural conditions of the receiver are far more important* in the communication process than the initial paradigm would imply. The anomalies have accumulated to the point that a new "receiver-centered" paradigm, or a paradigm in which interacting individuals together create meaning, is proposed as more adequate than the original source-message-receiver model. (p. 279, italics added)

Schramm (1983) objects to a one-way flow model, arguing that communication is not a one-way relationship in which a communicator "does something" to a passive audience. "Now the audience has as much to do with the effects as the communicator. Information flows both ways" (p. 14).

Chaffee pointed out that the concept of a mass audience becomes archaic, even though mass production of messages does not (Rogers & Chaffee, 1983). No longer is there a mass, undifferentiated audience receiving the same information at the same relative time, but instead audiences are characteristically specialized, often small and differentiated, with more in common with other consumers of the same content. Audience fragmentation—away from simultaneous nationally shared information content, and audience segmentation—development of special-interest channels or content with relatively homogenous audience segments, although not necessarily large in size—occur. Although there is no longer a mass audience of one medium, there is a potential mass audience for shared information across a variety of media when major events occur.

Pool (1983) suggested a change in research focus brought about by new technologies. The effect of mass media

is not the salient question to ask about an information retrieval system. If people have access to an enormous range of information and are able to choose what they want out of it, they may have all sorts of problems in skill and motivation in finding just what they want, but no one is telling them what ought to be heard or seen. This situation makes the user more interesting than the effects of the messages on that user. (p. 261)

Selective exposure research is an example of a receiver-oriented perspective already developed. The focus of this research is on why and how individuals expose themselves to information, rather than how media affect them. Zillmann and Bryant (1985) review current research directions. The earliest selective exposure research applied Leon Festinger's (1957) theory of cognitive dissonance to predict that information is selected on the basis of its consistency with attitudes, beliefs and behaviors. Information dissonant with such cognitions or behaviors is avoided (not selected) (Cotton, 1985). A universal principle is used to try to explain exposure, as did the magic bullet theory of effects.

The uses-and-gratifications approach to selective exposure has also been an active research area. Media exposure is believed to be motivated by anticipation of intrinsic gratifications (transitory mental or emotional responses) and in part, by utilitarian considerations or uses, such as guidance-seeking or utility for conversation (Atkin, 1985). Different individuals seek different uses and gratifications — an individual differences approach to a receiver-oriented model. A related individual differences approach is selectivity as a receiver trait, already suggested by Chen (1984) and exemplified by Heeter and Greenberg's (1985) analysis of cable viewing styles. Here, a model of the choice process in selecting programs to watch was developed, and viewers were found to engage in selectivity (examining options and changing channels) at different rates.

Increased user choice is only one element of technological change. The implications of this capability are summarized below as propositions for modifying our conceptualization of mediated communication.

P1: Information is always sought or selected, not merely sent.
P2: Media systems require different levels of user activity. (Users are always active to some extent.)
P3: Activity is a user trait as well as a medium trait. (Some media are more interactive than others; some receivers are more active than others.)

Degree of Responsiveness to the User

The enhanced potential for people and machines to exchange information raises the issue of whether those interactions should be considered communication. The nature of person–machine interactions varies widely across media systems.

An example of a simple person–machine interaction might be a videotex system in which users are frequently offered choices through a menu. The user selects a numbered option by pressing a key on the keypad. That selection is transmitted to a local or distributed intelligence that is programmed to receive and interpret the signal and to transmit or display the particular page of information the user requests. More sophisticated interactions can also occur. In Toronto, users of Teleguide could select restaurants by filling out multiple criteria electronic questionnaires that ask for desired price range, location, type of food, and types of credit cards accepted. Educa-

12. IMPLICATIONS OF NEW TECHNOLOGIES 229

tional psychologists built "teaching machines" before the introduction of personal computers, which provided the learner with programmed instruction and instant feedback about the correctness of responses.

At a more extreme level of person-machine interaction, users can write their own machine language computer programs, allowing them to control what the computer does, within the constraints of the language and the device (and the person). In some instances, the machines may exchange information with other machines, for example, a videotex mainframe may contact a restaurant's computer to log a reservation for a user. Eventually, the user's request would reach the people at the restaurant making seating arrangements. (Machine-to-machine exchanges are another area of philosophical interest to communication scholars, but those issues are beyond the scope of the present focus on human communication.)

A major issue is whether these interactions should be defined as communication. Hewes (cited in Rice & Associates, 1984) suggested that when we use computers, we communicate with the original system designers and database indexers, programmers, and so on, even though the original programmers may be long gone or far removed from the user's time and place and intent of use. Communication over traditional mass media is usually described as a message sent by a source to a receiver. Thus, when people read a book, they are communicating with the author who created those messages. Much use of new technologies directly parallels this model. For example, videotex users read pages of news that have been supplied to the system by "sources."

However, computers also introduce a form of person-machine exchange that does not necessarily parallel that model. When programmers write a computer program in machine language (binary code), they are likely to be doing so in order to use the computer as a tool, to produce some desired result. In a sense they may be considered to be communicating with the original creators of the machine or of machine language. But it is more the case that they are simply using the language that was created, much as we use spoken languages. Computer programmers are not seeking to be receivers or senders of mass communication messages. They are using programmed logic as a tool to interact with that structure to accomplish some result. It might be said that they are interacting with the computer, rather than with the original creators.

New technologies introduce a wide range of situations that fall somewhere between the two extreme models of computer programming and mass media consumption. Take the example of conducting a computerized bibliographic search. A large collection of bibliographic information exists in computer memory—too large to be useful in its entirety. The system has been programmed to interact with a user to select specific pieces of information to display. When users seek information by responding to or sending commands to the computer, they are operating in a simplified computer programming situation, interacting with the computer to accomplish a goal. When they are reading the actual bibliographic information once it has been selected, they are consumers of content created by a source for mass use.

Having suggested that persons and machines do interact, it becomes necessary to integrate that interaction with the concept of communication. Rice and Williams (1984) argue that person–machine interactions should be considered communication, pointing to cognitive psychologists' development of "mental model" theories of person–technology interaction. They cite a theory adapted by Borgman (1982) that posits that "humans, no matter their level of experience, develop images [of a technology] that lead to a conceptual representation of a device which is used in interacting with that device" (Rice & Williams, 1984, p. 65). This mental model theory permits co-orientation models of communication to be applied to human–machine interactions. For example, Newcomb's (1953) co-orientation model of communication (Figure 12.3) involves person "A" and person "B" and an external object, "X." From person A's perspective, A holds an attitude toward B and an attitude toward X. A also perceives that B holds an attitude toward A and toward X. Newcomb's theory assumes that there is a "strain toward symmetry" such that there is balance across these relationships. If A likes B and B likes X, A is influenced to like X. If A does not like B and B likes X, A may be influenced to dislike X. If B is a computer or videotex system (or TV channel) instead of a person, the mental model theory suggests that the strain toward symmetry would still apply. Thus, individuals approach machines in a manner similar to how they approach other humans. Perhaps they also approach person–machine interactions like they approach communication.

Fredin and Krendl (1984) apply the concept of schema (or script of expectations) to media, calling it a media frame. "A media frame can be de-

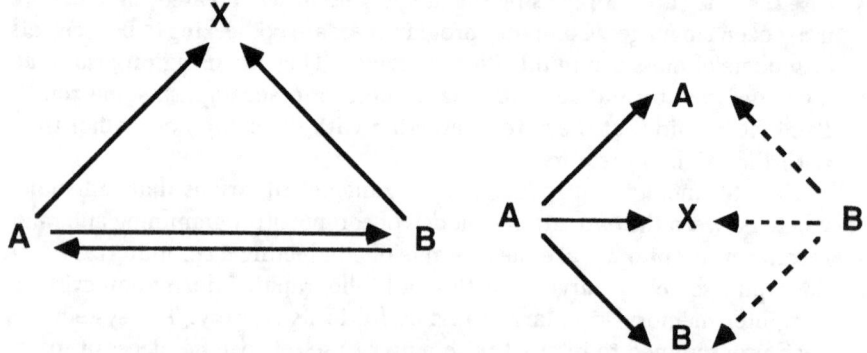

FIG. 12.3 Newcomb's co-orientation model of communication

fined as a structure of expectations individuals apply to organize and understand their experiences with a particular medium. It is evoked whenever the medium is being thought about or is present" (p. 2). The frame establishes a general relationship between the individual and the medium, and the medium and society. Fredin and Krendl demonstrated that eighth graders' media frames about computers changed after they used computers to access an electronic encyclopedia. Thus, a media frame evolves over time in response to experiences with a medium. Different people may have different media frames regarding the same media system, affecting their expectations about using the media system.

To say that person-machine interaction is not communication becomes increasingly difficult. Rice (1984) pointed out that even the legal distinction between communication and processing is blurring. He cited the AT&T divestiture as an example. "The distinctions between processing and communication are useful at the gross level: local distribution and long-haul transmission are officially communication but not processing. Value-added carriers provide both processing and communication, while service bureaus provide processing but not communications" (p. 34).

P4: Person-machine interactions are a special form of communication.

Degree of Monitoring System Use

The nature of feedback offered by some new technologies may need clarification and expansion. Arbitron and Nielsen rating companies have long provided estimates of audiences for TV and radio stations. Their measurement techniques include surveys (which are not as precise) and electronically monitored samples of households, used to estimate national audiences. These data are sold to the stations and to advertisers considering purchase of commercial time. This situation is quite different from that of a two-way cable system or a videotex system in which the system operator has the capability of monitoring all usage with great precision. (And, they are able to prepare their own reports for potential advertisers.) In such situations, the system operators have the potential to intricately link use with content and format features by precisely tracking use behavior. Westley and MacLean's (1957) model of mass communication included the concept of "feedback" (see Fig. 12.2). Purposive feedback on the part of the receiver includes letters to the editor that give media institutions some idea of the impact of their messages. Nonpurposive feedback is feedback the user does not initiate intentionally. In face-to-face communication, some body language may provide nonpurposive feedback to another communicator. Purchase behavior is used by advertisers as feedback on the effectiveness of advertisements, as is audience research. Some technologies permit a special kind of nonpurposive feedback that is not optional and rare, but built into the system itself. Continuous feedback, then, is the ongoing measurement of use behavior of a media system. This type of feedback is not an optional user response, but a monitoring of use which users may not be aware of and probably could not avoid if they wanted to. Some media systems can monitor use at point of purchase (e.g., movie theaters). Continuous feedback provided by some technologies is more extensive, including the ability to track behavior of particular users over time.

> P5: Continuous feedback is a special form of feedback in which use behavior is measured on an ongoing basis by a source (e.g., videotex programmer) or gatekeeper (e.g., cable operator) of all users.

Ease of Adding Information by Users

Media systems increasingly permit users to add information to the collection of information available to others using the system. In effect, the user can be a source of mass communication messages received by other users. Electronic bulletin boards are designed to be accessed by various users who add messages to the system for general consumption. Thus, the user is an essential information source (or information provider) for that system. Similarly, in some videotex systems, users can create pages of information and add them to the system. Videotex systems also offer "ask the expert" subroutines, where users "write in" questions and experts write in answers. The questions and the experts' answers are added to the system database, remaining there for a month or more. On Compuserve, users with valuable information are encouraged to formally become "information providers" as well as information users. A further challenge to the traditional one-way flow models of mass communication is this dissolution of the distinction between source and receiver.

> P6: The distinction between source and receiver is not present in all media systems.

Facilitation of Interpersonal Communication

Particularly with the various technologies used for conferencing (computer, video, and audio conferencing), users can exchange messages with other individuals in situations previously limited to face to face interactions. Telephony, for example, has long been a limited form of interpersonal communication, even though it is "mediated."

12. IMPLICATIONS OF NEW TECHNOLOGIES

> Because the new media are interactive and may be used in a variety of new situations—flexible interpersonal communication (for example, through electronic mail), group communication (through video conferencing), and private use of public information (through videotex)—the mediated communication is giving way to a continuum of communication behaviors. (Rice & Williams, 1984, p. 56)

This continuum ranges from interpersonal to mass communication, all of which can occur using mediated or unmediated systems. Rogers (Rogers & Chaffee, 1983, p. 25) claimed that "interactive communication represents a historical turning point away from the one-way transmission" of television and other traditional media, because "source and receiver cannot be distinguished in an interactive communication system." Conditions have already been identified under which a user can serve as an information provider to a system, offering messages for mass consumption. In the case of mediated interpersonal communication, all parties may communicate interpersonally with a specific other or others. Rogers (Rogers & Chaffee, 1983, p. 26) asked: will "participant" replace source and receiver? Will information exchange replace communication?

"One barrier [to a more general theoretical understanding of communication] has been the major division in communication research based on the distinction between interpersonal versus mass media channels" (Rogers & Chaffee, 1983, p. 24). That arbitrary distinction is breaking down some, in part due to interactive communication technologies.

> New communication technologies are no longer occurring just in mass media communication; they are now affecting interpersonal and small-group communication also. The miniaturization of computers is bound to affect the kind of research and theory that we produce, establishing entirely new communication situations. (Rogers & Chaffee, 1983, pp. 24–25)

> P7: Media systems may facilitate mass communication, interpersonal communication, or both.

This chapter has re-examined assumptions about the nature of communication in light of new technologies. Six dimensions of interactivity have been developed. Hopefully this perspective will encourage consideration of basic communication concepts both across different technologies and between mediated and nonmediated communication situations. As Chen (1984) stated: "Research that looks beyond the technology of each new medium to its underlying content and symbols will enable theoretical progress that does not stop at the borders of each machine" (p. 284).

REFERENCES

Atkin, C. (1985). Information utility and selective exposure to entertainment media. In D. Zillmann & J. Bryant (Eds.), *Selective exposure to communication* (pp. 63-92). Hillsdale, NJ: Lawrence Erlbaum Associates.

Berlo, D. (1960). *The process of communication.* New York: Holt, Rinehart & Winston.

Borgman, C. (1982). *Theoretical approaches to the study of human interaction with computers.* Stanford University Institute for Communication Research.

Chen, M. (1984). Computers in the lives of our children: Looking back on a generation of television research. In R. Rice & Associates (Eds.), *The new media* (pp. 269-286). Beverly Hills: Sage.

Cotton, J. (1985). Cognitive dissonance in selective exposure. In D. Zillmann & J. Bryant (Eds.), *Selective exposure to communication* (pp. 11-34). Hillsdale, NJ: Lawrence Erlbaum Associates.

DeFleur, M., & Ball-Rokeach, S. (1982). *Theories of mass communication.* New York: Longman & Associates.

Festinger, L. (1957). *A theory of cognitive dissonance.* Evanston, IL: Row & Peterson.

Fredin, E., & Krendl, K. (1984, November). *Computer frames: The evolution of thoughts concerning computers among adolescents.* Paper presented at the Midwest Association for Public Opinion Research (MAPOR), Chicago.

Heeter, C., & Greenberg, B. (1985). Cable and program choice. In D. Zillmann & J. Bryant (Eds.), *Selective exposure to communication* (pp. 203-224). Hillsdale, NJ: Lawrence Erlbaum Associates.

Lasswell, H. (1948). The structure and function of communication in society. In L. Bryson (Ed.), *The communication of ideas* (pp. 37-51). New York: Harper & Row.

Miller, G. (1983). Taking stock of a discipline. *Journal of Communication, 33*(3), 31-41.

Newcomb, T. (1953). An approach to the study of communication acts. *Psychological Review, 60*, 393-404.

Osgood, C. E. (1954). Psycholinguistics: A survey of theory and research problems. *Journal of Abnormal and Social Psychology,* XLIX, Morton Prince Memorial Supplement.

Paisley, W. (1983). Computerizing information: Lessons from a videotex trial. *Journal of Communication, 33*(1), 153-161.

Parker, E., & Dunn, D. (1972) Information technology: Its social potential. *Science, 176,* 1392-1399.

Pool, I., de Sola. (1983). What ferment?: A challenge for empirical research. *Journal of Communication, 33*(3), 258-261.

Pressey, S. (1964). Autoinstruction: Perspectives and problems. In E. Hilgard (Ed.), *Theories of learning and instruction* (pp. 153-181). Chicago: University of Chicago Press.

Rafaeli, S. (1985, May). *If the computer is a medium, what is the message: Explicating interactivity.* Paper presented at the International Communication Association convention, Dallas.

Reichenbach, H. (1951). *The rise of scientific philosophy.* Berkely: The University of California Press.

Rice, R. (1984). New media technology: Growth and integration. In R. Rice & Associates (Eds.), *The new media* (pp. 33-54). Beverly Hills: Sage.

Rice, R., & Williams, F. (1984). Theories old and new: The study of new media. In R. Rice & Associates (Eds.), *The new media* (pp. 55-80). Beverly Hills: Sage.

Rogers, E., & Chaffee, S. (1983). Communication as an academic discipline: A dialog. *Journal of Communication, 33*(3), 18-30.

Schramm, W. (1983). The unique perspective of communication: A retrospective. *Journal of Communication, 33*(3), 6-17.

Schramm, W., & Roberts, D. (1971). *The process and effects of mass communication.* Urbana: University of Illinois Press.

Shannon, C., & Weaver, W. (1949). *The mathematical theory of communication.* Urbana: University of Illinois Press.

Surlin, S., & Tate, E. (1976). All in the family. *Journal of Communication, 26*(4), 61–68.

Westley, B., & MacLean, M. (1957). A conceptual model for communication research. *Journalism Quarterly, 34,* 279–301.

White, R. (1983). Mass communication and culture: Transition to a new paradigm. *Journal of Communication, 33*(3), 279–301

Zillmann, D., & Bryant, J. (Eds.). (1985). *Selective exposure to communication.* Hillsdale, NJ: Lawrence Erlbaum Associates.

13

A Behavioral Systems Framework for Information Design and Behavior Change

Richard A. Winett
Kathryn D. Kramer
Virginia Polytechnic Institute and State University

Both government and private sector organizations often attempt to inform and to influence citizens and consumers through the use of information. For example, government may want to promote particular health, safety, or other consumer protection practices, and the private sector may try to develop and market certain information or information technology that either fits with or alters consumers' behavioral patterns. In both instances, a useful starting point would be a framework that integrates concepts about information processing, behavioral choice, and behavioral enactment. Principles and procedures for using information and information technology could be derived from these concepts, which are then applicable to real-life setting and are pertinent to such issues as information-technology development, information format, information delivery (channel and access), as well as *behavior-context* considerations.

Such a framework appears particularly important for various government information campaigns, instituted alone or in collaboration with universities and industry, that have been directed in recent years to such concerns as smoking prevention, drunk driving, and dietary change. Unfortunately, most campaigns have failed or had very modest results (Wallack, 1981). Clearly, some of the limited success is attributable to access problems (i.e., the inability to provide long enough or frequent enough exposure to information). However, it is also becoming apparent that part of the problem is conceptual. The relatively singular frameworks (e.g., "attitude change") for information (campaign) development, implementation, and impact analysis have generally not demonstrated effectiveness (McGuire, 1981). More integrative frameworks incorporating aspects from several disciplines or theories (e.g., psychology, communication, diffusion, marketing) have shown some limited success (Solomon & Maccoby, 1984). However, most of the tests of these frameworks have been rather molar (e.g., the Stanford community health projects, Farquhar et al., 1985), and it has not been possible to more specifically delineate concepts, principles, and procedures that are effective.

Developing a conceptual framework is especially needed in light of the various kinds of "new media," (i.e., interactive computer-communication systems) that have been developed since the 1960s (Rice, 1984). In some cases, the design and software of these systems have partly rested on psychological input concerning cognitive processes. However, there appear to be few instances of new media following a framework where cognitive processes (e.g., information acquisition) are linked to behavioral processes (i.e., performance) *both* at the time and place of interaction with the new media, *and for other* related times, places, and behaviors (Kiesler, Siegel, & McGuire, 1984). For example, an interactive system in a supermarket providing nutritional information need not only maintain consumer attention and use of the system, *but* presumably could follow concepts, principles, and procedures that would increase the probability of consumers acting on the information (i.e., shopping for more nutritious foods) over a long period of time. Unfortunately, although much research has focused on "person-machine" interactions, very little new media research has dealt with behavioral responses outside of the "machine setting" (Rice, 1984).

This pattern of research is similar to a large body of communication research that has been criticized for not focusing more on short- and long-term behavioral processes and outcomes (McGuire, 1981). This last point is illustrated more generally by an examination of McGuire's schema (shown in Table 13.1) for communication variables and research. Very briefly, two basic problems (discussed at length in Winett, 1986) exist:

1. There are some assumptions about the linkages of "early" (i.e., cognitive) dependent measures to "later" ones (i.e., behavior), assumptions that often receive only weak empirical support (i.e., different variables and processes are linked to different dependent measures; Bandura, 1986).

2. These assumptions and interests have led to much communication research on cognitive processes, and less research on behavioral processes, as illustrated in the figure (the + and − are based on the review of literature in Winett, 1986). Thus, a good deal of *new media* research is deficient because investigators have incorrectly assumed that the study of attitudes, perceptions, beliefs, and even reported intentions, are closely related to behaviors. Research has focused on these presumed antecedents at the expense of studying actual behaviors in appropriate contexts.

TABLE 13.1
A Basic Communication/Information Technology Model (from Winett, 1986, p. 16 based on McGuire, 1981)

Dependent Variables	Independent Communication Variables				
	Source	Message	Channel	Receiver	Destination
Exposure	+	+	+	+	−
Attending	+	+	+	+	−
Liking	+	+	+	+	−
Comprehending	+	+	+	+	−
Skills	−	−	−	−	−
Yielding (attitude change)	+	+	+	+	−
Memory	+	+	+	+	−
Information search & retrieval	+	+	+	+	−
Decision	+	+	+	+	−
Initiate behavior	−	−	−	−	−
Reinforced behavior	−	−	−	−	−
Maintenance	−	−	−	−	−

+ *Much* research & consideration   − *Minimal* research and consideration

BEHAVIORAL SYSTEMS FRAMEWORK

There appears to be a need for a framework applicable to diverse concerns such as the enactment of information campaigns and the development of information technology, which emphasizes cognitive and behavior linkages and behavior change in context. A framework is a system for organizing concepts, principles, and procedures. A framework may have a particular perspective, but is differentiated from a theory or theoretical system.

Winett (1986) has developed one such framework, "behavioral systems," and applied the framework to a number of different aspects of information development and impact (e.g., health campaigns, consumer policy, and new media). The framework integrates concepts from psychology (social cognitive theory, behavior analysis), communication, diffusion theory (particularly Bandura's, 1986, reconceptualization of diffusion theory), public health, and marketing. One hallmark of the framework is the attempt to use common concepts in conducting multilevel analyses (e.g., to understand setting and cultural resistance points for information), so as to properly frame information. Another hallmark is the attempt to use a common set of principles and procedures pertaining to message content, context, and delivery, for information used in a number of domains and channels. Bandura's social cognitive theory, which emphasizes the triadic influence of cognitive, behavioral, and environmental variables, has provided a fertile base for such principles and procedures.

A schema of the framework is presented in Fig. 13.1. This schema emphasizes the processes and concepts used in message development for a series of projects supported by the National Science Foundation (NSF), and in particular, for a recent project that focused on changing food-shopping purchases. Additional work using the framework, also in the area of nutritional change, is supported by the National Cancer Institute. Multilevel analyses are emphasized in the framework and used in conceptualizing and planning interventions. For example, understanding contemporary shopping behaviors in supermarket settings, and cultural and social barriers to change, are important for developing nutrition information campaigns. Information campaigns must realistically depict behaviors in context and provide workable strategies to overcome cultural and social barriers, points previously emphasized by social marketers (e.g., Manoff, 1985). For example, viewers of TV messages on beneficial nutritional practices need to be shown specific product substitutions in supermarkets, and how to prepare appropriate, alternative meals that might appeal to different family members.

Such specificity of content requires considerable formative and pilot research so that the specific content is developed for certain audience segments and then pilot-tested for effectiveness. Therefore, not surprisingly,

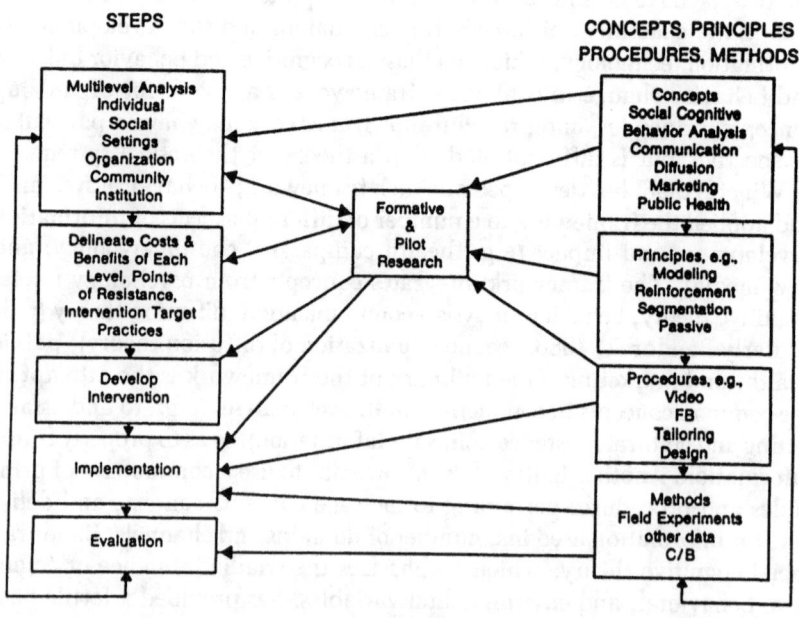

FIG. 13.1 Behavioral Systems Framework

13. INFORMATION DESIGN AND BEHAVIOR CHANGE

at the center of the framework is formative and pilot research. It is clear that many information compaigns have *failed* because of inadequate formative and pilot research (Rice & Paisley, 1981). Adequate formative and pilot research emphasizes behavioral processes in relevant contexts. The more typical formative and pilot research that tend to rely on questionnaires, focus groups, or reports of behavioral intentions is not appropriate for information campaigns or new media technologies with behavioral outcome targets. Rather, microanalyses of behaviors and settings must be performed and pilot-content tested for behavioral outcomes. For example, actual home observations of meals that are eaten and substitutions that are palatable are much preferred by behavioral researchers than are reports of such activities, and much preferred to more general assessments of nutritional knowledge and beliefs.

With regard to another domain, the framework not only ties together concepts, principles, and procedures for information design, but also appears to have predictive ability ("generality") across technologies and content. For example, on the one hand, various "prosocial TV" programs that resulted in documented viewer behavioral changes used a set of similar elements and variables. On the other hand, new media without certain elements seemed to be minimally used by consumers and was, therefore, likely to neither inform or influence (Winett, 1986, chapters 2, 5).

A final hallmark of the approach is the type of research seen as most appropriate for the framework. These points pertain to current media *and* evolving new media.

Although a number of research strategies can be used, microanalyses in formative research and experimental field studies to assess outcomes of overall procedures have been emphasized. Following the tenets of true experiments, the concepts and principles of the framework have been used to develop particular information strategies, generally tested out under real-world conditions, for appreciable periods of time. Clearly, as noted, the framework makes particular predictions about effectiveness (i.e., cognitive and behavioral change). In addition, and following a more basic research model, other measures in these field experiments have tracked linkages between cognitive and behavior change, assessed contextual factors influencing information impact and change, and investigated other processes or variables suggested as critical by different models of information impact. Further, the experimental methodology is in contrast to frequently used methods providing less causal inference, for example, in diffusion and communication research (post hoc surveys; Rogers, 1983). Indeed, Rogers (1983) has recommended that, where possible, the experimental approach be used in new diffusion research. By extension, this recommendation also is most appropriate for other communication and new media research.

As both a heuristic and a summary, we have attempted to place in one table much of what we feel is known about effective approaches to information and behavior. Therefore, Table 13.2 indicates effective and ineffective variables and elements of information strategies and campaigns. These variables and elements are derived from the framework, a review of relevant literature, and the use of classic communication variables.

Our more recent work (see following) has tried to incorporate all these effective variables and elements into information procedures. In addition, and as also is discussed later in this chapter, these same points (e.g., the emphasis on goal setting, feedback, and modeling procedures) form a basis for our proposed development of new media.

TABLE 13.2
Elements and Variables Related to Ineffective
and Effective Information Campaigns (from Winett, 1986)

	Ineffective	*Effective*
Message (format & content)	Poor quality decreases attention	High quality to enhance attention (e.g., comparable to commercial ad)
	Overemphasize quantity vs. quality	High quality may overcome some problems in limited exposure
	Vague or overly long messages; drab (e.g., "talking head")	Highly specific messages; vivid (e.g., behavioral modeling)
Channel	Limited exposure (e.g., late night PSAs)	Targeted exposure
	Inappropriate media (e.g., detailed print for behavior change)	Appropriate media (e.g., TV for behavior change)
Source	Not well attended to	Trustworthy, expert or competent; may be also dynamic and attractive
Receiver	Little formative research to understand audience characteristics	Much formative research to target message to audience
Destination	Difficult or complex behaviors resistant to change	Simple behaviors, or behaviors in a sequence, changeable and where long-term change can be supported by the environment
Conceptualization	Inappropriate causal chain (e.g., early events as predictors of later ones)	More appropriate causal chain and emphasize behavior change
	Little analysis of competing information and environmental constraints	Analysis of competing information and environmental constraints used to design messages
Goals	Unrealistic (i.e., expect too much change)	Realistic, specific, limited

13. INFORMATION DESIGN AND BEHAVIOR CHANGE

Finally, we are also becoming cognizant of the need to examine stages of behavioral change (acquisition, generality, sustained), and in particular, more thoroughly study processes involved in maintenance of behavioral changes (Bandura, 1986; Brownell, Marlatt, Lichtenstein, & Wilson, 1986).

RESEARCH LEADING TO THE DEVELOPMENT OF THE FRAMEWORK

Besides a recent book that has reviewed traditional communication and new media literature from the perspective of the behavioral systems framework (Winett, 1986), a number of projects under the auspices of the NSF have been seminal in formulating and then testing the framework. During the period 1979-1987, five field experiments were conducted that directly pertain to the framework. The first work (1979-1984) used residential energy conservation behaviors as a testing ground for concepts and principles derived from primarily social learning theory (Bandura, 1977), an early forerunner of the investigator's framework (e.g., Winett & Neale, 1979), and considerable prior work by the first author in a behavioral approach to environmental problems (Geller, Winett, & Everett, 1982). These field experiments, which lasted for periods of several months to more than a year, demonstrated the utility of several important concepts, principles, and procedures, and had a number of impacts:

1. Feedback and goal setting, conceptualized within social learning terms as a *consequence*, cognitive-behavioral procedure, could be refined (e.g., more clarity, simplicity, and specific goals) and have marked impacts on consumer behaviors, that is, large reductions in energy use (Winett et al., 1982) However, analyses indicated how feedback's effects were moderated by contextual factors (e.g., family budget share paid for home energy). These analyses led to a systems model of information impact and consumer behavior (Winkler & Winett, 1982) exemplified by the use of multilevel analyses as a key starting point in the behavioral systems framework.

2. Another ("antecedent") procedure derived from social learning theory, behavioral modeling, received extensive experimentation in this work (Winett et al., 1982). Behavioral modeling entails the active demonstration of desired behavior changes, and is a strategy particularly relevant for large-scale, media (video)-based strategies. Importantly, the development of effective behavioral modeling video programs involves not only attention to psychological variables and processes (e.g., reinforcement of models; the information acquisition—behavioral performance distinction; Bandura, 1986), but also integration and use of concepts, principles, and procedures from communication (Wright & Huston, 1983), diffusion (Rogers, 1983),

and social marketing (Manoff, 1985). For example, video programs must use formats and strategies to assure viewer attention, processing, and memory; messages must be tailored to particular audiences, who are shown how to overcome obstacles to adopting new practices. When the term *modeling* is used in this chapter it includes all of the aforementioned points.

At first examination, *feedback* and *modeling* appear to be different procedures involving very different processes. This is not the case. Both procedures require formats to make information easy to understand and remember and contextual factors to make information more salient. Both procedures also best use highly specific information tied directly to behaviors. Thus, both procedures, when effective, closely follow points noted in Table 13.1 (and see Winett & Kagel, 1984). In addition, the interactivity, tailoring, and immediacy of access and response provided by new media again suggests that feedback and modeling procedures may be even more effective within this new realm.

3. Psychology, marketing, communication, and diffusion research literatures enlarged the scope of the initial framework and were directly used in formulating the 20- to 30-minute video programs for the field experiments. These studies started on a small scale by showing the videos in small groups and in homes, with and without social interaction. Video programs used in all projects have been developed and produced in collaboration with the Learning Resource Center (LRC) at Virginia Tech. The LRC is an internationally recognized facility. In this way, it was assured that the video productions were of very high quality, one step in enhancing the internal validity of the studies. We feel that such careful step-by-step design, field testing, and refinement is absolutely essential for new media production.

The first studies showed that the modeling format was effective for information transfer (knowledge gain) and for behavior change (enactment of conservation practices and resultant energy savings). Similar information presented in a (video) discussion format was not effective (Winett et al., 1982). The modeling effects were highly replicable across populations and seasons (Winett et al., 1982).

Not surprisingly, a combination of feedback, goal setting, and modeling was most effective, and at times dramatically effective (Winett et al., 1982). For example, a modeling and feedback procedure resulted in savings of almost 50% of electricity used for air conditioning. However, it appeared that video modeling did not require extensive social contact to be effective (Winett, Love, Stahl, Chinn, & Leckliter, 1983), a point that is critical for its wide-scale applicability. In addition, carefully blending social cognitive, communication, diffusion, and social marketing principles resulted in a video program format that was effective when delivered over cable TV *without* accompanying personal contact (Winett, Leckliter, Chinn, Stahl, & Love, 1985).

13. INFORMATION DESIGN AND BEHAVIOR CHANGE 245

In this study, channel and access issues were also of importance. The project was conducted in collaboration with a cable TV system and, therefore, it was possible for the program to be shown four times during prime time.

In this study, following a baseline period, participants were randomly assigned to five conditions. A no-contact control condition only continued to have their outdoor electricity meter read. A no-contact media condition was only prompted by phone and letter to watch the program. A contact control condition had their outdoor meter read, but also each week completed forms related to comfort issues also investigated in this research (see the following). These forms were delivered and retrieved each week by staff persons blind to experimental conditions. A contact media condition, thus, was the same as the no-contact media condition, except for the form delivery and retrieval. Finally, a home visit, contact media condition was the same as the contact media condition, but also received a 45-minute home visit within several days of viewing the program to review and personalize the different procedures depicted in the program.

Thus, in this experiment, it was possible to assess the effects of the TV program alone, apart from personal contact. In addition, a special insert in the TV program asked viewers to place an "X" on a form used by viewers to rate the program. In this way, it was confirmed that 98% of experimental participants watched the program, and only 3% of controls watched.

The results of this study showed that viewing the TV program only once resulted in overall electricity savings of about 11%, and about 22% on electricity used for cooling. Results were about the same regardless of condition (i.e., the same effects with or without contact, or the more extensive home visit). Savings from the one viewing were maintained across the summer. A similar "booster" winter TV program produced similar effects, and there was some evidence for maintenance of effect with no TV programs during the next summer. The overall project appears to be one of the better demonstrations of how media can be developed and made effective by following specific guidelines (i.e., the points from Table 13.1 and social cognitive theory).

4. The work on home energy conservation also focused on the study of human comfort (i.e., a field-based, longitudinal approach to its study and alteration; Winett, Hatcher, Leckliter, Fort, Fishback, & Riley, 1981; Winett et al., 1983). As part of this research, we continuously measured temperature and humidity in participants' home and their perceived comfort. A "substitution strategy" was developed so that high energy use practices (e.g., extensive use of air conditioning) was replaced with low energy use practices (moderate air conditioning and window fans). A critical point here is that through this research we knew exactly what procedures reduced

energy use, but maintained comfort, and were acceptable to consumers. Such fine tuning of suggested strategies is essential if information campaigns are to be effective.

5. It was also apparent that concepts, principles, and techniques to present information to consumers were concerns that were quite central to economic theory and consumer policy (Winett & Kagel, 1984). For example, until recently, economic theory on consumer response to information has not considered that different types of information formats can have markedly different effects (Kahneman & Tverskey, 1984), a point demonstrated in the first author's comparison of modeling and discussion formats. Government and consumer agencies often attempt to present information to consumers to remedy asymmetries of information and market imbalances. Although extensive theory and principles have been developed on when and where information remedies should be used (Beales, Craswell, & Salop, 1981; Beales, Mazis, Salop, & Staelin, 1981; Mazis, Staelin, Beales, & Salop, 1981), there is much less consensus and research on *how* to make (e.g., third-party) information sources effective to inform and influence consumers (both topics are reviewed in Winett, 1986, chapter 6).

6. The conceptual development and demonstration of effective information remedies formed the backdrop of the last project that is reported in detail in the next section. That is, the regulatory concerns of effective consumer information and behavioral systems as the framework for such endeavors provided part of the rationale for that investigation.

7. It was also noted that much of the development of the framework to that point rested on our research focused on residential energy conservation. For some consumers, there were few constraints to changing energy-related practices in the home, and some of the practices required minimal effort or cost. That is, these behaviors may be "easy" to influence and require less consideration of contextual constraints (i.e., the multilevel analyses of the framework). Further development and tests of the framework could better rest with demonstrations with behaviors judged more difficult to influence.

8. The area of nutritious and economical food purchases was chosen as the testing ground. Active interest in the area involves presentation of third-party information to create more price competitiveness in the food (supermarket) marketplace (e.g., Devine, 1978; Greene, Rouse, Green, & Clay, 1984), and prominent health risks concerning dietary practices (high fat, low fiber, and low complex carbohydrate diets) and linkages to disease (cancer and cardiovascular diseases). As evidence has accumulated, these concerns have reached center stage. For example, professionals at the National Cancer Institute believe that 25% to 35% of site specific cancers are attributable to diet (Greenwald, Sondik, & Lynch, 1986). However, at-

tempts to modify food purchase and dietary practices have often been formidably resistant to change. For example, reviews of interventions for dietary change that focused on either individual, group, setting, organization, or community levels have generally shown no or minimal effects (reviewed in Winett, King, & Altman, in press). However, a zeitgeist appears to be forming that makes study in this area opportune and potentially more favorable.

In any case, we felt that the development of the behavioral systems framework, its conceptual base, principles, strategies, predictive ability, and *generality*, could receive a better test in an area where consensus exists on the difficulty of change, but where a changing context makes experimentation timely. These were the background points for our last NSF study that are briefly discussed here.

CURRENT PROJECT

Formative and Pilot Research

The current project is best seen as an initial effort into a more difficult realm than the prior research. As part of this effort, 6 months were spent conducting extensive formative and pilot research. This research included surveys and interviews to ascertain knowledge levels (nutrition and shopping), misinformation, current shopping and meal patterns and content, "behavioral flow" in supermarkets, points of resistance (e.g., cultural, ethnic) and influence, and acceptable change strategies.

A major contention was that information interventions would be most effectively delivered *outside* of the supermarket setting. This contention was based on the rapid pace of most shoppers and the existence of many competing sources of information already in supermarkets. However, partly based on the study's results, and partly based on ideas about strategically placing new media in supermarkets, this initial notion is being reconsidered.

Pilot research for the project included the development of 7- to 8-minute videotapes that were first used in focus groups for reaction, modified accordingly, and then used in pilot studies. In three pilot studies, the feedback procedures and forms were developed. In particular, the food-shopping checklist and reliability procedures described here received extensive pretesting.

In this way, the major study was started with a firm understanding of content and themes that would be deemed acceptable (and unacceptable) by potential participants and with procedures and methods that were workable. It also appears that the current project may be the only one to track all food purchases of many *individual* consumers over a relatively long time period.

Research Methods and Design. For this project, conducted in Blacksburg, Virginia, a door-to-door recruitment procedure within specified neighborhoods was used, which has been the recruitment method employed in all our prior studies. The participation rate (agree to participate/number contacted) of about 30% was appreciably less than in the prior work. This appears mostly attributable to the perceived difficulty in completing the food-shopping checklist. Although the 30% participation rate raises questions of selection bias and external validity, interestingly as a sample, a nutritional breakdown of the study sample's food purchases (see following) indicated that dietary practices closely followed national norms.

After a 7-week baseline period, participating homes were assigned to conditions using a stratified random assignment procedure (stratifying on neighborhood location and percent fat in food purchases). The design originally entailed a 2 × 2 design with a control condition. The variables in the design were feedback–no feedback and a modeling versus lecture format for the videotape. This second variable was conceptualized as a test of information *content* versus *context*. The 30-minute modeling videotape, within a storyline, used a combination of social–cognitive and communication principles that were effective (on cognitive and behavioral measures) in the prior research and received support from the literature. Many of the scenes were shot in supermarkets to demonstrate to viewers how to better negotiate this setting. Much of the approach centered on use of a *complete* shopping list as the major way to organize nutritious purchases at the lowest price, while reducing impulse buying. Other points focused on strategies to deal with cultural barriers (e.g., overcoming men's resistance to meatless dinners) with the depicted barriers and potential approaches to them based on the formative and pilot research.

The lecture videotape had word-by-word virtually the identical content as the modeling videotape, but was produced in a studio and delivered by an experienced and highly rated lecturer. In many ways, the lecture format was similar to public service announcements and many government-initiated information campaigns or information remedies.

The present study's comparison differs from the comparison of a modeling versus discussion tape format done in our prior work, in that the content of the tapes was identical. This was possible because a voice-over audio portion was often used in the modeling tape. In addition, all videotapes were viewed by participants alone in their home on project equipment with a noninteractive staff person present.

The feedback system revolved around the study's major dependent measure, weekly food purchases. All weekly food purchases were entered by participants on a food checklist that was hand-delivered and hand-retrieved (along with other forms) to participants on a weekly basis. All food items were computer-entered using software developed for the project by Dr. W. Bruce Walker.

Weekly purchases were all converted to grams and percent complex and simple carbohydrates, total carbohydrates, protein, saturated fat, total fat, and dollars spent weekly on food only. All participants had nutrition *goals* that were individualized given baseline nutrient levels, but that approximated the National Cancer Institute's nutritional goals (30% fat, 58% carbohydrates, 12% protein), and food expenditure goals of about 20% dollar reductions. On a standard form, participants in feedback conditions received a weekly nutritional breakdown in percent and the total amount of dollars for food purchases. Standard statements were used to express progress or lack of progress from baseline levels toward goals.

The food-checklist data received extensive item and price reliability checks using participants' detailed food-shopping receipts. These data were found to be of acceptable reliability (Kazdin, 1984).

Two conditions were added to this project for conceptual and practical reasons. The first procedure has particular importance and was called *participant modeling* (Bandura, 1986). In this procedure, all participants viewed the modeling videotape. Several days later, a staff person met separately with each participant in his or her home and developed a shopping list with them (the key nutritional and shopping strategy in the videotape). Next, each participant was taken on a shopping trip for their weekly shopping (similar to what was depicted in the video), following the videotape's guidelines, their shopping list, and interactive modeling procedures. Weekly feedback was provided by a 5-minute phone call.

Participant modeling is recognized as a particularly powerful behavior change strategy. It was used to examine the upper limits of change in nutrition and shopping practices, and to provide a *benchmark* for the video-feedback procedures. This was an important consideration since many prior studies have *failed to show any change* in nutritional practices.

In addition, the comparison on participant modeling and modeling and feedback follows a long history of interest in the communication and diffusion literature in interpersonal versus media-based procedures (Rogers, 1983), An early and simplistic consensus was that "media alone could not change behavior," a point countered by the investigator (Winett, 1986) and other researchers. In the present study, what was of particular interest relevant to this classic point was that the information procedures that were used had a firm basis in behavior change research, whereas the interpersonal procedures mirrored the information strategies and seemingly were the most powerful interpersonal approaches that reasonably could have been chosen. A comparison of the outcomes between the information and interpersonal procedures would, thus, shed light on this "axiom" of communication research.

A last procedure only included video modeling and a 45-minute general discussion in the home. This condition examined the effects of personal attention apart from the interactive instruction of participant modeling.

Thus, the study used a mixed factorial design (Keppel, 1982) and had these procedures: control, modeling-no feedback, modeling-feedback, lecture-no feedback, lecture-feedback, participant modeling, modeling-discussion. The order of effectivenes (percent nutrient change and reduction of expenditures) was hypothesized to be: participant-modeling, modeling-feedback, lecture-feedback, modeling-discussion, modeling, lecture.

As noted, the major measure was the weekly food items purchased by participants represented in nutrients (grams, percent) and cost. However, other self-report measures were used primarily on a pre-post basis. The purpose of these measures was to examine a "flow-through" (i.e., "hierarchy of effects") change process from attention to the video, knowledge change, retention of information, beliefs, intention to change, and self-efficacy with regard to instituting specific nutritional and shopping practices. In addition, participants were placed on a process of change measure, adapted for use for this project. Finally, detailed demographic and health risk (number of individual and family health risk indicators) data were also available from all participants, given the apparent saliency of these measures for health behavior change.

Overall, the self-report measures also allowed the examination of predictors of health behavior changes, with different theories and disciplines emphasizing different variables. For example, different theories emphasize health risk or costs of illness (Fuchs, 1975), health beliefs (Janz & Becker, 1984), or more specific psychological variables (Bandura, 1986). The data on "flow-through" and predictors were seen as information that could be included in, and enhance, the behavioral systems framework for subsequent research, as well as a way to substantiate hypothetical change processes.

Results. The major results of this study are summarized in Table 13.3. Examination of this table indicates that only conditions with feedback showed significant changes. For example, conditions where feedback was used showed a mean total fat reduction of 4.9%, whereas conditions without feedback showed essentially no change in total fat. However, modeling-feedback was considerably more effective than lecture-feedback, the former condition showing change on all measures except simple carbohydrates. Surprisingly, participant modeling was *not* more effective than modeling-feedback, although it is apparent that some important changes were more specifically enacted in participant modeling (e.g., the decrease in saturated fat). There was, unfortunately, no evidence for the effectiveness of modeling alone.

TABLE 13.3
Percent Change in Nutrient Content and Dollars Spent Weekly for Food Purchases During Intervention†

	Control	Modeling No FB	Modeling FB	Lecture No FB	Lecture FB	Participant Modeling FB	Modeling Discussion No FB
Complex Carb.	−1.2	−2.9	+5.4**	+1.9	+2.9	+1.5	−1.0
Simple Carb.	+1.2	+1.3	+0.1	−1.3	+0.6	+5.1	+0.3
Total Carb.	0.0	−1.6	+5.5*	+0.6	+3.5	+6.6*	−0.7
Protein	−1.6	−1.0	+0.8	+0.6	−1.1	−1.7	+1.2
Saturated Fat	+0.9	+0.4	−0.9*	−0.4	−1.2*	−2.2*	+0.7
Total Fat	+1.3	+1.8	−6.7*	−0.8	−2.6	−5.5*	−0.7
Dollars	−8.7	−12.5	−26.4*	−2.0	−15.6	−12.0	−2.7

†Only includes dollars spent on food
*$P < .05$ when compared to control condition
**$P < .01$ when compared to control condition

Although effect sizes appear small, it must be noted that the *degree of potential* change (e.g., from 40% fat to 30% fat) was minimal. However, the 6.7% reduction in percent fat by the modeling–feedback condition represents a 16.1% shift within the fat category of food and about a 60% reduction in fat toward the 30% goal. Further, we examined the percent of participating households during baseline and intervention that approximated (<32%) the National Cancer Institute's and the American Heart Association's recommended proportion of total fat. For all condition *except* modeling–feedback, during baseline *and* intervention, the percentage of households at or below the fat criterion was 19%. For modeling–feedback, the percentages were 10% during baseline, but 60% during intervention.

The overall effectiveness of modeling–feedback is a systematic replication of the first author's prior work (Winett et al., 1982). The relative nonsuperiority of participant modeling may be attributable to less than optimal procedures (although procedures conceptually and practically followed established guidelines; Bandura, 1986), or current limits to shopping-nutritional changes. In any case, the results suggest that in *some* instances media-based procedures may be about as effective as interpersonal ones (Winett, 1986). Further, and more generally, the study also supports the position that particular kinds of information procedures, which are crafted from appropriate formative research, and delivered to specific audiences, can result in behavioral change.

The failure to find any effects for the lecture alone and weak effects for lecture–feedback suggests that mere delivery of *content* even by a high-quality performer within this format is not sufficient to promote behavioral changes. Public service announcements and other third-party information remedies using this format, and that focus only on content, are likely to be ineffective (Winett & Kagel, 1984). This finding substantiates a major point of the research as first proposed (i.e., concerning information remedies) and is consistent with the points noted on Table 13.1. Content alone is often not persuasive or motivational.

It is our contention that modeling alone can be improved to be somewhat effective alone. On the one hand, data from participants suggested that the modeling video did not provide enough specific details on several topics (e.g., meal preparation). In addition, the most recent and incisive statements by the National Cancer Institute on diet and cancer were not included in the tape. On the other hand, microanalyses of individual purchases indicated that participants who saw the modeling video and changed their purchase patterns *did* follow the *particular* recommended strategies. That is, for some participants, the message was clearly received and acted on. Finally, modeling may be more effective if saliency, immediacy, and proximity (to behavior) issues are better addressed and use is made of new media systems.

It is also important to note that the use of modeling in small groups and over the cable TV system in the energy-related NSF work was preceded by more study and trials than for the current project. Data from the current project should be sufficiently useful so that modeling alone can be effective in subsequent work that we describe in the next section.

The additional self-report measures showed that the best predictors of change were the belief and health-risk measures. A schema based on these data and the effective procedures in the study suggested that a process of change flows from information saliency, to persuasion, to modeling, to other cognitive changes (i.e., enhanced self-efficacy to engage in certain behaviors), goal setting, behavioral enactment, feedback, and behavioral refinement. This process of change fits with the theory developed by Bandura (1986) and McGuire (1981), and needs to be further emphasized (and investigated) for information design and delivery in subsequent work.

Overall, we feel that the results support the viability of the behavioral systems framework as one approach to the study of information and behavior.

SOME FUTURE DIRECTIONS

As we noted, we considered the project that we just described as an initial foray into a difficult area, but one where there is increased evidence of dietary-disease links, and hence, urgency to modify the typical American diet. In addition, the procedures that were shown to be effective across a number of studies need to be appropriately embedded in new media information systems. Although the research suggested a number of possible directions, we have focused on one of them that we briefly present here.

As we noted, we believe that based on our prior work and participants' comments in the current project modeling alone could be effective. However, even if modeling alone was very effective, a major problem would still exist. That is, without considerable resources gaining access to the broadcast media, particularly television, for an extended campaign is highly unlikely.

Given this situation, we started to think about more specific, potentially less expensive new media, that could be directly targeted to certain audiences and be particularly salient to them. In addition, we, of course, wanted to build on our conceptual framework, principles, procedures, and previous and current findings.

We are designing, in collaboration with a major supermarket chain, and supported by The National Cancer Institute, the development of in-store and other site (e.g., shopping malls) public access, interactive information systems that fit the setting, are based on all the points noted in Table 13.1, and revolve around modeling, feedback, and goal setting. The use of new media particularly allowes for a degree of saliency, immediacy, and interactivity that promises to make these procedures more effective than in the last project we described.

In supermarkets, we envision systems having the following parts:

1. A modeling component using a minimally interactive videodisc format. Once inside a supermarket, a customer could activate the system and view 2- to 3-minute weekly segments. The segments will be part of an "unfolding" campaign based on a newly developed process of change model which extends over a 6-week period from a rationale to particular product substitutions and alternative meal suggestions. The campaign can then be altered and reshown. The segments will use all the modeling points previously noted, be based on considerable formative and pilot research, but be relatively brief so as to coincide with, and not interrupt, customer flow in the supermarket.

2. A simple, automated shopping list can be used for feedback on intended purchases. At home or in the store, customers can complete an opscan sheet that lists all potential major and some minor food purchases. With the use of a scanner, a stand-up computer, and a printer, it is possible to quickly provide feedback to customers on their intended purchases following procedures we used in the project described in the prior sections. To be maximally effective, feedback, as before, will be tied to specific goals. For example, the National Cancer Institute's goal for total fat consumption in 1990 is 30%, and for the year 2000, it is 25%. Customers will be able to immediately see how well the nutrition content of their intended purchases fits with this and other important goals. In addition, specific statements consistent with the feedback can also make product substitution suggestions.

3. A second feedback system may also be developed using the highly detailed receipt system that many supermarket chains have adopted. These receipts clearly list every product that was purchased (e.g., "Dannon Yogurt-Plain-one quart"), and it may be possible to both label products on the receipt ("low fat") and provide summary feedback as with the first system.

Although saliency and proximity to behaviors are advantages of the supermarket system, the quick pacing of the supermarket and an abundance of cues make it a less-than-ideal setting for information transfer and appropriate behavior change. Hence, we feel that systems in shopping malls, although reducing saliency and proximity, may be effective for nutrition change because individuals should have more time to interact with the system. Therefore, we are also investigating the use of video modeling and feedback systems in malls. Further, we also plan to develop specific prompting and incentive procedures so that customers make sustained use of the systems.

Clearly, many stores and mall areas are being inundated with "electronic merchandising" systems. However, as with other new media, it appears that few, if any, such systems have had a conceptual basis in a framework emphasizing cognitive–behavioral links; few have undergone extensive periods of formative and pilot research to develop content and formats; and apparently, few have received careful evaluations to assess individual and organizational impacts. And although some will disagree, few, if any, systems have been geared to be most beneficial to consumers.

It is also essential to track aggregate sales data at the level of the store. For example, it is important to know how increases in the purchase of some products compensate for decreases in purchases of other products. Further, critical concerns are what type of customer uses the new media system, and if the new media system attracts new customers to supermarkets or shopping malls.

If carefully executed, research on such systems also can have general application beyond the particular content, target audiences, and systems. For example, individuals who use new media systems in different settings can be tracked by tapping specific measures related to knowledge, beliefs, performance with the systems, and behaviors outside the "machine-setting." Such data can reveal much about the process of change as it relates to information and personal variables, information saliency, specific procedures, and setting influences. These findings, of course, can be used to develop more effective second generation systems.

This progression of conceptualization, formative and pilot research, the development of procedures and information systems, and process and outcome research illustrates the steps in the behavioral systems framework. The continuation of such research by us and other investigators assures more refinement, development, and application of that framework, particularly for new media that will be beneficial to consumers.

ACKNOWLEDGMENT

Research reported in this chapter was supported by grants from the National Science Foundation to the first author from 1979–1987.

REFERENCES

Bandura, A. (1977). *Social learning theory.* Englewood Cliffs, NJ: Prentice-Hall.
Bandura, A. (1986). *Social foundations of thought and action: A social cognitive theory.* Englewood Cliffs, NJ: Prentice-Hall.
Beales, H., Craswell, R., & Salop, S. C. (1981). The efficient regulation of consumer information. *Journal of Law and Economics, 24,* 491–539.

Beales, H., Mazis, M. B., Salop, S. C., & Staelin, R. (1981). Consumer search and public policy. *Journal of Consumer Research, 8*, 11-22.

Brownell, K. D., Marlatt, G. A., Lichtenstein, E., & Wilson, G. T. (1986). Understanding and preventing relapse. *American Psychologist, 41*, 765-782.

Devine, D. G. (1978). A review of the experimental effects of increased price information on the performance of Canadian retail food stores in the 1970s. *Canadian Journal of Agricultural Economics, 26*, 24-30.

Farquhar, J. W., Fortman, S. P., Maccoby, N., Haskell, W. L., Williams, P. T., Flora, J. A., Taylor, C. B., Brown, B. W., Solomon, D. S., & Hulley, S. B. (1985). The Stanford Five City Project: Design and methods. *American Journal of Epidemiology, 63*, 171-182.

Fuchs, V. R. (1975). *Who shall live?: Health, economics, and social choice.* New York: Basic Books.

Geller, E. S., Winett, R. A., & Everett, P. B. (1982). *Preserving the environment: New strategies for behavior change.* Elmsford, NY: Pergamon Press.

Greene, B. F., Rouse, M., Green, R. B., & Clay, C. (1984). Behavior analysis in consumer affairs: Retail and consumer response to publicizing comparative food price information. *Journal of Applied Behavior Analysis, 17*, 3-22.

Greenwald, P., Sondik, E., & Lynch, B. S. (1986). Diet and chemoprevention in NCI's research strategies to achieve national cancer control objectives. In L. Breslow, J. E. Fielding, & L. B. Lave (Eds.), *Annual review of public health* (Vol. 7, pp. 267-292). Palo Alto: Annual Reviews.

Janz, N. K., & Becker, M. H. (1984). The health belief model: A decade later. *Health Education Quarterly, 11*, 1-47.

Kahneman, D., & Tverskey, A. (1984). Choices, values, and frames. *American Psychologist, 39*, 341-350.

Kazdin, A. E. (1984). *Behavior modification in applied settings* (3rd ed.). Homewood, IL: Dorsey.

Keppel, G. (1982). *Design and analysis: A researcher's handbook.* Englewood Cliffs, NJ: Prentice-Hall.

Kiesler, S., Siegel, J., & McGuire, T. W. (1984). Social psychological aspects of computer-mediated communication. *American Psychologist, 39*, 1123-1134.

Manoff, R. K. (1985). *Social marketing: Imperative for public health.* New York: Praeger.

McGuire, W. J. (1981). Theoretical foundations of campaigns. In R. E. Rice & W. J. Paisley (Eds.), *Public communication campaigns* (pp. 67-83). Beverly Hills: Sage.

Mazis, M. B., Staelin, R., Beales, H., & Salop, S. (1981). A framework for evaluating consumers information regulation. *Journal of Marketing, 45*, 11-21.

Rice, R. E. (1984). *The new media: Communication, research, and technology.* Beverly Hills: Sage.

Rice, R. E., & Paisley, W. J. (Eds.). (1981). *Public communication campaigns.* Beverly Hills: Sage.

Rogers, E. M. (1983). *Diffusion of innovations* (3rd ed.). New York: The Free Press.

Solomon, D. S., & Maccoby, N. (1984). Communication as a model for health enhancement. In J. D. Matarazzo, S. M. Weiss, J. A. Herd, N. E. Miller, & S. M. Weiss (Eds.), *Behavioral health: A handbook for health enhancement and disease prevention* (pp. 209-221). New York: Wiley.

Wallack, L. M. (1981). Mass-media campaigns: The odds against finding behavior change. *Health Education Quarterly, 8*, 209-260.

Winett, R. A., Hatcher, J., Leckliter, I. N., Fort, T. R., Fishback, J. R., Love, S. Q., & Erlbaum Associates.

Winett, R. A., Hatcher, J., Leckliter, I. N., Fort, T. R., Fishback, J. R., Love, S. Q., & Riley, A. W. (1982). The effects of videotape modeling and feedback on residential thermal conditions, electricity consumption, and perceptions of comfort: Summer and winter studies. *Journal of Applied Behavior Analysis, 15*, 381-402.

Winett, R. A., Hatcher, J., Leckliter, I., Fort, T. R., Fishback, J. F., & Riley, A. (1981). Modifying perceptions of comfort and electricity used for heating by social learning strategies: Residential field studies. *ASHRAE Transactions*, 87, 555-567.

Winett, R. A., & Kagel, J. H. (1984). The effects of information presentation format on consumer demand for resources in field settings. *Journal of Consumer Research*, 14, 655-667.

Winett, R. A., King, A. C., & Altman, D. *Health psychology and public health: An integrative approach* (in press). Elmsford, NY: Pergamon Press.

Winett, R. A., Leckliter, I. N., Chinn, D. E., Stahl, B. N., & Love, S. Q. (1985). The effects of videotape modeling via cable television on residential energy conservation. *Journal of Applied Behavior Analysis*, 18, 33-34.

Winett, R. A., Love, S. Q., Stahl, B. H., Chinn, D., & Leckliter, I. N. (1983). Comfort standards and energy conservation strategies based on field experiments: A replication and extension of findings. *ASHRAE Transactions*, 17, 188-192.

Winett, R. A., & Neale, M. S. (1979). Psychological framework for energy conservation in buildings: Strategies, outcomes, directions. *Energy and Buildings*, 2, 101-116.

Winkler, R. C., & Winett, R. A. (1982). Behavioral interventions in resource conservation: A systems approach based on behavioral economics. *American Psychologist*, 37, 421-435.

Wright, J. C., & Huston, A. C. (1983). A matter of form: Potentials of television for young viewers. *American Psychologist*, 38, 835-844.

14

An Annotated Statistical Abstract of Communications Media in the United States

Dan Brown
East Tennessee State University

Jennings Bryant
University of Alabama

INTRODUCTION

The communications media are nearly ubiquitous in contemporary American life. Along with traditional media such as telephones, radio, and television, many new media may receive similar acceptance. For example, mobile telephone units may soon be in most automobiles, most businesses may soon use electronic mail. The transfer of information by means of machines is an accepted way of living in the United States, and the new communication devices appear to be gaining popularity at rates unprecedented by earlier media.

During the decade 1970–1980, the communications industry in the United States grew by an annual average rate of change equal to 1.9%. That rate increased during the 1980–1982 period to 2.1%, with 1,420,000 communications employees in 1982. Projections for growth of the industry during the period including 1982–1990 were 2.2%. The steady increase in growth rate is impressive, but the projections for 1990–1995 are even more so: 2.9% to a total of 1,950,00 employees. The figures for the radio and television broadcasting industry are higher than for the communications industry as a whole: from 139,000 employees in 1970 to 203,000 in 1980, yielding an average annual growth rate of 3.9%; to 221,000 employees in 1982, an average annual growth rate from 1980–1982 of 4.3%. The future appears, however, to foretell the reaching of a critical mass in broadcasting. The projected average rate of increase in the broadcast media from 1982–1990 falls slightly to 4.2% and then drops abruptly to 3.0% for the period between 1990–1995. Even with the drop in average rate of increase, the broadcasting industry is expected to continue to grow in total number of employees: to 308,000 in 1990 and 357,000 in 1995. We can more fully comprehend these changes and projections in light of the comparable figures for the growth of all industries: 2.2% growth during 1970–1980, a decline of 0.3% during 1980–1982, growth of 1.8% during 1982–1990 and 1.5% during 1990–1995 (U. S. Bureau of the Census, 1985).

One useful way in which to consider the scope of current developments in communications media is to place them into comparative historical context. Fortunately, investigations into the development of specific technological media innovations is supported by a substantial and diverse scholarly heritage. Some scholars have offered historical assessments of adoption trends based on archival data (e.g., De Fleur, 1966; Sterling, 1984); others have developed social–scientific models of diffusion and adoption with supporting evidence provided from diverse settings, situations, and disciplinary perspectives (e.g., Bandura, 1986; Rogers, 1983); still others have focused on models of forecasting the success of media innovations (e.g., Klopenstein, this volume). This chapter offers a relatively comprehensive historical examination of trends in the adoption of technological media innovations in the United States. Breadth rather than depth is the objective in that many communications media are examined, but little interpretation of data is provided. The result is a compilation of tables and graphs presenting patterns of adoption and use—a statistical history of the communications media in the United States. For some media, we attempted to provide data that illustrate message unit distribution (e.g., circulation). Whenever possible, official census data were employed. When such data were not readily available, alternative sources were utilized.

The Print Media

Some historians trace the printing press to ancient China. Marco Polo described Chinese printing in 1295, but the Western world traces its printing press to Johann Gutenberg, a 15th century German. In 1814, a two-cylinder press was developed that allowed simultaneous printing of both sides of the paper, turning out 1,100 copies per hour. Improvements by 1830 allowed the printing of 4,000 such double impressions per hour, making the mass production of newspapers a reality. Within a year after *The New York Sun* went on sale for a penny in 1833, the circulation of the newspaper rose to 8,000, and the era of the penny press had been defined. Table 14.1 and Fig. 14.1 and 14.2 illustrate this rapid growth that continued into the 20th century.

As the penny press newspapers catered to the masses, several magazines

TABLE 14.1
Newspaper Firms and Daily Newspaper Circulation 1704–1986

Year	Number	Circulation (millions)
1704	1	
1710	1	
1720	3	
1730	7	
1740	12	
1750	14	
1760	18	
1770	30	
1780	39	
1790	92	
1800	235	
1810	371	
1820	512	
1830	715	
1840	1,404	
1850	2,302	0.8
1860	3,725	1.5
1870	5,091	2.6
1880	9,810	3.6
1890	12,652	8.4
1900	15,904	15.1
1904	16,459	19.6
1909	17,023	24.2
1914	16,944	28.8
1919	15,697	33.0
1921	9,419	33.7
1923	9,248	35.5
1925	9,569	37.4
1927	9,693	41.4
1929	10,176	42.0
1931	9,299	41.3
1933	6,884	37.6
1935	8,266	40.9
1937	8,826	43.3
1939	9,173	43.0
1947	10,282	53.3
1950	12,115	53.8
1960	11,315	58.9
1965	11,383	60.4
1970	11,383	62.1
1975	11,400	60.7
1980	9,620	62.2
1981	9,676	61.4
1982	9,183	62.5
1983	9,205	62.6

(Continued)

TABLE 14.1
(Continued)

Year	Number	Circulation (millions)
1984	9,151	63.1
1985	9,134	62.8
1986	9,144	

Note: The data from 1704 through 1900 are from Lee (1973). The data from 1904 through 1947 are from U. S. Bureau of the Census (1976a). The number data after 1947 are from U. S. Bureau of the Census (1986).

targeting the middle-class audience sprang up during 1820–1842. By 1850, magazines offered previously published materials from other sources and reproduction of illustrations. Magazines in the 20th century moved from general to special interest publications. By 1929, magazine publishers sought national audiences that would attract advertisers. By the late 1950s, general interest magazines were on their last legs, and many of the old favorites

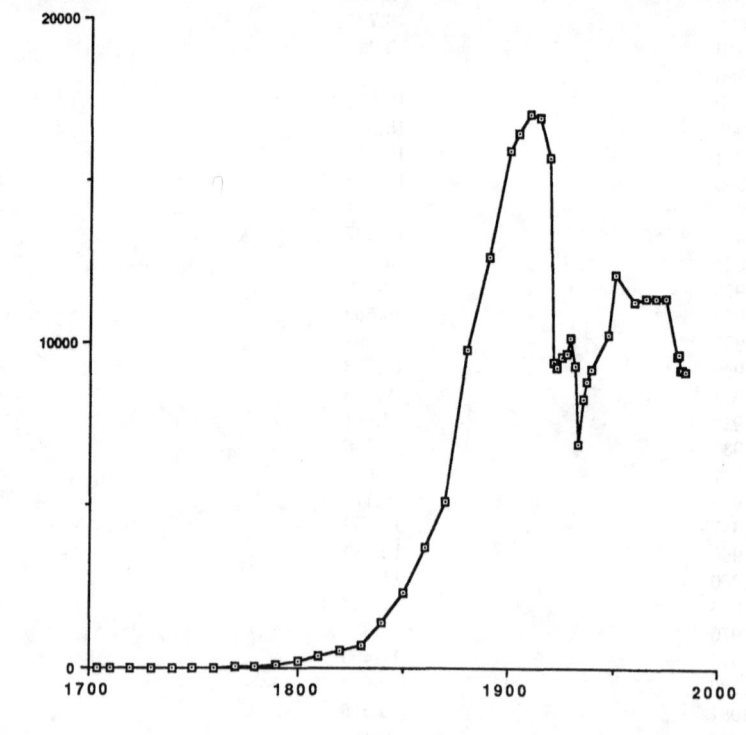

FIG. 14.1. Newspaper firms 1704–1986

14. STATISTICAL ABSTRACT

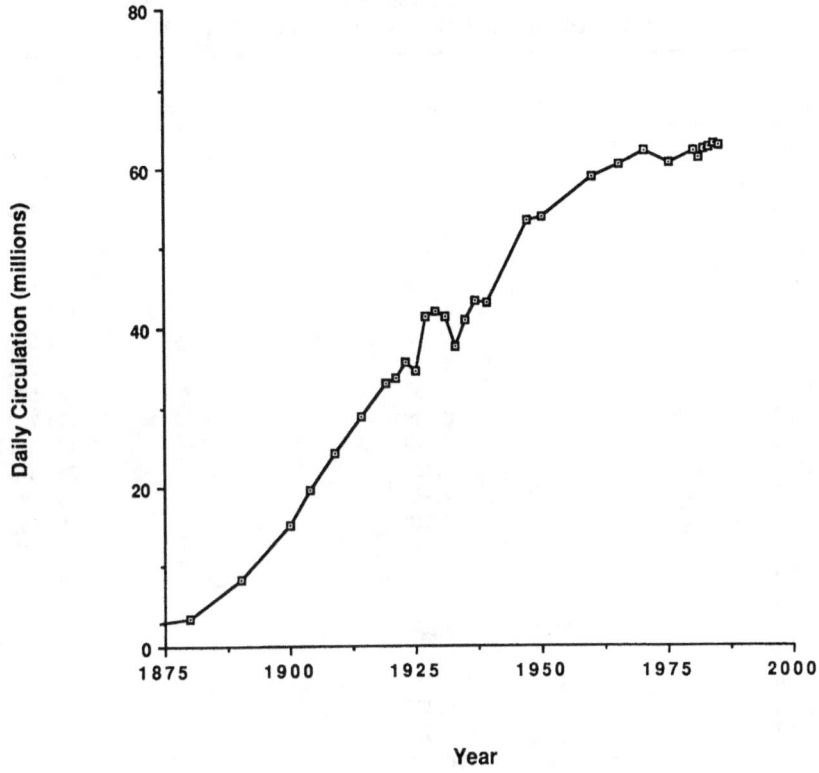

FIG. 14.2. Newspaper circulation 1850-1985

were dying out. The ranks of specialty publications that replaced them has more than doubled the number of 1950s periodical publications in the 1980s. Table 14.2 and Fig. 14.3 trace the 20th century growth of periodicals.

The *Bay Psalm Book* was published in America in 1640, and about 90,000 other titles were published in that era. Pamphlets were popular during the Revolutionary War, and publishing began to thrive in serving general, professional, and educational audiences. By the 1820s, paperback books arrived, although their spread was hampered by unfavorable postal rulings in the 1840s.

Soon after World War II, 25¢ paperbacks were marketed almost everywhere, and people who had never before purchased books became interested. By 1950, quality literary works began to appear in paperback. After the renewed emphasis on education that appeared in the late 1950s and early 1960s, the publication of educational books became quite profitable, and some of the nation's largest corporations entered publishing. Following total book sales of 1.56 billion in 1974, the number of volumes sold in-

TABLE 14.2
Published Periodical Titles and Circulation 1904–1986

Year	Titles	Circulation (thousands)
1904	1,493	17,418
1909	1,194	19,877
1914	1,379	28,486
1919	4,796	
1921	3,747	
1923	3,829	
1925	4,496	179,281
1927	4,659	191,000
1929	5,157	202,022
1931	4,887	183,527
1933	3,459	174,759
1935	4,019	178,621
1937	4,202	224,275
1939	4,985	239,693
1947	4,610	384,628
1954	3,427	449,285
1958	4,455	408,364
1960	8,422	
1965	8,990	
1970	9,573	
1975	9,657	
1980	10,236	
1981	10,873	
1982	10,688	
1983	10,952	
1984	10,809	
1985	11,090	
1986	11,328	

Note: The data from 1904 through 1958 are from U. S. Bureau of the Census (1976a). The data from 1960 through 1985 are from U. S. Bureau of the Census (1986).

creased every year until 1984. In the peak year of 1983, the 2.045 billion volumes sold represented a 31.1% increase over 1974 sales. The 1.6% decline from 1983 in 1984 to 2.013 billion books sold left the total 29% higher than the 1974 figure. Table 14.3 and 14.4 trace the publishing of book titles since 1880.

Telegraph

In the decade after the first patent in June 1840 on a wired electric telegraph system, the government entered and left the telegram-for-a-fee business because expenses ran nearly 10 times revenues. The Western Union

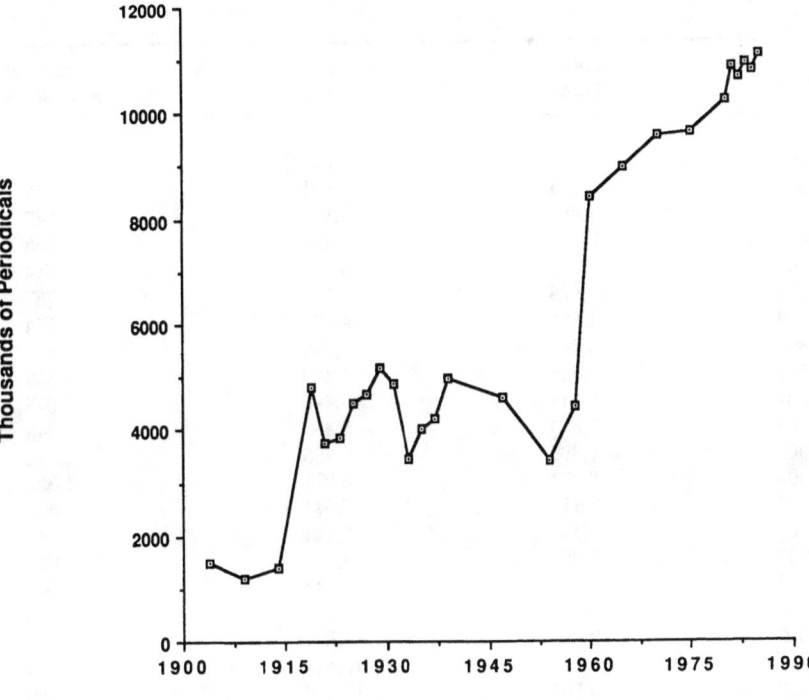

FIG. 14.3. Periodical titles 1904-1986

TABLE 14.3
Published Book Titles 1880-1984

Year	Total Titles	Number of New Books	Number of New Editions
1880	2,076		
1881	2,991		
1882	3,472		
1883	3,481		
1884	4,088		
1885	4,030		
1886	4,676		
1887	4,437		
1888	4,631		
1889	4,014		
1890	4,559	4,113	446

(Continued)

TABLE 14.3
(Continued)

Year	Total Titles	Number of New Books	Number of New Editions
1891	4,665		
1892	4,862	4,074	788
1893	5,134	4,281	853
1894	4,484	3,837	647
1895	5,469	5,101	368
1896	5,703	5,189	514
1897	4,928	4,171	757
1898	4,886	4,332	554
1899	5,321	4,749	572
1900	6,356	4,490	1,866
1901	8,141	5,496	2,645
1902	7,833	5,485	2,348
1903	7,865	5,793	2,072
1904	8,291	6,971	1,320
1905	8,112	7,514	598
1906	7,139	6,724	415
1907	9,620	8,925	695
1908	9,254	8,745	509
1909	10,901	10,193	703
1910	13,470	11,671	1,799
1911	11,123	10,440	783
1912	10,903	10,135	768
1913	12,230	10,607	1,623
1914	12,010	10,175	1,835
1915	9,734	8,349	1,385
1916	10,445	9,160	1,285
1917	10,060	8,849	1,211
1918	9,237	8,085	1,152
1919	8,594	7,625	969
1920	8,422	5,101	1,086
1921	8,329	5,438	1,008
1922	8,638	5,998	865
1923	8,863	6,257	921
1924	9,012	6,380	1,158
1925	9,574	6,680	1,493
1926	9,925	6,832	1,527
1927	10,153	7,450	1,449
1928	10,354	7,614	1,562
1929	10,187	8,342	1,845
1930	10,027	8,134	1,893
1931	10,307	8,506	1,801
1932	9,035	7,556	1,479
1933	8,092	6,813	1,279
1934	8,198	6,788	1,410
1935	8,766	6,914	1,852

(Continued)

TABLE 14.3
(Continued)

Year	Total Titles	Number of New Books	Number of New Editions
1936	10,436	8,584	1,852
1937	10,912	9,273	1,639
1938	11,067	9,464	1,603
1939	10,640	9,015	1,625
1940	11,328	9,515	1,813
1941	11,112	9,337	1,775
1942	9,525	7,786	1,739
1943	8,325	6,764	1,561
1944	6,970	5,807	1,163
1945	6,548	5,386	1,162
1946	7,735	6,170	1,565
1947	9,182	7,243	1,939
1948	9,897	7,807	2,090
1949	10,892	8,460	2,432
1950	11,022	8,634	2,388
1951	11,255	8,765	2,490
1952	11,840	9,399	2,441
1953	12,050	9,724	2,326
1954	11,901	9,690	2,211
1955	12,589	10,266	2,363
1956	12,538	10,007	2,531
1957	13,142	10,561	2,581
1958	13,462	11,012	2,450
1959	14,876	12,017	2,859
1960	15,012	12,069	2,943
1961	18,060	14,238	3,822
1962	21,904	16,448	5,456
1963	25,784	19,057	6,727
1964	28,451	20,542	7,909
1965	28,595	20,234	8,361
1966	30,050	21,819	8,231
1967	28,762	21,877	6,885
1968	30,387	23,321	7,066
1969	29,579	21,787	7,792
1970	36,071	24,288	11,783
1975	39,372		
1979	45,182		
1980	42,377		
1981	48,793		
1982	46,935		
1983	53,380		
1984	51,058		

Note: The data for 1880–1919 include pamphlets; 1920–1928, pamphlets included in total only; thereafter, pamphlets excluded entirely. Beginning 1959, the definition of "book" changed, rendering data on prior years not strictly comparable with subsequent years. Beginning 1967, the counting methods were revised, rendering prior years not strictly comparable with subsequent years. The data from 1904 through 1947 are from U. S. Bureau of the Census (1976a). The data from 1975 through 1983 are from U. S. Bureau of the Census (1984). The data from 1984 are from U. S. Bureau of the Census (1985).

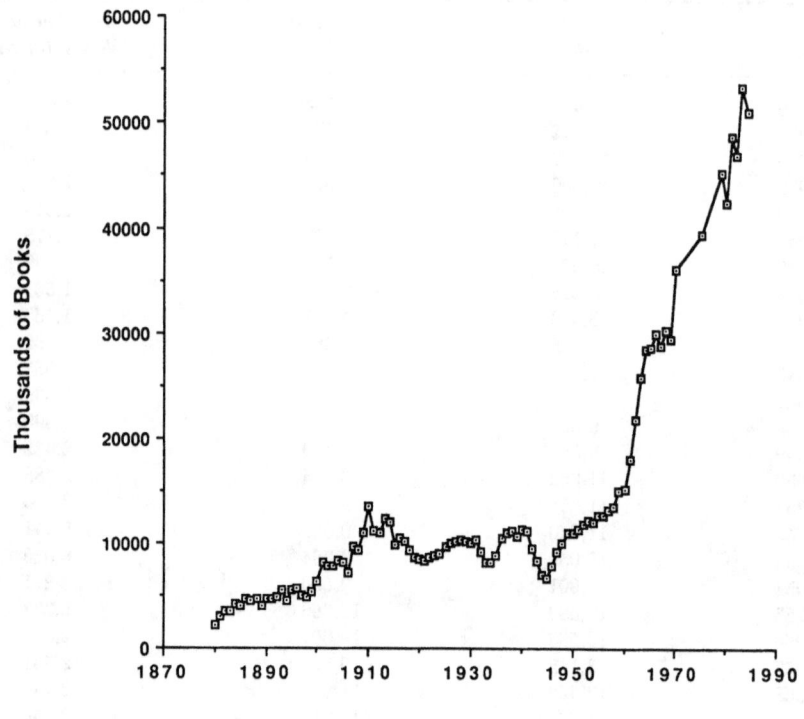

FIG. 14.4. Book titles 1880–1984

Telegraph Company dominated American telegraph business from the 1850s. By the mid-1860s, the company took over dozens of competitors and became the only company operating in the United States (Thompson, 1947). Smaller companies formed in later years to compete with Western Union in various regions or cities, but the older company remained dominant. Table 14.4 and Fig. 14.5 show the growth in the number of telegraph messages transmitted during the 19th century and the first half of the 20th century.

Telephone

Telephone service grew rapidly after the device was patented in March 1876. Table 14.5 and Fig. 14.6 illustrate telephone growth and penetration after that year.

Telephone answering machine sales amounted to $154 million in 1981. When the price of the machines declined to under $100 in 1983, sales rose 58%, and 1986 sales climbed to $450 million with nearly 5 million units

TABLE 14.4
Annual Revenue Telegraph Messages (millions) Transmitted 1866-1984

Year	Number of Messages		Year	Number of Messages	
1866	5.9		1912	----	(109.4)
1867	6.4		1913	----	
1868	7.9		1914	----	
1869	9.2		1915	----	
1870	9.2		1916	----	
1871	10.6		1917	129.3	(151.7)
1872	12.4		1918	134.0	
1873	14.5		1919	139.4	
1874	16.3		1920	155.9	
1875	17.2		1921	139.5	
1876	18.7		1922	149.2	(181.5)
1877	21.2		1923	158.5	
1878	23.9		1924	162.7	
1879	25.1		1925	185.2	
1880	29.2	(31.7)	1926	203.0	
1881	32.5		1927	103.4	(215.6)
1882	38.8		1928	211.6	
1883	41.2		1929	234.1	
1884	42.1		1930	212.0	
1885	42.1		1931	183.4	
1886	43.3		1932	143.1	(147.9)
1887	47.4		1933	143.6	
1888	51.5		1934	155.2	
1889	54.1		1935	176.3	
1890	55.9		1936	193.6	
1891	59.1		1937	200.7	(206.9)
1892	62.4		1938	185.6	
1893	66.6		1939	189.1	
1894	58.6		1940	191.6	
1895	58.3		1941	210.9	
1896	58.8		1942	223.1	
1897	58.2		1943	231.7	
1898	62.2		1944	225.5	
1899	61.4		1945	236.2	
1900	63.2		1946	212.1	
1901	65.7		1947	213.8	
1902	69.4	(91.7)	1948	191.0	
1903	69.8		1949	175.3	
1904	67.9		1950	178.9	
1905	67.5		1951	180.2	
1906	71.5		1952	151.7	
1907	74.8	(103.8)	1953	162.2	
1908	62.4		1954	152.6	
1909	68.1		1955	153.9	
1910	75.1		1956	151.6	
1911	----		1957	143.9	

(Continued)

TABLE 14.4
(Continued)

Year	Number of Messages	Year	Number of Messages
1958	131.9	1968	85.6
1959	131.0	1969	77.1
1960	124.3	1970	69.7
1961	117.3	1975	42.0
1962	112.5	1979	55.0
1963	104.2	1980	55.0
1964	97.4	1981	56.0
1965	94.3	1982	50.0
1966	92.7	1983	42.0
1967	89.1	1984	39.0

Note: Census data shown for some years in parentheses. The data from 1866 through 1970 are from U. S. Bureau of the Census (1976a). The data from 1975-1984 are from U. S. Bureau of the Census (1986).

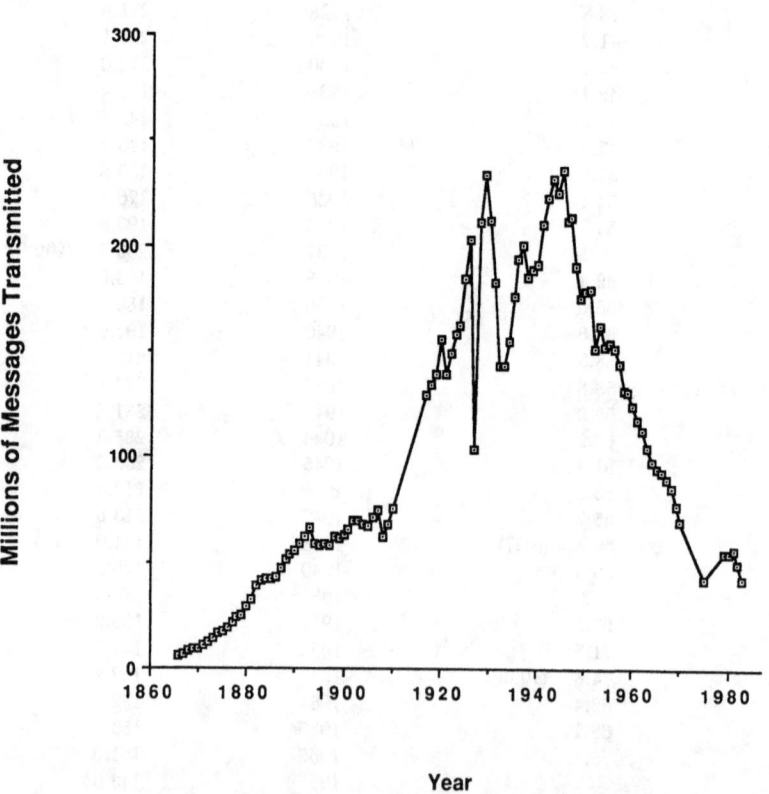

FIG. 14.5. Annual revenue telegraph messages transmitted 1866-1984

TABLE 14.5
Telephones 1876–1982

Year	Number of Telephones (thousands)	Percent of Households with Telephones
1876	3	
1877	9	
1878	26	
1879	31	
1880	48	
1881	71	
1882	98	
1883	124	
1884	148	
1885	156	
1886	167	
1887	181	
1888	195	
1889	212	
1890	228	
1891	239	
1892	261	
1893	266	
1894	285	
1895	340	
1896	404	
1897	515	
1898	681	
1899	1,005	
1900	1,356	
1901	1,801	
1902	2,371	
1903	2,809	
1904	3,353	
1905	4,127	
1906	4,933	
1907	6,119	
1908	6,484	
1909	6,996	
1910	7,635	
1911	8,349	
1912	8,730	
1913	9,543	
1914	10,046	
1915	10,524	
1916	11,241	
1917	11,717	
1918	12,078	
1919	12,669	
1920	13,273	35.0

(Continued)

TABLE 14.5
(Continued)

Year	Number of Telephones (thousands)	Percent of Households with Telephones
1921	13,817	35.3
1922	14,294	35.6
1923	15,316	37.3
1924	16,015	37.8
1925	16,875	38.7
1926	17,680	39.2
1927	18,446	39.7
1928	19,256	40.8
1929	19,970	41.6
1930	20,103	40.9
1931	19,602	39.2
1932	17,341	33.5
1933	16,628	31.3
1934	16,869	31.4
1935	17,424	31.8
1936	18,433	33.1
1937	19,453	34.3
1938	20,953	34.6
1939	20,831	35.6
1940	21,928	36.9
1941	23,521	39.3
1942	24,919	42.2
1943	26,381	45.0
1944	26,859	45.1
1945	27,867	46.2
1946	31,611	51.4
1947	34,867	54.9
1948	38,205	58.2
1949	40,709	60.2
1950	43,004	61.8
1951	45,636	64.0
1952	48,056	66.0
1953	50,373	68.0
1954	52,806	69.6
1955	56,243	71.5
1956	60,190	73.8
1957	63,624	75.5
1958	66,645	76.4
1959	70,820	78.0
1960	74,342	78.3
1961	77,422	78.9
1962	81,969	80.2
1963	84,453	81.4
1964	88,793	82.8
1965	93,656	84.6

(Continued)

14. STATISTICAL ABSTRACT

TABLE 14.5
(Continued)

Year	Number of Telephones (thousands)	Percent of Households with Telephones
1966	98,787	86.3
1967	103,752	87.1
1968	109,256	88.5
1969	115,222	89.8
1970	120,218	90.5
1975	130,000	
1979	153,000	
1980	157,000	93.0
1981	158,000	
1982	151,000	
1983	189,000	
1984	198,000	91.8
1985	205,000	92.2
1986	212,000	
1987	220,000	

Note: 1950–1982 data applies to principal carriers filing reports with FCC; earlier data applies to Bell and independent companies. Beginning in 1959, data includes figures from Alaska and Hawaii. The data for 1986 and 1987 are estimates. The data to 1970 are from U. S. Bureau of the Census (1976a). The data from 1970 through 1982 are from U. S. Bureau of the Census (1986). The data after 1982 are from U. S. Department of Commerce (1987).

sold, comparable to the number of cordless telephones that were purchased in 1986. Computerized business answering devices accounted for only $5 million in 1981 sales, but the 1986 figures were $310 million. Of the buyers, 64% were aged 25–44 and in the over-$25,000 annual income bracket. About 12% of the homes in America had answering machines by 1986.

Cellular telephone-users in America numbered about 1,000 in 1983, about 100,000 in 1984, and about 350,000 in 1985. In 1986, about 100 cellular telephone systems were operating in the United States, but numerous locales remained without service (Maney, 1986). The cost of cellular telephone service in 1984 was about $2,000 for installation, and dropped by half by 1986. Average 1986 monthly cellular phone bills ran around $125, a 16% decline from the $150 bill in 1984, according to a newsletter for cellular telephone users, *Telocator Network of America*. Charges were levied on both outgoing and incoming calls (28 to 48¢ per 1986 call), with a flat monthly fee ranging from $15 to $30.

Motion Pictures

Motion pictures took audiences by storm in the period of the 1920s to 1940s. Coinciding with the emergence of television in the late 1940s, motion pic-

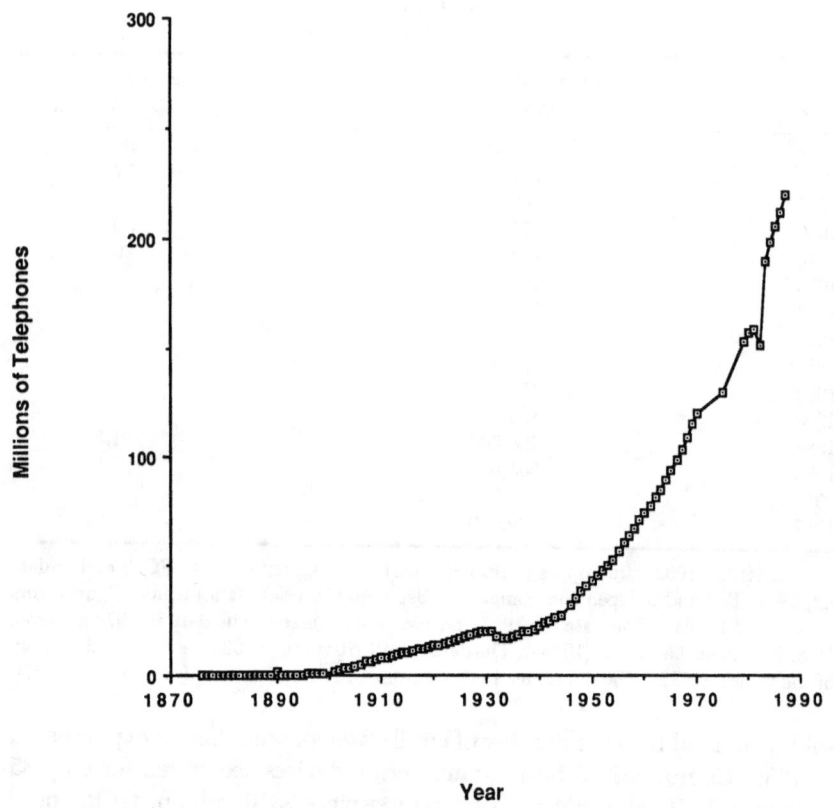

FIG. 14.6. Telephones sold 1876-1987

ture attendance declined. Table 14.6 and Fig. 14.7 trace motion picture attendance and box office receipts.

In the same pattern as with attendance at motion picture theaters, the number of theaters increased to more than 18,000 in the late 1940s and then began to fall. The decline continued until reaching about 9,000 theaters in the mid-1960s. Slow growth to about 11,000 theaters continued until 1975, when the number of screens replaced the number of theaters reported in annual census reports.

More rapid growth of almost 1,000 new screens per year occurred into the mid-1980s. As of August 1984, 19,589 theaters (85.5% indoors) were operating in the United States, up 3.7% from 1983. Indoor theaters numbered 18,327 by 1985, up 4.7% from 1984. "The total number of indoor and outdoor theaters was expected to increase in 1986 as major theater chains bought more theaters and as major motion picture distributors began reentering the movie exhibition business after being excluded in the industry's

TABLE 14.6
Motion Picture Attendance and Box Office Receipts 1922–1987

Year	Average Weekly Movie Attendance (millions)	Box Office Receipts ($ million)	Weekly Attendance per Household
1922	40		1.56
1923	43		
1924	46		1.71
1925	46		
1926	50		1.78
1927	57		
1928	65		2.23
1929	80	720	
1930	90	732	3.00
1931	75	719	
1932	60	527	1.97
1933	60	482	
1934	70	518	2.24
1935	80	556	
1936	88	626	2.71
1937	88	676	
1938	85	663	2.52
1939	85	659	
1940	80	735	2.29
1941	85	809	
1942	85	1,022	2.33
1943	85	1,275	
1944	85	1,341	2.29
1945	85	1,450	
1946	90	1,692	2.37
1947	90	1,594	
1948	90	1,506	2.22
1949	70	1,451	
1950	60	1,376	1.38
1951	54	1,310	
1952	51	1,246	
1953	46	1,187	
1954	49	1,228	1.04
1955	46	1,326	
1956	47	1,394	
1957	45	1,126	
1958	40	992	.79
1959	42	958	
1960	40	951	.76
1961	42	921	
1962	43	903	
1963	42	904	
1964	44	913	
1965	44	927	.77

(Continued)

TABLE 14.6
(Continued)

Year	Average Weekly Movie Attendance (millions)	Box Office Receipts ($ million)	Weekly Attendance per Household
1966		964	
1967		989	
1968		1,045	
1969		1,099	
1970	18	1,162	.29
1971	14	1,214	.22
1972	15	1,375	.22
1973	16	1,500	.23
1974	18	1,725	.26
1975	20	2,115	.28
1976	20	2,036	.27
1977	20	2,372	.27
1978	22	2,643	.29
1979	22	2,821	.28
1980	20	2,749	.25
1981	21	2,966	.25
1982	23	3,453	.28
1983	23	3,766	.27
1984	23	4,031	.27
1985	20	3,749	.23
1986		3,885	
1987		3,830	

Note: An estimate is reported for 1987. The data to 1970 are from U. S. Bureau of the Census (1976a). The data from 1970, 1975, and 1979 through 1985 are from U. S. Bureau of the Census (1986). The box office receipts data from 1971 through 1974 are from U. S. Bureau of the Census (1975). The box office receipts data from 1976 are from U. S. Bureau of the Census (1977). The box office receipts data from 1977 and 1978 are from U. S. Bureau of the Census (1981).

early days for antitrust reasons" (U. S. Department of Commerce, 1986, p. 61-2). By the end of 1986, the National Association of Theater Owners reported 22,145 screens, "with 1900 new screens scheduled for opening in 1987" (Lawlor, 1987).

Richard Hollingstead opened an "Automobile Movie Theater" in 1933 in Camden, New Jersey. In 1950, 1,000 drive-ins were operating. The outdoor theaters peaked in 1958 at 4,063 screens. Although none have been built since the mid-1970s (O'Driscoll, 1987), the total number of such theaters remained at about 4,000 until 1980. Dropping each year after 1980, drive-ins declined by 23.3% from 1980 to 1983. However, during 1984 and 1985 their numbers declined by less than 1% each year in the face of rising land values and real estate taxes.

14. STATISTICAL ABSTRACT

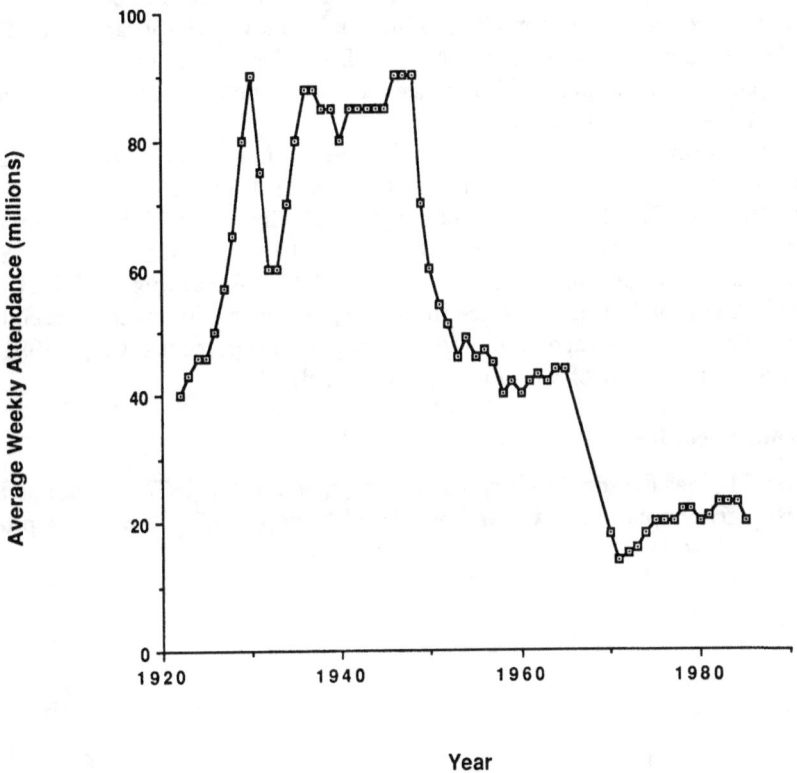

FIG. 14.7. Average weekly motion picture attendance 1922–1987

The 318 motion picture production projects getting under way in 1984 was the highest total in over 10 years and up 28% over 1983. New projects by the major producers were up 8% over 1983 to 130 motion pictures, the highest since the 126 starts in 1972. Production by independent studios was up 46% over 1983 to 188 films (U. S. Department of Commerce, 1985, p. 62-2). Production in 1985 was the highest in 12 years, with 330 film starts by major studios and independent producers worldwide. The starts by major studios were down in 1985 to 105 from 130 in 1984. However, independent projects were up by 20% to 225 (U. S. Department of Commerce, 1987, p. 61-2).

Overseas activity by the motion picture industry is one of the most successful business enterprises in the United States. American films are distributed in more than 100 countries around the world, and American television programs in more than 90 countries. More than half (167) of the new film projects by American producers in 1985 were overseas endeavors. Of these projects, independent productions were up 24% over 1984 to 129, whereas the major studio overseas films were down 15% from 1984 to 38. The motion picture industry exports $1.2 billion in business activity each year (U. S. Department of Commerce, 1985, p. 62-1). For an examination of motion picture attendance and box office receipts in the United States, see Table 14.6 and Figs. 14.7 and 14.8.

Some people have forecast doom for the motion picture industry with the growth of home video, pointing to decreasing attendance at motion picture theaters. Theater employment topped 131 million in 1975, but the number of theater employees declined 9 of the 10 succeeding years (U. S. Department of Commerce, 1985, pp. 62-1, 62-3). According to Robert J. Mulligan of the Office of Service Industries, however, "(b)ox office receipts should show an average annual growth rate of 3.5 percent through 1991" (U. S. Department of Commerce, 1987, p. 61-3).

Sound Recording

After Thomas Edison developed a "talking machine" in 1877, devices such as the "graphophone," "gramophone," and "zonophone" followed. Despite

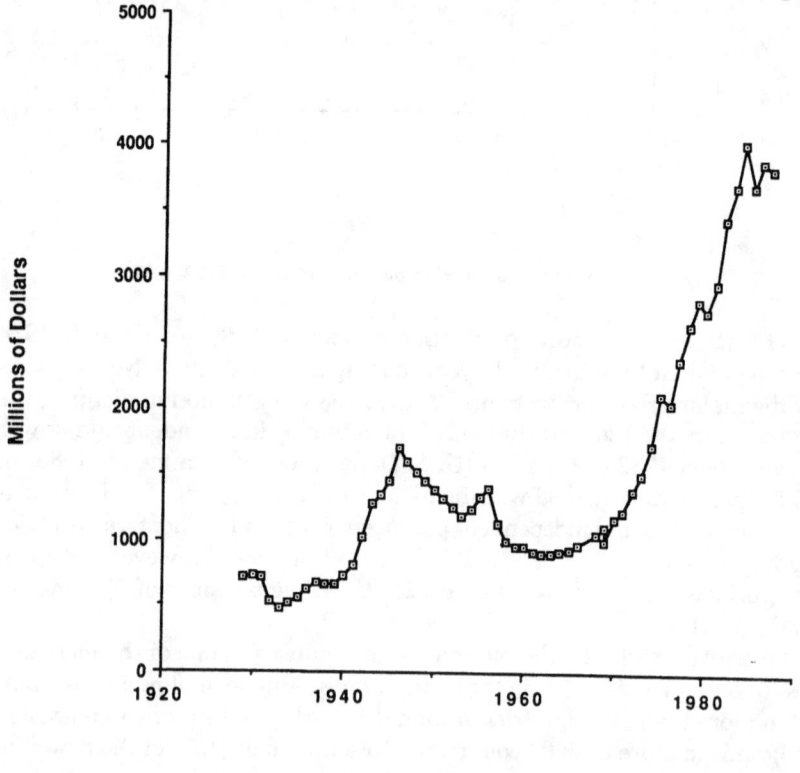

FIG. 14.8. Motion picture box office receipts 1929–1987

relatively high prices, early phonographs were popular. Table 14.7 and Fig. 14.9 trace the growth in popularity of phonographs.

Beginning in 1922, radio interrupted the progress of the phonograph industry, and sales of both players and records dropped by 50% in 1924 over the previous year. By 1927, the phonograph industry called off its battle against radio and introduced radio-phonograph players. During World War II, however, the government restricted the use of shellac for the war effort. Because the material was needed for producing records, production

TABLE 14.7
Phonograph Shipments 1899-1984

Year	Phonographs Shipped (thousands)
1899	151
1909	345
1914	514
1919	2,230
1921	596
1923	997
1925	642
1927	988
1929	603
1947	760
1952	830
1953	1,494
1954	3,919
1955	2,743
1956	3,949
1957	4,765
1958	4,050
1959	4,200
1960	3,242
1961	3,343
1962	3,668
1963	3,699
1964	3,242
1965	4,057
1966	4,323
1967	3,828
1968	3,705
1969	3,941
1970	4,106
1972	5,184
1973	6,135
1974	4,807
1975	3,420
1976	3,855
1977	4,625

(Continued)

TABLE 14.7
(Continued)

Year	Phonographs Shipped (thousands)
1978	4,545
1979	9,087
1980	8,919
1981	8,431
1982	8,192
1983	8,599
1984	8,378

Note: The data from 1899 to 1970 except 1955, 1957, 1958, and 1959 are from U. S. Bureau of the Census (1976a). The data from 1955, 1957, and 1958 are from U. S. Bureau of the Census (1959a). The data from 1959 are from U. S. Bureau of the Census (1959b). The data from 1970, 1975 through 1978 are from U. S. Bureau of the Census (1979). The data from 1972 through 1974 are from U. S. Bureau of the Census (1975). The data from 1979 through 1983 are from U. S. Bureau of the Census (1984). The data from 1984 are from U. S. Bureau of the Census (1985).

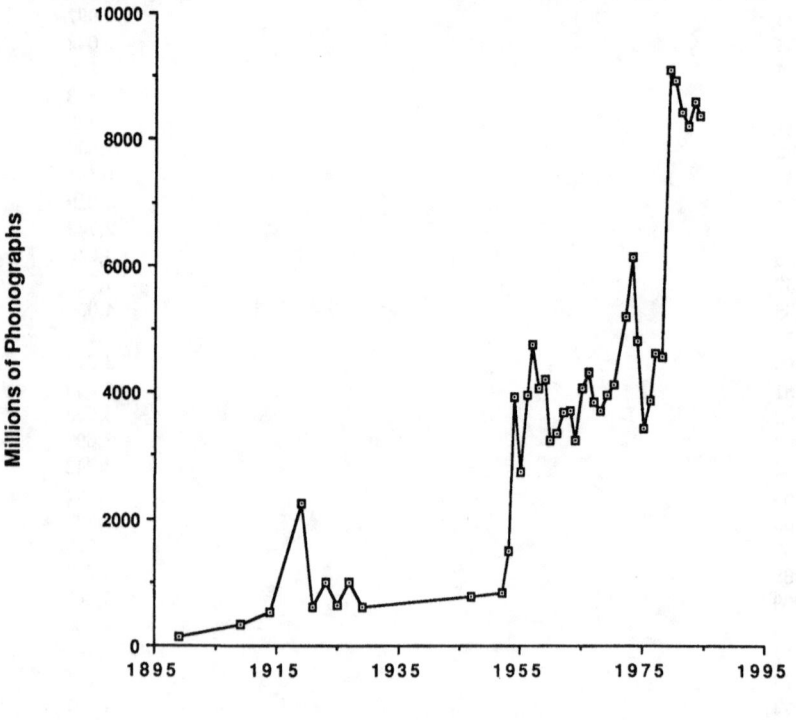

FIG. 14.9. Phonographs shipped 1899–1984

fell dramatically. Musicians also went on strike from 1942 through 1944 to protest recorded music as threatening their jobs. The record industry received a boost during World War II from the practice initiated by Capitol records of giving away records to radio stations for promotional purposes.

In 1948, the 33⅓ long-playing record (LP) entered the market, as did the 45-rpm extended play (EP) record, and players were introduced that would play at three speeds: 33⅓, 45, and 78 rpm. During the years 1947-1949, record sales dropped as people waited to see which standard would dominate. By the 1950s, the 78 rpm record had become obsolete, and the others became standards for singles (45 rpm) and albums (33⅓ rpm). High fidelity sound record players were introduced in 1954 and stereophonic sound in 1958, and record sales rose by more than 100% over the figures from the previous year.

In 1947, the 3M Company introduced magnetic recording tape, a new technology offering improvements in sound quality, multitrack recording, and lower costs. The first patent was issued for such a device to Valdemar Poulsen in 1900, but applications occurred slowly. The Nazis used magnetic recording in the 1930s. Americans used it to preserve scientific data in 1950, the year when the first digital tape transport was introduced. Four-track tape arrived in 1959, bringing tape into a competitive price range with records. Tape cartridges and cassettes soon followed. By the early 1960s, audio tape cartridges for use in automobiles were popular, and Philips of the Netherlands introduced the cassette recorder in 1963. From 1981 to 1984, sales of automobile audio cassette players, 88% of which were in sets with radios, rose 17.6% to 4.97 million units. Only 4.96 million players sold in 1985, but the retail value of 1985 models exceeded that of 1984 players by 2.3%, reaching $858 million. Table 14.8 and Fig. 14.10 trace the growth of audio tape players.

Revenues from sales of recordings during 1974-1978 nearly doubled. In the early 1980s, predictions abounded that the slumping recorded music business was doomed. However, the $4.4 billion in 1984 sales exceeded the previous high in 1978 of $4.1 billion. Sales in 1984 of prerecorded audio cassettes rose by 32% over 1983 figures. The 1984 total cassette revenues of $2.1 billion reflected their leading position in the industry. Table 14.9 and Figs. 14.11 and 14.12 illustrate sales of prerecorded music from the early 1970s to the mid-1980s.

The 1985 level of LP/EPs plus audio cassettes shipped surpassed in the 1973 quantities shipped by 240%. Although sales of LP/EPs were down, interest in recorded music was up, partly due to the advent of music video and new technologies such as laser compact disc (CD) players.

Retailing for several hundred dollars at introduction in 1983, the price of CD players in 1986 ranged from $150-$200. Table 14.10 and Fig. 14.13 document the rapid acceptance by the public of CD technology.

TABLE 14.8
Audio Tape Recorder/Player Shipments 1955–1985

Year	Number of Shipments (thousands)
1955	360
1956	400
1957	500
1958	400
1959	500
1960	425
1961	500
1962	720
1963	828
1965	3,445
1966	5,000
1967	4,581
1968	5,573
1969	6,929
1970	8,459
1971	8,747
1972	10,268
1973	12,000
1974	10,400
1975	11,200
1979	20,973
1980	24,082
1981	28,877
1982	28,886
1983	30,783
1984	28,384
1985	28,842

Note: The data from 1955, 1960, and 1961 are from U. S. Bureau of the Census (1962). The data from 1956 are from U. S. Bureau of the Census (1958). The data from 1957 and 1958 are from U. S. Bureau of the Census (1959a). The data from 1959 are from U. S. Bureau of the Census (1959b). The data from 1962 and 1963 are from U. S. Bureau of the Census (1964). The data from 1965, 1970, and 1972 through 1975 are from U. S. Bureau of the Census (1976b). The data from 1966 are from U. S. Bureau of the Census (1968). The data from 1967 are from U. S. Bureau of the Census (1969). The data from 1968 and 1969 are from U. S. Bureau of the Census (1970a). The data from 1971 are from U. S. Bureau of the Census (1970b). The data from 1979 through 1984 are from U. S. Bureau of the Census (1985). The data from 1985 are from U. S. Bureau of the Census (1986).

Radio

Commercial radio broadcasting began in 1920. Regular licensing began in 1921, and experimental networking over telephone lines began by 1922. NBC formed the first formal network in 1926. All stations were AM until

14. STATISTICAL ABSTRACT

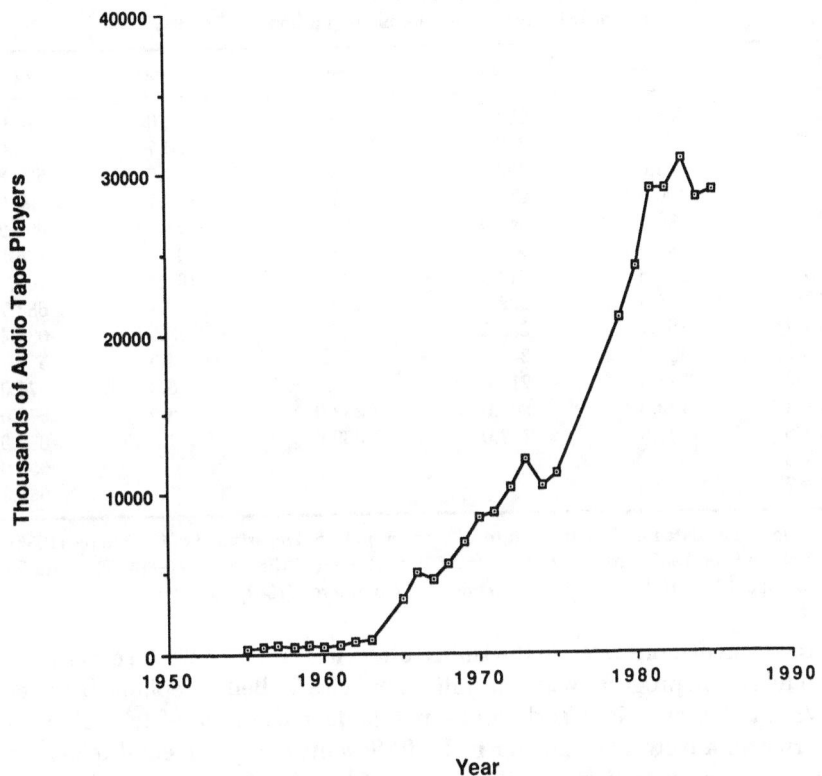

FIG. 14.10. Audio tape players shipped 1955-1984

the FCC authorized 15 FM stations October 31, 1940, and commercial FM broadcasting began January 1, 1941. As of June 30, 1987, 10,889 radio stations were authorized, of which 10,128 were on the air and the others had received construction permits (Summary of broadcasting, 1987, p. 111). Table 14.11 and Fig. 14.14 trace the growth of radio set sales.

In 1985, 95.9 million audio units were sold at for $7.04 billion. Sales volume in units exceeded the 1981 figure by 2.3%, whereas dollar values increased by 6.8%. During 1981-1985, radio-set-only sales declined for home models by 1.3% and 2.0% for car radios. However, during the same period, sales of in-dash cassette player-radio combinations increased by 39% to 4.03 million units. The retail value of those units increased by 62.7% to $789 million (U. S. Bureau of the Census, 1985, p. 751).

Television

Wireless picture transmission was patented in 1884, and mechanical tele-

TABLE 14.9
Prerecorded Music Unit Shipments (millions) 1973-1987

Year	Singles	LPs/EPs	Cassettes	8-tracks	Total
1973	228.0	280.0	15.0	91.0	614.0
1974	204.0	276.0	15.3	96.7	592.0
1975	164.0	257.0	16.2	94.6	531.8
1976	190.0	273.0	21.8	106.1	590.9
1977	190.0	344.0	36.9	127.3	698.2
1978	190.0	341.3	61.3	133.6	726.2
1979	195.5	318.3	82.8	104.7	701.1
1980	164.3	322.8	110.2	86.4	683.7
1981	154.7	295.2	137.0	48.5	635.4
1982	137.2	243.9	182.3	14.3	577.7
1983	125.0	210.0	237.0	6.0	578.0
1984	132.0	205.0	332.0	6.0	675.0
1985	121.0	167.0	339.0	4.0	631.0
1986					658.0
1987					663.3

Note: The data for all years prior to 1983 are from U. S. Department of Commerce (1986). The data from 1983 through 1985 are from U. S. Bureau of the Census (1986). The data for 1986 and 1987 are from U. S. Department of Commerce (1987).

vision was demonstrated in the United States in 1925. In 1927, an experimental television program was transmitted by wire by Bell Telephone between Washington and New York, and a public demonstration of television occurred in a New York theater in 1930. Seventeen experimental television stations were operating by 1937, and the *Milwaukee Journal* applied in 1939 to become the first commercial television broadcaster. After a 1940 hearing, the FCC authorized commercial television to begin operating on July 1, 1941, and the first grant for regular television operation was issued to WNBT, New York (Federal Communications Commission, 1979, p. 12). As the 1940s waned, television set ownership accelerated and continued to do so for the next 40 years. Table 14.12 and Fig. 14.15 document this growth.

As set ownership grew, so did station operation. In 1948, the FCC imposed a freeze on new frequency allocations for television stations to combat interference, temporarily slowing the increase in new stations that continued into the 1980s. Sterling (1984) has documented the growth of broadcast stations through 1983. As of June 30, 1987, 1,588 television licenses had been authorized, of which 1,315 were on the air, with the others having had construction permits approved (Summary of broadcasting, 1987, p. 111).

A 1985 survey of 13,000 households by the Electronic Industries Association revealed that 98% of American homes had television, and 91% had

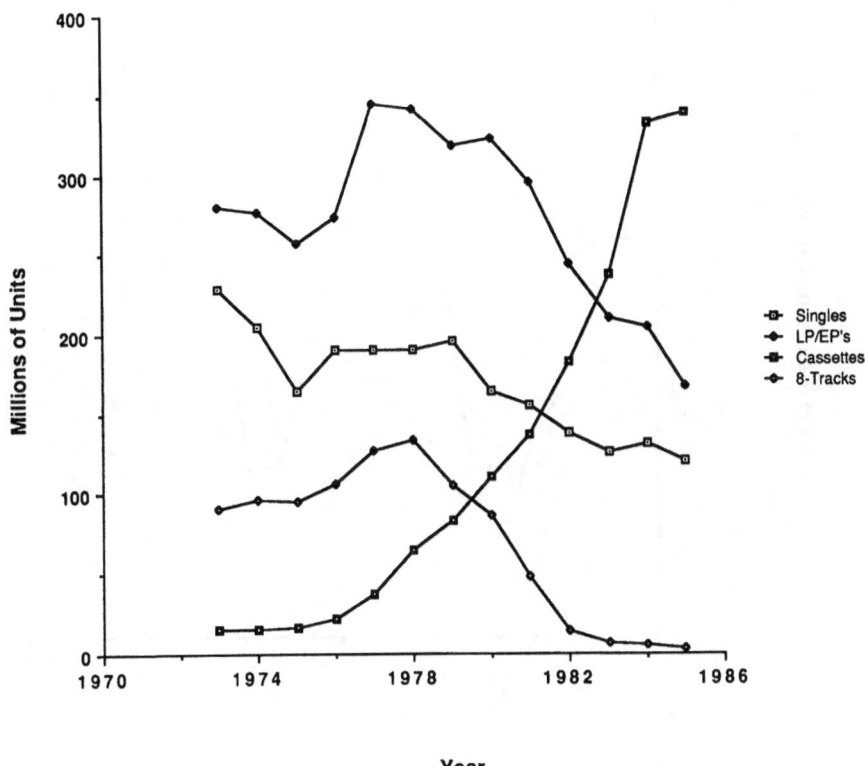

FIG. 14.11. Types of prerecorded music units shipped 1973–1986

TABLE 14.10
Compact Disc Player Shipments 1983–1986

Year	Disc Shipments (millions)	Player Shipments (thousands)	Penetration (percent)
1983	1	45	0
1984	6	200	1.6
1985	23	850	6.4
1986	50 (estimate)	1,500	7.0

Note: The data for discs through 1985 from U. S. Bureau of the Census (1986). The data for discs and players for 1986 are from Hillkirk (1986). The data for players through 1985 are from U. S. Bureau of the Census (1986). The data for penetration for 1984 and 1985 are from Graham (1986). The data for penetration for 1986 are from Lewyn (1987).

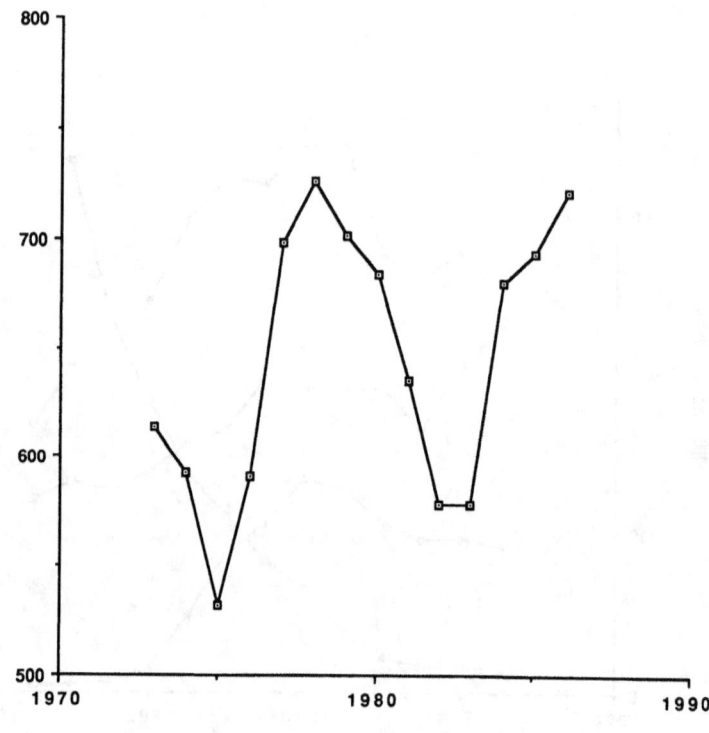

FIG. 14.12. Total prerecorded music units shipped 1973-1986

TABLE 14.11
Radio Set Production and Penetration 1922-1985

Year	Sets Produced (thousands)	Households with Sets (thousands)	Percent Penetration
1922	100	60	
1923	500	400	
1924	1,500	1,250	
1925	2,000	2,750	
1926	1,750	4,500	
1927	2,350	6,750	
1928	3,250	8,000	
1929	4,428	10,250	
1930	3,789	13,750	40.3

(Continued)

TABLE 14.11
(Continued)

Year	Sets Produced (thousands)	Households with Sets (thousands)	Percent Penetration
1931	3,594	16,700	
1932	2,446	18,450	
1933	4,157	19,250	
1934	4,479	20,400	
1935	6,030	21,456	
1936	8,249	22,869	
1937	8,083	24,500	
1938	7,142	26,667	
1939	10,763	27,500	
1940	11,831	28,500	80.3
1941	13,642	29,300	
1942	4,307	30,600	
1943		30,800	
1944		32,500	
1945		33,100	
1946	15,955	33,998	
1947	20,000	35,900	91.8
1948	16,500	37,623	
1949	11,400	39,300	93.4
1950	13,468	40,700	
1951	11,928	41,900	
1952	10,431	42,800	
1953	12,852	44,800	
1954	10,028	45,100	
1955	14,133	45,900	95.9
1956	13,518	46,800	95.7
1957	14,505	47,600	95.8
1958	11,747	48,500	96.1
1959	15,622	49,450	96.1
1960	17,127	50,193	95.1
1961	17,374	50,695	94.7
1962	19,162	51,305	93.7
1963	18,282	52,300	94.6
1964	19,176	54,000	96.2
1965	24,119	55,200	96.1
1966	23,595	57,200	97.6
1967	21,698	57,500	97.1
1968	22,566	58,500	96.2
1969	20,549	60,600	97.4
1970	34,049	62,000	97.8
1971		65,400	
1972		67,200	
1973	37,652	69,400	
1974	33,231	70,800	

(Continued)

TABLE 14.11
(Continued)

Year	Sets Produced (thousands)	Households with Sets (thousands)	Percent Penetration
1975	25,276	72,600	98.6
1976	31,656	74,000	
1977	41,800	75,800	
1978	32,478	77,800	
1979	28,550	79,300	
1980	27,012	79,968	99
1981	27,881	81,600	99
1982	26,518	82,691	99
1983	28,188	83,078	99
1984	27,391	84,553	99
1985	27,528	85,921	99

Note: Authorization of new radio stations and production of radio sets for commercial use was stopped from April 1942 until October 1945. 1959 is the first year for which Alaska and Hawaii are included in the figures. The figures prior to 1970 refer to sets produced, whereas figures after 1970 refer to sets shipped. The data prior to 1970 are from U. S. Bureau of the Census, (1976a). The production data from 1970, 1975, and 1978 through 1981 are from U. S. Bureau of the Census (1982). The production data from 1973 are from U. S. Bureau of the Census (1974). The production data from 1974 through 1977 are from U. S. Bureau of the Census (1978). The production data from 1981 through 1985 are from U. S. Bureau of the Census (1986). The households with sets data from 1970 and 1971 are from U.S. Bureau of the Census (1972). The households with sets data from 1972 are from U. S. Bureau of the Census (1972b). The households with sets data from 1973 and 1974 are from U. S. Bureau of the Census (1975). The households with sets data from 1975 through 1977 are from U. S. Bureau of the Census (1978). The households with sets data from 1978 and 1979 are from U. S. Bureau of the Census (1981).

at least one color television set. The survey also revealed that 70% of American homes owned at least one black-and-white television set, and 2% owned a projection television unit.

Cable TV

Cable television began in the late 1940s to provide a means of delivering quality television signals to areas that could not receive satisfactory direct broadcast transmissions. By 1950, 70 cable systems were operating in the United States, serving 14,000 subscribers (Federal Communications Commission, 1979, p. 14). As Table 14.13 and Fig. 14.16 show, cable systems began rapid growth in the 1960s that continued into the mid-1980s.

In 1986, 72.8% of all American cable operations catered to fewer than 4,000 subscribers, and 48.7% served fewer than 1,000 homes. However,

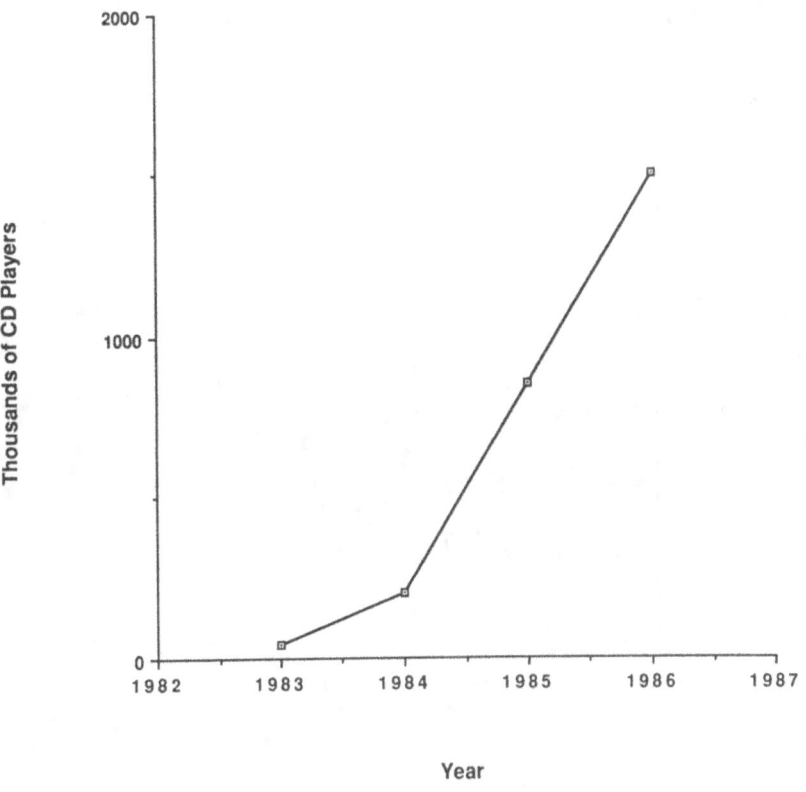

FIG. 14.13. Compact disc players shipped 1983–1986

only 13% of all cable system subscribers are served by systems that reach fewer than 4,000 homes, and 3.7% of cable subscribers access systems serving fewer than 1,000 homes (U. S. Bureau of the Census, 1985, p. 534). Arbitron estimated 1986 cable penetration to be 45.5% (i.e., over 39 million households), an increase of 1.5% over fall 1985 (44.8%; over 38 million households) (National Association of Broadcast, 1986). A. C. Nielsen estimated cable penetration at 46.8% (up 5% since February 1985), or more than 40 million households (National Association of Broadcasters, 1986).

Satellites and Home Receivers

Telstar I, launched in July 1962 by AT&T and NASA, was the first communications satellite. Early Bird began in April 1965 the trend toward geosynchronous orbits followed by all current communications satellites. In 1975, 17 satellites, including INTELSAT, INMARSAT, and all domestic

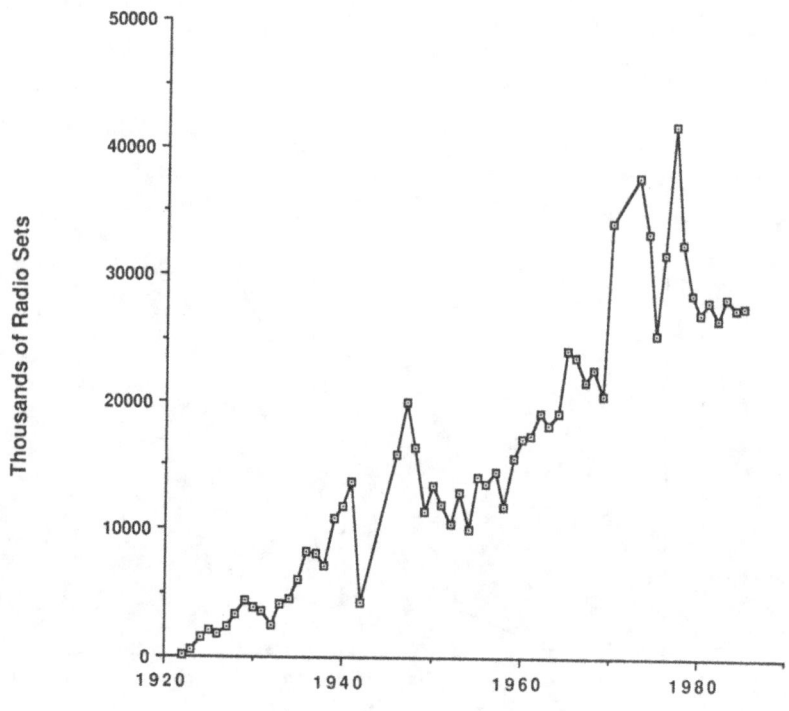

FIG. 14.14. Radio sets produced 1922–1985

TABLE 14.12
Television Sets Production and Penetration 1946–1986

Year	Sets Produced (thousands)	Households with Sets (thousands)	Percent Penetration
1946	6	8	
1947	179	14	
1948	975	172	
1949	3,000	940	
1950	7,464	3,875	9
1951	5,385	10,320	
1952	6,096	15,300	
1953	7,216	20,400	
1954	7,347	26,000	
1955	7,757	30,700	
1956	7,387	34,900	

(Continued)

TABLE 14.12
(Continued)

Year	Sets Produced (thousands)	Households with Sets (thousands)	Percent Penetration
1957	6,399	38,900	
1958	4,920	41,924	
1959	6,349	43,950	
1960	5,708	45,750	87
1961	6,178	47,200	
1962	6,471	48,855	
1963	7,130	50,300	
1964	8,107	51,600	
1965	8,382	52,700	
1966	7,285	53,850	
1967	5,104	55,130	
1968	5,813	56,670	
1969	5,309	58,250	
1970	4,852	59,550	95
1972	13,508		
1973	17,368		
1974	15,280		
1975	11,453	68,500	97
1976	12,896	69,600	
1977	14,771	71,200	
1978	16,300	72,900	
1979	16,074	74,500	
1980	17,004	76,300	98
1981	16,804	79,900	98
1982	17,127	81,500	98
1983	19,700	83,300	98
1984	21,014	83,800	98
1985	20,639	84,900	98
1986		85,900	98

Note: 1959 is the first year for which Alaska and Hawaii are included in the figures. The data dealing with sets produced to 1965 and the data dealing with households with television to 1971 are from U. S. Bureau of the Census (1976a). The data dealing with sets produced from 1965, 1968, and 1969 are from U. S. Bureau of the Census (1970a). The data dealing with sets produced from 1966 and 1967 are from U. S. Bureau of the Census (1968). The data dealing with sets produced from 1970 through 1974 are from U. S. Bureau of the Census (1975). The data dealing with sets produced from 1975 through 1978 are from U. S. Bureau of the Census (1979). The data dealing with sets produced from 1979 through 1983 are from U. S. Bureau of the Census (1984). The data for sets produced from 1984 and the data dealing with households with television from 1980 through 1984 are from U. S. Bureau of the Census (1985). The data for set penetration for all years and all data for 1985 and 1986 are from U. S. Bureau of the Census (1986).

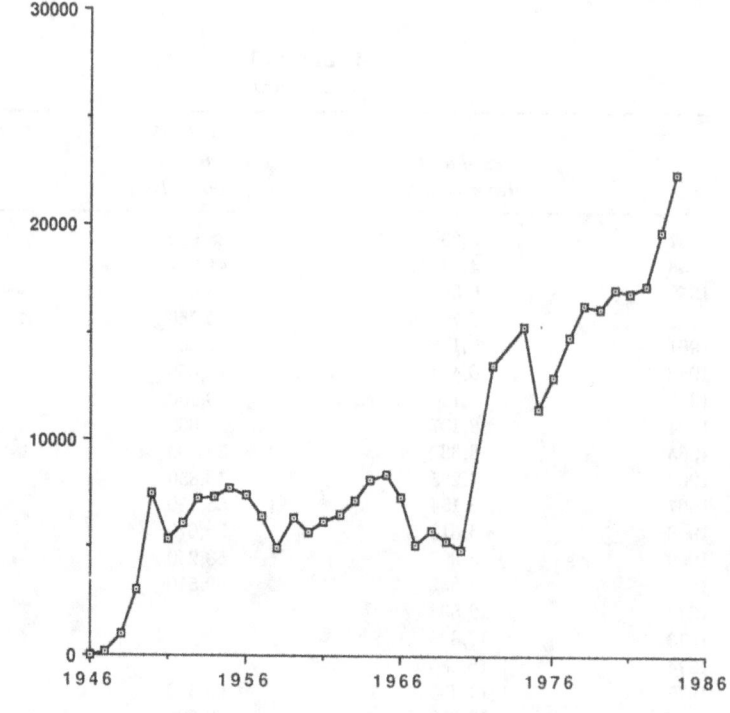

FIG. 14.15. Television sets produced 1946–1986

Table 14.13
Cable Television Systems, Subscribers, and Penetration 1952–1986

Year	Systems	Subscribers (thousands)	Penetration (Percent)
1952	70	14	
1955	400	150	
1960	640	650	
1965	1,325	1,275	
1967	1,770	2,100	
1968	2,000	2,800	
1969	2,260	3,600	
1970	2,490	4,500	
1971	2,639	5,300	
1972	2,841	6,000	
1973	2,991	7,300	

(Continued)

TABLE 14.13
(Continued)

Year	Systems	Subscribers (thousands)	Penetration (percent)
1974	3,158	8,700	
1975	3,506	9,800	
1976	3,681	10,800	
1977	3,832	11,900	
1978	3,875	13,000	
1979	4,150	14,100	
1980	4,225	16,000	
1981	4,375	18,300	25.3
1982	4,825	21,000	29.0
1983	5,600	25,000	37.2
1984	6,200	30,000	41.2
1985	6,600	31,275	44.6
1986	7,600	36,933	46.8

Note: All figures as of February of the sample year. The systems and subscribers data are from U. S. Bureau of the Census (1986). The penetration data are from U. S. Bureau of the Census (1986).

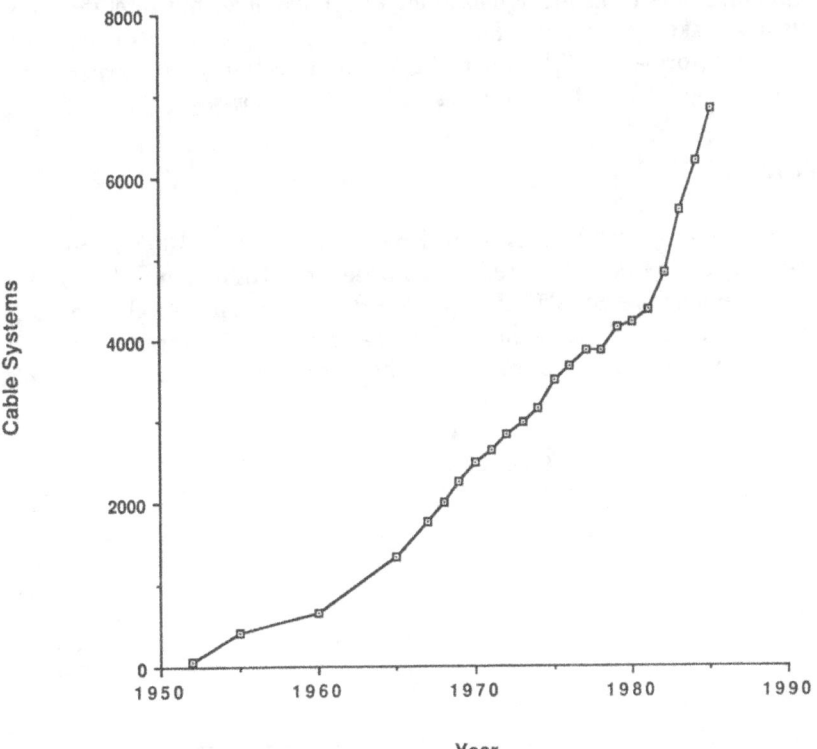

FIG. 14.16. Cable television systems 1952–1986

satellites, were in orbit. The comparable figures for 1980 had swelled to 37 and to 43 in 1983. By 1986, the United States had 135 domestic and military orbiting satellites. According to the director general of INTELSAT, the satellites serviced 66% of America's international telephone activity, 98% of television broadcasts, and 90% of data transmissions (Clark, Payne, & Griffiths, 1986). Earth stations numbered 48 in 1975 and 4,873 in 1980. By the mid-1980s, 93% of TV stations and 85% of radio stations had the capability of receiving satellite signals.

By 1986, 1.7 million households owned satellite dishes. The market practically crashed after the peak in 1985 (see Table 14.14 and Fig. 14.17) when major program suppliers announced plans to scramble transmissions and to charge fees to dish owners who previously had received programs for free.

Facsimile

Among the many services that satellites make possible are facsimile machines that allow the transmission of printed pages between distant places. Facsimile machines transmit signals along telephone lines, but satellite transmission makes the process feasible across much greater distances. The machines (formerly "Telecopiers," a Xerox trademark) have experienced enormous growth in the 1980s, as Table 14.15 shows.

VCRs

In 1956, the Ampex Corporation demonstrated its VR-1000 video Tape Recorder/Reproducer that used 2-inch wide tape. Toshiba introduced a less expensive machine in 1959 that produced video quality suitable for non-broadcasting purposes. By the late 1960s and early 1970s various manufacturers offered videotape recorders that used smaller tape: one-inch,

TABLE 14.14
Satellite Dish Sales 1980–1986

Year	Dishes Sold
1980	4,000
1981	20,000
1982	60,000
1983	225,000
1984	525,000
1985	700,000
1986	280,000

Note: The 1986 figure is estimated. The data from 1980 through 1983 are from Lewyn (1986). The data for 1984 through 1986 are from U. S. Department of Commerce (1987).

14. STATISTICAL ABSTRACT

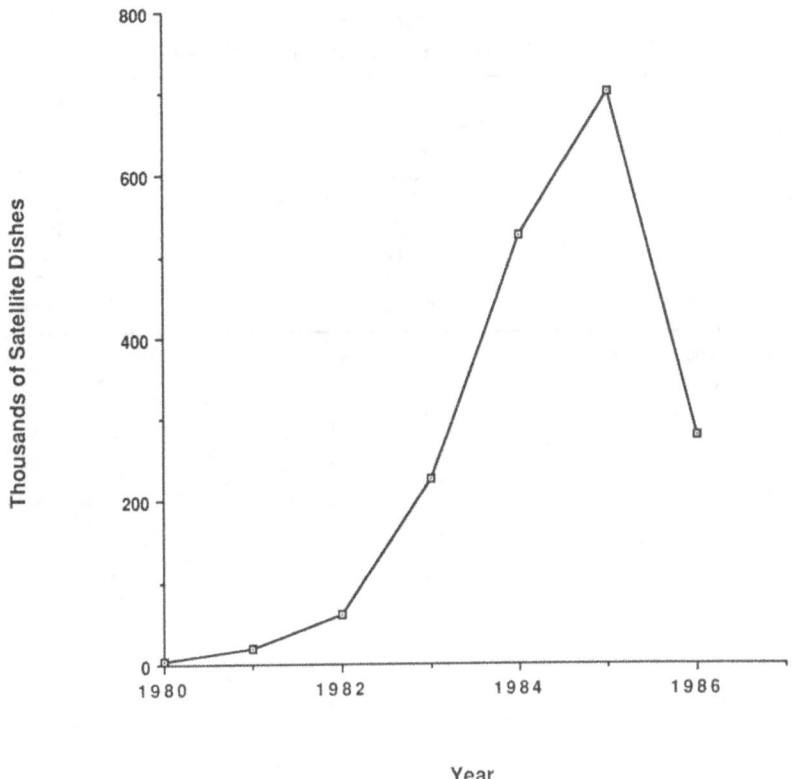

FIG. 14.17. Satellite dish sales 1980-1986

three-quarter-inch, or one-half-inch sizes. Cartridge loading also came into use, and Sony introduced its $1,300 Betamax in 1975 as the first machine primarily targeted to home users. Between 1975 and 1986, as Table 14.16 and Fig. 14.18 illustrate, 31.9 million VCRs were sold. A sales peak was reached in 1986 when sales were leading 1985 totals by 13.9% (Television Digest, 1986), but sales were down by 0.5% during the first half of 1987.

According to the Electronics Industry Association, 517,000 camcorders (small VCRs incorporated into video cameras) were sold in 1985. Sales for the first half of 1987 reached more than 500,000, up by 49% over the first half of 1986.

A 3-year survey sponsored by Columbia Pictures/Coca Cola revealed that theater attendance in 1983-1985 was down to 100 million from 113 million in 1983. Large increases in videocassette rentals occurred during the period in every age group: total rentals increased from 30 to 262.4 million units; among people 10-19 years, from 6.9 to 58.4 million; 20-29 years, 7.9 to 69.9 million; 30-39, 7.2 to 69.6 million; 40-49 years, 5 to 37.1 mil-

TABLE 14.15
Facsimile Machine Shipments and Sales 1981–1986

Year	Machines Shipped	Sales Value ($ millions)
1981	56,200	266.8
1982	63,900	283.0
1983	75,400	316.3
1984	89,000	340.6
1985	156,800	497.1
1986 (est.)	205,700	592.9

Note: From Memmott (1986).

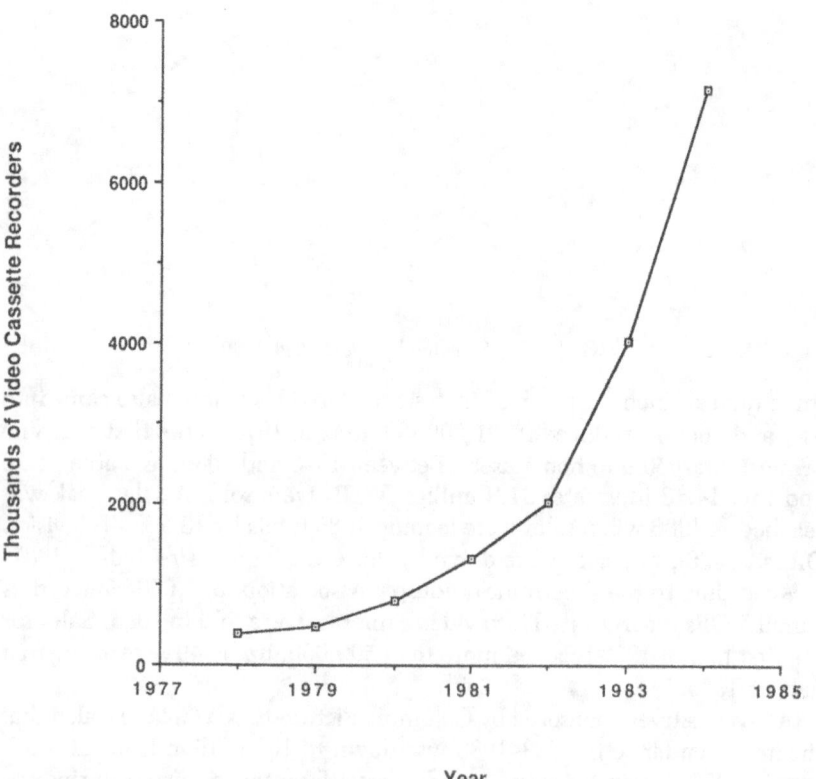

FIG. 14.18. Videocassette recorders shipped 1978–1986

TABLE 14.16
Home Video Units Shipped 1978–1985

Year	Videocassette Recorders (VCR) (thousands)	Percent VCR Penetration	Videodisc Players (thousands)
1978	402		
1979	478		
1980	804	1.1	
1981	1,330	1.8	160
1982	2,030	3.1	240
1983	4,020	5.5	312
1984	7,143	10.6	188
1985	11,912	20.8	179
1986		36.0	

Note: The data from 1978 are from U. S. Bureau of the Census (1982). The data from 1979 through 1984 are from U. S. Bureau of the Census (1984). The data from 1985 are from U. S. Bureau of Census (1986). The penetration data are from U. S. Bureau of the Census (1986).

lion; and among people over 50 years, 3 to 27.4 million videocassette rentals. Also during the same period, the proportion of homes owning a VCR increased from 9% to 30% (Green, 1986, p. 1A; U. S. Department of Commerce, 1987, p. 61-6).

A survey of 1,000 people in 1985 by the Newspaper Advertising Bureau revealed that 56% of VCR owners said they went to the movies as often as before their VCR purchase. Less movie attendance was reported by 41%, whereas only 2% reported that they went to the movies more often after purchasing a VCR (Capousis, 1986, p. 1D). Data reported in the *U. S. Industrial Outlook 1987* revealed that total 1985 revenues from sales and rentals of prerecorded videotapes amounted to $4.55 billion, "considerably higher than box office receipts for the year" (U. S. Department of Commerce, 1987, p. 61-3).

LINK Resources estimated 1987 prerecorded video cassette sales to reach $4.5 billion and $5 billion in 1988. Videocassette rentals in 1987 drew an estimated $3.5 billion in revenue for about 1.3 million rental transactions. Rentals in 1988 were estimated to remain at 1987 levels (Graham, 1987).

Videodiscs

Early development of videodisc technology was well under way in the early 1960s, but the first machine (Discovision) to be offered for public sale in December 1978 (Gross, 1986, p. 156) sold for $700. Discs retailed from

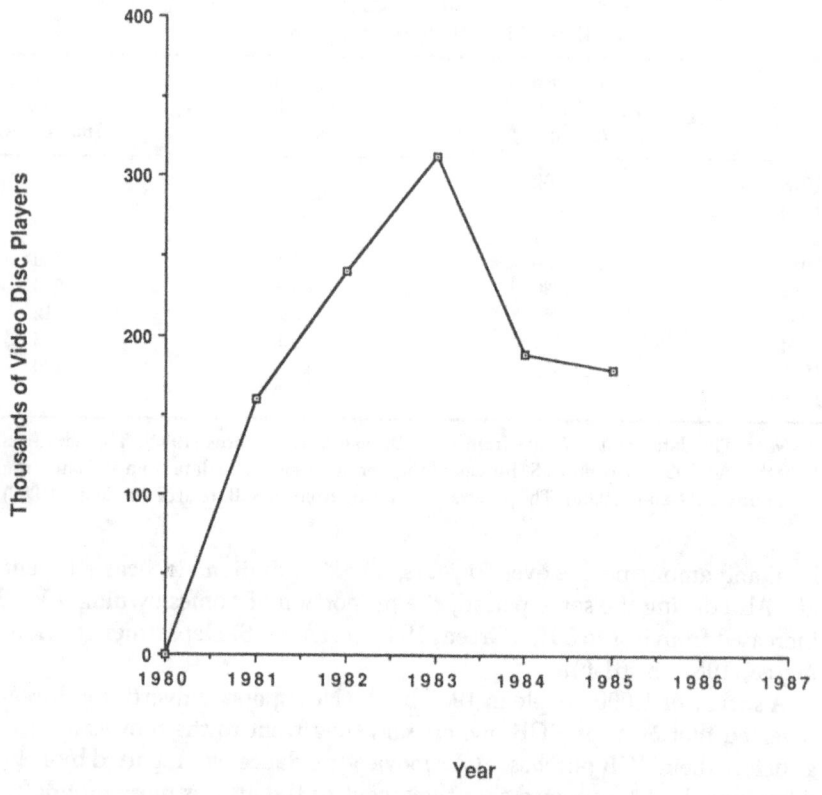

FIG. 14.19. Videodisc players shipped 1981-1985

$6-$16. Only 25,000 DiscoVision machines were sold. Sales of videodisc players during 1981-1984 respectively reached 160,000; 240,000; 312,000; and 188,000. Figure 14.19 traces 1980 shipments of videodisc players.

SYNTHESIS

By 1986, electronic devices were becoming commonplace in American homes. Radio was available in 99% of these households, television in 98%, color television in 91%, cable television in 46%, audio systems in 88%, telephones in 92%, push button telephones in 53%, microwave ovens in 45%, VCRs in 36% (44% by 1987), garage door openers in 14%, telephone answering devices in 13%, and compact disc players in 4% (Capousis, 1986, p. 1E; Mullins, 1986, p. 1A; U. S. Bureau of the Census, 1986, p. 531). The presence of personal computers in 17% of 1986 American homes provided further evidence of acceptance of new technologies for everyday use. Table 14.17 and Fig. 14.20 illustrate trends in sales of personal computers, and other chapters in this volume treat in greater detail the diffusion of computers and related technologies such as teletext and videotex.

Remarkable growth during 1985–1986 occurred among some of the newer technologies. For example, telephone answering devices were in use in only 5% of American households in 1985. Television experienced similar rapid growth in the late 1940s and early 1950s, but television required 3 years to accomplish the kind of proportional gains in penetration of American homes that telephone answering devices accomplished in that one year. Clearly, adoption of technological innovation has increased at greater rates as the overall level of technological sophistication reached higher levels.

Dimmick and Rothenbuhler (1984) observed that choices made by consumers determine the results of competition among industries. Winett (1986) referred to this perspective as the "ecological model" because it involves interdependency of uses of various media with the manner in which consumers live. For example, Winett pointed out that teletext may not appeal to all people because reading newspapers and magazines does not fit well with being tied to a terminal. We like to take such materials to various locales when we read, and the requirement of ready access to a screen may serve as a block to adopting teletext. As the ecological model succeeds in explaining the lack of American enthusiasm for teletext, the model accounts for the fabulous success of telephone answering devices. Winett also said that the ecological model is not particularly useful in making predictions about the acceptance of new media in the long run or when sudden unexpected disruptions influence media availability.

Winett argued for a "modest view" of acceptance of new media, and history seems to offer support. Television did not kill radio and motion pictures. The older media merely adapted themselves to new market pressures,

TABLE 14.17
Personal Computer Shipments and Home Use 1978–1985

Year	Number of PCs Shipped (thousands)	Homes with PCs (millions)
1978	212	
1979	246	
1980	371	
1981	1,110	0.75
1982	3,530	3.00
1983	6,900	7.64
1984	7,700	11.99
1985	7,100	14.96

Note: The data from 1978 are from U. S. Bureau of the Census (1983). The data from 1979 and 1980 are from U. S. Bureau of the Census (1984). The data from 1981 through 1985 are from U. S. Bureau of the Census (1986).

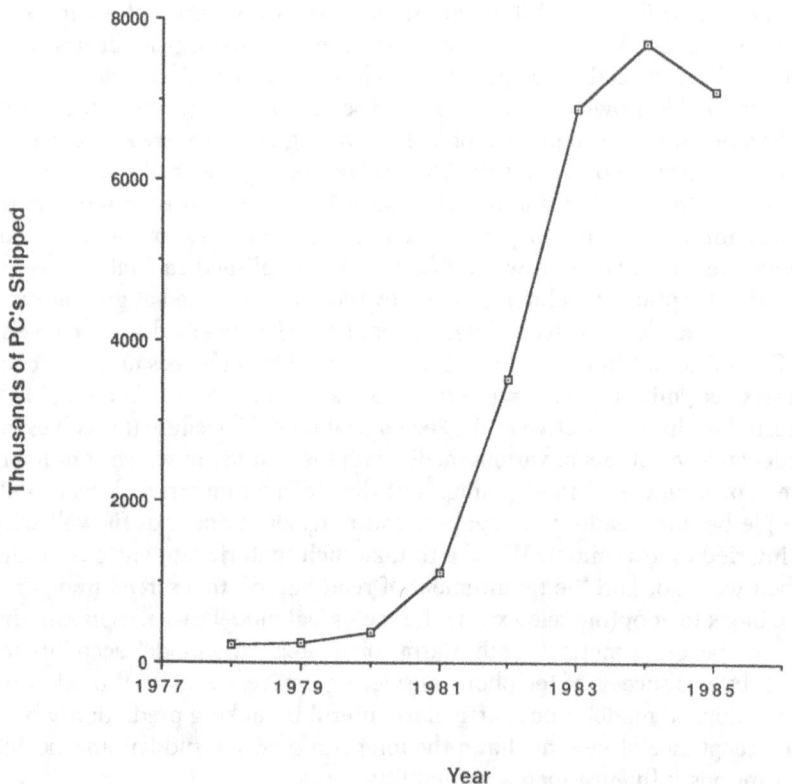

FIG. 14.20. Personal computers shipped 1978-1985

finding new ways to appeal to audiences. In the 1980s, VCRs provided the new challenge to the theater industry, but motion pictures were still in demand, increasingly for home viewing. The pressure of VCRs was on the environment for viewing rather than on the product being viewed. As the 1980s ebb, only the channel, not the content, is under fire (Rice, 1984).

REFERENCES

Bandura, A. (1986). *The social foundation of thought and action: A social cognitive theory.* Englewood Cliffs, NJ: Prentice-Hall.
Capousis, H. E. (1986, June 2). What's hot in USA homes. *USA Today*, p. 1E.
Clark, E., Payne, S., & Griffiths, D. (1986, May 19). Is the U. S. headed for a satellite crisis? *Business Week*, p. 49.
De Fleur, M. L. (1966). *Theories of mass communication.* New York: D. McKay.
Dimmick, J., & Rothenbuhler, E. W. (1984). Competitive displacement in the communica-

tion industries: New media in old environments. In R. E. Rice (Ed.), *The new media: Communication, research, and technology* (pp. 287-304). Beverly Hills: Sage.
Federal Communications Commission. (1979, May). *A short history of electrical communication* (Information Bulletin). Washington, DC: Author.
Graham, J. (1986, July 7). Sales of CD players are soaring. *USA Today*, p. 1D.
Graham, J. (1987, August 11). Video buffs are sold on buying. *USA Today*, p. 1D, 2D.
Green, T. (1986, May 15). Fans tune in VCRs, tune out theaters. *USA Today*, p. 1A.
Gross, L. (1986). *The new television technologies* (2nd ed.). Dubuque, IA: William C. Brown.
Hillkirk, J. (1986, August 19). CDs create new kind of mania. *USA Today*, p. 1B.
Lawlor, J. (1987, June 30). Cineplex blockbuster opens today. *USA Today*, pp. 1B, 2B.
Lee, A. (1973). *The daily newspaper in America*. New York: Octagon Books.
Lewyn, M. (1986, July 16). Sending a new signal. *USA Today*, p. 4B.
Lewyn, M. (1987, May 29). Video CDs to debut tomorrow. *USA Today*, pp. 1B, 2B.
Maney, K. (1986, July 2). Future's on line for cellular phones. *USA Today*, p. 4B.
Memmott, M. (1986, August 12). Facsimile machines link USA. *USA Today*, pp. 1B, 2B.
Mullins, M. E. (1986, April 25). *USA Today*, p. 1A.
National Association of Broadcasters. (1986, April). *Broadcast Marketing & Technology News*. Washington, DC: Author.
O'Driscoll, P. (1987, June 22). A tradition refuses to flicker out. *USA Today*, pp. 1D, 2D.
Rice, R. E. (1984). *The new media: Communication, research, and technology*. Beverly Hills: Sage.
Rogers, E. M. (1983). *Diffusion of innovations* (3rd ed.). New York: The Free Press.
Sterling, C. H. (1984). *Electronic media: A guide to trends in broadcasting and newer technologies 1920-1983*. New York: Praeger.
Summary of broadcasting. (1987, July 27) *Broadcasting*, p. 111.
Television Digest. (1986, July). *Broadcast Marketing & Technology News*, p. 2.
Thompson, R. L. (1947). *Wiring a continent: The history of the telegraph industry in the United States, 1832-1866*. New York: Arno Press.
U. S. Bureau of the Census. (1958). *Statistical abstract of the United States: 1958* (79th ed.). Washington, DC: U. S. Government Printing Office.
U. S. Bureau of the Census. (1959a). *Statistical abstract of the United States: 1959* (80th ed.) Washington, DC: U. S. Government Printing Office.
U. S. Bureau of the Census. (1959b). *Statistical abstract of the United States: 1960* (81st ed.). Washington, DC: U. S. Government Printing Office.
U. S. Bureau of the Census. (1962). *Statistical abstract of the United States: 1962* (83rd ed.). Washington, DC: U. S. Government Printing Office.
U.S. Bureau of the Census. (1964). *Statistical abstract of the United States: 1964* (85th ed.). Washington, DC: U. S. Government Printing Office.
U. S. Bureau of the Census. (1968). *Statistical abstract of the United States: 1968* (89th ed.). Washington, DC: U. S. Government Printing Office.
U. S. Bureau of the Census. (1969). *Statistical abstract of the United States: 1969* (90th ed.). Washington, DC: U. S. Government Printing Office.
U. S. Bureau of the Census. (1970a). *Statistical abstract of the United States: 1970* (91st ed.). Washington, DC: U. S. Government Printing Office.
U.S. Bureau of the Census. (1970b). *Statistical abstract of the United States: 1971* (92nd ed.). Washington, DC: U. S. Government Printing Office.
U. S. Bureau of the Census. (1972). *Statistical abstract of the United States: 1972* (93rd ed.). Washington, DC: U. S. Government Printing Office.
U. S. Bureau of the Census. (1974). *Statistical abstract of the United States: 1974* (95th ed.). Washington, DC: U. S. Government Printing Office.

U. S. Bureau of the Census. (1975). *Statistical abstract of the United States: 1975* (96th ed.). Washington, DC: U. S. Government Printing Office.

U. S. Bureau of the Census. (1976a). *Statistical history of the United States: From colonial times to the present.* New York: Basic Books.

U. S. Bureau of the Census. (1976b). *Statistical abstract of the United States: 1976* (97th ed.). Washington, DC: U. S. Government Printing Office.

U. S. Bureau of the Census. (1977). *Statistical abstract of the United States: 1977* (98th ed.). Washington, DC: U. S. Government Printing Office.

U. S. Bureau of the Census. (1978). *Statistical abstract of the United States: 1978* (99th ed.). Washington, DC: U. S. Government Printing Office.

U. S. Bureau of the Census. (1979). *Statistical abstract of the United States: 1979* (100th ed.). Washington, DC: U. S. Government Printing Office.

U. S. Bureau of the Census. (1981). *Statistical abstract of the United States: 1981* (102nd ed.). Washington, DC: U. S. Government Printing Office.

U. S. Bureau of the Census. (1982). *Statistical abstract of the United States: 1982-1983* (103rd ed.). Washington, DC: U. S. Government Printing Office.

U. S. Bureau of the Census. (1983). *Statistical abstract of the United States: 1984* (104th ed.). Washington, DC: U. S. Government Printing Office.

U. S. Bureau of the Census. (1984). *Statistical abstract of the United States: 1985* (105th ed.). Washington, DC: U. S. Government Printing Office.

U. S. Bureau of the Census. (1985). *Statistical abstract of the United States: 1986* (106th ed.). Washington, DC: U. S. Government Printing Office.

U. S. Bureau of the Census. (1986). *Statistical abstract of the United States: 1987* (107th ed.). Washington, DC: U. S. Government Printing Office.

U. S. Department of Commerce. (1985). *U. S. industrial outlook 1985.* Washington, DC: U. S. Department of Commerce, U. S. Bureau of Economic Analysis and U. S. Bureau of Labor Statistics.

U. S. Department of Commerce. (1986). *U. S. industrial outlook 1986.* Washington, DC: U. S. Department of Commerce, U. S. Bureau of Economic Analysis and U. S. Bureau of Labor Statistics.

U. S. Department of Commerce. (1987). *U. S. industrial outlook 1987.* Washington, DC: U. S. Department of Commerce, U. S. Bureau of Economic Analysis and U. S. Bureau of Labor Statistics.

Winett, R. (1986). *Information and behavior: Systems of influence.* Hillsdale, NJ: Lawrence Erlbaum Associates.

Author Index

Page numbers in *italics* show where complete bibliographic entries are given.

A

Abboud, M. B., 46, *57*
Aboubakr, Y., 46, *57*
Adler, M. N., 88, *103*
Adler, R. P., 21, *40*
Agostino, D. E., 184, *193*
Ajzen, I., 32, 37, *38*
Alisky, M., 168, *176*
Altman, D., 247, *257*
Anderson, D. R., 207, *214*
Anderson, J. K., 27, *40*
Anderson, R. E., 61, 62, 70, 71, 80, *81*
Arlen, G., 106, 117, 118, *121*
Armara, R. C., 23, *38*
Asher, W., 22, 31, 35, 37, *38*
Assmus, G., 31, *38*
Atkin, C., 74, *82*, 167, *176*, 228, *234*
Atwater, T., 111, *121*

B

Baer, W. S., 116, *121*
Bagdikian, B. H., 199, *214*
Baker, B., 54, 57
Ball-Rokeach, S., 75, *82*, 219–220, *234*
Bandura, A., 75, *81*, *82*, 238, 239, 243, 249, 250, 252, 253, 255, 260, *300*
Bantz, C. R., 78, 181, 193, *194*
Barakat, S., 49, *57*
Barbieri, R., 21, *38*
Barker, M., 47, *57*
Barnes, B. E., 13, *17*
Barnett, G. A., 120, *121*, 149, *161*
Barnett, H. J., 202, *214*
Barwise, T. P., 6, 7, *17*, 201, 205, *214*
Bass, F. M., 34–35, *38*
Bauer, R. A., 182, *193*
Beales, H., 246, 255, *256*
Beck, P. W., 28, *38*
Becker, H. J., xxv, *xxvii*
Becker, M. H, 250, *256*
Beebe, J. H., 199, 200, 201, 202, *215*
Beltran, L. R., 164, 170, *176*
Berenson, C., 33, *40*
Berlo, D., 221, *234*
Beville, H. M., Jr., 4, 5, 11, 15, 16, *17*, 32, 24, 37, *38*, 204, *214*
Biehal, G., 111, *121*

303

Bierbaum, T., 45, 57
Bishop, S. C., 119, 122
Bloch, H., 205, 212, 216
Blumler, J., 18, 76, 77, 82, 83, 181, 182, 193, 194, 213, 214
de Bock, H. 195
Bolter, J. D., 147, 162
Bolton, T., 34, 38
Bordeleau, P., 160, 162
Botein, M., 211, 214
Boucher, W. J., 40
Bouthilet, L., 65, 84
Bowes, J. E., 66, 82
Boyd, D., 12, 126, 128, 130, 133, 144, 163, 165, 169, 170, 176, 184
Boyd-Barrett, O., 164, 176
Breslow, L., 256
Bright, J. R., 24, 25, 31, 32, 38
Brown, B. W., 238, 256
Brown, D., 259
Brown, J. R., 65, 66, 82
Brown, N. A., 111, 121
Brownell, K. D., 243, 256
Bruno, A. V., 207, 214
Bryant, J., 7, 19, 66, 82, 176, 207, 214, 216, 227-228, 234, 235, 259
Burdine, B. H., xviv, xxvii
Burns, D, xx, xxvii
Burke, T., xxvii
Bussenius, W., 54
Butler, J. M., 110, 121

C

Capousis, H. E., 297, 298, 300
Capuzzi, C., 106, 121
Cardozo, R. N., 31, 34, 41
Carey, J., 36, 38
Caron, A. H., 147, 151, 161
Carroll, J. M., 73, 82
Carroll, P. B., xvi, xxvii
Cathcart, R., 148, 162
Chaffee, S. H., 7, 17, 63-64, 65, 74, 79, 80, 82, 83, 217, 226, 233, 234
Chambers, J. C., 33, 38
Chen, M., 72, 84, 226, 228, 233, 234
Chinn, D. E., 244, 257
Chiruvolu, P., 167, 176
Christian, C., 148, 161
Christians, C., 21, 39

Chu, G. C., 66, 82
Clark, E., 294, 300
Clay, C., 246, 256
Clemons, E. K., 106, 121
Coates, J. F., 27, 38
Coffin, R., Jr., 44
Coleman, J., 76, 82
Collins, M. A., 7, 18, 207, 214
Comstock, G., 65, 82
Cook, T. D., 199, 214
Coopman, J., 51, 57
Corder-Bolz, C. R., 74, 82
Cornell, N. W., 22, 40
Cornog, M., 106, 122
Cotton, J., 228, 234
Covvey, H. D., 77, 82
Cramond, J. K., 66, 82
Craswell, R., 246, 255
Curran, J., 215
Czepiel, J., 76, 82

D

Daley, H., 70, 71, 75, 76, 84, 149, 162
Dalkey, N. C., 26, 38
Danzinger, J. N., 67, 76, 82
Darmon, R., 207, 214
Darvis, R. C., 26, 38
Day, K., 149, 161
Daynes, R. R., 27, 38
DeFleur, M. L., 75, 82, 219-220, 234, 260, 300
Dervin, B., xxvii, 82
Devine, D. G., 246, 256
Devins, S., 47, 57
Dickerson, M. D., 149, 161
Didsbury, H. F., Jr., xxvii
Dimmick, J., 299, 300-301
Dobrow, J. A., 170, 176
Dodds, W., 34, 38
Donohue, G., 81, 84
Dorfman, A., 164, 176-177
Dorr, A., 77, 83
Dozier, D., xvii, xxvii, 110, 121
Douzou, S., 147, 151, 161
Duncan, R., 76, 85
Dunn, D. A., 117, 122, 225, 234
Durand, R. M., 190, 194
Dutton, W. H., 61, 62, 63, 64, 67, 68, 69, 71, 76, 79, 82, 83, 149, 162

AUTHOR INDEX

E

Eccles, J. S., 74, 83
Edwardson, M., 119, 121
Eguchi, H., 215
Ehrenberg, A. S. C., 6, 7, 17, 201, 205, 207, 210, 214
Ehrman, H., 44, 57
Encel, S., 21, 38
Ettema, J. S., 16, 17, 32, 38, 111-112, 113, 115, 116, 121
Evans, C., 61, 66, 82
Everett, P. B., 243, 256

F

Farivar, B., 34, 40
Farquhar, J. W., 238, 256
von Feilitzen, C., 65, 82
Ferguson, B. J., 66, 85
Festinger, L., 227, 234
Fielding, J. E., 256
Fink, E. L., 11, 12, 18, 131, 144, 202, 210, 215
Finn, T. A., 106, 121
Fishback, J. F., 245, 257
Fishbein, M., 32, 37, 38
Fisher, B. A., 181, 193
Fisher, J. C., 30, 38
Fisher, J. F., 108, 121
Fleischauer, B. P., 62, 85
Flichy, P., 148, 162
Flora, J. A., 238, 256
Forester, T., 61, 66, 82
Forsythe, V. L., 48, 57
Fort, T. R., 245, 257
Fortman, S. P., 238, 256
Fowles, J., 27, 39
Foxall, G. R., 32, 38
Franca, B. A., 22, 40
Fredin, E., 230-231, 234
Frey, F. W., 129, 144
Fuchs, V. R., 250, 256
Fulk, J., 68, 74, 82
Furu, T., 65, 82

G

Ganley, C. D., 128, 144, 165, 169, 171, 174-175, 177
Ganley, O. H., 128, 144, 165, 169, 171, 174-175, 177
Garramone, G. M., 118, 121
Geller, E. S., 243, 256
Gensch, D. H., 6, 17, 205, 214
Gentry, J. W., 149, 161
Gerbner, G., 8, 17, 199, 206, 210, 211, 213, 214
Gershuny, J., 65, 82
Gerson, E. M., 73, 83
Giron, M. V., 47, 57
Giroux, L., 147, 151, 161
Glasser, T. L., 200, 214
Godet, M., 23, 28, 35, 39
Goldberg, A. G., 26, 40
Goldberg, L., 108, 121
Golding, P., 199, 211, 215
Gonzales, I., 69, 82
Goodhardt, G. J., 7, 17, 18, 205, 207, 214
Graham, J., 285, 297, 301
Graham, M., 26, 28, 30, 39
Green, R. B., 246, 256
Green, T., 297, 301
Greenberg, B. S., 12, 18, 65, 83, 87, 88, 103, 206, 209-210, 214, 228, 234
Greenberg, E., 202, 214
Greenberger, M., 21, 39, 121, 122, 123
Greene, B. F., 246, 256
Greenwald, P., 246, 256
Griffin, R., 68, 84
Griffiths, D., 294, 300
Gronhaug, K., 66, 85
Gross, L., xvi, xxvii, 8, 17, 199, 206, 210, 211, 213, 214, 297, 301
Grosshopff, R., 47, 57
Grovhaug, K., 149, 162
Guback, T., 170, 177
Gumpert, G., 148, 162
Gunter, B., 131, 144
Gurevitch, M., 7, 17, 18, 65, 76, 77, 83, 181, 182, 194, 213, 214, 215
Gutierrez, F., 201, 216
Guzda, M. K., xvii, xxvii

H

Haas, H., 65, 83
Hagelin, T., 53, 57
Handford, G., 65, 85

Harris, A. C., 118, *121*
Harris, L., 61, 62, 70, 71, 80, *81*
Harvey, M. G., 184, *193*
Haskell, W. L., 238, *256*
Hatcher, J., 243, *256*
Head, S. W., 133, *144*, 167, *177*
Headen, R. S., 6, *18*, 207, *214*
Heald, K. A., 62, *85*
Heeler, R. M., 35, *39*
Heeter, C., 12, *18*, 206, 209–210, *214*, 217, 228, *234*
Helmer, O., 26, *38*
Henricksen, F., 6, *18*
Hewes, D., 229
Hilgard, E., *234*
Hill, K., 27, *39*
Hillkirk, J., 285, *301*
Himmelweit, H. T., 65, *83*
Hirsch, M., 55, *57*
Hirsch, P. M., 200, 201, 206, 213, *214*, *215*
Hockheimer, J. L., 7, *17*
Holbeck, J., 76, *85*
Holley, J. H., 108
Holt, S. A., 6, 13, *18*
Hooper, R., 108, 109, 110, 117, *122*
Hudson, H. E., 130, *144*
Hulley, S. B., 238, *256*
Hustad, T. P., 35, *39*
Huston, A. C., 243, *257*
Hutchesson, B. N. P., 30, *39*

I, J

Jacklin, P., 200, *215*
Jamison, D., 167, *176*
Janisch, H., 53, *57*
Janke, R. V., 119, *122*
Janz, N. K., 250, *256*
Jeffries-Fox, B. C., xvi, *xxvii*
Jeffries-Fox, S., xvi, *xxvii*
Johnson, R. C., 184, *193*
Johnston, J., *38*, *121*
Jones, M. G., 111, *122*
Judge, S., 53, *57*
Jun, S. H., 62, 63, 64, 68, 69, 76, 79, *82*
Jurgensmeyer, J. E., 119,. *122*

K

Kagel, J. H., 244, 246, 252, *257*
Kahn, H., 28
Kahneman, D., 246, *256*
Kaplan, B. M., 12, *18*
Katz, E., *18*, 65, 66, 76, 77, 82, *83*, 129, 130, 131, 132, *144*, 164, 167, *177*, 181, 182, *193*, *194*, 213, *214*
Katzman, N., 65, *82*
Kazdin, A. E., 249, *256*
Kendzierski, D. A., 199, *214*
Kent, K. E. M., 118, 119, *121*
Keppel, G., 250, *256*
Kerr, P., 53, 54, *57*
Kiesler, S., 74, *83*, 238, *256*
Kiewit, D. A., 13, *18*
Killion, K. C., 6, 11, *18*
Kim, K., 149, *161*
Kindred, J., 45, *57*
King, A. C., 247, *257*
Kinear, T. C., *122*
Kippax, S., 65, 77, *83*
Kitchen, P. J., 184, *194*
Klapper, J. T., 198, *215*
Kling, R., 67, 73, 76, *82*, *83*
Klompmaker, J., 6, *18*, 207, *214*
Klofenstein, B. C., 21, 22, 27, 29, 33, 37, *39*, 260
Kolette, D., 62, 66, *83*
Koughan, M., 21, *39*
Kovaric, P., 61, 64, 69, 71, 77, 82, *83*, 149, *162*
Kraemer, K. L., 67, 76, 82, *83*
Kramer, K. D., 237
Krendl, K., 230–231, *234*
Krugman, D. M., 6, *18*, 21, *39*
Ksobiech, K. J., 201, 207, *215*
Kupferberg, N., 119, *122*
Kurian, G. T., 130, *144*

L

Lambert, Z. V., 190, *194*
Lave, L. B., *256*
Lancaster, G. A., 35, *39*
Lasswell, H., 221, *234*
Lautenberg, F. R., 80, *83*
Lazar, J., 65, *84*
Lazarsfeld, P., 66, *83*

AUTHOR INDEX

Leckliter, I. N., 243, 244, 245, *256*, *257*
Ledingham, J. A., 108, 118, *122*
Lee, C., 164, *177*
Lehman, M., *xxvii*
Lent, J. A., 126, 128, 130, 133, *144*, 168, 169, 170, *176*
Lerner, D., 129, *144*, 164, *177*
Levin, H. J. 200, *215*
Levine, M. S., 190, *194*
Levy, M. R., 11, 12, *17*, *18*, 131, *144*, 182, 183, 184, *194*, 202, 210, *215*
Levy, P., 66, *83*
Lewyn, M., 285, 294, *301*
Lhoest, H., 174, *177*
Lichtenstein, E., 243, *256*
Lieberman, D., 63–64, 79, 80, *83*
Lin, C., 125, 166, 168, 173
Linder, S. B., 65, *83*
Linstone, H. A., 24, 26, *39*
Lipinski, H., 21, *40*
Lipinski, R., 88, *103*
Livingston, V., 16, *18*
Lorch, E. P., 207, *214*
Love, S. Q., 244, *257*
Lu, D., 13, *18*
Lull, J., 209, *215*
Lynch, B. S., 246, *256*

M

Maccoby, N., 238, *256*
MacLean, M., 220–221, 231, *235*
Mahajan, V., 34, 35, *39*, *41*
Mahmoud, E., 36, *39*
Mahoney, W., 183, *194*
Makrididakis, S., 22, 28, *39*, *41*
Malone, T. W., 72, 73, *83*
Mander, J., 65, *83*
Manning, W. G., 199, 200, 201, 202, *215*
Manoff, R. K., 240, *256*
Marlatt, G. A., 243, *256*
Martin, J., xvi, *xxvii*, 30, *39*
Martino, J., 24, 26, 29, 30, *39*
Mattelart, A., 164, *176–177*
Mattos, S., 165, *177*
Mazis, M. B., 246, *256*
McAllister, N. H., 77, *82*
McAnany, E., 167, *177*
McCain, T., 201, *215*
McCarthy, S. J., 110, 118, *122*

McCombs, M. E., 65, *82*, 211, *215*
McConnell, M., 119, *121*
McFail, J. C., 165, *177*
McFarlan, F. W., 106, 119, *121*, *122*
McGuire, T. W., 238, *256*
McGuire, W. J., 238, 239, 253, *256*
McLaughlin, M., *84*, *121*
McLeod, J., 74, *82*
McPhail, B. M., 28, *39*
McPhail, T. L., 28, *39*, 53, *57*
McQuail, D., 7, *18*
Meade, N., 30, *40*
Meehan, E. R., 16, *18*, 200, *215*
Meeks, B. N., xxv, *xxvii*
Melanson, J., 46, *57*
Memmott, M., 296, *301*
Menzel, H., 76, *82*
Mercier, P. A., 148, 160, *162*
Messaris, P., 74, *83*
Millar, V. E., 106, *122*
Miller, D., 149, *161*
Miller, G., 226, *234*
Miller, K., 68, *83*
Miller, P. V., 7, *18*
Miller, T., 120, *122*
Mody, B., 167, *177*
Monet, J., 56, *58*
Monge, P., 68, *83*
Morgan, M., 199, 210, 211, 213, *214*
Morrison, J. L., 26, *40*
Morse, R. C., xvi, *xxvii*
Mosco, V., xvi, *xxvii*
Moss, M., 36, *38*
Motavalli, J., 118, *122*
Moyer, R., 35, *40*
Muller, D., 149, *162*
Muller, E., 34, *39*
Mullick, S. K., 33, *38*
Mullins, M. E., 298, *301*
Murdock, G., 199, 211, *215*
Murphy, R. D., 49, *58*
Murray, J. P., 65, 77, *83*
Myers, P., 27, *40*

N

Naisbitt, J., 26, *40*
Neale, M. S., 243, *257*
Neale, W. C., 120, *122*
Neufeld, M. L., 106, *122*

Neuman, W. R., 109, *122*, 199, 213, *215*
Neustadt, R. M., 108, *122*
Newcomb, H. M., 213, *215*
Newcomb, T., 230, *234*
Nicol, J., 77, *83*
Nicholls, J. A. P., 29, *41*
Nie, N., 117, *122*
Nilles, J. M., 61, 62, 66, *83*, *84*
Nimkoff, M. F., 65, *84*
Ninan, T. N., 175, *177*
Noam, E., *214*, *216*
Noelle-Neumann, E., 200, 211, *215*
Nordenstreng, K., 164, *177*
Northrop, A., 67, 76, *83*
Nyhan, M., 21, *40*, 88, *103*

O

O'Brien, T., 27, *40*
Ogan, C. L., 43, 169, *177*
Ogburn, W. F., 65, *84*
Ojala, M., 119, *122*
Olien, C., 81, *84*
Olusa, C. S., 48, *58*
Olshavsky, R., xvii, *xxvii*, 36, *40*
Oppenheim, A. N., 65, *83*
Osgood, C. E., 218-219, *234*
Overduin, H., 111, *121*
Owen, B. M., 199, 200, 201, 202, 203, *215*, *216*

P

Paisley, W., 69, 72, *84*, 222, *234*, *256*
Palmgreen, P., *19*, 166, *177*, 181-182, *194*, *214*
Papert, S., 73, *84*
Parente, J., 27, *40*
Parker, E. B., 117, *122*, 225, *234*
Pasquali, A., 164, *177*
Paulu, B., 131, *144*
Payne, S., 294, *300*
Pearce, J., *84*
Pearl, D., 65, *84*
Pemberton, J., 111, *122*
Perse, E. M., 183, *194*
Peterson, R., 35, *39*
Peterson, T., 165, 167, *178*
Pfeffer, J., 68, 74, *84*

Pizante, G., 118, *121*
Plassard, F., 148, 160, *162*
Polley, C., 49
Poltrack, D. F., 13, *17*, 201, *215*
Pond, E., 47, *58*
Pool, I. de Sola, 22, 31, *40*, 63, *84*, 148, *162*, 164, *177*, 227, *234*
Porter, M. E., 106, *122*
Powell, R. A., 183, *194*
Power, J. G., 68, 74, *82*
Pressey, S., 222, *234*
Proulx, S., 160, *162*
Pry, R. H., 30, *38*

R

Rafaeli, S., 67, *84*, 221, 223, *234*
Rapparini, R., xvi, *xxvii*
Read, W. H., 164, 170, *177*
Reardon, G., 89, *103*
Reeves, B., 66, *84*
Reichenbach, H., 226, *234*
Renfro, W. L., 26, *40*
Rice, R., xvii, *xxvii*, 4, 16, *18*, 21, 32, *40*, 69, *84*, 110, *121*, 147, *162*, 217, 221, 229, 230, 231, 233, *234*, 238, 256, 300, *301*
Ricklefs, R., xvi, *xxvii*
Riley, A., 245, *257*
Roberts, D., 63-64, 65, 74, 79, 80, *82*, *83*, *84*, 221, *235*
Roberts, S. K., xxii, *xxvii*
Robinson, G., *215*
Robinson, J., 65, *84*
Robinson, R., *84*
Rogers, E. W., 4, 16, *18*, 21, 32, 33-34, *40*, 62, 63, 64, 66, 68, 69, 70, 71, 75, 76, 79, *82*, *84*, 113, *121*, 148, 152, *162*, 164, 176, *177*, 217, 226, 233, *234*, 241, 243, 249, *256*, 260
Roman, J. W., xxi, *xxvii*
Rosenblum M., 165, *177*
Rosengren, K., *19*, 166, *177*, 182, *194*, *214*
Rosenthal, E. M., 15, *18*
Roslow, S., 29, *40*
Rothe, J. T., 184, *193*
Rothenbuhler, E. W., 299, *300-301*
Rouse, M., 246, *256*
Rowland, W., *215*

AUTHOR INDEX

Rubens, W. S., 5, 6, 14, 15, 16, *18*
Rubin, A. M., 65, 78, *84*, 181, 182, 183, 184, 192, 193, *194*
Rubin, R. B., 182, 192, *194*
Ruchinskas, J. E., 21, *40*
Rust, R. T., 6, *18*, 207, *214*

S

Sabatelli, R., xvi, *xxvii*
Sachar, E. B., xviv, *xxvii*
Sackman, H., 27, *40*, 105–106, 117, *122*
Salancik, G. R., 23, *38*, 68, 74, *84*
Salop, S. C., 246, *255*, *256*
Salvaggio, J. L., xxiii, *xxvii*
Sandberg, D. E., xxi, *xxvii*
Sarett, C., 74, *83*
Sata, K., *215*
Scardigli, V., 148, 160, *162*
Schmemann, S., 46, *58*
Schmidt, B. C., 212, *215*
Schmitz, J., 68, 74, *82*
Schnaars, S. P., 33, *40*
Schramm, W,. 66, *82*, 164, 165, 167, *178*, 221, 227, *234*, *235*
Schiller, H. I., 119, *122*, 164, *178*
Setzer, F. O., 22, *40*
Shaman, P., 6, *17*, 205, *214*
Shannon, C., 218, 219, *235*
Shaw, D., 211, *215*
Shoemaker, F., 62, 76, *84*
Shoeman, M. E. F., *38*
Siebert, F. S., 165, 167, *178*
Sieck, S. K., 109, *123*
Siegel, G., 120, *121*
Siegel, J., 238, *256*
Simmonds, W. H. C., 24, *39*
Signorielli, N., 199, 200, 210, 211, 213, *214*, *215*
Singh, C. U., 175, *177*
Singleton, L. A., xv, *xvii*, 21, *40*
Slack, J. D., xv, *xxvii*
Smale, A., 174, *178*
Smith, A., 111, *123*
Smith, D. D., 33, *38*
Solomon, D. S., 238, *256*
Sondik, E., 246, *256*
Spinrad, xvii, *xxviii*
Sproull, L., 74, *83*
Staelin, R., 246, *256*

Stahl, B. H., 244, *257*
Stanton, T., xx, *xxviii*
Steinfield, C. W., 61, 64, 67, 69, 71, 74, 82, *84*, 149, *162*
Sterling, C. H., xxiii, *xxviii*, 260, *301*
Stewart, C. M., 106, *121*
Stone, G. C., 68, *84*
Storch, C., 118, *123*
Straubhaar, J. D., 12, 125, 126, 128, 130, *144*, 163, 165, 166, 168, 169, 170, 173, *176*, *178*, 184
Swartz, S., xvi, *xxvii*
Sun, S. W., 209, *215*
Surlin, S., 220, *235*
Svenning, L. L., 21, *40*

T

de Tarle, A., 55, *57*
Tate, E., 220, *235*
Taylor, C. B., 238, *256*
Taylor, R., 77, *84*
Terry, H. A., 184, *193*
Thomas, J., 68, *84*
Thomas, S., *xxvii*
Thomas S. V., 199, *214*
Thompson, L. M., 13, *17*
Thompson, R. L., 268, *301*
Tiedge, J. T., 201, 207, *215*
Tigert, T., 34, *40*
Tinsley, E., 46, *58*
Titchenor, P., 81, *84*
Trost, M., 183, *194*
Turnstall, J., 164, 170, *178*
Tull, D. S., 33, *40*
Turing, A. M., 150, *162*
Turkle, S., 72, *84*
Turoff, M., 26, *39*, *40*
Turner, T., 108
Tverskey, A., 246, *256*
Twiss, B. C., 29, 35, 36, *40*
Tydeman, J. H., 21, *40*, 88, *103*
Tyler, M., xxii, *xxvii*

U,V,W

Urban, C. D., 115, *123*
Varis, T., 164, 169, 170, *177*, *178*
Veith, R. H., 109, *123*

Venit, S., xx, *xxviii*
Venkatesh, A., 66, 85, 149, *162*
Vince, P., 65, *83*
Vitalari, N., 66, 85, 149, *162*
Vladeck, B. C., 62, *85*
Vogel, M. E., 62, *85*
Voigt, J., *xxvii*, 82
Von Hippel, E., 32, 36–37, *40*
Waggoner, M. D., 26, *40*
Wakshlag, J., 3, 5, 6, 7, 10, *19*, 201, 202, 205, 206, 207, *216*
Wallace, B., 106, *123*
Wallack, L. M., 237, *256*
Wang, G., 183, *195*
Wartella, E., 66, 84, *215*
Waterman, D., 201, *215*
Watkins, B., *215*
Weaver, D. H., xxiv, *xxviii*, 111, *123*
Weaver, W., 218, 219, *235*
Webster, J. G., 3, 4, 6, 7, 8, 10, 11, 13, *18–19*, 197, 201, 202, 205, 206, 207, 208, 209, 212, 213, *215*, *216*
Wedell, G., 129, 130, 131, 132, *144*, 164, 167, *177*
Weilbacher, W. M., xxiii, *xxviii*
Wells, A., 164, *178*
Wenham, B., 51–52, *58*
Wenner, L., *19*, 166, *177*, 182, *194*, 214
Werba, H., 56, *58*
Westley, B., 220–221, 231, *235*
Wharton, F., 45, *58*
Wheelwright, S. C., 22, 39, *41*
White, R., 167, *178*, 226–227, *235*
Whitney, C., *215*
Whitson, T., *38*
Wilde, R. J., 65, 66, *82*

Wildman, S. S., 200, 201, 203, *216*
Wilhoit, C. G., *195*
Williams, F., 66, 72, 85, 217, 230, 233, *234*
Williams, M. E., 120, *123*
Williams, P. T., 238, *256*
Williams, T. M., 65, *85*
Wilson, C. C., 201, *216*
Wilson, G. T, 243, *256*
Wind, V., 31, 32, *41*
Windahl, S., 182, 183, *194*, *195*
Winett, R. A., 237, 238, 239, 241, 242, 243, 244, 245, 246, 249, 252, *256*, 257, 299, *302*
Winn, M., 65, *85*
Wirth, M. O., 205, 212, *216*
Wise, G., 31, *41*
Withington, F. G., 31, *41*
Wober, M., 89, *103*
Woollacott, J., *215*
Wright, C., 35, *39*
Wright, J. C., 243, *257*
Wu, T., 70, 71, 75, 76, 84, 149, *162*

Y, Z

Yorke, D. A., 184, *195*
Young, D., 56, *58*
Yin, R. K., 62, *85*
Zacks, R., 44, 46, *58*
Zaltman, G., 76, *85*
Zillmann, D., 7, *19*, 66, 82, *176*, 207, 214, *216*, 227–228, *234*, *235*
Zwimpfer, L., 21, *40*, 88, *103*

Subject Index

A

A. C. Nielsen Company, 8, 10, 12, 14, 15, 17, 65, 102, 200–201, 204, 205, 231
   Automated Measurements of Lineups (AMOL), 14
   Cable On-Line Data Exchange (CODE), 10–11
   Home Video Index, 15–16
Advertising, xxiii–xxiv, 7, 52, 100–101
   on teletext, 100–101
American Heart Association, 252
Arbitron, 12, 15, 231
Attention, 13, 207, 244
Attentional inertia, 207
Audience measurement firms, 4, 223
   A. C. Nielsen, *see* A. C. Nielsen Company
   Arbitron, *see* Arbitron
   Audits of Great Britain, *see* Audits of Great Britain
   Gordon S. Black Corporation, *see* Gordon Black
   Louis Harris & Associates, *see* Louis Harris
   MARPLAN, Ltd., *see* MARPLAN, Ltd.
Audits of Great Britain (AGB), 12–13, 14, 15, 102

electronic labels, 14

B

Behavior-context considerations, 237
Behavioral systems analysis, 237–257
BITNET, xxv
Books, diffusion of, 263–268
Broadband cable, 217
British Broadcasting Corporation (BBC), 87, 89, 164

C

Cable television, 8, 9, 13, 33, 34, 35, 36, 37, 43, 45, 51, 55, 69, 106, 118–119, 136, 200–201, 202–203, 204–205, 222, 224, 226, 244, 288–289, 292–293, 298
   conversion chart, 9
   diffusion of, 288–289, 292–293, 298
   growth, 21, 33, 34–35, 36, 37
Cable television networks
   Black Entertainment Television, 10

311

SUBJECT INDEX

Cable News Network, 54
HBO, 54
MTV, 13
VH-1, 54
Cabletext, 222
Camcorders, 295
CBS/Fox International, 44
Communication policy, 43-58
  control of pornography, 46-47, 49
  politics of VCRs, 44-52
Communication revolution, xv
Communications industry, 259-260
Compact disc, audio, 30, 281, 284, 285, 289
Computer Data Services, xxii
Computers, xvii, xviv-xxi, xxiii-xxiv, 4, 8, 22, 33, 37, 43, 56, 61-85, 147-162, 223, 298-300
  advances in, xx
  computer literacy, 160
  connectivity, xxi-xxiii, 217, 229
  conferencing, 225
  diffusion of, 149, 298-299, 300
  factors in use of, 70-78
    integrated model, 77-78
    personal attributes, 75-77
    social status, 70-73
    sociocultural setting, 73-75
  family use of, 61-63, 68-78
  impacts of home use, 63-65
  in organizations, 67-68
  interactive computer-communication systems, 238
  motivations to adopt, 152
  networks, 16
  person-machine exchange, 229
  software, xx-xxi, xxiii
  supercomputer, xviv-xx
  use with teletext, 88
Consumer buyer intent surveys, 31

D

Diaries, 5-6, 10
Diffusion and adoption
  and forecasting, 33-34
  conditions for, xxiii-xxv
  early adopters, 108, 117-118, 119, 149
  of individual media, 260-300

of new media, xv, xvii, xxiv-xxi, xxiii-xxv, 22, 46, 49, 61-63, 106, 112-113, 125, 148, 165-178, 238, 239, 244, 260-300
  problems in forecasting, 21-41
  rate of, xii, 165-178

E

Ecological models, 299
Electronic bulletin boards 224
Electronic Equipment Exporters Association, 133
Electronic Industries Association, 284-285, 295
Electronic mail, 67, 73, 259
Electronic publishing, xxvi-xxvii, 107, 116
Exposure
  assessment of, 3-19
  sampling, 14-16
  use of ratings, *see* ratings

F

Facsimile
  diffusion of, 294, 296
  Telecopiers, 294
Federal Communications Commission (FCC), 43, 284
Feedback, 221, 223, 244, 254
Fiber optics, 217
Film, 43, 50-52, 224
  diffusion of motion pictures, 273-278
Forecasting, 21-41, 148
  accuracy of, 33
  definitions of, 23-24
  history of, 22-23
  issues in, 30-31
  math models, 34-35
  methods of, 24-37
    Delphi, 25, 26-27
    growth curves, 25, 29-30
    historical analogy, 25, 28-29
    monitoring, 25-26
    scenarios, 25, 28-29
  of new media, 24
  stages of, 24-25
  technological, 24-37
Formative research, 240-241, 247-253, 255

SUBJECT INDEX 313

Four Theories of the Press, 165
Fragmentation of audiences, 203-206
Futures research, 23

G

Garage door openers, 298
Gatekeeper, 220, 232
General Agreement in Tariffs and Trade (GATT), 50
Gordon S. Black Corporation, 62

H

HACE (Home Administration, Communication, and Entertainment), xvii, xxvi-xxvii
Home banking, 108, 109, 111-116, 117

I

Independent Broadcasting Authority (IBA), 87, 89
Information-processing paradigm, 147
Information utility, 105-107
Integrated services digital networks (ISDN), 117
Interactive media, 63, 69, 72, 105-123, 147-148, 217-235, 238, 254
Interactivity, 221-233, 244
  dimensions of, 221-225
  implications of, 225-233
International communication, 12, 125-145
International Journal of Forecasting, 23
International Telecommunication Union, 55

J,K,L

Journal of Forecasting, 22-23
Knowledge gap, 81
Library-building (VCR), 11
Local area networks (LAN), xviv-xx
Low power television (LPTV), 43
Louis Harris & Associates, 61, 62, 70, 71, 74, 75, 80, 83

M

Magazines, diffusion of, 260-265
MARPLAN, Ltd., 89-90
Master antenna television, 43
Mathematical theory of communication, 218
McBride Commission, 170
Media effects, 7, 181, 197, 199, 203, 210-211, 227, 237-239
  attitude change, 237-238
  impacts of home computing, 63-65
  limited effects models, 7, 220-221
  network effect, 207
  powerful effects, 8, 66, 200, 219, 228
  social categories perspective on, 219
  social relations perspective on, 219
  spiral of silence, 211
  Westley-MacLean model of, 220-221, 231
Message abundance, 8-11
Meters (ratings), 5-6, 10, 12
  peoplemeter, 12-13
  passive vs. active metering, 13
Modeling, 244, 249-254
  participant modeling, 249-250
Motion Picture Association of America (MPAA), 44, 52
Motion Picture Export Association of America (MPEAA), 52-53, 54, 133, 175

N

National Association of Broadcasters, 62, 289, 300
National Association of Theater Owners, 276
National Cable Television Association, 202, 215
National Cancer Institute, 240, 246, 249, 252, 253, 254
National Science Foundation, 240, 247, 255
New World Information Order, 50
Newspapers, xvii-xviv, xxvi-xxvii, 99-100, 103, 106, 108, 129, 135, 139, 223, 260-263
  diffusion of, 260-263
Newspaper Advertising Bureau, 297

O,P

Octo-Puce, 150-151
Old media vs. new media, 198-203
Pay-per-view television, 43, 51
PBX, xxii-xxiii
Phonograph, 30
  diffusion of, 278-281
Piracy (of broadcast signals or films), 43-44, 52-56, 170
Playback, 126, 140
Polarization of audiences, 203, 206-210
Potential reappropriation perspective, 149-150

Q,R

QUBE, xvi
Radio, xvii-xviii, xxiii, 30, 36, 99-100, 102, 129, 135, 139, 164, 223, 259, 282-283, 286-288, 290
  diffusion of, 282-283, 286-288, 290
Radio Free Europe/Radio Liberty, 133
Ratings, 5-6, 11-12, 223
Reconceptualizing communication, 217-235
Regulatory policies, 22
Ritual of discovery, 154

S

Sampling, 14-16, 89-90, 151-152, 185-186
Satellite Instructional Television Experiment (SITE), 167
Satellites, xviv, xxii-xxiii, 21, 43, 52-66, 167, 289, 294-295
  diffusion of, 289, 294-295
  direct broadcast satellites (DBS), 51-56
  Early Bird, 289
  INMARSAT, 289
  INTELSAT, 289, 294
  Telstar I, 289
  VSAT, xxii, 36
Selective attention, 220
Selective exposure, 7, 12, 206-207, 223-224, 227-228
Selective perception, 220
Social cognitive theory, 239-241
Social learning theory, 243
Social marketing, 244
Southern New England Telephone, 62

T

Tape recorders (audio)
  diffusion of, 281-283
  digital, 30
Technological innovation forecasting method, 25
Tele Haiti, 54
Telecommunications, xxi-xxiii, 28, 125, 217
Teleconferencing, 21, 224-225, 233
Telegraph, diffusion of, 264, 268, 269-270
Telephone, 22, 30, 31, 117, 148, 223, 224, 232, 259, 268, 271-273, 274, 294, 298
  answering machine sales, 268, 273
  cordless, 273
  diffusion of, 271-273, 274, 298
  graphophone, 278
  gramophone, 278
  mobile units, 259
  zonophone, 278
Telephony, 232-234
Teleshopping, 109, 118
  J. C. Penny's Telaction, 118
Teletext, xvi, xxii, 16, 21, 37, 87-103, 218, 223
  in the United Kingdom, 87-103
  brief history of, 87-89
  problems in using, 97-98
  use of, 89-97
Teletext systems
  Ceefax, xvi, 87, 88, 93-94, 96-97, 98-99, 101
  Oracle, 87, 88, 93-94, 96-97, 98-99, 101
  Teletex, xvi
Television, xvii-xvix, xxiii-xxvii, 8, 29, 30, 34, 36, 51, 55, 62, 65-66, 74, 91-92, 99-100, 103, 119, 129, 134, 139, 143, 150, 163, 164, 197-216, 221-223, 226, 241, 244-245, 259, 283-284, 288, 290-292, 294, 298, 299
  and channels, 201-203
  channel loyalty, 207

diffusion of, 283-284, 288, 290-292
patterns of audience exposure, 197-216
programming, 198-202
subscription television, 36-45
Time-series analysis, 32-33
Time-shifting (with VCRs), 11, 45, 125, 131, 134, 140, 188, 189, 190, 192

U

U. S. Bureau of the Census, 260, 261-262, 264, 267, 273, 276, 280, 282, 283, 284, 285, 288, 289, 291, 293, 297, 290, 299, 301-302
U. S. Department of Commerce, 273, 276, 277, 278, 284, 294, 297, 302
U. S. Information Agency, 133
Uses and gratifications, 7, 77, 181-195, 201, 228

V

Video Inquiry Parliamentary Committee (U. K.), 47
Video Recordings Bill (U. K.), 47
Video telephone, 70
Videocassette recorder (VCR), xviii, 8, 10-14, 21, 28, 29, 30, 33, 35, 43-52, 54, 56, 125-145, 163-178, 181-195, 200-201, 202, 203, 206, 210, 222, 224, 226, 294-297, 298, 300
 diffusion of, 294-297
 politics of, 44-52, 163
 reasons for worldwide adoption, 125-144
 uses of and gratifications from, 181
Videodisc, 21, 27, 28, 29, 31, 33, 37, 254, 297-298
 Discovision, 297-298

Videogames, 33
 computer games, 73
Videotex, xv-xvii, xxi-xxiii, xxiv, xxvi, 8, 16, 21, 26, 32, 34, 36, 37, 69, 104-123, 218, 222, 223, 226, 228-229, 232, 233
Videotex systems
 American Airline's Sabre, 119
 BellSouth's Transtext Universal Gateway, 117
 BISON, xvi
 BSR, After Dark, 109, 119
 CompuServe, 107, 119
 CNR Partners, 107
 Covidea, xvi, 117
 Dialog/Knowledge Index, 107, 119
 Dow Jones News/Retrieval, 107, 119, 120
 First Hand, 111-116, 120
 Green Thumb, 222
 International Market-Net, xvi
 Keycom, xvi
 Keyfax, 105, 111
 Knight-Ridder's Viewtron, xv, 105, 109, 111
 Knight-Ridder's Vu-Text, 120
 Lexis, 109
 Medlars, 109
 Pacific Bell's Project Victoria, 117
 Prestel, 109, 110, 117
 Teleguide, 228
 The Source, 107, 119, 222
 Time-Mirror's Gateway, xv, 105, 108, 111
 Time Video Information Service, 110, 118
 Trintex, xvi, 107

Z

Zapping, 12, 126, 184
Zipping, 12, 126, 184

For Product Safety Concerns and Information please contact our EU representative GPSR@taylorandfrancis.com
Taylor & Francis Verlag GmbH, Kaufingerstraße 24, 80331 München, Germany